Hard Truths and the Duty to Change: Recommendations from the Independent Review Commission on Sexual Assault in the Military

At the direction of President Biden, on February 26, 2021, Secretary of Defense Austin established the 90-Day IRC on Sexual Assault in the Military. The Commission, chaired by Lynn Rosenthal, was charged with conducting "an independent, impartial assessment" of the military's current treatment of sexual assault and sexual harassment. The IRC officially began its review on March 24, 2021. This is the report of this commission.

It is published as a convenience to those who may wish to have a quality professionally printed copy of the report.

Edited 2021 Ocotillo Press
ISBN 978-1-954285-78-1

Ocotillo Press
Houston, TX 77017
Books@OcotilloPress.com

Contents

Foreword

A Letter to Service Members of the U.S. Military

We heard you. This report is a reflection of your voice - your struggles and your challenges.

To the junior enlisted: We talked with you on ships, on bases and installations; we talked with you from places within the U.S. and abroad; you reached out to us on our website, and through veterans and military service organizations. Your voices never stopped ringing in our ears as we worked through our recommendations. After all, you make up nearly half the entire force. You deserve to have your voices heard when policies, regulations, and laws are being considered that directly affect you. So, we reached out to you, and you reached out to us.

We listened when you told us that the climate of your unit was highly dependent on the quality of your leadership. We heard you when you said there were commanders who supported and mentored you but there were also those who turned away from harassment and abuse, eroding your trust. You told us about "toxic accountability" but you also told us about leaders who went above and beyond to protect and defend you. You begged us to replace boring PowerPoint trainings and engage you in meaningful dialogue instead. You admitted that sometimes you were confused about what behavior was acceptable and what crossed the line. We heard about the times when you stepped in to stop inappropriate or predatory behavior. You explained to us how you watched certain teammates go from being energetic and enthusiastic to depressed and withdrawn after a sexual assault. You told us you wanted change.

To everyone, we recognize that you came into the military for different reasons, from different backgrounds, with different goals. You wear different uniforms, have different jobs, and different career paths. But you swear the same oath and would lay down your lives for each other. You are the promise of continued freedom, and you deserve excellence. You deserve excellence in training, in leadership, mentorship, and resiliency. You also deserve dignity and respect, and the opportunity for advancement based solely on your grit, skill, and merit.

We thank you for your valued contributions to this report and for standing in the breach. The future is in your hands. We are counting on you.

Sincerely,

The Independent Review Commission (IRC) on Sexual Assault in the Military

Lynn Rosenthal   Dr. Debra Houry   LTC Bridgette Bell   Dr. Indira Henard

Cindy Dyer   Neil Irvin   CPT Kris Fuhr (ret.)   Kristina Rose   Meghan A. Tokash

James R. Schwenk   Maj. General James Johnson (ret.)   Dr. Kyleanne Hunter   Kayla Williams

Overview

At the direction of President Biden, on February 26, 2021, Secretary of Defense Austin established the 90-Day IRC on Sexual Assault in the Military. The Commission, chaired by Lynn Rosenthal, was charged with conducting "an independent, impartial assessment" of the military's current treatment of sexual assault and sexual harassment. The IRC officially began its review on March 24, 2021.

To accomplish the goals outlined in its charter, the IRC recruited twelve highly-qualified experts from outside of the Department of Defense (DoD) and the Services, with experience in the fields of civilian criminal justice, victim advocacy, policy and program development for sexual violence[1] prevention and response, public health, and research. During the 90-Day period, the IRC gathered input from key stakeholders across DoD, the Military Departments and Services, and external organizations. In particular, the IRC sought the views and perspectives from the individuals who would be most impacted by its recommendations: commanders; enlisted Service members; and survivors—including active duty Service members, individuals recently separated from service, and veterans.

In June 2021, the IRC presented Secretary Austin with its report and recommendations addressing four broad areas: accountability, prevention, climate and culture, and support and care of victims.[2] These four lines of effort are equally important—and therefore interdependent—in stopping sexual harassment and sexual assault in the military.

The IRC developed more than 80 recommendations (28 recommendations and 54 sub-recommendations). The full set of recommendations are detailed in four separate reports, with highlights included in this overview. In addition to these recommendations, the IRC identified common themes illustrative of the current state of sexual assault and sexual harassment in the military. These themes are presented below.

Common Themes

Broken Trust

When it comes to sexual assault and harassment, the IRC concluded that there is a wide chasm between what senior leaders believe is happening under their commands, and what junior enlisted

---

[1] Sexual violence refers to sexual activity when consent is not obtained or not given freely. Anyone can experience sexual violence. The person can be, but is not limited to, a friend, intimate partner, coworker, neighbor, or family member. Source: Basile, K., Smith, S., Breiding, M., Black, M., & Mahendra, R. (2014). *Sexual Violence Surveillance: Uniform Definitions and recommended Data Elements, Version 2.0.* Centers for Disease Control and Prevention (CDC), National Center for Injury Prevention and Control. https://www.cdc.gov/violenceprevention/pdf/sv_surveillance_definitionsl-2009-a.pdf

[2] Those who have experienced sexual assault may refer to themselves as survivors or as victims. Some prefer "survivor" to indicate that they lived through the assault, while others prefer "victim" to indicate that someone harmed them. "Victim" is used in the military justice systems. This document uses these terms interchangeably and always with respect for those who have been subjected to these crimes.

Service members actually experience. This is true across the enterprise. As a result, trust has been broken between commanders and the Service members under their charge and care.

Leadership is Paramount

Preventing, responding to, and supporting Service members who are the victims of demeaning language, sexual harassment, and sexual assault is a command responsibility. Commanders must be held accountable for their unit climates and for their action—or inaction—when it comes to protecting their people.

The Military Justice System is Not Equipped to Properly Respond to Special Victim Crimes

Special victim crimes disproportionately impact certain victims because who they are, or what motivated the crime. These crimes are often interpersonal in nature, in which the victim and the alleged offender may have a pre-existing relationship or acquaintance. Special victims—particularly survivors of sexual assault and domestic violence—deserve all critical decisions about their case to be made by a highly trained special victim prosecutor who is independent from the chain of command.

Sexual Harassment and Sexual Assault Exist on a Continuum of Harm

Sexual assault does not stand alone, but rather exists on a continuum of harm which may begin with sexual harassment and escalate into sexual assault. This is particularly true in the military, where survivors of sexual harassment are at significantly higher risk of later experiencing sexual assault.[3] To think of them as two separate problem sets is to fundamentally misunderstand the challenge the Department–and the force–face, especially with regard to unit climates.

Victims Bear a Heavy Burden

The IRC spoke with hundreds of survivors of sexual assault during the 90-Day review. One-on-one interviews and panel discussions brought to light the substantial burdens placed on victims as they navigated the military justice and health systems. Many survivors with whom the IRC spoke had dreamt their entire lives of a career in the military; in fact, they loved being in the military and did not want to leave, even after experiencing sexual assault or sexual harassment. But because their experience in the aftermath of the assault was handled so ineptly or met with hostility and retaliation, many felt they had no choice but to separate.

---

[3] Matthews, M., Morral, A.R., Schell, T.L., Cefalu, M., Snoke, J., Briggs, R.J. (2018). *Organizational Characteristics Associated with Risk of Sexual Assault and Sexual Harassment in the U.S. Army*. RAND Corporation. https://www.rand.org/pubs/research_reports/RRA1013-1.html

Critical Deficiencies in the Workforce

The workforce dedicated to Sexual Assault Prevention and Response (SAPR) is not adequately structured and resourced to do this important work. Many failures in prevention and response can be attributed to inexperienced lawyers and investigators, collateral-duty (part-time) SAPR victim advocates, and the near total lack of prevention specialists. These failures are not the fault of these personnel, but rather of a structure that de-emphasizes specialization and experience, which are necessary to address the complexities of sexual assault cases and the needs of victims.

Outdated Gender and Social Norms Persist Across the Force

Although the military has become increasingly diverse, women make up less than 18 percent of the total force.[4] With these dynamics, many women who serve report being treated differently than their male counterparts. In the IRC's discussions with enlisted personnel, many Service women described feeling singled out or the subject of near daily sexist comments, as one of few women in their units.

Little is Known about Perpetration

The most effective way to stop sexual harassment and sexual assault is to prevent perpetration. However, the Department lacks sufficient data to make evidence-based decisions in this domain. As a result, the impact of prevention activities in military communities, particularly activities aimed at reducing perpetration, remains relatively unknown.

Points of Strength that Show Promise for the Future

Despite these challenges, the IRC also found points of strength throughout the force. These promising observations were gleaned from installation visits, as well as discussions with junior enlisted Service members, noncommissioned officers (NCOs), survivors, commanders, and response personnel. As one junior enlisted Service member commented "not everything is broken." For example:

- The Army is making strides to better identify both promising and toxic leaders through the Battalion Commander Assessment Program (BCAP) and the Colonels Command Assessment Program (CCAP).[5]
- The Navy leads the Services in developing and retaining experienced courtroom litigators. Since 2007, the Navy's Military Justice Litigation Career Track (MJLCT) has been vital to the

[4] Of total force members in 2018 (i.e., Active Duty, Reserve, and Guard members from all Services), 82 percent identify as male and 71 percent identify as White. *Source*: Military One Source. (2019). 2018 Demographics: Profile of the Military Community. https://download.militaryonesource.mil/12038/MOS/Reports/2018-demographics-report.pdf, pp. 6-7.

[5] Denton, C.J. (2021). BCAP: The Battalion Command Assessment Program. *Army.mil.* https://www.army.mil/article/243040/bcap_the_battalion_command_assessment_program

Navy's ability to prosecute special victim cases and maintain the successful Victims' Legal Counsel (VLC) Program.[6]

- In the Marine Corps, the Marine and Family Programs Division is promoting better understanding of the connections between sexual assault and other forms of interpersonal violence and self-harm, as well as emphasizing primary prevention lessons like how to understand what healthy relationships look like in the workplace and at home.[7]
- The Air Force has launched an Interpersonal Violence (IPV) pilot program across ten installations in the U.S., providing legal services to members of the military community who are survivors of dating, domestic or workplace violence or sexual assault.[8]
- Three state National Guards have implemented pilot programs to provide proactive case management that links Service members with histories of trauma to resources and support.

These examples of promising efforts and strong commitments across the Services are evidence that change is possible. The IRC intends this report not as an indictment of the military, but rather as an opportunity to take long overdue action. At the end of this 90-day immersive process, we conclude that this is not an impossible problem to solve. By harnessing the strengths of commander leadership, investing in prevention, and building a qualified workforce, real progress can be made.

Key Recommendations

Cross-Cutting Recommendations

- Ensure Service members who experience sexual harassment have access to support services and care.
- Professionalize, strengthen, and resource the Sexual Assault Prevention and Response workforce across the enterprise.
- Improve the military's response to domestic violence—which is inherently tied to sexual assault.
- Improve data collection, research, and reporting on sexual harassment and sexual assault to better reflect the experiences of Service members from marginalized populations—including LGBTQ+ Service members, and racial and ethnic minorities.
- Establish the DoD roles of the Senior Policy Advisor for Special Victims, and the DoD Special Victim Advocate.

---

[6] Additionally, the Navy has developed specific precept language to enable the advancement of career military litigators.

[7] Marine Corps Community Services. (n.d.). Prevention. https://usmc-mccs.org/prevention/

[8] DeKunder, D. (2021, May 4). Program provides legal services for survivors of interpersonal violence, sexual assault. *Joint Base San Antonio News*. https://www.jbsa.mil/News/News/Article/2594830/program-provides-legal-services-for-survivors-of-interpersonal-violence-sexual/

Accountability

- Create the Office of the Special Victim Prosecutor in the Office of the Secretary of Defense (OSD) and shift legal decisions about prosecution of special victim cases out of the chain of command.
- Provide independent trained investigators for sexual harassment and mandatory initiation of involuntary separation for all substantiated complaints.
- Offer judge ordered military protective orders for victims of sexual assault and related offenses, enabling enforcement by civilian authorities.

Prevention

- Equip all leaders with prevention competencies and evaluate their performance.
- Establish a dedicated primary prevention workforce.
- Create a state-of-the-art prevention research capability in DoD.

Climate and Culture

- Codify in DoD policy and direct the development of metrics related to sexual harassment and sexual assault as part of readiness tracking and reporting.
- Use qualitative data to select, develop, and evaluate the right leaders for Command positions.
- Apply an internal focus on sexual violence across the force in DoD implementation of the 2017 National Women, Peace and Security Act.
- Fully execute on the principle that addressing sexual harassment and sexual assault in the 21st century requires engaging with the cyber domain.

Victim Care and Support

- Optimize victim care and support by establishing a full-time victim advocacy workforce outside of the command reporting structure.
- Expand victim service options for survivors by establishing and expanding existing partnerships with civilian community services and other Federal agencies.
- Center the survivor by maximizing their preferences in cases of expedited transfer, restricted reporting, and time off for recovery from sexual assault.

These recommendations, and more, are **detailed in the Appendices** to this report, which include individual reports for each line of effort.

Acknowledgements

The members of the IRC would like to acknowledge the many individuals who helped to make this report possible. Most importantly, we are grateful to the survivors who shared their painful stories in hopes of sparing others. We want to thank Secretary of Defense Austin for establishing the IRC and entrusting us with this important task. We are grateful to the Chairman of the Joint Chiefs of Staff, General Milley, for sharing his candid views and asking important questions. The IRC appreciated meeting with the Military Service Secretaries and Chiefs for sharing their insights. We were fortunate to have had a brilliant group of consultative and subject matter experts from DoD and the Services, who were generous with their time and knowledge. The DoD Sexual Assault Prevention and Response Office (SAPRO) deserves special recognition for responding to an overwhelming number of requests for information. There were many others, both military and civilian, who gave the IRC perspectives on military life and culture, all with the aspiration of a military that is free from sexual assault and sexual harassment. We offer the recommendations in this report in that same spirit.

Dedication

From the military veteran IRC members, this is for our sisters and brothers. Many of us lived the double burden of both preparing for and serving in war, only to also be betrayed by those we stood with shoulder-to-shoulder. While navigating the systems to deal with our sexual harassment and assaults we were told, “what do you expect?” or encouraged to keep our head down grit through it. To our sisters and brothers still serving, we say "enough." We will not stand idly by and let the culture tell you that you should expect to be harmed, or that you are alone. When we donned the cloth of our Nation, we swore an oath to uphold the Constitution–that all are created equal. Our military has long fought for the dignity and respect of others across the seas, cities, forests, and deserts—in every climate and place. Yet we must also look inward at the war that exists within our ranks. As long as the scourge of sexual assault and harassment persists, we have work to do to ensure that all are equal. Our work on the IRC has been a continuation of our oath, and our promise to you that we will continue to work for you.

From the civilian members of the IRC, we must say that we are acutely aware that we cannot know the sacrifice of military Service. We cannot fully understand the effects of long deployments on Service members and their families. We cannot know the intense preparation for warfighting or the difficulties of returning from combat. We have not experienced the stamina it takes to live the 24-hour life of a Soldier, Airman, Marine, Guardian, or Sailor. We were honored to serve on the IRC with our colleagues who do know all of this. As sexual assault experts and advocates, we only know that sexual harassment and assault should not be a cost of serving our country.

<u>A final note:</u> Towards the conclusion of the IRC, we learned of the sudden passing of Tonya McKennie, the subject matter expert from the Navy who assisted the Victim Care and Support line of effort. Tonya, who was a Regional Sexual Assault Response Coordinator in San Diego, was a gifted advocate who cared passionately about serving victims of sexual assault. She provided invaluable assistance to the entire IRC. We are grateful that we had the opportunity to work with her and are deeply saddened by her passing. This report is dedicated to her memory.

Introduction

Our nation's military is centered on the commander, who is responsible for everything a command does and fails to do. Instilling a command climate where everyone is treated with dignity and respect is a command responsibility. Preventing, responding to, and supporting Service members who are the victims of demeaning language, sexual harassment, and sexual assault is a command responsibility. Failure to do so, whether intentional or not, is a command failure. Commanders must be held accountable for their command climates and for their actions, or inaction including lack of supervision, when it comes to protecting their people.

Enlisted leaders are also essential in maintaining a command climate of dignity and respect, and in preventing, responding to, and supporting victims of sexual harassment and sexual assault. Small unit commanders rely heavily on enlisted leaders to implement command policy. Together, commanders, their subordinate officers, and enlisted leaders in all small units are the key to stopping demeaning language, sexual harassment, and sexual assault. If many commands can do so successfully, every command can do so. There simply are no excuses.

Command responsibility starts at the top with the Commander-in-Chief and includes every leader in the chain of command, down to the most junior commander. But the effort to resolve this scourge must be broader than commanders and enlisted leaders. It must include everyone who leads based on their grade or rank, and on peers who step forward to interrupt degrading or harmful behavior. The scope and intransigence of this problem require an all-hands on-deck solution.

DoD has long believed that morale and unit cohesion are indispensable elements in maintaining good order and discipline and mission accomplishment. Few things corrode morale and unit cohesion more than a command climate that favors some over others. The racial tension in the military in the 1960s and 1970s,[9] too often resulting in fights and riots, is testimony to the destructive power of command climates that are not based on treating everyone with dignity and respect. There is a direct link between unhealthy command climates and mission failure. The military's problem with sexual harassment and sexual assault is proof that too many small units have unhealthy command climates.

This report addresses accountability, climate and culture, prevention, and support and care of victims. These pillars are equally important—and therefore interdependent—in stopping sexual harassment and sexual assault in the military. Each must receive constant attention by commanders and enlisted leaders. Focusing on these issues cannot be seen by leaders as a distraction from the warfighting mission; indeed, if the military is to succeed in that mission, it cannot fail to address sexual harassment and sexual assault. Leaders have many responsibilities that demand their attention, but they cannot take days off from stopping the degradation of some Service members by others.

[9] Webb, S.C., & Herrmann, W.J. (2002). *Historical Overview of Racism in the U.S. Military*. Defense Equal Opportunity Management Institute. https://apps.dtic.mil/dtic/tr/fulltext/u2/a488652.pdf

Current State

Many of those who have served our nation in uniform look back on that service fondly and with reverence. They particularly recall the feeling of being part of a team in a small unit dedicated to a common cause—the defense of our nation—that was much bigger than each of them. In a very real sense, they literally entrusted their lives to the Service members with whom they served. This bond of trust was strong, pervasive, and deeply meaningful.

But some Service members found that trust betrayed. These Service members were demeaned by other Service members, their battle buddies, due to their sex or gender, or some aspect of who they are. They were sexually harassed and sexually assaulted by the Service members with whom they were proud to serve, with whom they had bonded so closely in service to our nation. The very persons they trusted the most betrayed that trust.

When this trust is violated—physically or emotionally—the wounds cut deep. For many survivors of military sexual assault, the betrayal of this sacred bond is an added layer of trauma. Add on to that the sudden and confusing schism that too often forms within the once close-knit unit when other members of the team decide they need to pick sides.

Victims of sexual assault and sexual harassment in the military are all too often doubly betrayed: by the Service member(s) who harmed them, and by the commanders who failed to protect them—or neglected to support them after reporting the harm they experienced. No one should ever have to serve under such conditions.

There are many reasons survivors of sexual assault never report, and some of them are not unique to military culture. But there are aspects of military life that make the experience of sexual assault and the decision to report even more challenging. Military units are small by design: Service members generally live, eat, and work in the same area, and because of this closeness, spend their off-hours together. This creates a small universe for the average junior enlisted Service member—the very person who is at the highest risk for sexual assault and sexual harassment.[10]

The decision to report an assault or harassment is compounded by the very real fear of retaliation, reprisal, and being ostracized from their unit/family. Or, some assaults happen while Service members are on temporary duty away from their unit, such as a training course needed for promotion. In this context, the decision to report an assault or harassment is compounded by the fear that the survivor might lose their coveted slot in the course, have to stay longer, or not graduate with their peers.

---

[10] Of active duty women in paygrades E-1 to E-4, 9.1 percent experienced a sexual assault in the past 12 months, the highest estimated rate among all women. Alleged offenders were most often male military members of a similar or higher rank. Source: Breslin, R., Davis, E., Hylton, K., Hill, A., Klauberg, W., Petusky, M., Klahr, A. (2019). *2018 Workplace and Gender Relations Survey of Active Duty Members: Overview Report.* Report No. 2019-027. Alexandria, VA: Office of People Analytics, 67-68. https://apps.dtic.mil/sti/citations/AD1072334

The effects of sexual assault and sexual harassment on Service members are well- documented. Many survivors spend the rest of their lives battling physical, mental, and emotional trauma as a consequence of the harm they endured. DoD owes America's daughters and sons a safer place to live and work; and if harm comes to them, a safer place to report and recover.

Finally, it must be stated that Service members do not bear the burden of sexual violence equally. For example, gay and bisexual men experience sexual assault at a rate nine times higher than heterosexual men in the military; lesbian and bisexual Service women are sexually assaulted at double the rate of heterosexual Service women.[11] Victims of sexual harassment and sexual assault can experience these harms differently, in connection with their gender, sexual orientation or gender identity, race, or ethnicity. Service members may be the target of sexual assault, harassment, hazing, bullying, or other abuses because of who they are—or who they are perceived to be.

Efforts-to-Date

In 2010, the SAPRO Director explained, "changing attitudes, behaviors, and beliefs related to sexual assault takes between eight and ten years to achieve."[12] In those intervening eleven years, however, DoD estimates[13] that roughly 135,000 active duty Service members (65,400 women and 69,600 men) have been sexually assaulted and about 509,000 active duty Service members (223,000 women and 286,000 men) have experienced sexual harassment.[14] These hundreds of thousands of Service

---

[11] Morral, A.R., & Schell, T.L. (2021). *Sexual Assault of Sexual Minorities in the U.S. Military.* Santa Monica, CA: RAND Corporation. https://www.rand.org/pubs/research_reports/RRA1390-1.html

[12] Isikoff, M. (2011). Lawsuit Claims Pentagon Ignored Military Rape Victims. *NBC News.* https://www.nbcbayarea.com/news/politics/did_pentagon_turn_blind_eye_to_rape_victims_/1909120/

[13] DoD estimates the number of Service members who have been sexually assaulted and sexually harassed in the 12 months prior to survey administration, which the Department has administered every two years since 2010. Sexual harassment figures for 2014 were estimated based on the proportion of those who indicated an experienced of sexual harassment on the *RAND Military Workplace Study (RMWS)* multiplied by the active duty end-strength that year. Sexual harassment data were not available for men in 2006. These figures do not represent incidents that could have occurred during years that DoD did not conduct a survey. In addition, this number does not necessarily represent unique Service members (i.e., some Service members may have experienced sexual assault and/or sexual harassment in separate survey years), nor does it account for Service members who recorded several incidents within the same survey period.

[14] Breslin, R., Davis, E., Hylton, K., Hill, A., Klauberg, W., Petusky, M., Klahr, A. (2019). *2018 Workplace and Gender Relations Survey of Active Duty Members: Overview Report.* Report No. 2019-027. Alexandria, VA: Office of People Analytics. https://apps.dtic.mil/sti/citations/AD1072334; Davis, L., Grifka, A., Williams, K., Coffey, M., Van Winkle, E. P., & Hurley, M. (2017). *2016 Workplace and Gender Relations Survey of Active Duty Members: Overview Report* (No. 2016-050). Alexandria, VA: DMDC. https://apps.dtic.mil/dtic/tr/fulltext/u2/1032638.pdf; Morral, A. R., Gore, K. L., & Schell, T. L. (2015). *Sexual Assault and Sexual Harassment in the U.S. Military: Volume 1. Design of the 2014 RAND Military Workplace Study.* Santa Monica, CA: RAND National Defense Research Institute. https://www.rand.org/content/dam/rand/pubs/research_reports/RR800/RR870z2 1/RAND_RR870z2-1.pdf; Defense Manpower Data Center. (2013). *2012 Workplace and Gender Relations Survey of Active Duty Members: Tabulation Volume.* Report No. 2012-065. Arlington, VA: DMDC. https://sapr.mil/public/docs/research/WGR_ActiveDuty_2012_Report.pdf; Rock, L., Lipari, R.N., Cook, P.J., & Hale, A.D. (2011). *2010 Workplace and Gender Relations Survey of Active Duty Members: Overview Report of Sexual Assault.* Report No. 2010-025. Arlington, VA: DMDC. https://sapr.mil/public/docs/research/DMDC_2010_WGRA_Overview_Report_of_Sexual_Assault.pdf; Lipari, R. N., Cook, P.

members who experienced sexual harm are clear evidence that culture has not changed, and that leaders have failed to "move the needle," as Chairman Milley recently acknowledged.[15] This has not been for lack of trying, nor lack of oversight. Since 2010, there have been more than ten DoD Inspector General (IG) engagements to review and improve prevention and response.[16] In addition, there have been:

- Over 50 Secretary of Defense-directed initiatives to improve prevention and response;
- Over 150 Congressional provisions operationalized related to sexual assault;
- Over 200 recommendations from government panels and task forces assessed for applicability to the SAPR mission space; and
- Over 60 Government Accountability Office (GAO) sexual assault-related recommendations assessed to measure prevention and response efforts and to inform future programming.[17]

There is recent evidence that progress is achievable. In 2016, DoD demonstrated positive, incremental change with a statistically significant *reduction* in sexual assault prevalence from 2014 and a 10-year low in Service members who experienced sexual assault in the past year. Devastatingly, these gains did not last, contemporaneous with changes in leadership that quickly undermined efforts to drive down the scourge.

In 2018, sexual assault prevalence increased by 44 percent among women (men's prevalence stayed the same).[18] More than 20,000 Service members were the victims of sexual assault that year (13,000 women and 7,500 men).[19] Fewer than 8,000 per year reported that assault, according to the Department's own annual surveys.[20] The sexual harassment numbers are bleaker, with about one in every four active duty women reporting experiences of sexual harassment.[21] Yet DoD received only 1,781 reports of sexual harassment in FY20.[22] Military leadership has failed America's daughters and sons, and the Service members know it.

J., Rock, L., & Matos, K. (2007). *2006 Gender Relations Survey of Active Duty Members.* Report No. 2007-022. Arlington, VA: DMDC. https://sapr.mil/public/docs/research/DMDC_2010_WGRA_Overview_Report_of_Sexual_Assault.pdf

[15] Ryan, M. & Lamothe, D. (2021, May 6). 'We haven't moved the needle' on Sexual Assault in the Military, General Says. *The Washington Post.* https://www.washingtonpost.com/national-security/military-sexual-assault/2021/05/06/a8f51a7c-ae98-11eb-8109-f8ba1ea2eeab_story.html

[16] DoD SAPRO. (n.d.). *Policy and Strategy.* https://www.sapr.mil/sites/default/files/Policy%20and%20Strategy%20Overview%20Slicksheet_Reference_0.pdf

[17] Ibid.

[18] Breslin, R., Davis, E., Hylton, K., Hill, A., Klauberg, W., Petusky, M., Klahr, A. (2019). *2018 Workplace and Gender Relations Survey of Active Duty Members: Overview Report.* Report No. 2019-027. Alexandria, VA: Office of People Analytics, 26. https://apps.dtic.mil/sti/citations/AD1072334

[19] Ibid.

[20] DoD SAPRO. (2021). Appendix B: Statistical Data on Sexual Assault. *Fiscal Year 2020 Annual Report on Sexual Assault in the Military*, 11. https://www.sapr.mil/sites/default/files/Appendix_B_Statistical_Data_On_Sexual_Assault_FY2020.pdf

[21] Id., 44.

[22] DoD SAPRO. (2021). Appendix F: Sexual Harassment Assessment. *Fiscal Year 2020 Annual Report on Sexual Assault in the Military.* https://www.sapr.mil/sites/default/files/Appendix_F_Sexual_Harassment_Assessment_FY2020.pdf/

Section I: IRC Mission, People, and Process

On March 24, 2021, the work of the 90-Day IRC on Sexual Assault in the Military officially began. To accomplish the goals outlined in its charter, the IRC recruited twelve independent, highly-qualified experts (HQEs) from outside of DoD and the Services, with experience in the fields of civilian criminal justice, victim advocacy, policy and program development for sexual violence prevention and response, public health, and research. Five of the twelve HQEs are former military commanders, and two have served as judge advocates. All Military Departments are represented among the IRC's experts. Together, the HQEs were charged with forming recommendations across four lines of effort: accountability; prevention; climate and culture; and victim care and support. The IRC Charter outlined the scope for each line of effort:

- **Line of Effort 1, Accountability**: Recommend policy changes and propose actions to improve prevention and response efforts on sexual assault, harassment, and other readiness-detracting behaviors; assess the role of the Uniform Code of Military Justice (UCMJ) in addressing the prevalence of sexual assault and harassment, survivor likelihood of reporting, and ability to appropriately bring alleged perpetrators to justice; and, assess the feasibility, opportunities, and risks from changes to the commander's role in military justice.
- **Line of Effort 2, Prevention**: Conduct a comprehensive assessment of ongoing prevention efforts to determine where gaps may exist, and determine where additional resources may be needed; and, provide recommendations that achieve an enduring, Department-wide prevention infrastructure, and equip leaders with data, people, resources, policy, and tools to stop sexual assault.
- **Line of Effort 3, Climate and Culture**: Identify and propose evidence-based approaches to improve climate and culture to ensure that all Service members feel safe; empower Service members to use available support services; enable Service members to report without fear of reprisal from leadership or peers; and, ensure Service members are able to serve with dignity and respect.
- **Line of Effort 4, Victim Care and Support**: Conduct a review of clinical and non-clinical victim services to ensure services are comprehensive, evidence-based, and available to all victims regardless of reporting status; and, provide recommendations that include mental health care, physical health care, and care that is trauma-informed and victim-centered.

The IRC sought to both establish its independence and build on the expertise that lies within DoD and the Services. This was accomplished by creating working groups for each line of effort, made up of DoD officials and Service leaders supported by subject matter experts (SMEs) from within the Services.[23] The HQEs were empowered with the final decision-making authority on the

[23] See Appendix G for the list of Consultative and Support team members.

recommendations.[24] The diverse backgrounds and expertise of the HQEs set the stage for rich dialogue and well-informed discussions across all four lines of effort.

Altogether, the IRC's recommendations present an overview of the problem, and offer targeted solutions for commanders of all ranks, the Services, and the Department to build trust and restore confidence in the military's ability to prevent and respond to sexual assault and sexual harassment.

Approach

The IRC took a multidisciplinary approach to reviewing policies, programs, and processes governing the military's response to sexual assault and sexual harassment. In crafting the recommendations, the Commission sought input from the Services; DoD components;[25] military and veteran service organizations; victim advocacy groups;[26] and, survivors, through a combination of individual interviews, virtual listening sessions, group discussions, and written feedback. In total, the IRC met with more than 600 individuals in the course of the 90-day timeline.

Each line of effort reviewed pertinent Congressional legislation, reports from DoD, Federal agencies, and civil society, and examined the research specific to their focus area. As a complement to these desk reviews, the IRC held live briefings with leading experts in military justice, sexual violence prevention and response, spanning academia, research institutes, and the Federal government. The IRC also commissioned over 150 requests for information from the Service SMEs.

It was important to the Commission that the recommendations be informed by, and give voice to, the experiences and insights of Service members—the majority of whom live and serve far outside of the Pentagon. Although travel was limited by COVID-19, the IRC visited six installations, covering five states.[27] To hear from Service members outside the U.S., the IRC also held virtual discussion groups with installations in Europe and the Pacific. Through a combination of in-person and virtual site

---

[24] Two HQEs represented Federal agencies (i.e., the CDC and the Department of Veterans Affairs) and were non-voting members of the IRC.

[25] DoD Components include the Office of Force Resiliency, SAPRO, the Office of People Analytics, Accessions Policy, the Office of Government Counsel, OSD Promotions Policy, Joint Staff, OSD Policy, Family Advocacy Program (FAP), the Defense Equal Opportunity Management Institute, and the Office for Diversity, Equity, and Inclusion (ODEI).

[26] The IRC met with the following stakeholder groups: Aequitas, Air Force Association, American Progress Women's Initiative, Association of the U.S. Army, Blue Star Families, Center for Council on Foreign Relations Women & Foreign Policy Program, Disabled American Veterans, Enlisted Association of the National Guard of the U.S., Esposas Militares Hispanas USA, Military Family Advisory Network, Military Officers Association of America, Minority Veterans of America, Modern Military Association, National Center on Domestic and Sexual Violence, National Crime Victims Law Institute, National Coalition Against Domestic Violence, National Military Family Association, National Organization for Victim Assistance (NOVA), National Women's Law Center, Not in My Marine Corps, Protect Our Defenders, Service Women's Action Network, TAPS, Time's Up, Ujima: The National Center on Violence Against Women in the Black Community, US Army Warrant Officers Association (The Military Coalition), Vietnam Veterans of America, and Wounded Warrior Project.

[27] To respect the promise of anonymity to all who spoke with the IRC, the IRC is not sharing the full set of installations with whom it met.

visits, the IRC met with enlisted personnel, commanders, and victim services providers[28] from all Services, and National Guard and Reserve units representing nine states.

Hearing from Survivors

Speaking with survivors provided pivotal context and foundation for all of the IRC's recommendations. The IRC used multiple outreach mechanisms to connect with as many survivors as possible during its limited timeframe, and heard from those currently serving, recently separated Service members, and veterans.[29] The IRC spoke with survivors through in-person interviews on installations, individual phone conversations, and several virtual panel discussions.

The IRC is indebted to Chief Nolita Whiten, who courageously shared her story, and graciously gave up her time and expertise to serve as a consultative expert for the IRC's victim care and support line of effort.

The HQEs also sought written testimony from survivors in the military community through an online form operated by the Safe Helpline. Between March 24 and June 2, 2021, the IRC received 237 anonymous submissions. While every survivor's experience is unique, the IRC received responses that shared several common themes, including messages of hope that the IRC would bring change and improvements to the current system. Figure 1 captures recurring categories of responses from Service members and survivors submitted through the Safe Helpline.

---

[28] The IRC met with SAPR/SHARP VAs, SARCs, and program managers, as well as FAP victim advocates and clinicians, and Military Equal Opportunity staff.

[29] The IRC heard from survivors of all ages—including veterans who served during the Vietnam War. The insights and experiences these veterans shared with the IRC are a testament to the enduring impacts of trauma, but also the incredible resilience of survivors.

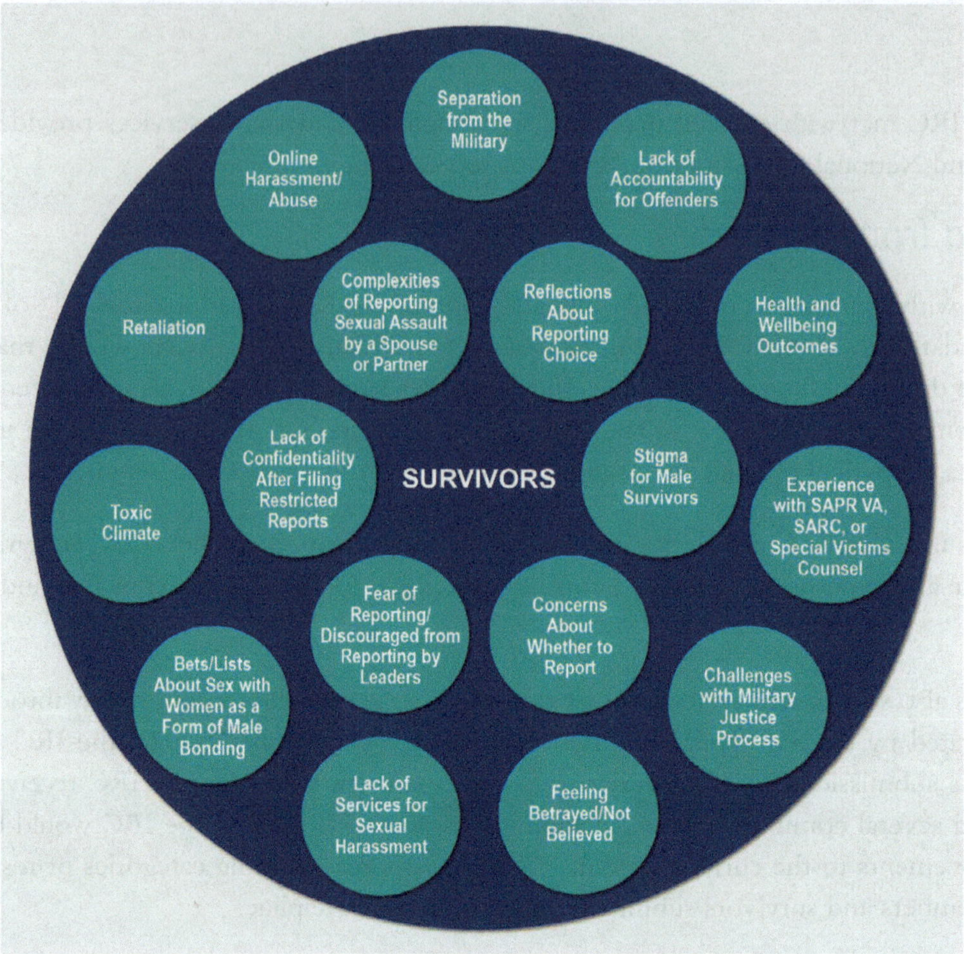

Figure 1. IRC Survivor Feedback Themes

Meeting with Enlisted Personnel

Enlisted personnel represent more than 80 percent of the total force, and junior enlisted Service members (paygrades E1-E4) face the highest risk for both experiencing and perpetrating sexual assault.[30] These young Service members are directly supervised by NCOs (paygrades E5-E6), who have a strong influence on unit climate. Given these considerations, the IRC organized discussion groups with junior enlisted and NCOs as a key aspect of its installation visits. In total, the IRC met with more than 171 enlisted personnel during these visits.[31]

---

[30] Breslin, R., Davis, E., Hylton, K., Hill, A., Klauberg, W., Petusky, M., Klahr, A. (2019). *2018 Workplace and Gender Relations Survey of Active Duty Members: Overview Report.* Report No. 2019-027. Alexandria, VA: Office of People Analytics, 67-68. https://apps.dtic.mil/sti/citations/AD1072334

[31] The IRC worked with DoD SAPRO to develop a process for the installations to use in selecting junior enlisted Service members, NCOs, and survivors to participate, virtually and in-person. This process was informed by prior, similar efforts undertaken by the Department, such as the Military Justice Experience Surveys.

To encourage full candor in these meetings, all comments were not-for-attribution, and discussion group participants were not placed in a group with anyone representing their chain of command.[32] Following a process similar to the Fort Hood IRC, the Commission engaged these Service members in a semi-structured conversation to take the pulse on key areas related to sexual harassment and sexual assault, including (but not limited to):

- The role of command in setting the tone for climate;
- Perceptions on leadership's handling of sexual assault and sexual harassment;
- Knowledge of others who have experienced sexual assault;[33]
- The presence (or absence) and frequency of sexual harassment in their units; and,
- Views of the SAPR/SHARP program, and related training and education.[34]

Meeting with the Services' Senior Enlisted Advisors

Hearing from the Service senior enlisted leadership helped the IRC to better understand some of their most pressing issues, as well as gain insight into how changes in policy, law, and regulation would affect them. After all, the Service Senior Enlisted leaders interact with their troops every day. To that end, the IRC invited each of them to discuss proposed recommendations, and to learn their perspectives on what would make the most impact in the life of the enlisted Service member. The members of Commission are grateful for their time, their wisdom, and their candor. These leaders' dedication and commitment to their troops and the issues that affect them was apparent.

Section II: Statement of the Problem

1. Broken Trust

Since the beginning of our nation, military justice has been a commander-centric system. Commanders are responsible for all that a unit does and does not do, so they have complete authority in matters of discipline. Implicit in this broad grant of authority is the issue of trust: trust by commanders in subordinates to follow the orders of commanders, and trust by subordinates in commanders that commanders will wield this broad grant of authority fairly in order to do justice and thus assist in maintaining good order and discipline.

---

32 To clarify none of the NCOs at E-5 or E-6 paygrades were leaders of the more junior ranks participating. Of note, while meeting with the Service members in the discussion groups on site, several volunteered the information that they felt they were selected by their leadership because they were "squared away" and would represent their units well to the IRC.

33 Some of the junior enlisted personnel self-identified as survivors/volunteered this information in the course of the dialogue. Participation in the discussion groups was not based on whether Service members identified as victims of sexual assault or sexual harassment.

34 Senior research consultants on contract with DoD SAPRO from Booz Allen Hamilton were dialed in to each of the junior enlisted discussion groups and took notes for the IRC's records and review of each meeting. Key themes were pulled out as executive summaries of the transcribed meetings.

Service members have the expectation of trust in their commanders to respond fairly to allegations of sexual harassment and sexual assault, while also demonstrating compassion for victims. Yet too many commanders have failed to do so.

> "I have experienced sexual harassment and one sexual assault throughout my career… During my 19 years, I have not reported a single incident. I have no trust in my safety or the system to protect me. I have kept my career, but have I kept my dignity?"
>
> -Survivor, as told to the IRC through the DoD Safe Helpline

Victims told the IRC that they do not trust commanders to do justice in sexual harassment and sexual assault cases for a variety of reasons. In addition to a perceived conflict of interest, they see commanders as: complicit (allowing precursor demeaning language and actions to go unchecked); or, are more focused on combat readiness, logistics, and other higher priority matters than on caring for their troops. They also do not understand how a commander with limited legal training can be trusted to make quintessential legal decisions such as deciding whether there is probable cause to charge someone with a crime and whether there is evidence sufficient to obtain and sustain a conviction to warrant sending a charge to a court-martial. Even victims who respected their commanders said their commanders should not be making those decisions.

These observations led the IRC to conclude that there is a wide chasm between what senior leaders believe is happening under their commands, and what junior enlisted Service members actually experience[35]. As a result, trust has been broken between commanders and the Service members under their charge and care. On the topic of sexual harassment and sexual assault, the IRC's many discussions with commanders often stood in stark contrast with the emergent truths from speaking with junior enlisted personnel or hearing from survivors. This is not for lack of concern. Many commanders recognize sexual harassment and sexual assault are corrosive to the force, they simply lack the capacity to fix it. The IRC focused on developing recommendations to help rebuild that broken trust.

2. The Military Justice System is Not Equipped to Properly Respond to Special Victim Crimes

Special victim crimes are cases that disproportionately impact victims because of the type of offense committed (i.e., sexual assault), who they are (trait of the victim), or what motivated the crime (intent of the offender). Victims of these crimes frequently experience re-victimization and re-traumatization

[35] This specific determination was largely drawn from the experiences and insights directly shared with the IRC by junior enlisted personnel through interviews, installation visits, and virtual discussion groups; however, the focus of the IRC's recommendations to restore this fractured trust are equally applicable across the force to Service members of all ranks.

in the processing of their cases.[36] Often interpersonal in nature, special victim crimes may also involve victims who have intersectional identities that create additional barriers to justice.[37] Not infrequently, special victims can experience multiple crimes that overlap with sexual assault. For example, victims of sexual assault may have been harmed by a fellow Service member, but also by a spouse or intimate partner. For men—particularly gay, bisexual, and transgender Service members—sexual assault often occurs in the context of bullying and hazing.[38] In addition, certain victims are always special victims, regardless of the crime committed against them, due to their age, or their relationship with the offender (i.e., children under the age of sixteen, an intimate partner, a spouse, or a dating partner). Special victim cases also include crimes of bias or hate based on the victim's sex, gender, race, ethnicity, color, religion, national origin, sexual orientation, or gender identity.

These special victims require and deserve all critical decisions about their case to be made by a highly trained special victim prosecutor who is independent from the chain of command. A commander's position within the unit leads to an inherent appearance of a conflict of interest. Further, commanders are not lawyers, and they do not receive adequate training regarding victimization, implicit bias, and the impact these concepts have on the administration of justice.

> "Prosecuting special victim cases requires highly specialized prosecutors who understand the victim as a whole person, and equally understand why the offender chose them."
>
> -Former JAG, as told to the IRC in an interview

Only prosecutors have the technical training to make the purely legal decisions that affect victims' access to justice. These lawyers are uniquely positioned to assess whether a case is a special victims case, to decide whether and what charges should be preferred, to determine the likelihood of conviction, to engage with other lawyers in plea negotiations, to offer grants of immunity to trial witnesses, and to issue subpoenas. These decisions should be in the sole discretion of lawyers who, unlike commanders, are directly involved in interviewing witnesses, reviewing all available evidence, and preparing the case for trial. These specialized, independent judge advocates should report to a Director leading a DoD-wide Office of Special Victim Prosecutors.

Unless and until the aperture is expanded to include all categories of special victim crimes, and cases are handled by highly trained and experienced special victim prosecutors, the military justice system will never be equipped to properly respond to special victim cases.

---

36 Orth, U. (2002). Secondary victimization of crime victims by criminal proceedings. *Social Justice Research, 15*(4): 313–325.

37 Kilpatrick, D.G., & Acierno, R. (2003). Mental health needs of crime victims: Epidemiology and Outcomes. *Journal of Traumatic Stress, 16*(2): 119–32.

38 Morral, A. R., & Schell, T. L. (2021). Sexual *Assault of Sexual Minorities in the U.S. Military*. Santa Monica, CA: RAND Corporation. https://www.rand.org/pubs/research_reports/RRA1390-1.html

3. Leadership is Paramount

It has been argued that removing commanders' authority in determining whether to try sexual assault cases would effectively be telling them they "no longer have skin in the game"—or worse, that some commanders may "no longer care" about sexual assault and its impact on their units. The IRC challenges those suppositions, and believes they do a fundamental disservice to these senior leaders. When it comes to sexual assault and sexual harassment, commanders are, and will continue to be, responsible for maintaining good order and discipline with their commands; this includes:

- Establishing and maintaining a command climate of dignity and respect for all;
- Using strategies to prevent sexual harassment and sexual assault; and,
- Ensuring victims who have made the brave decision to come forward are afforded care and consideration including preventing retaliation within the unit.

The transfer of technical legal decisions concerning complex, interpersonal crimes to independent military prosecutors cannot negate, nor diminish, the commitment and concern that caring leaders have for the Service members under their command. Commanders will continue to have a bevy of tools at their disposal, ranging from adverse administrative action to nonjudicial punishment.[39] Leaders must use these tools to hold Service members accountable, but also concentrate their efforts on prevention, climate and culture, and ensuring victim care and support.

> "It goes back to making sure commanders are educated, and they actually enforce the rules, and don't just sweep it under the rug. I've seen that. If the commander does that, we have a good area of operations. At the end of the day, the soldiers and NCOs run the unit, but the commander enforces rules to standard."
>
> - Junior Enlisted, as told to the IRC during a listening session

---

39 Sexual assault reports are far more likely to result in nonjudicial punishment, administrative discharge, or other adverse administrative action rather than be referred to court-martial. Source: DoD SAPRO. (2021). *Fiscal Year 2020 Annual Report on Sexual Assault in the Military.* https://www.sapr.mil/sites/default/files/DOD_Annual_Report_on_Sexual_Assault_in_the_Military_FY2020.pdf

"Zero tolerance is actually 100 percent tolerance."

-NCO, as told to the IRC during a listening session

Commanders can and must continue to set an example, praise good behavior, and quell inappropriate conduct as soon as it occurs. In the more egregious circumstances when a Service member's conduct rises to the level of a sexual assault, the commander has a new powerful weapon in her or his arsenal–an experienced, independent special victim prosecutor. Commanders still retain the most important role: looking after the welfare of their troops.

A broken culture is the root of the sexual harassment and sexual assault policy failures over the past two decades. Only leaders can fix this, so the Services must select the right leaders. Many Service members report command climates where demeaning language and sexual harassment are the norm and go unchecked by the commander and enlisted leaders.[40] They also report instances of retaliation and ostracism after reporting that harassment, or disclosing sexual assault.[41] This is a different type of betrayal, but often just as harmful. Many of these incidents could have been prevented. Concerned leaders could have created command climates where demeaning gender-based comments, sexual harassment, and sexual assault were not tolerated. They had all the authority to do so, but too many leaders failed to lead. These incidents had additional corrosive effects on good order and discipline: broken trust between Service members and their leaders, and the military they volunteered to serve.

Commanders must also shift their mindset on sexual harassment and sexual assault and see tackling them as part of their main effort. Instances of sexual violence reduce a unit's combat effectiveness and overall operational readiness and must receive the appropriate level of attention from commanders. Yet in hearing from hundreds of survivors, the IRC took away that many commanders simply do not treat sexual harassment and sexual assault with the same level of time or attention that they treat a broken vehicle. After decades of applying Band-Aids to fix a gaping wound, efforts-to-date have done little but maintain the status quo because too many leaders—at all echelons of the enterprise—continue to believe that sexual violence is a distraction from the military's core warfighting mission, and therefore not something it must take seriously.

"When you respect someone, you don't violate their person, their property, or their opportunity."

-Senior Enlisted Advisor, as told to the IRC during a listening session

[40] Sadler, A., Mengeling, M., Booth, B., O'Sea, A., & Torner, J. (2017). The Relationship between the U.S. Military Officer Leadership Behaviors and Risk of Sexual Assault in Reserve, National Guard and Active Component Servicewomen in Nondeployed Locations. *American Journal of Public Health, 107*(1), 147-155.

[41] Breslin, R., Davis, E., Hylton, K., Hill, A., Klauberg, W., Petusky, M., & Klahr, A. (2019). *2018 Workplace and Gender Relations Survey of Active Duty Members: Overview Report*. Report No. 2019-027. Alexandria, VA: Office of People Analytics, 38. https://apps.dtic.mil/sti/citations/AD1072334

4. Sexual Harassment and Sexual Assault Exist on a Continuum of Harm

Sexual violence is not neatly compartmentalized into discrete behaviors or events, but rather exists on a continuum of harm, which begins with sexual harassment and escalates into sexual assault.[42] To think of them as two separate problem sets is to fundamentally misunderstand the challenge the Department–and the force–face. Research by RAND[43] illuminates these intersections: Service members who experience sexual harassment and gender discrimination suffer higher rates of sexual assault. Roughly one in three Service members who were the victims of sexual assault stated that the offender initially targeted them with sexual harassment.

> "Many of the services offered to individuals reporting a sexual assault are not available to individuals reporting sexual harassment. There was no one to coordinate me getting emotional assistance, legal services to understand my rights, or options to get out of there."
>
> -Civilian SAPR VA, as told to the IRC through the DoD Safe Helpline

Left unchecked, sexual harassment significantly contributes to a unit's sexual assault risk. In units with above-average rates of sexual harassment, the risk for sexual assault increases by a factor of 1.5 among women, and 1.8 – almost 2-fold – among men.[44] LGBTQ+ Service members are especially impacted.[45] But while sexual harassment may be a precursor to sexual assault in the military environment, the experience of victims[46] should not be discounted, or seen as "less serious." Service members who experience sexual harassment can also suffer from post-traumatic stress disorder, depression, anxiety, and other health impacts, including suicide.[47]

---

[42] DoD. (2019). *National Defense Authorization Act for Fiscal Year 2020.* https://www.congress.gov/116/plaws/publ92/PLAW-116publ92.pdf

[43] RAND. (2017). *Improving Oversight and Coordination of Department of Defense Programs That Address Problematic Behaviors among Military Personnel.* Santa Monica, CA: RAND Corporation. https://www.rand.org/pubs/research_reports/RR1352.html

[44] Schell, T., Cefalu, M., Farris, C., & Morral, A. (2021). *The Relationship Between Sexual Assault and Sexual Harassment in the U.S. Military: Findings from the RAND Military Workplace Study.* Santa Monica, CA: RAND Corporation. https://www.rand.org/pubs/research_reports/RR3162.html

[45] Schuyler, A., Klemmer, C., Mamey, M., Schrager, S., Goldbach, J., Holloway, I., & Castro, C. (2020). Experiences of Sexual Harassment, Stalking, and Sexual Assault During Military Service Among LGBT and Non-LGBT Service Members. *Journal of Traumatic Stress, 33*(3). https://doi.org/10.1002/jts.22506

[46] Although DoD uses the term "complainant" to describe those who report a sexual harassment, the IRC uses the terms victim and survivor to denote Service members who experienced either sexual assault or sexual harassment.

[47] Stander, V.A. & Thomsen, C.J. (2016). Sexual Harassment and Assault in the U.S. Military: A Review of Policy and Research Trends. *Military Medicine, 181*(1): 20–27. https://doi.org/10.7205/MILMED-D-15-00336https://doi.org/10.7205/MILMED-D-15-00336

It is therefore concerning that DoD policies governing sexual harassment entirely miss this connection with sexual assault and do not address the continuum of sexual harm or provide victims with access to support services. This is also true at the Service level, with the exception of the Army Sexual Harassment and Assault Response Program.[48]

Rather, sexual harassment is addressed within the Department's diversity, equity, and inclusion, and equal opportunity policies.[49, 50, 51] While the linkages between workplace equity and workplace safety are important, this approach comes at the expense of establishing a clear response for victims to receive support. Instead, DoD policies subsume sexual harassment within policies governing other forms of harassment and discrimination. These policies are led by various DoD components, lending to a fractured approach without any one entity specifically responsible for, or specialized in, the area of sexual harassment. Outside the Army, this translates into the complete absence of support services[52] for Service members who experience sexual harassment, as the designated response personnel—Equal Opportunity Advisors[53]—are equipped only to receive complaints and support commanders in resolving complaints.

> "It's not just about conviction [for the victims]; it's about how they were treated in the process."
>
> -Senior NCO, as told to the IRC during a listening session

5. Victims Bear a Heavy Burden

In the military, no one is more consequential to the wellbeing and recovery of survivors of sexual assault and sexual harassment than their commanders. Commanders who grasp the seriousness of these crimes and are equipped to respond can make a measurable difference in survivors' lives. In meeting with survivors, the IRC learned of caring, compassionate leaders who facilitated lifesaving arrangements for victims under their command. Many well-meaning commanders, however, lacked a

---

[48] Headquarters Department of the Army. (2020, July 24). Army Command Policy: Army Regulation 600-20. https://armypubs.army.mil/epubs/DR_pubs/DR_a/ARN30511-AR_600-20-002-WEB-3.pdf

[49] DoD. (2020). *DoDI 1350.02: DoD Military Equal Opportunity Program.* https://www.esd.whs.mil/Portals/54/Documents/DD/issuances/dodi/135002p.pdf?ver=2020-09-04-124116-607

[50] DoD. (1992). *DoDI 1440.1: the DoD Civilian Equal Employment Opportunity Program.* https://prhome.defense.gov/Portals/52/Documents/nofear/DoDDirective1440%201.pdf

[51] DoD. (2020). *DoDI 1020.03: Harassment Prevention and Response in the Armed Forces.* https://www.esd.whs.mil/Portals/54/Documents/DD/issuances/dodi/102003p.PDF?ver=DAAzonEUeFb8kUWRbT9Epw%3D%3D

[52] For example, victim advocacy, safety planning, or other trauma-informed care to assist Service members who have experienced sexual harassment. This may include helping the Service member to address any immediate safety needs, understand their reporting options, and identify any behavioral health services that may be helpful.

[53] These personnel have different titles depending on the Service. For example, the Navy has Command Managed Equal Opportunity (CMEO) Managers. https://www.mynavyhr.navy.mil/Support-Services/21st-Century-Sailor/Equal-Opportunity/Resolving-an-Issue/

basic awareness of how trauma impacts victims or inadvertently took actions that breached the confidentiality of a Restricted Report.[54] Some commanders want to help, but do not know how. This makes the support of a professionally trained victim advocate especially critical, as these personnel can equip commanders with the information and tools they need to best ensure the safety and recovery of victims.

> "After my sexual assault, three other women came forward in three months. During that time, he was never detained. He started stalking me – I had to move barracks six times. I had two different prosecution teams and four different SVCs. My victim advocate deployed before the trial."
>
> -Survivor, as told to the IRC in an interview

One-on-one interviews with survivors of sexual assault in the military revealed the substantial burdens placed on victims as they navigated the military justice and health systems. Many women and men with whom the IRC spoke had dreamt their entire lives of a career in the military; in fact, they loved being in the military and did not want to leave, even after experiencing sexual assault or sexual harassment. But because their experience in the aftermath of the assault was handled so ineptly or met with hostility and retaliation, many felt they had no choice but to separate. These individual experiences are reflected in research. Data from the 2014 RAND Military Workplace Study indicate that exposure to sexual assault doubled the odds that a member would separate from the military in the ensuing 28 months.[55] RAND estimates that in 2014, the military lost more than 16,000 person-years to sexual assault and harassment, incurring the replacement costs. The impact of these separations on both the individual and the military are significant, resulting in broken lives and a fractured workforce.

At times, getting the proper care and response after a sexual assault in the military seems as if it is based on pure luck. There are so many places where the system can break down and when it does, it can stem from any combination of poor training, bias, and the inability of command and other officials to grasp the seriousness of this kind of violation. The IRC heard from several survivors whose experiences illustrate these shortcomings:

---

[54] A Service member who experiences sexual assault may choose to make a Restricted or Unrestricted Report to a DoD authority. Victims make a Restricted Report to specified individuals (e.g., SARCs, SAPR VAs, or healthcare providers), enabling confidential access to care and services. These reports are not referred for investigation and do not involve review by command authorities. Given the desire for confidentiality, the victim is not asked to provide extensive details about the sexual assault. SARCs therefore record limited data about these victims and the alleged offenses in the Defense Sexual Assault Incident Database (DSAID). Unlike a Restricted Report, an Unrestricted Report of sexual assault is referred for investigation to a Military Criminal Investigation Organization, and command is notified of the alleged incident. DoD collects data on Unrestricted Reports from the cases entered into DSAID by SARCs. A victim can choose to participate in the justice system by converting a Restricted Report to an Unrestricted Report at any time. Source: DoD SAPRO. (2021). Appendix B: Statistical Data on Sexual Assault. *Fiscal Year 2020 Annual Report on Sexual Assault in the Military.*

[55] Morral, A. R., Matthews, M., Cefalu, M., Schell, T. L., & Cottrell, L. (2021). *Effects of Sexual Assault and Sexual Harassment on Separation from the U.S. Military: Findings from the 2014 RAND Military Workplace Study*. Santa Monica, CA: RAND Corporation. https://www.rand.org/pubs/research_reports/RR870z10.html, 24.

- One survivor had four different special victims counsel over the course of her case, requiring her to retell her story multiple times;
- A severely traumatized survivor requested an expedited transfer, only to be expedited to a ship that immediately deployed, leaving her feeling more isolated than ever;
- A survivor made a Restricted Report of sexual assault, but it was changed to Unrestricted because the commander "guessed" she had made it, violating her privacy and her trust;
- A survivor's advocate communicated with her for one month, then not again for two and a half years (to ask if she wanted to speak with the IRC);
- One survivor traveled across the U.S. to return to the installation where she had been assaulted to attend the court martial, only to have the judge fall asleep during the proceedings;
- One survivor was asked by the command what she had done to invite the assault and whether she had been flirting with the man who attacked her.

This list could go on and on. The IRC listened to many Service members whose stories are a testament to this hard truth: when things go wrong in the system for survivors, they can go disastrously wrong.

Making a report of sexual assault in the military is a brave choice. It takes tremendous courage to come forward, especially knowing the negative consequences that could result. Most of the victims the IRC spoke with said they regretted making a report, either Restricted or Unrestricted. Many said that there was no confidentiality in the process—everyone in the unit learned about the report, one way or another. Victims were often shunned and ostracized afterwards by their peers and leaders. Many had trouble getting time off to go to medical and legal appointments or taking care of themselves in the aftermath of the assault. Bias and rape myths pervaded their interactions. Some victims told the IRC about being accused of lying to harm someone's career or get out of work.

> "I wasn't sleeping. I have violent nightmares. I started drinking to cope. I was harassed by command for going to psych. I regretted ever reporting."
>
> -Survivor, as told to the IRC in an interview

Yet, there is every reason to believe that Service members who have experienced sexual assault or sexual harassment can resume their military career and be productive and successful. It all depends upon the way in which the military responds to a report of sexual harassment or assault, the options and interventions available for the survivor, the environment they return to, and whether or not there is ongoing support available. Unfortunately, there is no guarantee that a Service member will have positive experiences with any of these, much less all of them.

6. Critical Deficiencies in the Workforce

The IRC found that the workforce dedicated to SAPR is not adequately structured and resourced to do this critical work. Many failures in prevention and response can be attributed to inexperienced lawyers and investigators, collateral-duty SAPR VAs, and the near total lack of actual prevention specialists. These failures are not the fault of these personnel, but rather of a structure that de-emphasizes specialization and experience, which are necessary to address the complexities of sexual assault cases and the needs of victims. This holds true across the various disciplines that make up the military's approach to sexual assault.

> "I am the only full-time victim advocate for 18,000 people."
>
> - Civilian SAPR VA, as told in an interview to the IRC

DoD and the Services Lack a True Prevention Capability

> "Giving someone a water bottle with the hotline number is too late—that's response, not prevention. They tend to get conflated."
>
> - SARC, as told to the IRC in a listening session

When asked about sexual assault and sexual harassment, Service leaders frequently invoke the need for prevention. This important commitment is not, however, matched by the resources or capabilities of the current workforce. Prevention is a specific discipline rooted in science and public health. For more than a decade, evidence-informed strategies for the prevention of sexual violence have been developed and tested, including some in the military. Nevertheless, the Services continue to confuse sexual assault response and awareness (e.g., training on reporting, conducting awareness campaigns) with prevention. Examples include teal pancake breakfasts,[56] dance contests,[57] and golf tournaments[58] to raise awareness of the SAPR program on base. Although these activities are well meaning, they trivialize the seriousness of the issue, and alienate Service members who have experienced sexual assault. Moreover, these kinds of events are not rooted in prevention science.

Across the Services, these events are evidence that prevention and awareness are regularly conflated. As a result, SARCs are called upon to design initiatives and events that have little to do with research-based prevention programs. Military personnel leading prevention activities are often double-hatted

---

[56] Szoldra, P. (2021, April 14). Army unit urges soldiers to 'be a hero, eat a pancake' for sexual assault. Task & Purpose. https://taskandpurpose.com/news/army-sexual-assault-awareness-teal-pancakes-hero/

[57] Marine Corps Community Services. (2016). The Sexual Assault Prevention Innovation Award Winner Did What? https://usmc-mccs.org/articles/the-sexual-assault-prevention-innovation-award-winner-did-what/

[58] Levering, L. (2021, April 29). It Takes a Team: Fort Gordon observes Sexual Assault Awareness and Prevention Month. *Army.mil.* https://www.army.mil/article/245735/it_takes_a_team_fort_gordon_observes_sexual_assault_awareness_and_prevention_month

or tasked as collateral duty sexual assault responders. These personnel generally do not have the expertise to design, implement, and evaluate comprehensive prevention activities, through no fault of their own. The IRC learned that unfunded prevention mandates have also contributed to this problem, requiring the Services to shoehorn people and programs to make it work.

Commanders must also play a role in prevention, but leaders at every level lack the knowledge, skills, and abilities necessary to be a force for the prevention of sexual harassment and sexual assault. In particular, primary prevention—stopping sexual violence before it starts—is not well understood across the enterprise.[59,60]

Leading in prevention requires more than a one-time awareness campaign or simple statements of support. In the same way that the military evaluates constantly shifting environments to develop winning combat strategies, DoD and the Services must conduct a comprehensive scan of its capabilities to determine the optimum full-time prevention workforce and invest the resources necessary to accomplish the mission.

> "I regularly run into commanders only wanting to assign their most dispensable leaders to SARC/ [SAPR] VA positions. And that has ended disastrously for us in some cases."
>
> -Former SARC, as told to the IRC in a listening session

Serving Victims Cannot be a "Part Time" Effort and Requires a Professional Response

In the military, the majority of victim advocacy is conducted by Service members as a collateral duty[61] or developmental assignment. The IRC met collateral-duty SAPR Vas and SARCs who were assigned to these roles without any regard for their strengths and abilities. Even when these collateral-duty personnel cared about victims and wanted to do a good job, they lacked the knowledge and ability to do so. Many had little, if any, experience in social services, and would soon rotate out of the position.

The assumption that a mechanic or logistics specialist will have the skills to effectively address the complexities of sexual assault is an affront to victims. Importantly, though, the IRC also met collateral-duty SAPR VAs and SARCs who volunteered for the positions and were excited to be part of the solution. DoD and the Services should consider how to best harness the interest and

---

[59] DoD. (2020). DoDI 6400.09: DoD Policy on Integrated Primary Prevention of Self-Directed Harm and Prohibited Abuse or Harm. https://www.esd.whs.mil/Portals/54/Documents/DD/issuances/dodi/640009p.pdf?ver=2020-09-11-104936-223

[60] Primary prevention can include improving physical environments in barracks and installations, teaching basic sexual education and developing healthy communication skills for sexual activities, and strengthening and enforcing policies that prohibit hazing, stalking, and harassment, and increasing knowledge about military culture and violence prevention.

[61] For example, across the Services, collateral duty sexual assault response personnel come from a range of military occupational specialties, such as aircraft maintenance or logistics. The expectation is that these Service members will spend the majority of their time in their primary job, and tack on additional hours to help staff their unit's SAPR or SHARP program.

enthusiasm of these young Service members without expecting them to serve in jobs that should be filled by experienced, full-time professional advocates.

Sexual Assault Cases Require Specialized, Trained Military Justice Practitioners

"As a combat veteran, I recognize that the military can't protect my daughter from sexual assault 24/7…it just can't. But it does have the responsibility to competently defend her…and it didn't."

-Father of a survivor, as told to the IRC in an interview

The IRC found that military justice practitioners are hard-working, dedicated, and earnest. They too, however, lack the experience and specialization needed to effectively handle complex sexual assault cases. Service Judge Advocate General (JAG) Corps leadership, apart from the Navy, do not allow judge advocates who specialize in criminal litigation to stay in these positions for their careers. This creates a lack of confidence in military lawyers by both Service members and the public. After hearing from current and former military practitioners, as well as sexual assault victims who participated in the military justice court-martial system, it is apparent that the Service's JAG refusal to allow talented practitioners to remain in career litigation billets harms both victims and accused. Those litigating special victim cases do not possess the characteristics and skills to perform their job, which in turn fosters institutional incompetence. Former military judges and judge advocates who spoke with the IRC described junior prosecutor courtroom performance as ranging from "terrible" to "incompetent." However, in trials where seasoned special victim prosecutors participated as co-counsel to the more inexperienced and often junior counsel, the quality of government practice increased exponentially.

In sum, the IRC found that these workforce deficiencies, namely lack of specialization and experience, were apparent throughout each sector of prevention and response. To address these critical gaps across the workforce, the IRC recommends career tracks for military justice personnel; the establishment of a dedicated primary prevention workforce; and the restructuring of the victim care and support workforce to largely eliminate collateral duty for these essential positions. Gaps in manpower, personnel, and training should be considered to create a workforce that can be sustainable over time.

7. Outdated Gender & Social Norms Persist Across the Force

Although the military has become increasingly diverse, women make up less than 18 percent of the total force, and less than 30 percent of the force identifies as some racial minority.[62] With these dynamics, many women who serve report being treated differently than their male counterparts. In

[62] Of total force members in 2018 (i.e., Active Duty, Reserve, and Guard members from all Services), 82 percent identify as male and 71 percent identify as White. Source: Military OneSource. (2019). 2018 Demographics: Profile of the Military Community. https://download.militaryonesource.mil/12038/MOS/Reports/2018-demographics-report.pdf, pp. 6-7.

the IRC's discussions with enlisted personnel, many Service women described feeling singled out or the subject of near daily sexist comments, as one of few women in their units. Their perceptions are reinforced by research.

When women are considered "less than" by their male peers or leaders, unit climates are breeding grounds[63] for gender discrimination, sexual harassment, and sexual assault. Career fields that are especially male dominated can be at higher risk for sexual assault. According to RAND, the highest risk career field for women is field artillery, with more than 1 in 10 Service women experiencing sexual assault in 2018.[64]

"I heard that they made a list of who I could have slept with to get my job. I was the joke to them."

-Service woman NCO, as told to the IRC through the DoD Safe Helpline

Across the force, sexual violence is an outgrowth of lingering "subcultures of misogyny," as recently described by the Commandant of the Marine Corps.[65] These subcultures don't only exist in real life—they also thrive online. The IRC also spoke with multiple survivors of sexual assault and sexual harassment who were targeted through social media and other electronic means. Indeed, cyberharassment and technology-facilitated[66] abuse was a recurring theme in the submissions from Service members to the IRC through the DoD Safe Helpline. Their stories are reinforced by DoD data, which demonstrates that cyberharassment contributes to hostile unit climates, and is, for some victims, the primary means by which they experience abuse. Among active duty women, 30 percent who have experienced sexual harassment indicate the harassment took place online, on social media or by other electronic means.[67,68]

---

[63] Flood, M., & Pease, B. (2009). Factors Influencing Attitudes to Violence Against Women. *Trauma, Violence & Abuse, 10*(2). www.jstor.org/stable/26636200: 125–142.

[64] Matthews, M., Morral, A.R., Schell, T.L., Cefalu, M., Snoke, J., Briggs, R.J. (2018). *Organizational Characteristics Associated with Risk of Sexual Assault and Sexual Harassment in the U.S. Army*. RAND Corporation. https://www.rand.org/pubs/research_reports/RRA1013-1.html

[65] Senate Armed Services Committee. (2020, March 5). Statement of the Honorable Thomas B. Modly Acting Secretary of the Navy, Admiral Michael M. Gilday, Chief of Naval Operations, and General David H. Berger, Commandant of the U.S. Marine Corps on Fiscal Year 2021 Department of the Navy Budget before the Senate Armed Services Committee. https://www.armed-services.senate.gov/imo/media/doc/Modly--Gilday--Berger_03-05-20.pdf

[66] Technology-facilitated abuse includes specific behaviors or crimes under the UCMJ, such as: Article 117a, nonconsensual distribution of intimate digital images and Article 130 stalking. Additionally, technology-facilitated abuse describes forms of harmful behavior or interpersonal violence that are communicated through social media, or other internet-based platforms/applications. For example, retaliation for reporting a sexual assault can take place online by posting a derogatory comment or even a threat to someone's social media page. Similarly, a Military Protective Order can be violated via electronic communications if the subject contacts the victim through electronic means, i.e., email, chat, messenger, or other social media application.

[67] Breslin, R., Davis, E., Hylton, K., Hill, A., Klauberg, W., Petusky, M., Klahr, A. (2019). *2018 Workplace and Gender Relations Survey of Active Duty Members: Overview Report*. Report No. 2019-027. Alexandria, VA: Office of People Analytics. https://apps.dtic.mil/sti/citations/AD1072334

[68] Cyberharassment is also linked to sexual assault. DoD's own surveys indicate that one-third of victims who report experiencing sexual assault felt they had been the target of retaliation through online ostracism or maltreatment. Source:

The IRC was confronted with the challenges posed by stubborn gender stereotypes in listening sessions with junior enlisted Service members. These meetings exposed a profound disconnect between the lessons that sexual assault and sexual harassment trainings seek to teach, and the behaviors, attitudes, and beliefs of junior enlisted Service members towards SAPR/SHARP. These young Service members told the IRC that training makes men afraid that they will be falsely accused rather than providing skills and knowledge to be part of positive change.[69] They spoke of outdated training that seemed to reinforce rape myths, rather than address misinformation.

In particular, the IRC heard from young men Service members who expressed confusion regarding what behaviors could result in a "SHARP violation." Some interpreted information sessions about SHARP/SAPR to say: "don't touch a female; don't look at a female; and don't talk to a female" to avoid getting in trouble. This perception was reinforced by women Service members, who expressed feeling at times like men in their units would simply avoid them, contributing to social isolation to the detriment of unit cohesion. These perceptions are widespread. For example, in a new survey on women in Army Special Forces, one male officer said, "I am afraid that female who fails to meet the standards, she can end my career by claiming SHARP."[70] In fact, this sentiment is so pervasive across the force that SHARP has become a verb (e.g., Service members might "get Sharped" or victims may make false accusations and "SHARP" an innocent Service member). Even the junior enlisted Service members, with whom the IRC spoke shared sincere concern over the problem of sexual assault and wanted to be engaged in solutions, held these misconceptions. False reporting is a commonly held rape myth across the general population,[71] but is especially concerning in the military, where sexual assault is significantly underreported,[72] and baseless reports are rare.[73]

In addition to sexism, harmful beliefs and attitudes on race, ethnicity, sexual orientation, gender identity, and others have a connection to how Service members experience sexual harassment and sexual assault. As others have rightly observed, "our military is a reflection of our own society."[74] The IRC met with survivors whose experiences with sexual assault and sexual harassment were impossible to divorce from their race or ethnicity, or sexual orientation or gender identity. Another

---

DoD. (2017). *Fiscal Year 2016 Annual Report on Sexual Assault in the Military.* https://sapr.mil/public/docs/reports/FY16_Annual/FY16_SAPRO_Annual_Report.pdf

69 These observations were made in IRC junior enlisted listening sessions virtual and site visits.

70 Britzky, H. (2021, May 18). 'Stop the social experiment'—New Survey Spotlights Bias Against Women in Army Special Ops. *Task and Purpose.* https://taskandpurpose.com/news/army-special-operations-women-survey/

71 Ibid.

72 DoD SAPRO. (2021). Appendix C: Metrics and Non-Metrics on Sexual Assault. *Fiscal Year 2020 Annual Report on Sexual Assault in the Military.* https://www.sapr.mil/sites/default/files/Appendix_C_Metrics_and_NonMetrics_on_Sexual_Assault_FY2020.pdf

73 In 2020, 33 out of 3,358 sexual assault cases were not taken for action due to allegations determined to be "false or baseless." Source: DoD. (2021). Appendix B: Statistical Data on Sexual Assault. *Fiscal Year 2020 Annual Report on Sexual Assault in the Military.*

74 Shinkman, P.D. (2021). How the Military Attempts to Right Racial Wrongs. *U.S. News.* https://www.usnews.com/news/national-news/articles/2021-04-20/military-racism-george-floyd-and-new-attempts-at-change-air-force-chief-gen-brown-discusses-the-future-of-the-armed-forces

Service member described to the IRC how difficult it was, as a male survivor, to report the sexual assault and ask for help, because he feared stigma from peers, who would scrutinize his sexuality. The military cannot effectively prevent sexual assault and sexual harassment without a holistic effort to promote a culture in which *all* Service members feel like they belong. [75]

8. Little is Known about Perpetration

The most effective way to stop sexual harassment and sexual assault is to prevent perpetration, but the Department lacks sufficient data to make evidence-based decisions in this domain. The bulk of research on sexual violence in the military has focused on victims;[76] however, without complementary research on perpetration—and the unique risk factors that drive some Service members to sexually harass or assault others—the military lacks half of the total information needed to paint the full picture of how and why sexual violence occurs. Despite the evidence that sexual harassment is strongly tied to sexual assault risk, there is also little to no research on sexual harassment prevention within the Department.[77, 78] As a result, the impact of prevention activities in military communities, particularly activities aimed at reducing perpetration, remains relatively unknown. This lack of insight regarding the motivation, predictive behaviors, and impact of prevention programs on perpetrators is especially concerning because *some efforts may actually cause harm*, if not implemented with care. For example, a growing body of research indicates that some men who hold hostile attitudes towards women may endorse increased sexual aggression after exposure to anti-violence messaging.[79]

---

[75] These themes are addressed in a spoken word performance created by Rashan Legard, a survivor and platoon leader with the 96th Aviation Support Battalion, 101st Combat Aviation Brigade at Fort Campbell, Kentucky. An article on the Army's website says the performance "shines a spotlight on mental health, LGBTQ discrimination, respect for women, and race." See: Rico, Antonieta. Officer shares harrowing experience of assault to drive culture change. Army Resilience Directorate.
https://www.army.mil/article/246894/officer_shares_harrowing_experience_of_assault_to_drive_culture_change. 27 May 2021.

[76] The need to gather data on perpetration was emphasized in many IRC working group meetings as an urgent research gap for the Department and the Services.

[77] In addition, the majority of research does not capture social trends and processes occurring at the interactional, team, unit, community, or organizational levels.

[78] In 2020, the DoD published the first ever DoD Sexual Assault Prevention and Response Research Agenda which identifies ten research priorities. The agenda guides and informs SAPR research across the Department but is not directive in nature or enforceable. Additionally, although the various forms of sexual violence share common risk and protective factors, the current research agenda is not integrated (i.e., inclusive of suicide, substance misuse, etc.), and therefore misses important opportunities to discover or test cross-cutting interventions.

[79] Malamuth, N.M., Huppin, M., & Linz, D. (2018). Sexual assault interventions may be doing more harm than good with high-risk males. *Aggression and Violent Behavior, 41*: 20-24. https://doi.org/10.1016/j.avb.2018.05.010

Section III: Recommendations

For full details, please see the report for each line of effort and the cross-cutting recommendations in the corresponding Appendices.

Cross-cutting Recommendations

- DoD should immediately make sexual harassment victims eligible for SAPR services and undertake a review of all policies and structures tasked with addressing elements of the military's sexual harassment response.
- DoD must undertake a comprehensive approach to professionalizing, strengthening, and resourcing the workforce for SAPR across the board.
- DoD must improve the military's response to domestic violence, which is inextricably tied to sexual assault, by taking key actions to enhance accountability, inform prevention through better data collection, and increase access to victim care and support for Service members, their families and partners who experience relationship abuse, including sexual assault.
- DoD needs to improve data collection, including qualitative research and quantitative survey tools, to better reflect the experiences of Service members whose intersecting identities, such as race, ethnicity, sexual orientation, gender and gender identity, may place them at higher risk for sexual harassment and sexual assault.
- The Secretary of Defense should establish, alongside the OSD Office of the Special Victim Prosecutor, the complementary role of the Senior Policy Advisor for Special Victims. The Senior Policy Advisor should be supported by the new position of the DoD Special Victim Advocate.

Recommendations by Line of Effort

Line of Effort 1: Accountability

1.1 **Creation of the Office of the Special Victim Prosecutor within the Office of the Secretary of Defense.**

1.2 **Independent, trained investigators for sexual harassment and mandatory initiation of involuntary separation for all substantiated complaints.**

1.3 **Judge-ordered Military Protective Orders for victims of sexual assault and related offenses.**

1.4 **Professionalized career billets for military justice personnel handling special victim crimes.**

1.5 **Judge-alone sentencing in all noncapital general and special courts-martial and establishment of sentencing parameters.**

1.6 Expedite processing of proposed Executive Orders regarding military justice, including those currently awaiting issuance related to sexual assault, sexual harassment, and other special victim crimes.[80]

1.7 Modify the UCMJ in several key areas to increase uniformity, reliability, and consistency in the military justice system.

1.7 a The Secretary of Defense should direct the Defense Advisory Committee on Investigations, Prosecution, and Defense of Sexual Assault in the Armed Forces (DAC-IPAD) to study Article 32 Preliminary Hearings.

1.7 b The Secretary of Defense should direct the DAC-IPAD to study Article 34, Advice to Convening Authority Before Referral to Trial.

1.7 c The UCMJ should be amended to establish a preponderance of the evidence standard for non-judicial punishment.

1.7 d Article 25 of the UCMJ should be amended to establish random selection of panel members.

1.7 e The Secretary of Defense should direct the Services to establish funding appropriate for defense counsel control of their own resources.

1.7 f Article 128b. of the UCMJ should be amended to include dating violence.

1.8 Study caseloads to attain the optimum timeline for the military justice process.

Line of Effort 2: Prevention

2.1 Equip all leaders with prevention competencies and evaluate their performance.

2.1 a The Under Secretary of Defense for Personnel and Readiness (USD(P&R)) should define the competencies leaders must have to oversee prevention.

2.1 b The Services and the National Guard Bureau (NGB) should develop and hold leaders appropriately accountable for prevention.

2.1 c The Services and the NGB should equip all leaders to develop and deliver informed prevention messages in formal and informal settings.

2.2 Establish a dedicated primary prevention workforce.

2.2 a USD(P&R) should develop a model for a dedicated and capable prevention workforce.

2.2 b USD(P&R) should develop a professional credential for the prevention workforce.

2.2 c The Services should determine the optimum full-time prevention workforce, and equip all echelons of active duty, reserve, and guard organizations.

---

[80] The IRC notes that this recommendation, which supports the Department's efforts to enumerate sexual harassment as a specified offense under the general Article 134, was previously endorsed by the 2019 Sexual Assault Accountability and Investigation Task Force. See: https://media.defense.gov/2019/May/02/2002127159/-1/-1/1/SAAITF_REPORT.PDF

2.3 Implement community-level prevention strategies unique to Service members' environments.

- **2.3 a** The Services and the NGB should resource and implement prevention strategies at organizational and community levels.
- **2.3 b** USD(P&R) should identify a non-clinical OSD-level Office of Primary Responsibility for alcohol policy and develop relevant policy guidance and oversight.

2.4 Modernize prevention education and skill-building to reflect today's generation of Service members.

2.5 Identify and actively support Service members with the most effective prevention interventions.

- **2.5 a** The Services and the NGB should institute a pilot program to link Service members with resources and support.
- **2.5 b** The Services and the NGB should employ virtual platforms to provide support to all Service members.

2.6 Create a state-of-the-art DoD prevention research capability.

- **2.6 a** DoD should establish a dedicated research center for the primary prevention of interpersonal and self-directed violence.
- **2.6 b** USD(P&R), the Services, and the NGB should continually review and update all policies that unnecessarily restrict data collection on important populations of Service members.
- **2.6 c** The Secretary of Defense should immediately authorize operational testing of the Air Force Compatibility Assessment with a cross-Service pre-accession sample, allowing for important research and intervention development.
- **2.6 d** USD(P&R) should commission research on gender and masculinities to develop effective social marketing strategies to facilitate primary prevention efforts.

2.7 Establish a comprehensive National Guard primary prevention strategy.

- **2.7 a** The NGB should develop Army National and Air National Guard prevention strategies aligned with DoD's Prevention Plan of Action, based on the National Guard's unique construct and missions.
- **2.7 b** USD(P&R) should submit a legislative proposal providing authorization and funding for the NGB to conduct recurring National Guard unit inspections and staff assistance visits for prevention oversight and assistance.

2.8 USD(P&R) should update the Department's prevention strategy, including the DoD Prevention Plan of Action, to incorporate approved IRC recommendations.

Line of Effort 3: Climate and Culture

3.1 USD(P&R) should codify in policy and direct the development and implementation of metrics related to sexual harassment and sexual assault as part of readiness tracking and reporting.

3.2 USD(P&R) should direct the Services to educate the force about sexual harassment and sexual assault within the context of the Services' core values.

3.3 DoD must execute on the principle that addressing sexual harassment and sexual assault in the 21st century requires engaging with the cyber domain.

- **3.3 a** Collect data to measure the problem of cyberharassment (and related harms).
- **3.3 b** Educate leaders on cyberharassment and technology-facilitated sexual harassment and sexual assault.
- **3.3 c** Hold Service members appropriately accountable who engage in cyberharassment and other forms of technology-facilitated sexual harassment and sexual assault.

3.4 DoD should ensure that there is an internal focus on preventing sexual harm and gender-based violence across the force in implementing the 2017 National Women, Peace, and Security (WPS) Act.

- **3.4 a** Elevate and standardize the gender advisor workforce.
- **3.4 b** Use qualitative data as part of indicators for Defense Objective One of the WPS Strategic Framework.
- **3.4 c** Integrate a gender analysis into the military's planning & operational frameworks.
- **3.4 d** Review and revise Professional Military Education (PME) and DoD schoolhouse curricula to mainstream WPS priorities.
- **3.4 e** Congress should support DoD's inclusion of Personnel & Readiness in WPS implementation and codify in legislation.

3.5 Use qualitative data to select, develop, and evaluate the right leaders for command positions.

- **3.5 a** Use qualitative data to select and develop the right leaders.
- **3.5 b** Include a meaningful narrative section in performance evaluations for officers and NCOs.

3.6 Building a climate for the reduction of sexual harassment and sexual assault as a fundamental leader development requirement.

3.7 USD(P&R) should undertake a series of enhancements to the climate survey process to ensure that timely, actionable data can be used to improve unit climate on sexual harassment and assault.

- **3.7 a** USD(P&R) should develop a standardized "pulse survey" tool that would enable unit-level commanders to collect real-time climate data on sexual harassment and sexual assault from Service members in their units between required administrations of the Defense Organizational Climate Survey (DEOCS).

3.7 b The Secretary of Defense should direct the Services to develop a formal system to share climate survey data at the unit level and initiate and evaluate corrective action plans.

3.7 c USD(P&R) should accelerate efforts to develop a validated "Climate Benchmark" to measure healthy and unhealthy climate at the unit level.

3.7 d The Secretary of Defense should assess whether current DoD policies, relevant components, and the Service-level Equal Opportunity workforce have the capacity to help commanders resolve climate issues.

3.8 The Services should publish the nature and results of all disciplinary actions related to sexual misconduct and disseminate this information to troops periodically.

Line of Effort 4: Victim Care and Support

4.1 Optimize the victim care and support workforce.

4.1 a Move SARCs and SAPR VAs from the command reporting structure.

4.1 b Eliminate collateral duty for SARCs and SAPR VAs, with exceptions for ships, submarines, and isolated installations.

4.1 c Explore the co-location of SAPR and SHARP with other special victim services, such as FAP, to improve coordination, collaboration, and consistency in victim support.

4.1 d Train Independent Duty Corpsmen to be Sexual Assault Medical Forensic Examiners so patient care and evidence collection can be provided in deployed and isolated environments.

4.2 Expand victim service options to meet the needs of all survivors of sexual assault and sexual harassment.

4.2 a Increase access to and visibility of civilian community-based care.

4.2 b Authorize Service members to access the full spectrum of VA services for conditions related to military sexual assault and sexual harassment confidentially, and without a referral.

4.2 c Expand access to CATCH to include victims of sexual harassment and enable Service members to self-service access to CATCH.

4.2 d Create survivor-led peer support programs that allow for in-person, virtual, and telephone interaction.

4.2 e Amplify victims' rights and services in the post-trial period.

4.3 Center the survivor to facilitate healing and restoration.

4.3 a Implement the No Wrong Door approach to sexual harassment, sexual assault, and domestic abuse across the Services and NGB.

4.3 b Institute a "Commander's Package" from the SAPR VA with recommendations for victim care and support.

4.3 c Allow survivors flexibility to take non-chargeable time off for seeking services or time for recovery from sexual assault.

4.3 d Increase victim agency and control of the response process by: maximizing adherence to survivor preference on reporting status, and centering survivor preferences in expedited transfers.

4.3 e Study the methods our allies have used to make amends to survivors, including restorative engagement to acknowledge harm, and potential victim compensation.

4.4 Re-envision training and research to improve victim care and support.

4.4 a Establish a Defense Sexual Assault and Sexual Harassment Center of Excellence that administers a core curriculum of trauma and response trainings for all SAPR VAs and SARCs, chaplains, and other response personnel.

4.4 b Develop training to build the capacity of SARCs and SAPR VAs to provide culturally competent care to Service members from communities of color, LGBTQ+ Service members, religious minorities, and men

4.4 c Revise and update training modules on appropriate response to sexual assault and sexual harassment in PME for officers and NCOs.

4.4 d Use an action research model to identify root problems, test interventions, and create best practices with survivors' input

Section IV: Way Forward

The U.S. military is highly socialized to change. From permanent changes of station to deployments to implementing and executing new laws, change is a constant. It is always happening. In deciding whether to adopt and implement the IRC's recommendations, every stakeholder needs to have the courage to challenge the status quo. The courage to change must come from the Department and the Services, but it also must come from Congress. For the past decade, many lawmakers have said that change is needed, but the Department requires resources. Congress, therefore, needs to take action by providing meaningful resources at the enterprise level. Moving the needle on sexual harassment and assault will require new investments in victim services and prevention. While it was beyond the scope of this analysis, the IRC anticipates that such investments will result in cost savings to the military in productivity, health, mental health, and other costs related to sexual harassment and assault.[81]

[81] Based on CDC data, the individual lifetime cost of rape is estimated to be $122,461 per victim; across the U.S. population, this is estimated at nearly $3.1 trillion (in 2014 dollars). Costs are based on combined expenses from medical care to victims, criminal justice responses, lost work productivity among victims and offenders, and others. Peterson, C., DeGue, S., Florence, C., & Lokey, C. N. (2017). Lifetime Economic Burden of Rape Among U.S. Adults. American journal of preventive medicine, 52(6), 691–701. https://doi.org/10.1016/j.amepre.2016.11.014

Congressional Oversight

The IRC is mindful that DoD and the Services have been working to implement a considerable number of Congressional requirements focused on SAPR. According to a 2021 GAO report,[82] between 2004 and 2019, Congress enacted 249 requirements that largely cover victim advocacy and support, management and oversight, and military justice, with a smaller number addressing prevention. This has resulted in ongoing shifts to policy and implementation plans related to sexual assault and harassment. The IRC recommendations also include items for legislative actions, including changing the role of commanders in military justice decisions. The IRC recommends that legislative changes to the UCMJ be prioritized for Congress in this year's National Defense Authorization Act (NDAA) with implementation dates of 2023. The IRC urges Congress to consider reasonable timeframes for implementation and importantly, evaluation of new provisions. To improve accountability on sexual assault prevention and response, Congress should also encourage greater transparency of Service-level spending in these areas.

Timeline & Implementation

Each IRC recommendation is important to the overall effort of establishing command climates of dignity and respect, stopping sexual assaults and related misconduct, and supporting victims. Accordingly, each should be implemented as swiftly as possible with due regard for taking the time necessary to implement carefully and fully. Some recommendations require legislation, implementation by the President, and the establishment of new organizations, policies, and procedures, along with the requisite training, by the Department. Others may be implemented much more quickly. The priorities noted here in no way diminish the critical importance of the other recommendations, but rather identify pressing issues for near-term and immediate action:

- Given the vital importance of victim services, and the serious deficiencies identified in this report, the recommendations in this area should be prioritized. The manpower study and desk audit (Recommendation 4.1b) should be initiated within three months from the date of this report. Additional Victim Care and Support recommendations should be prioritized for action as soon as possible, but no later than 6 months from the date of this report.

The following recommendations require policy changes that are long overdue and therefore should be prioritized for immediate action by the Department:

- Issuing policy guidance enabling SAPR VAs to provide response services to sexual harassment victims;
- Determining who should serve as investigators for formal sexual harassment complaints outside of the chain of command, taking into account the comfort level of victims in talking to

---

82 GAO. (2021). Sexual Assault in the Military: Continued Congressional Oversight and Additional DoD Focus on Prevention Could Aid DoD's Efforts. https://www.gao.gov/assets/gao-21-463t.pdf

investigators and the capacity of each proposed group to understand and investigate sexual harassment cases (see Recommendation 1.2);

- Reissuing DoD's policy on "Domestic Abuse Involving DoD Military and Certain Affiliated Personnel,"[83] which critically expands the DoD definition of "intimate partner" to include dating partners when defining eligibility for military-provisioned services regarding intimate partner violence (including sexual assault in the context of a relationship); and,
- Lifting restrictions on Service-level research on sexual minorities under the USD(P&R) policy memorandum, "Repeal of Don't Ask Don't Tell and Future Impact on Policy" dated January 28, 2011 (see Recommendation 2.6 b).

Many of the recommendations from the IRC's Accountability line of effort require Congress to amend the Uniform Code of Military Justice and make fundamental changes to military justice. These changes will take a considerable amount of time to fully implement. Accordingly, Appendix B discusses the appropriate timeline for implementing these recommendations. Similarly, Appendix C discusses the appropriate timeline for implementing the IRC's Prevention recommendations.

Because oversight of the Department's efforts in this area is important, the DAC-IPAD should be reconstituted without delay. The IRC also recommends that the Defense Advisory Committee for the Prevention of Sexual Misconduct be established as soon as possible.

Areas for Further Study

The IRC attempted to address as many issues as possible under its Charter. Given the limitations of a 90-day timeframe, not all concerns raised by stakeholders could be fully examined. Below are several areas that have been identified for further study. [84]

Military Service Academies

Although time constraints prevented the IRC from a separate in-depth focus on the Military Service Academies, the IRC kept the Academies in mind while framing the recommendations. Because the cadets and midshipmen are on active duty and subject to the UCMJ[85], they will benefit from the changes to military justice policy, practice, and procedure; however, implementation of the IRC's recommendations should include an analysis of their unique requirements.

---

[83] DoD. (2017). DoDI 6400.06: Domestic Abuse Involving DoD Military and Certain Affiliated Personnel. https://www.esd.whs.mil/Portals/54/Documents/DD/issuances/dodi/640006p.pdf

[84] A complete write-up of these issue areas can be found in Appendix F.

[85] Similarly, while the IRC did not examine the unique considerations of sexual assault and sexual harassment in the U.S. Coast Guard, pursuant to 10 U.S.C. § 101 and 14 U.S.C. § 101, the Coast Guard is a military service and a branch of the Armed Forces of the United States at all times. Coast Guard officers and enlisted members are subject to the UCMJ pursuant to 10 U.S.C. § 802 (Article 2), and the Coast Guard is part of the military justice system as implemented in the MCM (2019 ed.). The IRC welcomed the participation of the Coast Guard on its Accountability consultative team.

Long-term Behavioral Health and Victim Care

Stigma is a significant barrier to seeking behavioral health services in the military community because the culture sets the expectation that Service members should be able to handle problems on their own.[86] A major obstacle to survivors of sexual assault seeking long-term support for trauma is the fear of losing benefits, or being declared "unfit for duty." The IRC recommends DoD and the Services continue to study the impact of stigma on survivors' use of behavioral health services.

Administrative Separation Boards, Grade Determination Boards, and Boards of Inquiry

The IRC heard from many survivors (and several commanders) about their frustrations with the Service's various administrative boards, in that Service members with substantiated sexual assault allegations whose commanders initiate separation are afforded the opportunity to prove that they should nonetheless remain in the military. These administrative boards are comprised of Service members hand-selected by command[87] and with no legal training. The IRC heard resounding concerns that these Boards are not impartial and frequently decide to retain Service members despite substantiated incidents of sexual harassment or sexual assault. The IRC believes an extensive review of these Boards should be conducted by the DAC-IPAD to determine if there are systemic issues regarding their structure and decisions.

Victim Collateral Misconduct

Victims of sexual assault may have engaged in minor misconduct, such as underage drinking or fraternization, associated with the sexual assault incident. The thorny issue of whether and how to dispose of such misconduct currently rests with the victim's commander—which can create a chilling effect on victims' decisions to report their assault or even seek services. DoD is in the process of issuing a "Safe-to-Report" policy required by Congress[88] regarding collateral misconduct of victims of sexual assault and may include an outright prohibition on punishing victims who engage in minor collateral misconduct. The IRC supports the inclusion of such a prohibition. If enacted, the Department should consider assessing whether retroactive expungement of such records for previous victims, who did not receive the protections afforded by the new policy, would best attain justice. If the new policy does not include this type of prohibition, and due to the IRC's broken trust findings (See Recommendation 1.1), the Department should consider what role the proposed Special Victim Prosecutor, rather than commanders, should have in meting out collateral misconduct.

---

[86] Kaplan, D. (2019). *Reducing Military Mental Health Stigma to Improve Treatment Engagement: Guidance for Clinicians.* Psychological Health Center of Excellence, Department of Defense. https://www.pdhealth.mil/news/blog/reducing-military-mental-health-stigma-improve-treatment-engagement-guidance-clinicians

[87] The commander who selects the board members is typically at higher level than the commander who issued the nonjudicial punishment or reprimand, which may result in a process that is frustrating for both victim and the commander who issued disciplinary action for the substantiated allegation.

[88] Section 539A of the NDAA for FY21.

Guard and Reserve

A key principle undergirding the IRC's recommendations is the importance of equal access to justice, and consistent quality for victim care and support across the Total Force; however, the Guard and Reserve face unique challenges that simply do not allow them to develop perfectly parallel policies. DoD and Congress should support the efforts of the Guard, and the Reserves, to find solutions to the complex state and federal jurisdictional questions surrounding sexual harassment and sexual assault of these Service members. The Prevention section of this report includes recommendations specific to the Guard.

Civilian Workforce

Although this report focused on Service members, the IRC is mindful that the Department also employs nearly 900,000 DoD civilians across the globe,[89] and significant challenges remain in how DoD and the Services respond to sexual harassment and sexual assault affecting civilian personnel. The IRC recommends a continued focus on implementing the recommendations included in the GAO report, "Sexual Harassment and Assault: Guidance Needed to Ensure Consistent Tracking, Response, and Training for DoD Civilians."[90]

Final Thoughts

In the battle against sexual harassment and sexual assault in the military, there can be no middle ground. Leaders can either be "all in" for a culture free from sexual harassment and sexual assault, or they can allow for a culture of impunity to persist. Commanders must establish clear rules with concrete examples of what a healthy command climate of dignity and respect looks like. They must emphasize those rules at every opportunity, and seamlessly weave these standards for conduct into the fabric of their unit's day-to-day operations.

Service members closely observe when commanders enforce what they teach, so no breach can go uncorrected. Even "low-level" offensive statements require reprimand and consequence so that Service members know that commanders are living by the popular military saying, "the standard you walk by is the standard you accept." This vigilance and expectation of respect must also extend to the online environment, which is an extension of unit climate.

The IRC believes that the hard truths uncovered here are not intractable problems. Realizing a more inclusive and safer military is achievable—provided DoD, the Services, and Congress commit to

---

89 Davidson, J. (2021). Most reports by civilians of sexual assault go unrecorded in Defense Department database. *The Washington Post*. https://www.washingtonpost.com/politics/defense-civilians-sexual-assault/2021/02/19/306c0150-729e-11eb-a4eb-44012a612cf9_story.html

90 90 GAO. (2021). *Sexual Harassment and Assault: Guidance Needed to Ensure Consistent Tracking, Response, and Training for DoD Civilians*. https://www.gao.gov/assets/gao-21-113.pdf

taking a whole-of-body approach through investments in prevention, climate and culture, accountability, and victim care and support.

Appendix A: Cross-cutting Recommendations

See supplemental appendix.

Appendix B: Rebuilding Broken Trust: Recommendations for Accountability in the Military Justice System

See supplemental appendix.

Appendix C: Equipping the Force and Empowering Prevention: Recommendations to Prevent Sexual Harassment and Sexual Assault in the U.S. Military

See supplemental appendix.

Appendix D: The Imperative of Leadership in the War Against Sexual Assault: Recommendations for Climate & Culture

See supplemental appendix.

Appendix E: Honoring Our Duty to Survivors of Military Sexual Assault: Recommendations on Victim Care & Support

See supplemental appendix.

Appendix F: Areas for Further Study

See supplemental appendix.

Appendix G: IRC Founding Documents

See supplemental appendix.

Appendix A: Cross-cutting Recommendations

Through the course of its work, the Independent Review Commission (IRC) on Sexual Assault in the Military identified several overarching themes ripe for specific recommendations that were not exclusive to any one line of effort in its Charter. The following are high-level recommendations for the Department of Defense (DoD) to consider as it works to improve prevention and response to sexual assault and sexual harassment in the military.

Implement an Enduring & Comprehensive Policy Response to Sexual Harassment

DoD's approach to sexual harassment is fractured across several components and should be addressed in direct coordination with Sexual Assault Prevention and Response (SAPR) policies to reflect the established continuum of harm.[1] DoD must undertake a comprehensive review of policies and structures tasked with addressing elements of the military's sexual harassment response. In the interim, the IRC recommends DoD issue policy guidance enabling SAPR Victim Advocates (VAs) to provide response services to sexual harassment victims, so that no one is turned away who needs support.[2]

Restructure the SAPR Workforce

To move the needle on sexual violence prevention and response, DoD and the Services must restructure the workforce. The military is an organization of decisive action; however, the perception that action is lagging in the area of sexual violence cannot be overstated. The current workforce structure, including lack of career tracks for military justice personnel, the use of collateral-duty SAPR VAs, and double-hatted prevention specialists, is inadequate to address the scope of the problem. To correct these deficiencies, the IRC recommends that DoD take a comprehensive approach to restructuring the workforce that professionalizes and strengthens each of the critical disciplines, including public health experts, lawyers, investigators, and victim advocates.

Additionally, the IRC recommends the establishment of a dedicated primary prevention workforce, separate from the response personnel. As these efforts roll out, they should be articulated as comprehensive approach to SAPR. By redesigning the SAPR workforce, DoD will fill critical gaps and build long-term capacity to achieve its goals.

---

[1] Research by RAND illuminates these intersections: Service members who experience sexual harassment and gender discrimination suffer higher rates of sexual assault. Source: RAND. (2017). Improving Oversight and Coordination of Department of Defense Programs That Address Problematic Behaviors among Military Personnel. Santa Monica, CA: RAND Corporation. https://www.rand.org/pubs/research_reports/RR1352.html

[2] For example, victim advocacy, safety planning, or other trauma-informed care to assist Service members who have experienced sexual harassment. This may include helping the Service member to address any immediate safety needs, understand their reporting options, and identify any behavioral health services that may be helpful.

Improve DoD's Response to Domestic Violence

Because spousal and intimate partner relationships can also include sexual violence, the IRC could not comprehensively accomplish the mission in its Charter without including domestic violence alongside sexual assault and sexual harassment. Indeed, in the IRC's site visits and interviews with junior enlisted personnel, sexual assault by a spouse or intimate partner was repeatedly mentioned. In the general population and the military community, intimate partner violence frequently overlaps with sexual assault. Roughly 32 percent of active duty women and 30 percent of wives of active duty men have experienced domestic violence in the form of sexual violence, physical violence, or stalking at some point in their lifetimes.[3] Sexual assault in intimate partner relationships is also a lethality indicator. Decades of research have established that sexual abuse by spouses or intimate partners often takes place as part of a continuum of controlling and coercive behaviors that together indicate high risk for domestic violence homicide.[4, 5]

DoD must improve the military's response to domestic violence, which is inextricably tied to sexual assault, and therefore reflected in key aspects of the IRC's recommendations across all four lines of effort. The IRC recommends several actions to enhance accountability, inform prevention through better data collection, and increase access to victim care and support for Service members, their families and partners who experience relationship abuse, including sexual assault in the context of an intimate partner relationship.

- Designated independent judge advocates should replace commanders in deciding whether to charge a suspect with a crime (preferral), and whether that charge should be tried at court-martial (referral) in domestic violence cases, as the IRC recommends for sexual assault, sexual harassment, and other special victim crimes (see Recommendation 1.1).[6]

---

[3] Black, M., & Merrick, M. (2013). *Prevalence of Intimate Partner Violence, Sexual Violence, and Stalking among Active Duty Women and Wives of Active Duty Men—Comparisons with Women in the U.S. General Population, 2010*. CDC, National Center for Injury Prevention and Control, 1. https://www.sapr.mil/public/docs/research/2010_National_Intimate_Partner_and_Sexual_Violence_Survey-Technical_Report.pdf

[4] Campbell, J., Webster, D., Mahoney, P., O'Sullivan, C., White, M., Eliacin, J., Roehl, J., Guertin, K., & Semple, K. (2005). *Intimate Partner Violence Risk Assessment Validation Study, Final Report*. National Institute of Justice. https://www.ncjrs.gov/pdffiles1/nij/grants/209731.pdf

[5] Ibid.

[6] This concept stands in contrast to the current approach in the military justice system, which withholds initial disposition decisions for certain sexual assault offenses to the first O6 level commander. By default, nonsexual domestic violence crimes are excluded from the withholding policy, and therefore are subject to the general command concept of withholding initial disposition decisions "at the lowest level." Because the DoD does not track how many domestic violence cases get charged verses those that are handled at the nonjudicial level, the IRC considered feedback from scoping sessions with victims, military prosecutors and special victim counsel who opined that intimate partner/domestic violence cases rarely—if ever—see the inside of a courtroom.

The recent GAO report on domestic abuse, as well as multiple military justice practitioners with whom the IRC spoke, have raised multiple concerns with this approach, which presupposes that anything less than a sex crime is inherently less serious in nature (and therefore appropriately handled via other means, such as nonjudicial punishment). Unfortunately, domestic violence is typically a crime that involves repeated patterns of threatening and abusive behavior, which requires swift intervention and accountability for the offender. One of the most concerning aspects of this approach is that anything

- DoD should establish a mechanism to track prevalence of domestic abuse/intimate partner-related sexual assault by collecting information on the victim-perpetrator relationship in the Workplace and Gender Relations Surveys of Active Duty Members (WGRA), and Workplace and Gender Relations Surveys of Reserve Component Members (WGRR).[7]
- The Under Secretary of Defense for Personnel and Readiness (USD(P&R)) should immediately publish the reissuance of DoD Instruction (DoDI) 6400.06, "Domestic Abuse Involving DoD Military and Certain Affiliated Personnel," which expands the DoD definition of "intimate partner" to include dating partners in eligibility for Family Advocacy Program (FAP) services, and contains several measures to improve coordination between FAP and SAPR/Sexual Harassment Assault Response and Prevention (SHARP) to maximize victims' options in seeking support for intimate partner-related sexual assault.[8]

The IRC also recommends DoD heed the observations from the Government Accountability Office (GAO) May 2021 Report, and urgently develop the statutorily required database to track all reported domestic violence incidents, and collect command action—disciplinary and administrative—taken to address domestic violence.[9] The Office of the Secretary of Defense (OSD) oversight for this database should be led by the Deputy Secretary of Defense, or USD(P&R), to ensure sustained attention to the problem of domestic violence commensurate with its seriousness and Congressional interest.

Improve DoD Data to Better Reflect the Experiences of Service Members with Intersectional Identities

The experience of sexual violence is not divorced from Service members' multilayered identities. Data collection, research, and data reporting must be designed with an intentionally intersectional approach, because victims of sexual harassment and sexual assault can experience these harms differently, in connection with their gender, sexual orientation or gender identity, race, ethnicity, or other characteristics of who they are. For example, new data from RAND shows that just 12 percent of Service members identify as "other than heterosexual," but account for 43 percent of sexual assaults

short of a court-martial conviction of domestic violence will allow Service member abusers to maintain possession of their personal firearms. DoD has implemented the Lautenberg amendment (18 U.S.C. § 922(g)(9)) by prohibiting military abusers who have been convicted of domestic violence by a general or special court-martial from possessing a firearm, but not those disciplined through summary court-martial conviction, nonjudicial punishment, or administrative actions. This is worrisome, considering that abusers' access to firearms increases risk of domestic violence homicide five-fold. Source: Campbell J.C., Webster D., Koziol-McLain J., et al. (2003). Risk factors for femicide in abusive relationships: results from a multisite case control study. *American Journal of Public Health, 93*(7), 1089-1097.

[7] This recommendation should not be considered a substitute for the enduring need for the Department to develop a robust prevalence metric for all forms of domestic violence—including abuse experienced by civilian military spouses and intimate partners.

[8] DoD. (2017). *DoDI 6400.06: Domestic Abuse Involving DoD Military and Certain Affiliated Personnel*. https://www.esd.whs.mil/Portals/54/Documents/DD/issuances/dodi/640006p.pdf

[9] Since 2006, GAO has recommended DoD track command action for domestic violence cases. It has recommended (for the third time) DoD do so in the May 2021 report. Source: GAO (2021, May 6). *Domestic abuse: Actions Needed to Enhance DoD's Prevention, Response, and Oversight.* Report No. GAO-21-289. https://www.gao.gov/products/gao-21-289

in the military.[10] Approximately 1 in 3 Black Service members report experiencing past-year racial/ethnic harassment.[11]

Prevalence data from the civilian population clearly demonstrate the disproportionate impact of sexual and intimate partner violence among women of color, particularly Black women, and American Indian/Alaska Native women.[12] Curiously, DoD sexual assault and harassment prevalence data do not reflect this same pattern.[13] More information is needed to better understand how racial/ethnic minority Service members experience sexual violence. These Service members may simultaneously be the targets of racial harassment and sexual harassment, perhaps making both more difficult to detect or report.

DoD must improve data collection (including qualitative research and quantitative survey tools) and data reporting to better reflect the experiences of service members whose marginal identities (e.g., racial, ethnic, sexual, and gender minorities), may place them at higher risk for sexual harassment and sexual assault in the military.

Improve Data Collection and Data Reporting on Sexual Assault

- DoD should require the collection of data regarding sexual orientation and gender identity in Defense Sexual Assault Incident Database (DSAID);[14]
- DoD should require the collection of data regarding sexual orientation and gender identity on the WGRA and WGRR;[15]
- DoD should ensure the WGRA and WGRR publish both past-year prevalence, prior to joining the military prevalence, and lifetime prevalence of sexual assault by race and ethnicity, sexual orientation, and gender identity;

---

[10] Morral, A.R. & Schell, T.L. (2021). *Sexual Assault of Sexual Minorities in the U.S. Military*. RAND Corporation. https://www.rand.org/pubs/research_reports/RRA1390-1.html

[11] Daniel, S., Claros, A.Y., Namrow, N., Siebel, M., Campbell, A., McGrath, D., & Klahr, A. (2019). *2017 Workplace and Equal Opportunity Survey of Active Duty Members: Executive Report*. Report No. 2018-023. Alexandria, VA: Office of People Analytics. https://taskandpurpose.com/app/uploads/2021/01/27/2017-Workplace-and Equal-Opportunity-Survey-Report.pdf.

[12] Black, M.C., Basile, K.C., Breiding, M.J., Smith, S.G., Walters, M.L., Merrick, M.T., Chen, J., & Stevens, M.R. (2011). *The National Intimate Partner and Sexual Violence Survey (NISVS): 2010 Summary Report*. Atlanta, GA: CDC, National Center for Injury Prevention and Control.

[13] Breslin, R., Davis, E., Hylton, K., Hill, A., Klauberg, W., Petusky, M., Klahr, A. (2019). *2018 Workplace and Gender Relations Survey of Active Duty Members: Overview Report.* Report No. 2019-027. Alexandria, VA: Office of People Analytics, 67. https://apps.dtic.mil/sti/citations/AD1072334

[14] DSAID is the Department's authoritative, centralized case-level database used to collect and maintain information on sexual assaults involving members of the Armed Forces, including tracking and reporting on sexual assault-related retaliation data. DoD SAPRO operates DSAID and works collaboratively with the Services to implement and sustain the system. Source: DoD SAPRO. (2021). Defense Sexual Assault Incident Database (DSAID). https://www.sapr.mil/?q=dsaid-overview

[15] The WGRA offers critical insights regarding the estimated prevalence and characteristics of sexual assault, sexual harassment, and gender discrimination in the active component; Service member experiences with reporting those types of incidents; and perceptions of unit culture and climate. The *WGRR* captures key insights as to the estimated prevalence and characteristics of sexual assault, sexual harassment, and gender discrimination in the Reserve component, Service member attitudes and beliefs vis-à-vis these issues, and perceptions of unit climate.

- To improve the ability to compare rates of sexual assault[16] among service members of color with rates in the general population, the DoD Sexual Assault Prevention and Response Office (SAPRO) should work with the Centers for Disease Control and Prevention (CDC) Division of Violence Prevention to ensure that future reports of the military supplement to the National Intimate Partner and Sexual Violence Survey include a breakdown of past-year and lifetime prevalence by race/ethnicity. These data should be reported with the most granularity possible (e.g., specific racial and ethnic groups rather than "minority" and "not minority").[17]

Improve Data Collection and Data Reporting on Sexual Harassment

- DoD should ensure the WGRA and WGRR publish sexual harassment prevalence data by race and ethnicity, sexual orientation, and gender identity;
- DoD should evaluate ways to better collect data, via existing DoD-wide surveys, on the role of race/ethnicity on the experience of sexual harassment (i.e., racialized sexual harassment) in the military; and,
- DoD should require the Services and the National Guard Bureau to publish the following data for all sexual harassment complaints:
    - A breakdown of service members who filed complaints ("complainants") by gender, gender identity and sexual orientation, race and ethnicity;
    - A breakdown of all substantiated, unsubstantiated, and dismissed sexual harassment complaints by gender, gender identity and sexual orientation, race and ethnicity;
    - A breakdown of offender characteristics for complaints by gender, gender identity and sexual orientation, race, and ethnicity; and,
    - A breakdown of offender characteristics for substantiated complaints by gender, gender identity and sexual orientation, race and ethnicity.

Improve Data Collection and Data Reporting on Others Forms of Harassment and Discrimination that May Contribute to Risk for Sexual Violence

- DoD should require the collection of data regarding sexual orientation and gender identity on the Workplace and Equal Opportunity Survey of Active Duty (WEOA) and the Workplace and Equal Opportunity Survey Reserve Component Members (WEOR);[18]

---

[16] As well as intimate partner violence, including sexual assault in relationships.

[17] As consistent with Office of Management and Budget guidelines, the Department currently clusters specific racial and ethnic groups into "minority" and "not minority" on some scientific surveys.

[18] The WEOA assesses self-reported experiences of, and the climate surrounding, racial/ethnic harassment and discrimination in the active duty military. The WEOR estimates the level and consequences of racial/ethnic harassment and discrimination in the Reserve Component.

- DoD should ensure the Workplace and Equal Opportunity surveys of military members publish past-year prevalence rates for racial/ethnic harassment by gender identity and sexual orientation; and
- DoD should evaluate ways to better collect data, via existing DoD-wide surveys, on the role of gender in the experience of racial/ethnic harassment and discrimination in the military.

Improve and Expand Qualitative Research on Racial and Ethnic Minority Service Women Who Experience Sexual Assault, and Multiple Forms of Harassment

- DoD should commission qualitative research to better understand the experiences of racial/ethnic minority service women and their perceptions of climate, attitudes and experiences with sexual assault and sexual harassment, and gender and racial discrimination. Focus groups of service women and racial/ethnic minority women veterans could inform answers to questions such as:
  - Do you feel like your identity (e.g., race, sex, sexual orientation) has impacted your experience in the military in any way? If so, how?
  - How have your experiences been similar or different to those of your peers of the same gender?
  - How have your experiences been similar or different from those of your peers of the same race?

- DoD SAPRO should dedicate a segment of its iterations of the Military Service Gender Relations (MSGR) Focus Groups to understanding the experiences of racial and ethnic minority service members and survivors.[19]

Appoint a Senior Policy Advisor for Special Victims and a DoD Special Victim Advocate to Facilitate Change

The Secretary of Defense should establish, alongside the OSD Office of the Special Victim Prosecutor (Recommendation 1.1), the complementary roles of the Senior Policy Advisor for Special Victims and the DoD Special Victim Advocate (SVA). These Senior Executive Service civilian positions would report to the Deputy Secretary of Defense and reside in the immediate office of USD(P&R). The Senior Advisor for Special Victims and the SVA will work closely with the Office of the Special Victim

---

[19] The MSGR Focus Groups capture the overall perceptions and findings gleaned from active duty Service members and SAPR/SHARP responders who participated in focus groups in locations around the continental U.S. participants in these focus groups are often asked about the culture of their installation and who influences the culture for Service members, the influence of gender discrimination and sexual harassment on work culture and morale, and how leadership and the SAPR/SHARP responder can better prevent and respond to incidents of sexual assault and sexual harassment reported by Service members.

Prosecutor to ensure coordination and collaboration on Service-wide victim needs and support during the military justice system process.

The Senior Policy Advisor for Special Victims would serve as the lead coordinator and advisor for all special victim policies across DoD and the Services and oversee implementation of IRC recommendations as identified for action by the Secretary. Reporting directly to the Senior Policy Advisor for Special Victims, the DoD SVA will serve as DoD's primary representative for military special victims' rights and interests and help bridge the gap between policy at the DoD level, and execution at the Service level. The SVA will advise DoD leaders on all special victim-related matters, including policy, procedures, training, education, and programmatic issues. The SVA will not provide direct services to individual Service members but will ensure that survivors are regularly consulted (e.g., through focus groups, written input) when new and ongoing DoD sexual assault-related policy and implementation are being examined. The SVA will have direct communication with the SAPR/SHARP Directors at the Service level to facilitate standardization in the quality of care and support for victims across the entire enterprise.

The establishment of these positions would not affect any other organizational structure or assignment of responsibilities in the Department, including other offices whose functions directly affect special victims, such as SAPRO, FAP, and the Office for Diversity, Equity, and Inclusion. The Senior Policy Advisor for Special Victims would provide those offices with independent advice and comments from the perspective of special victims on all issues being addressed by those offices.

Rebuilding Broken Trust: Recommendations for Accountability in the Military Justice System

Independent Review Commission on Sexual Assault in the Military

Contents

List of Figures

Acknowledgements

The findings and recommendations in this report are the result of discussions, scoping sessions, and ultimately, the generous time and expertise from a diverse group of individuals. The Accountability experts of the Independent Review Commission (IRC) on Sexual Assault in the Military sincerely thank everyone they consulted during their review, including the survivors who graciously agreed to relive their experiences in the service of the IRC's work to improve the military justice system. Finally, the IRC's Accountability experts are grateful for the contributions of the Services' subject matter experts and consultative group members.

Background

On February 26, 2021, the Secretary of Defense ordered the establishment of an IRC to conduct an independent assessment of the Department of Defense's (DoD) efforts against sexual harassment and sexual assault. The IRC officially began its work on March 24, 2021 and was charged with forming recommendations across four lines of effort: accountability; prevention; climate and culture; and victim care and support.

This report is issued by the highly qualified experts (HQEs) leading the Accountability line of effort. The IRC Accountability experts were charged with the following tasks:

- Recommend policy changes and propose actions to improve prevention and response efforts on sexual assault, harassment, and other readiness-detracting behaviors;
- Assess the role of the Uniform Code of Military Justice (UCMJ) in addressing the prevalence of sexual assault and harassment, survivor likelihood of reporting, and ability to appropriately bring alleged perpetrators to justice; and
- Assess the feasibility, opportunities, and risks from changes to the commander's role in military justice.

The recommendations in this first report are necessary, but insufficient. Although the recommendations from the Accountability experts were the first to be issued, their success is interdependent with the proposals from other lines of effort focusing on prevention, climate and culture, and victim services. Each line of effort concentrates largely on the role of the commander, which is central to the response at every level. Taken as a whole, the IRC's recommendations will present a comprehensive view of the problem, and offer targeted solutions for commanders of all ranks, the Services, and the Department to build trust and restore confidence in the military's ability to prevent and respond to sexual assault and sexual harassment.

To facilitate the implementation of these proposed changes, the IRC recommends the retention of a select team of HQEs to provide continuity and oversight, capitalizing on the institutional knowledge developed during the IRC recommendation process.

Introduction

Since the beginning of United States (U.S.) history, military justice has been a commander-centric system. Commanders are responsible for all that a unit does and does not do, so they have complete authority in matters of discipline. Implicit in this broad grant of authority is the issue of trust: trust by commanders in subordinates to follow the orders of commanders, and trust by subordinates in commanders that commanders will wield this broad grant of authority fairly in order to do justice and thus assist in maintaining good order and discipline. When it comes to sexual harassment and sexual assault, across too many commands in all of the Services, that bond of trust appears to be broken.

It is not surprising that commanders face a crisis of confidence in their leadership. For many years, a long series of senior military officials have assured Congress, the American people, and the young enlisted women and men under their care and command that they understood the gravity of the sexual harassment and sexual assault problem,[1] and that they would fix it, pledging a commitment to "zero tolerance." Even the Chairman of the Joint Chiefs of Staff has acknowledged that the military has "not moved the needle" on this problem.[2]

Clearly, the status quo is not working: in 2018, sexual assault prevalence increased by 44 percent among women Service members. Every year, more than 20,000 Service members are the victims of sexual assault (13,000 women and 7,500 men).[3] Fewer than 8,000 per year reported that assault, according to the Department's own data.[4] The sexual harassment numbers are bleaker, with about 1 in every 4 active duty women responding to survey questions that they have been sexually harassed.[5] This is a 13 percent increase in two years, yet the crime is severely underreported–only 1,781 complaints (2

---

[1] The IRC has crafted recommendations to prevent and respond to the full continuum of sexual harm in the military, which begins with sexual harassment and escalates into sexual assault. To think of them as two separate problem sets is to fundamentally misunderstand the challenge the Department–and the force–face.

[2] Burns, R. (2021). *Top General Drops Opposition to Change in Sex Assault Policy*. The Times-Tribune. https://hosted.ap.org/thetimes-tribune/article/e343b149e17bfa5cc104ea354bdf8065/top-general-drops-opposition-change-sex-assault-policyv

[3] Breslin, R., Davis, E., Hylton, K., Hill, A., Klauberg, W., Petusky, M., Klahr, A. (2019). *Workplace and Gender Relations Survey of Active Duty Members: Overview Report*. Report No. 2019-027: Office of People Analytics, vi. https://apps.dtic.mil/sti/citations/AD1072334

[4] DoD SAPRO. (2021). Appendix B: Statistical Data on Sexual Assault. *Fiscal Year 2020 Annual Report on Sexual Assault in the Military*, 7-8. https://www.sapr.mil/sites/default/files/Appendix_B_Statistical_Data_On_Sexual_Assault_FY2020.pdf

[5] Breslin, R., Davis, E., Hylton, K., Hill, A., Klauberg, W., Petusky, M., Klahr, A. (2019). *Workplace and Gender Relations Survey of Active Duty Members: Overview Report*. Report No. 2019-027: Office of People Analytics, ix. https://apps.dtic.mil/sti/citations/AD1072334

percent) were filed in Fiscal Year (FY) 2020 (FY20).[6] The military has failed America's sons and daughters; and the Service members know it.

The report from the Fort Hood Independent Review Committee (FHIRC) is equally devastating, clearly demonstrating pervasive sexual harassment with too little meaningful commander or enlisted leader intervention. When it comes to sexual harassment and sexual assault, across the enterprise, there persists a dangerous chasm between the perception of senior leaders and the realities of Service members, particularly those at the junior enlisted level.

The gravity of this gap in understanding is underscored by the research, which shows that sexual harassment in the military, left unchecked, leads to sexual assault. In units with above-average rates of sexual harassment,[7] the risk for sexual assault increases by a factor of 1.5 among women, and 1.8–almost 2-fold–among men. LGBTQ+ Service members are especially impacted.[8] There is also a demonstrated association between the experience of victims who feel betrayed by the military's response to these harms, and suicide risk.[9, 10] This link was borne out in many conversations, as well as written submissions survivors shared with the IRC. This problem is more than serious, it is deadly.

Nearly every junior enlisted Service member with whom the IRC met–women and men–said demeaning language and sexual harassment were regular features of life in their units. Some said that noncommissioned officers (NCOs) intervened appropriately, while others said no intervention occurred, or worse – they led it, setting a hostile climate for their unit and singling out anyone who dared to question them or defend their more vulnerable peers. Enlisted women repeatedly shared they have given up on saying anything because "no one cares" so they just "suck it up and move on." Those statements are a scathing indictment of today's command climate and culture, of those commanders and enlisted leaders who do not lead, and of those more senior who fail to supervise closely.

The wounds from these demeaning gender-based comments, sexual harassment, and sexual assault are uniquely harmful to the American Service member. They are not wounds inflicted by an enemy

---

[6] DoD SAPRO. (2021). Appendix F: Sexual Harassment Assessment. *Fiscal Year 2020 Annual Report on Sexual Assault in the Military*, 4-5. https://www.sapr.mil/sites/default/files/Appendix_F_Sexual_Harassment_Assessment_FY2020.pdf

[7] Schell, T., Cefalu, M., Farris, C., & Morral, A. (2021). *The Relationship Between Sexual Assault and Sexual Harassment in the U.S. Military: Findings from the RAND Military Workplace Study.* Santa Monica, CA.: RAND Corporation. https://www.rand.org/pubs/research_reports/RR3162.html

[8] Morral, A. & Schell, T. (2021). *Sexual Assault of Sexual Minorities in the U.S. Military*. Santa Monica, CA: RAND Corporation. https://www.rand.org/pubs/research_reports/RRA1390-1.html.

[9] Monteith, L.L., Bahraini, N.H., Matarazzo, B.B., Soberay, K.A., & Smith, C.P. (2016). Perceptions of Institutional Betrayal Predict Suicidal Self-Directed Violence Among Veterans Exposed to Military Sexual Trauma. *Journal of Clinical Psychology, 72*(7): 743–755. https://doi.org/10.1002/jclp.22292

[10] Andresen, F.J., Monteith, L.L., Kugler, J., Cruz, R.A., & Blais, R.K. (2019). Institutional betrayal following military sexual trauma is associated with more severe depression and specific posttraumatic stress disorder symptom clusters. *Journal of Clinical Psychology*, *75*(7): 1305–1319.

in a faraway land, but by battle buddies, shipmates, or fellow marines, airmen, and guardians, often in spaces where Service members should be the safest. In the words of the Chairman of the Joint Chiefs of Staff, this treatment is "fratricide."[11]

Many of these incidents could have been prevented. Concerned leaders could have created command climates where demeaning gender-based comments, harassing behaviors, and sexual assault were not tolerated. They had all the authority to do so, but too many leaders failed to lead. These incidents had additional corrosive effects on good order and discipline: broken trust between Service members and their leaders, and the military they volunteered to serve.

The scars of these wounds linger and intensify long after the original harm as they are exacerbated by systemic problems throughout the military justice process. Unlike virtually any other workplace in the country, in the military, the employees' supervisor is charged with the determination of legal action for sexual harassment and sexual assault reported under their watch. When commanders are placed in the role of truth-seeker in sexual assault cases, Service members perceive their leaders are forced to make the difficult decision of whether to believe victim or accused. Their perceptions are not wrong. In fact, they are exacerbated when the victim and the alleged offender are in the same unit, overseen by the same commander who must decide who to believe. This is further complicated when the alleged offender is a high performer who may be needed in the ranks.

This broken trust manifests itself in junior enlisted Service members having a general distrust of their enlisted leaders and commanders, a specific distrust in having their commanders make disciplinary decisions in sexual assault and sexual harassment cases, and an overall distrust in a commander-centric military justice process. The IRC focused on developing recommendations to help rebuild that broken trust.

Despite this, the IRC believes that commanders, and their enlisted leaders, remain the key to solving the sexual assault and sexual harassment problem in the military. Commanders are specially trained and entrusted with maintaining good order and discipline and taking care of their people. They do this by fostering a command climate of dignity and respect. They simply must make solving this problem their priority, which can only be achieved with closer supervision of their troops, and putting a stop to demeaning language, sexual harassment, and sexual assault every time they see it or hear it.

List of Recommendations

Below are the eight recommendations developed by the Accountability experts. Recommendations that require legislation should take effect no earlier than October 1, 2023. For recommendations that do not require legislation, but require Presidential action, the IRC recommends implementation as part of the next annual review by the Joint Services Committee on

[11] Kenney, C.M. (2019, July 11). Milley: 'Not going to be intimidated into making stupid decisions.' *Stars and Stripes*. https://www.stripes.com/news/us/milley-not-going-to-be-intimidated-into-making-stupid-decisions-1.589885

Military Justice. For all other recommendations, the IRC advises implementation as quickly as possible.

1.1 Creation of the Office of the Special Victim Prosecutor in the Office of the Secretary of Defense.

1.2 Independent, trained investigators for sexual harassment and mandatory initiation of involuntary separation for all substantiated complaints.

1.3 Judge-ordered Military Protective Orders for victims of sexual assault and related offenses.

1.4 Professionalize career billets for military justice personnel handling special victim crimes.

1.5 Judge-alone sentencing in all noncapital general and special courts-martial and establishment of sentencing parameters.

1.6 Expedite processing of proposed Executive Orders regarding military justice, including those currently awaiting issuance related to sexual assault and other special victim crimes.

1.7 Modify the UCMJ in several key areas to increase uniformity, reliability, and consistency in the military justice system.

- **1.7 a** The Secretary of Defense should direct the Defense Advisory Committee on Investigations, Prosecution, and Defense of Sexual Assault in the Armed Forces (DAC-IPAD) to study Article 32 Preliminary Hearings.
- **1.7 b** The Secretary of Defense should direct the DAC-IPAD to study Article 34, Advice to Convening Authority Before Referral to Trial.
- **1.7 c** The UCMJ should be amended to establish a preponderance of the evidence standard for non-judicial punishment.
- **1.7 d** Article 25 of the UCMJ should be amended to establish random selection of panel members.
- **1.7 e** The Secretary of Defense should direct the Services to establish funding appropriate for defense counsel control of their own resources.
- **1.7 f** Article 128b of the UCMJ should be amended to include dating violence.

1.8 Study caseloads to attain the optimum timeline for the military justice process.

Methodology

The IRC determined on early that it needed to gather relevant information from as many practitioners and experts in the fields of military and civilian criminal justice as possible. In particular, it met separately with individuals and groups of: commanders; trial counsel; military judges; defense counsel; special victims' counsel/victims' legal counsel (SVCs/VLCs); highly qualified civilian experts; former court-martial panel members; and military criminal investigative organizations (MCIOs). The IRC also held virtual discussions with: more than 170 active duty, reserve, and guard enlisted members representing each Service, from installations in the U.S., Europe, and the Pacific; representatives from 28 Military Service Organizations (MSOs), Veteran Service Organizations (VSOs), and survivor advocacy groups;[12] and heard from more than 200 survivors of sexual assault and sexual harassment through a combination of virtual panels, individual meetings, and written testimonies.

The Accountability experts also met with legal scholars who represent the full spectrum of diverse and opposing opinions related to military justice. Additionally, the IRC's Accountability experts reviewed a wide range of studies, reports, scholarly articles, opinion pieces, and Congressional bills. With this information, the IRC began a multi-faceted approach to developing recommendations based on considerable analysis and internal debate. Initial recommendations were further informed by consultations with military justice experts to allow the team to tailor final recommendations to help instill confidence in victims, accused, and the American public in the handling of sexual harassment and sexual assault allegations by the military justice process.

The Accountability line of effort limited its review to the tasks assigned in the IRC Charter, specifically to sexual harassment, sexual assault, and related crimes. The IRC did not attempt to assess military justice as it relates to other crimes, or to military justice as a whole. Therefore, the IRC expresses no opinion regarding those matters that exceed their Charter.

Recommendation 1.1: Creation of the Office of the Special Victim Prosecutor

For sexual assault, sexual harassment, and other special victim cases, designated independent judge advocates should replace commanders in deciding whether to charge a suspect with a crime (preferral), and whether that charge should be tried at court-martial (referral). These independent judge advocates should report to a civilian-led Office of the Special Victim Prosecutor, housed in the Office of the Secretary of Defense (See: Recommendation 1.4: Professionalize Career Billets for Military Justice Practitioners and Military Criminal Investigators). The Special Victim Prosecutor should be

[12] The IRC met with the following stakeholder groups: Aequitas, Air Force Association, American Progress Women's Initiative, Association of the United States Army, Blue Star Families, Center for Council on Foreign Relations Women & Foreign Policy Program, Disabled American Veterans, Enlisted Association of the National Guard of the United States, Esposas Militares Hispanas USA, Military Family Advisory Network, Military Officers Association of America, Minority Veterans of America, Modern Military Association, National Center on Domestic and Sexual Violence, National Crime Victims Law Institute, National Coalition Against Domestic Violence, National Military Family Association, National Organization for Victim Assistance (NOVA), National Women's Law Center, Not in My Marine Corps, Protect Our Defenders, Service Women's Action Network, TAPS, Time's Up, Ujima: The National Center on Violence Against Women in the Black Community, US Army Warrant Officers Association (The Military Coalition), Vietnam Veterans of America, and Wounded Warrior Project.

independent from the chains of command of both the victim and the alleged offender in order to be seen as a neutral and detached decision-maker and be free from outside pressure.

The DoD Office of the Special Victim Prosecutor should be a lean, efficient, state of the art execution organization utilizing existing special victim billets, with a Director who is an Senior Executive Service (SES) career civil servant with extensive civilian and military special victim criminal justice experience. The scope of the Special Victim Prosecutor's authority should be limited to cases including special victim crimes and attempts, solicitation, and conspiracy to commit them. Congress may expand the authority of the Special Victim Prosecutor. The creation of the Office of the Special Victim Prosecutor is critical to the success of moving the needle in special victim prosecutions. The military is at a historic moment: judge advocates who try these cases can no longer be generalists housed under the Services. In order to make meaningful change and to regain trust in Service members and the American public, the Special Victim Prosecutor must be led by a civilian director under the Secretary of Defense.

As part of this effort to improve trust in the military justice process, the Secretary of Defense should issue a memorandum on the integrity of the military justice system patterned after the August 6, 2013 memorandum on that topic issued by the then-Secretary.

Defining Special Victim Crimes

Special victim crimes are cases that disproportionately impact victims because of who they are, or what motivated the crime. These crimes are often interpersonal in nature, in which the victim and the alleged offender may have a pre-existing relationship or acquaintance. These are also crimes that require greater specialization and a sensitivity to the complex dynamics that are often present in these cases. Many sexual assault victims also have intersectional identities that result in compounded barriers to justice and place them at higher risk of re-traumatization as they engage in the criminal legal system and investigative processes.[13,14]

> "Sexual assault with the intent to harm because of bias against a group looks more like a hate crime."
>
> -Drs. Andrew Morral & Terry Schell, RAND

Most special victim cases will be defined by the crime committed: sexual assault, sexual harassment, stalking, domestic violence (including dating violence[15]), retaliation, reprisal, and non-consensual distribution of digital images. Not infrequently, special victims can experience multiple crimes that overlap with sexual assault. For example, victims of sexual assault may have been harmed by a fellow Service member, but also by a spouse or intimate partner. For men,

[13] Kilpatrick, D.G. & Acierno, R. (2003). Mental health needs of crime victims: Epidemiology and Outcomes. *Journal of Traumatic Stress, 16*(2): 119–132.

[14] Orth, U. (2002). Secondary victimization of crime victims by criminal proceedings. *Social Justice Research, 15*(4): 313–325.

[15] These offenses, including strangulation and wrongful broadcast or distribution of intimate visual images, were passed in the National Defense Authorization Act (NDAA) for FY19.

sexual assault often occurs in the context of bullying and hazing. These intersections make the special victims framework particularly compelling, as specialization is needed to handle these sensitive cases.

In addition, certain victims are always special victims, regardless of the crime(s) committed against them, due to their age, or their relationship to the offender (i.e., children under the age of sixteen, older adults (65+), individuals with disabilities, a spouse, intimate partner, dating partner, or immediate family member). It is axiomatic that the level of sophistication and unique training necessary to both assess and prosecute these case requires they be handled by Special Victim Prosecutors.

Finally, because certain other victims share common characteristics with the special victims covered by the previous list of crimes, such as being victimized because of who they are, re-traumatization through the military justice process, and facing disparities in treatment due to their status, we include bias or hate crimes on the basis or the perceived basis of the victim's sex, gender, race, ethnicity, color, religion, national origin, sexual orientation, or gender identity. These crimes also include bullying and hazing. Including these crimes parallels special victim units in the civilian community and takes advantage of the greater capacity Special Victim Prosecutors have to address these cases. Congress may expand the category of special victim crimes as deemed appropriate. Figure 1 illustrates the categories of special victim crimes and offenses (note: the examples provided within each category are not exhaustive).

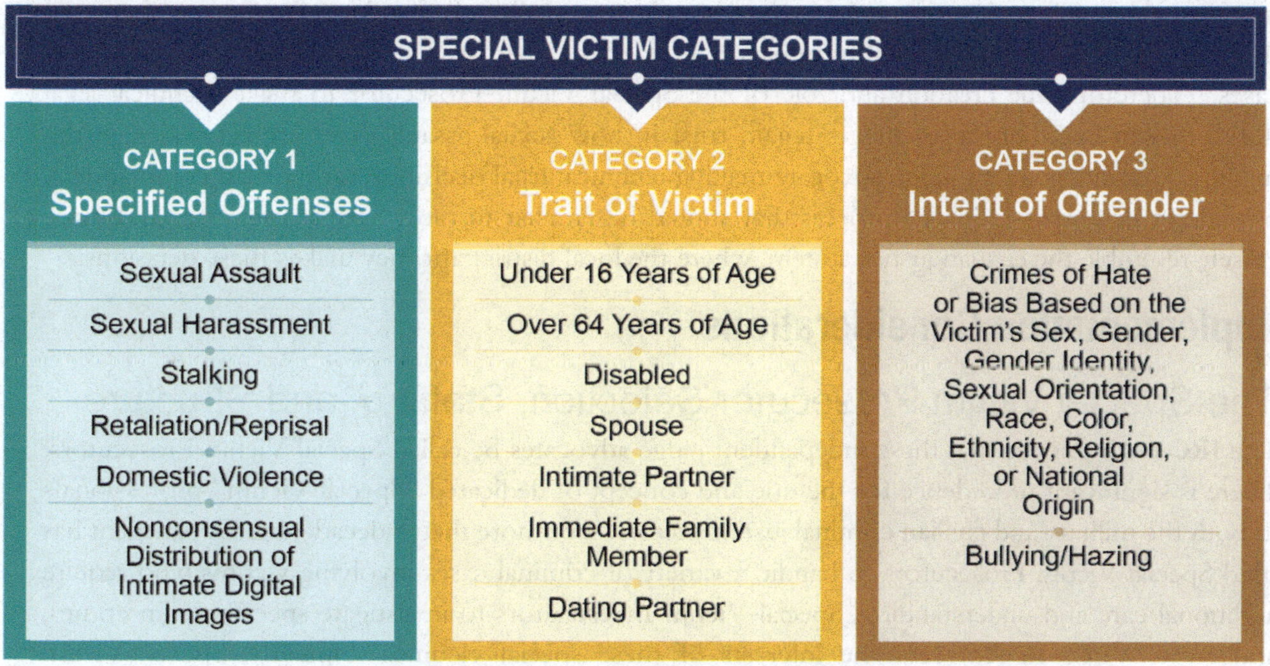

Figure 1. Special Victim Categories of Crimes and Offenses

Rationale for this Change: Broken Trust

Victims told the IRC that they do not trust commanders to do justice in sexual harassment and sexual assault cases for a variety of reasons. In addition to a perceived conflict of interest, they see commanders as: complicit (allowing precursor demeaning language and actions to go unchecked); or, are more focused on combat readiness, logistics, and other higher priority matters than on caring for their troops. They also do not understand how a commander with limited legal training can be trusted to make quintessential legal decisions such as charging someone with a crime. Even victims who respected their commanders said their commanders should not be making those decisions.

From the opposite perspective, that of the suspect, comes a similar distrust of the commander. Suspects have always had a distrust of their commanders making military justice decisions. In general, they feel that the commander is more concerned with taking firm disciplinary measures to instill good order and discipline than ensuring justice is done. Many commanders sincerely seek to "send a message" of zero tolerance for sexual assault and sexual harassment, but do so in reverse: rather than taking preventive measures to stop these corrosive behaviors from happening in the first place, they have misguidedly used their disposition authority to send cases to courts-martial that a specialized prosecutor knows have little chance of obtaining and sustaining a conviction. In support of this, the IRC heard from individuals and groups of commanders of all levels who believe forwarding cases with insufficient evidence to obtain and sustain a conviction–regardless of outcome–sends a strong discipline message. However, the IRC also heard that the practice of referring a case to trial to "send a message" that ends in an acquittal harms both victims and accused. Moreover, this philosophy and the associated disappointing trial outcomes are anathema to American concepts of justice and erode public confidence in military justice.

Shifting legal functions from commanders to specially trained and experienced lawyers will support a more equitable military justice system for both survivors and alleged offenders. Service members told the IRC that the commander is the primary source of the distrust in the handling of sexual assault cases. Therefore, the creation and role of the Special Victim Prosecutor to make technical legal decisions can help Service members regain trust in how sexual assault cases are processed in the military. An independent judge advocate making technical legal decisions, rather than commanders, provides a new military justice process that should be familiar to most Service members and more closely resemble the civilian justice system, where the local district attorney makes these decisions.

Implementation Considerations

The Special Victim Prosecutor Selection, Staffing, and Structure

The IRC recommends that these independent judge advocates be called Special Victim Prosecutors. There is significant precedence for the title and concept of dedicated "Special Victim" professionals in both the military and civilian criminal justice sectors. For more than a decade, the Department has used Special Victim Prosecutors to handle a variety of criminal cases involving victims who require additional care and understanding, Special Victim Investigators to investigate special victim crimes, and SVCs/VLCs to represent the interests of these special victims. Similarly, Special Victim Professionals have been widely used in the civilian criminal justice sphere since the first Special Victim Unit was created in the Manhattan District Attorney's Office in 1976.[16]

---

[16] Fairstein, L. (2018, May 21). 'The Real SVU': We kicked open the courtroom doors and got justice for sex-crime victims." *USA Today*.
https://www.usatoday.com/story/opinion/2018/05/21/real-svu-sex-crimes-me-too-special-victims-unit-column/627082002/

Currently, each of the Services have some trial counsel who receive additional training in developing and prosecuting special victim cases. What they are called varies by Service. The Army and Air Force use the title "special victim prosecutors." The Marine Corps uses the term "special victim qualified trial counsel." The Navy has a separate Military Justice Litigation Career Track (MJLCT) that uses Specialist I, Specialist II, and Expert designations for their special victim litigators. The Navy's MJLCT will be further detailed in Recommendation 1.4: Professionalize Career Billets for Military Justice Practitioners and Military Criminal Investigators.

This recommendation, as well as Recommendation 1.4: Professionalize Career Billets for Military Justice Practitioners and Military Criminal Investigators, builds upon the existing framework of the Services' special victim prosecutors, special victim qualified trial counsel, and experts in the MJLCT. These practitioners would remain in their positions if they are appropriately qualified and so desire, but under this recommendation, would be retitled as Assistant Special Victim Prosecutors and report to and work for the most experienced and newly minted Special Victim Prosecutors who report to the Director, Office of the Special Victim Prosecutor under the Secretary of Defense.

The Special Victim Prosecutors would be appointed by the Secretary of Defense from nominees submitted by the Secretaries of the Military Departments from among O-6 judge advocates experienced in military justice with the necessary judgment and maturity to serve in the billet. The Secretary of Defense, after considering the recommendations from the Secretaries of the Military Departments, would determine how many Special Victim Prosecutors to appoint, where to locate them, whether to request that the Military Department include them in deployments, and what support staff they need. The Secretaries of the Military Departments would be responsible for staffing, equipping, and funding those offices. To the extent possible, these new offices should use existing military justice personnel and resources. The Secretary of Defense would have the discretion to delegate his authority over all Special Victim Prosecutors to a Presidentially-appointed, Senate-confirmed position in OSD, resulting in a lean, streamlined, state of the art prosecution organization utilizing existing special victim billets.[17]

---

[17] Currently, the Army has 29 trial counsel qualified as special victim prosecutors; the Navy has 95 MJLCT practitioners, approximately 76 of whom are in designated litigation billets presently; the Air Force has 15 special victim qualified circuit trial counsel; and the Marine Corps has 33 special victim qualified trial counsel.

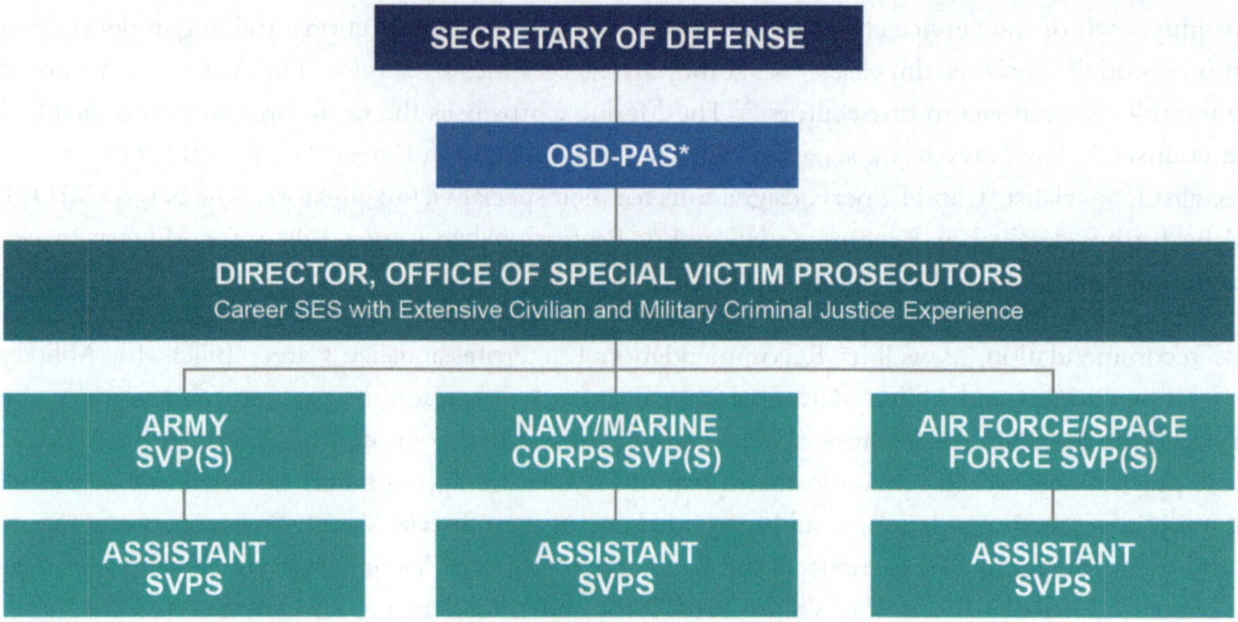

* The Secretary of Defense may decide to delegate his authority over the Office of Special Victim Prosecutors to a Presidentially appointed, Senate confirmed position in the Office of the Secretary of Defense.

Figure 2. Structure of the Office of Special Victim Prosecutors

The Secretary of Defense should have the discretion to appoint one lead Special Victim Prosecutor for each Service (e.g., Special Victim Prosecutor of the Army) who would be a judge advocate of similar qualifications, and who would supervise the Special Victim Prosecutors in their Service.

The Service Special Victim Prosecutors would report to and work for the Director, Office of Special Victim Prosecutors, who would be a career SES civil servant with extensive experience in litigation specializing in special victim cases in the civilian and military sectors, and a detailed understanding of military justice. The Director will oversee all the Services' Special Victim Prosecutors, who are the preferral and referral authorities. The Director would report to the Secretary of Defense. The Director's authority would include authority to direct the use of common forms, reporting requirements, and common policies, procedures, and practices. It would not include authority over any of the discretionary decisions made as part of the military justice process.

Guiding Principles

While there is a direct parallel between the Special Victim Prosecutor and District Attorneys and U. S. Attorneys, the Special Victim Prosecutor would be a new and unique part of the military justice process. Accordingly, the Accountability experts recommend three guiding principles for making this change to shape the Department's implementation.

Independence

The overall concept of independence of the Special Victim Prosecutor is much like the independence of a special counsel or special prosecutor, whose concepts are analogous and most likely familiar to the American public. In the civilian sector, special prosecutors are utilized when an inherent conflict of interest exists for the usual prosecuting authority. In the current military system, the commander functions as the prosecuting authority. Because the IRC heard time and time again that there is a lack of trust in the command, the DoD Office of the Special Victim prosecutor must be independent.[18]

The DoD Office of the Special Victim Prosecutor structure must be, and must be seen as, independent of the chains of command of the victim and of the accused all the way through the Secretaries of the Military Departments. Anything less will likely be seen as compromising what is designed to be an independent part of the military justice process, thus significantly undermining this recommendation. This includes independence from the Judge Advocates General (TJAGs) of the Service Departments.

Specialization and Experience

Special Victim Prosecutors and their Assistants must be well-trained and experienced in handling special victim cases. This need for specialization was identified by everyone with whom the IRC consulted (See: Recommendation 1.4).

Providing Commanders with the Opportunity to be Heard

Commanders of the victim and alleged offender should have the opportunity to provide their candid input to the Special Victim Prosecutor regarding case disposition. However, this input is not binding on the Special Victim Prosecutor.

Scope of Duties

The Special Victim Prosecutor should make the decision whether each case investigated by an MCIO is a special victim case. Each substantiated sexual harassment case referred to the Special Victim Prosecutor by the independent investigator discussed in Recommendation 1.2: Sexual Harassment Allegation Investigations and Mandatory Initiation of Involuntary Separation is by the nature of that substantiation a special victim case. The Secretary of Defense may provide for other cases arising in other situations (e.g., command investigated cases) to be referred to the Special Victim Prosecutor for a decision regarding whether the case is a special victim case.

The Special Victim Prosecutor should decide whether charges should be preferred in special victim cases. A Special Victim Prosecutor, Assistant Special Victim Prosecutor, trial counsel, or Service member under their supervision should prefer the specific charges. Any charge under any Article of the UCMJ may be preferred in a special victim case.

In special victim cases, the Special Victim Prosecutor should decide whether preferred charges should be forwarded to an Article 32 Preliminary Hearing Officer for review. Under regulations prescribed by the Secretary concerned, the Special Victim Prosecutor may request that a Preliminary Hearing

---

[18] The IRC agrees with the Shadow Advisory Report (April 2020) that independence of a Special Victim prosecutor reduces case referral inconsistency across jurisdictions and that these prosecutors would be immune to other factors such as "concern over an operational command's reputation for criminality, [or] personal familiarity with the accused..." Source: Shadow Advisory Report Group of Experts. (2020). *Alternative Authority for Determining Whether to Prefer or Refer Charges to Felony Offenses Under the Uniform Code of Military Justice*. A Shadow Advisory Report to the Senate Committee on Armed Services and the House Committee on Armed Services, 7. https://www.caaflog.org/uploads/1/3/2/3/132385649/shadow_advisory_report__april_20_2020_.pdf

Officer be provided by the trial judiciary from military judges or military magistrates appointed under Article 26a of the UCMJ.

The Special Victim Prosecutor should decide whether to refer preferred charges to a special or general court-martial. This recommendation requires that the Secretary of Defense take appropriate actions to ensure that the Special Victim Prosecutor is not ineligible to refer charges solely by virtue of the fact that the Special Victim Prosecutor decided to have charges preferred in a special victim case. The Special Victim Prosecutor would consider the victim's preference for jurisdiction in making the referral decision.

The Special Victim Prosecutor should refer the charges to a court-martial under regulations prescribed by the Secretary concerned. The Special Victim Prosecutor should not: have the authority to direct a convening authority to convene a court, because doing so would make the convening authority subject to the authority of the Special Victim Prosecutor; nor should the Special Victim Prosecutor be a convening authority, because doing so would result in one of the parties to a case establishing the court that will hear the case. The Special Victim Prosecutor should have the authority to decide whether to withdraw or dismiss any referred charge, and whether to conduct a retrial when authorized by an appropriate court.

In special victim cases where charges are referred to court-martial, the Special Victim Prosecutor should decide whether to enter into a pretrial agreement, whether to grant immunity to witnesses, whether to issue subpoenas and whether to approve and fund government counsel's requests for expert witnesses and other expenses incident to trying a case. Though not exhaustive, the duties of the Special Victim Prosecutor may be summed up in Figure 3.

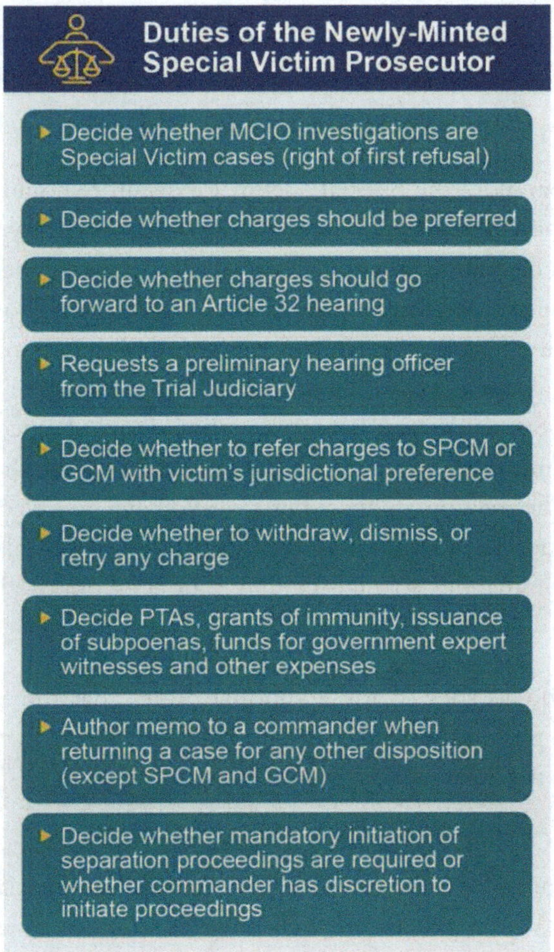

Figure 3. Duties of the Newly-Minted Special Victim Prosecutor

Non-Referred Cases

In special victim cases, when returning the case to the commander of the suspect (e.g., after deciding not to prefer charges or not to refer preferred charges to court-martial), the Special Victim Prosecutor should provide the commander with a memorandum formally returning the case to the commander for such action as the commander deems appropriate other than referring special victim crimes to a special or general court-martial. The memorandum should state that the commander may take any action deemed appropriate, including referral to special or general court-martial, for crimes based on evidence in the case that are completely unrelated to the special victim crimes in the case (e.g., an unrelated simple assault or larceny not involving a special victim).

The memorandum should also explain the basis for the Special Victim Prosecutor's decision (e.g., insufficient evidence, victim preference) and specifically state that the commander may impose nonjudicial punishment, refer to a summary court-martial, or impose or initiate administrative corrective measures such as counseling, letter of reprimand/letter of caution, or grade reduction (when authorized by Service regulation).

For cases that are not preferred, but for which the Special Victim Prosecutor finds the offense(s) to be substantiated, mandatory initiation of separation proceedings will occur (See: Recommendation 1.2).

Regarding administrative separation, the Special Victim Prosecutor should state whether the Special Victim Prosecutor has substantiated an allegation that requires mandatory initiation of separation or whether the commander has discretion to initiate such proceedings. When appropriate, the Special Victim Prosecutor should state specifically that the Special Victim Prosecutor's decision not to proceed does not mean that the Special Victim Prosecutor found that there was insufficient evidence to support the commander taking these additional disciplinary/corrective steps. If the Secretary of Defense determines that the Special Victim Prosecutor should include recommendations on specific disciplinary/corrective measures the commander should consider taking, the Secretary should so state in implementing guidance. The Accountability experts would have no objection to doing so, provided that the implementing guidance addresses avoiding any appearance of unlawful command influence or other pressure on the commander to take certain action as opposed to exercising his or her independent judgment.

The Secretary of Defense should specify any additional duties that the Special Victim Prosecutor should perform, and should provide the Special Victim Prosecutor with the necessary authority to perform such other duties as the Secretary deems appropriate.

Asserting Jurisdiction in Special Victim Cases

The Special Victim Prosecutor has the right of first refusal in special victim cases; it is the determination of the Special Victim Prosecutor that governs whether a case is a special victim case. This decision should be made as early in the investigative process as is practicable. The decision should be communicated as quickly as possible to the commanders of the victim and suspect, the investigators, the victim, and the suspect.

Standards Used by Special Victim Prosecutors in Decision-Making

In making preferral, referral, and other military justice decisions, Special Victim Prosecutors should use the same standards (e.g., Article 30, UCMJ, for preferral) used in non-special victim cases.

Staff Judge Advocates and Special Victim Prosecutors

Staff judge advocates should not have a role in advising Special Victim Prosecutors.

Defining the Commanders' Role Before and After the Special Victim Prosecutor Asserts Jurisdiction

Commanders retain a vital role in special victim cases before and after the Special Victim Prosecutor asserts jurisdiction in a case. After an allegation, and during the investigation, commanders are responsible for the care of victims and suspects, including ensuring to the extent of their authority that victims and suspects are treated with dignity and respect by the other members of their commands and by others they contact. Commanders decide on any appropriate restraint of the suspect including issuing stay away/military protective orders (see Recommendation 1.3: Judge-Ordered Military Protective Orders for Victims of Sexual Assault and Related Offenses). Before the assertion of jurisdiction, the Special Victim Prosecutor has no direct role in the case or in dealing with any person involved with the case (e.g., victim, accused, witness).

After the Special Victim Prosecutor asserts jurisdiction in a case, commanders continue with their responsibility for the care of victims and suspects, and making decisions regarding the restraint of the suspect. Commanders should notify the Special Victim Prosecutor prior to taking any action affecting the suspect, the victim, or the special victim case, and should consider any input the Special Victim Prosecutor may provide.

The establishment of Special Victim Prosecutors should not affect the authority of commanders to issue search authorizations, but should result in an initial withholding of authority to take disposition action in special victim cases. The Secretary of Defense should provide detailed withholding guidance.

Convening Courts-Martial in Special Victim Cases

The Special Victim Prosecutor should refer charges to a court-martial according to regulations prescribed by the Secretary concerned. Commanders retain the authority to administratively convene courts-martial. Members of the court-martial should be selected through a random selection process (See: Recommendation 1.7: Modify the UCMJ) to address the concern that commanders hand pick members to deliver desired court-martial results. The convening authority should continue to make availability decisions, such as excusing members who have personal, family, or professional (e.g., deployed far from the place of the court-martial) conflicts with serving as a member. The convening authority should not apply the criteria in the first sentence of subsection (e)(2) of Article 25, UCMJ, to the randomly selected members (detail as members those best qualified by reason of age, education, training, experience, length of Service, and judicial temperament). Instead, determining the qualifications for Service as a member should be left to the voir dire process at the court-martial.

Post-Trial Action in Special Victim Cases

Given that the discretion of the convening authority to grant any post-trial clemency is very limited, and primarily for the benefit of the defendant's family, the convening authority in special victim cases should exercise the limited post-trial authority the law allows. Allowing the Special Victim Prosecutor to also act on post-trial matters appears to be a conflict of interest. The Special Victim Prosecutor may provide views to the convening authority on the suitability of such action in special victim cases.

The ability of the convening authority to provide relief to a convicted defendant after he has been found guilty at a court-martial has been severely restricted. Prior to June 24, 2014, a convening authority had nearly unfettered discretion to provide clemency to a convicted defendant. That is, the convening authority could dismiss in total or lessen the findings of guilt and reduce, commute, or suspend jail sentences, money forfeitures, rank reductions, or any other sentence of the court.

For offenses committed from June 24, 2014, through December 31, 2019, convening authorities were prohibited from setting aside findings of guilt in any case where there was a conviction under Articles 120(a), 120(b), 120b, or 125 (sex offenses); where the maximum sentence of confinement for the offense exceeded two years; where the adjudged confinement exceeded six months; or where the adjudged sentence included a punitive discharge. In such cases, a convening authority also could not disapprove, commute, or suspend confinement for more than six months or a punitive discharge unless very specific exceptions applied.

Finally, for offenses committed on or after January 1, 2019, the convening authority has very limited discretion to grant any relief on findings or sentence to an individual convicted of any crime under the UCMJ. For any sex crime, or any other crime in which the maximum available punishment is greater than two years of confinement, or for which a sentence included a discharge from the military or greater than six month of confinement, the convening authority may not do anything to the findings of guilty. Nor can he or she touch the part of a sentence that provides for death, confinement, or a punitive discharge.[19]

There are two exceptions when the convening authority may take action. The first is when the Special Victim Prosecutor recommends some form of clemency because the defendant has provided substantial assistance in the investigation or prosecution of another person who has committed an offense. The second is when the military judge recommends that the convening authority suspend the discharge or confinement in excess of six months, in which case the convening authority may take that action, but no greater action.

The only other discretion the convening authority has is to defer or waive parts of a sentence under limited circumstances: the deferral (postponement) of reduction in rank and forfeitures and the waiver (forgiveness) of forfeitures for the benefit of the family members of the defendant. Essentially, a defendant may request that any reduction in rank be postponed (because reduction in rank decreases pay and allowances which could, in turn, be paid to the dependents). As well, the convening authority may authorize the waiver of forfeitures of pay, but this money does not go to the defendant. Rather, it goes into the separate bank account of the dependents of the defendant. In this way it provides financial relief for the family members who may be wholly financially dependent on the defendant, thus allowing time for the dependents to make life adjustments.

Other Options Considered

The IRC received many different recommended approaches to reforming the military justice system's response to sexual assault and harassment. These included:

- In the U.S., all military justice, except for purely military crimes, be turned over to local District Attorneys and U.S. Attorneys

[19] The Convening Authority can reduce, commute, or suspend portions of sentences that include a reprimand, forfeitures, fines, reduction in grade, or hard labor without confinement. Source: Article 60a(b)(2), Uniform Code of Military Justice (UCMJ), 10 U.S.C. § 860a.

- In the U.S., all sexual harassment, sexual assault and related crimes be turned over to local District Attorneys and U.S. Attorneys
- Independent civilian prosecutors be hired by the Department and authorized to adjudicate all crimes except purely military offenses
- Independent judge advocates adjudicate all crimes in the military including purely military offenses
- Independent judge advocates adjudicate all crimes in the military except purely military offenses
- Independent judge advocates adjudicate all sexual harassment, sexual assault and related crimes in the military
- One consolidated disposition authority at the three or four-star level in each Service adjudicate all sexual harassment, sexual assault, and related crimes in the military
- Military Justice Improvement Act of 2019[20]
- I am Vanessa Guillén Act of 2020[21]
- Status quo

The IRC concluded that referring cases to local District Attorneys and U.S. Attorneys was far too complex and difficult to be efficient or effective, and that introducing a civilian prosecutor into the military justice system would be a significant complicating factor with a benefit that could more easily be obtained through an independent judge advocate as we recommend. Regarding the scope of the independent judge advocate's duties, the IRC decided to aim at the problem that formed the basis for the Commission: sexual harassment, sexual assault, and related crimes. Finally, because of the breadth and depth of the lack of trust by junior enlisted Service members in commanders, it was determined that the status quo or any variation on the status quo that retained commanders as disposition authorities in sexual harassment, sexual assault, and related cases would fail to offer the change required to restore confidence in the system. The proposed solution was precisely crafted to target the specific problem set in the IRC charter.

Issuing a Secretary of Defense Memorandum on the Integrity of the Military Justice Process

The basis for Recommendation 1.1: Creation of the Office of the Special Victim Prosecutor is the loss of trust in commanders and in the military justice process. One way to help regain that lost trust is for Secretary Austin to issue a memorandum setting forth his expectations (and if coordinated with the White House, the expectations of President Biden as Commander-in-Chief) regarding integrity in the military justice process. There is precedent for doing so. Then-Secretary Chuck Hagel issued such a memorandum on August 6, 2013, which included a quote from the Counsel to the President.[22] That

[20] Military Justice Improvement Act of 2019. S.1789, 116th Cong. (2019). https://www.congress.gov/116/bills/s1789/BILLS-116s1789is.pdf; the IRC also reviewed the Military Justice Improvement and Increasing Prevention Act (2021).

[21] I am Vanessa Guillén Act of 2020. H.R.8270, 116th Cong. (2020). https://www.congress.gov/116/bills/hr8270/BILLS-116hr8270ih.pdf

[22] Hagel, C. (2013, August 6). Integrity of the military justice process [Memorandum]. Department of Defense. https://www.stripes.com/SECDEFMemorandum/theMilitaryJusticeProcess.pdf

memorandum became instrumental in overcoming allegations of unlawful command influence and the appearance of unlawful command influence being raised in sexual assault cases at that time. But much more important today, such a memorandum could be used by commanders to set the standard for integrity in military justice, establishing exactly what is expected from everyone involved. Key parts of the 2013 memorandum are:

- "This memorandum reiterates my expectations and those of the President regarding the integrity of the military justice process. Every military officer and enlisted member of the Department of Defense is to be made aware of its contents."
- "Central to military justice is the trust that those involved in the process base their decisions on their independent judgment. Their judgment, in turn, must be based purely on the facts of each individual case, not personal interests, career advancement, or an effort to produce what is thought to be the outcome desired by senior officials, military or civilian."
- "There are no expected or required dispositions, outcomes, or sentences in any military justice case, other than what result from the individual facts and merits of a case and the application to the case of the fundamentals of due process of law."
- "The integrity of the military justice process is too important to risk any misunderstanding of what the President and I expect from those involved in it."

As part of the effort to improve trust in the military justice process, the Secretary of Defense should issue a memorandum on the integrity of the military justice system patterned after the August 6, 2013 memorandum on that topic issued by the then-Secretary.

Outcome Metrics

The creation of the independent role of the Special Victim Prosecutor, overseen by the DoD Office of the Special Victim Prosecutor, will enhance the military justice workforce with the infusion of a cadre of highly skilled and trauma-informed litigators. These Special Victim Prosecutors will abide by their ethical guidelines for initiating and declining prosecutions, which in a justice-driven system should always prevail. This shift will result in better quality of cases both preferred and referred, which will increase the military's conviction rate exponentially over time.

The overall effect on military justice and those who participate in the system will be positive. With a state-of-the art office of specialized litigators handling special victim prosecutions, higher conviction rates will encourage victim reporting. Higher conviction rates, coupled with a well-trained force of career prosecutors will encourage more accused to enter into pretrial agreements thereby resolving cases short of a trial which results in certainty of conviction for the government and obviates the need for a victim to have to testify at trial. These outcomes will also increase confidence in the public that the military is correcting its course in the prosecution of special victim cases. These theories of change are directly tied to the IRC's charter and more specifically the Accountability line of effort's focus areas, including survivor likelihood of reporting, the ability to appropriately bring alleged perpetrators to justice, and the positive opportunity from changes to the commander's role in military justice.

Conviction Rates and Guilty Pleas: A Comparison with the Civilian Justice Response to Sexual Assault

Sexual assault cases are complicated and obtaining convictions and justice for victims requires expertise at all levels of the investigation and prosecution. This is true in both the military and civilian justice systems. To better understand the advantages of shifting legal decisions in sexual assault cases from commanders to specialized prosecutors, the Accountability experts compared military data on conviction rates and case processing with results from a recently published study released by the Department of Justice (DOJ) in 2019.[23] Ironically, the purpose of the DOJ study was to analyze the low number of sexual assault convictions obtained in the civilian justice system, in an effort to diagnose common challenges based on high case attrition. It examined reports of sexual assault over a three-year period in six sites across urban, suburban, and rural jurisdictions, representing diverse law enforcement agencies and communities.[24] The results of this study do not paint a flattering portrait of the civilian justice system response to sexual assault. Case attrition from initial report to ultimate prosecution is high and overall convictions are low; however, a comparison of the data suggests that the military's response is even worse. Figure 4 displays comparable prosecution data between the military and civilians for penetrative sexual assault cases:

	FY17 DoD Unrestricted Reports of Sexual Assault	2008-2010 Civilian Sexual Assault Reports (DOJ Data)
Number of Penetrative Sexual Assaults Reported	2,505	2,887
Number of Cases Available for Review and Subsequent Action	1,431 (57.1%)	1,404 (48.6%)
Number of Cases in Which Evidence Supported Command Action (Military) or Arrest of Subject (Civilian)	432 (17.2%)	544 (18.8%)
Total Number of Cases Preferred (Military) or Filed (Civilian)	368 (14.7%)	354 (12.3%)

Figure 4. Military & Civilians Prosecute Penetrative Sexual Assault Cases at Comparable Rates[25]

[23] Morabito, M. S., Williams, L. M., Pattavina, A. (2019). *Decision making in sexual assault cases: replication research on sexual violence case attrition in the U.S.* (NCJ 252689). Washington, DC: U.S. Department of Justice, National Institute of Justice. https://www.ojp.gov/pdffiles1/nij/grants/252689.pdf

[24] The study covered reports of sexual assault by women victims between 2008 to 2010. Sites were from states in the Northeastern, Southern, and Western U.S.

[25] Notes: A subset of the Unrestricted Reports from the FY17 Longitudinal Analysis are presented here. This figure shows the outcomes, as of FY19, for all Unrestricted Reports made in FY17 by victims alleging a penetrative crime (i.e., sexual assault, rape). Source: DoD SAPRO. (2020). Appendix B: Statistical Data on Sexual Assault. *Fiscal Year 2019 Annual Report on Sexual Assault in the Military*, 40.
https://www.sapr.mil/sites/default/files/DOD_Annual_Report_on_Sexual_Assault_In_The_Military_FY2019_Consolidated.pdf
Cases reported by women and girls 12 years and older involving penetrative sexual assault (i.e., rape, sodomy, and statutory rape); excludes forcible fondling. Source: Morabito, M. S., Williams, L. M., Pattavina, A. (2019). *Decision making*

- This figure reflects that both the civilians and the military prosecute cases at similar rates.
- Neither jurisdiction "weeds out" cases at significantly higher rates than the other.
- Both jurisdictions are prosecuting challenging and difficult to prove cases at similar rates.

Figure 5 examines conviction rates of penetrative sexual assault cases between the military and civilian systems:

Case Outcome	FY17 DoD Penetrative Sexual Assaults	FY18 DoD Penetrative Sexual Assaults	2008-2010 Civilian OJP Sexual Assaults
Total Number of Cases Preferred or Charged	517	433	354
Number of Cases that Resulted in a Guilty Plea	22 (4.2%)	31 (7.2%)	153 (43%)
Number of Cases Dismissed or Otherwise Not Pursued Criminally	282 (54.5%)	154 (35.5%)	152 (42.9%)
Number of Cases that Went to Contested Court-Martial or Trial	213 (41.2%)	248 (57.3%)	49 (13.8%)
Conviction Rate at Contested Court-Martial or Trial (Not Including Guilty Pleas)	*69 (32.4%)*	*141 (56.9%)*	*36 (73.4%)*
Overall Conviction Rate (conviction after contested trial or through guilty plea)	17.6%	39.7%	53.3%

Figure 5. Prosecutor-led Systems Achieve Higher Rates of Conviction in Sexual Assaults[26]

- Despite prosecuting cases at comparable rates, civilian prosecutors obtain higher conviction rates overall, and higher conviction rates after contested courts-martial or trials.
- Of significant importance is the civilian prosecutor's success in obtaining a conviction via a defendant's plea of guilty without the delay, re-traumatization, and uncertainty victims suffer with a trial: **Civilian Prosecutors obtained guilty pleas in 43 percent of all cases involving a charged suspect.**

The Accountability experts spoke with military justice practitioners (trial counsel, special victim prosecutors, defense counsel, and special victim counsel) about why the military obtains significantly

in sexual assault cases: replication research on sexual violence case attrition in the U.S. (NCJ 252689). Washington, DC: U.S. Department of Justice, National Institute of Justice. https://www.ojp.gov/pdffiles1/nij/grants/252689.pdf

The number of cases reported in FY17 that were considered for possible action by commanders. Source: DoD SAPRO. (2020). Appendix B: Statistical Data on Sexual Assault. *Fiscal Year 2019 Annual Report on Sexual Assault in the Military*, 40.
https://www.sapr.mil/sites/default/files/DOD_Annual_Report_on_Sexual_Assault_In_The_Military_FY2019_Consolidated.pdf

[26] Notes: Defense Advisory Committee on Investigation, Prosecution, and Defense of Sexual Assault in the Armed Forces. (2020). *Report on Investigative Case File Reviews for Military Adult Penetrative Sexual Offense Cases Closed in Fiscal Year 2017*. Defense Advisory Committee on Investigation, Prosecution, and Defense of Sexual Assault in the Armed Forces. (2020). *Fourth Annual Report*. Morabito, M. S., Williams, L.M., Pattavina, A. (2019). *Decision making in sexual assault cases: replication research on sexual violence case attrition in the U.S.* (NCJ 252689). Washington, DC: U.S. Department of Justice, National Institute of Justice. https://www.ojp.gov/pdffiles1/nij/grants/252689.pdf. Of 299 cases preferred and completed in FY20, convictions were obtained in 107, resulting in an overall conviction rate of 35.8 percent. Source: DoD SAPRO. (2021). Appendix B: Statistical Data on Sexual Assault. *Fiscal Year 2020 Annual Report on Sexual Assault in the Military*, 26.
https://www.sapr.mil/sites/default/files/DOD_Annual_Report_on_Sexual_Assault_in_the_Military_FY2020.pdf

fewer convictions, and specifically fewer convictions via pleas of guilty, compared with their civilian counterparts. These practitioners attributed this shortage to several factors.

These military justice practitioners told the IRC that lower rates of conviction and guilty pleas are inevitably tied to the lack of experience among military prosecutors trying sexual assault cases. This lack of experience is not only crippling when preparing and prosecuting a sexual assault case, but also inhibits a prosecutor from knowing when and how to engage in the plea negotiation process. The IRC's recommendation to establish a cadre of experienced special victim prosecutors (See: Recommendation 1.4: Professionalize Career Billets for Military Justice Practitioners and Military Criminal Investigators) will specifically address this problem.

An additional reason offered for the military's lower conviction rates and guilty pleas in particular is the number of stakeholders who must all agree to the terms of the guilty plea. Military justice practitioners explained to the IRC that a plea in the military can realistically only be obtained when the victim, special victim prosecutor, defendant, defense counsel, judge, commander, and the commander's staff judge advocate–seven parties–*all agree* on the terms of the plea agreement. By contrast, guilty pleas in civilian courts require the approval of five parties: the victim, prosecutor, defendant, defense counsel, and judge. The additional requirement of having the commander and his or her staff judge advocate also approve of the terms of the plea agreement appears to create an additional hurdle to overcome.

Bottom line: comparing the military and civilian justice systems reinforces the need to rethink the existing military structure for decision-making in sexual assault cases. The civilian study shows a higher rate of overall convictions, convictions via guilty pleas, and convictions at trial. Furthermore, the civilian data reflects similar rates of charging and decisions not to pursue criminal charges as their military counterparts. This means that the military's lower conviction rates and guilty pleas cannot be explained by a greater willingness to "take the tough cases."

Recommendation 1.2: Sexual Harassment Allegation Investigations and Mandatory Initiation of Involuntary Separation

The investigation of all sexual harassment should be performed by an independent, well-trained body that is outside the chain of command. The findings of whether to substantiate the allegation(s) should be made by the investigator, subject to a legal review, and the substantiated findings be reviewed by the Office of the Special Victim Prosecutor for consideration of criminal charges. Substantiated allegations not criminally charged should be referred back to the first O-6 in the chain of command for consideration of any other available non-punitive and adverse administrative action (e.g. nonjudicial punishment, or reprimands). Notwithstanding any other action taken by the commander, all substantiated findings of sexual harassment and other discriminatory behavior will result in *mandatory initiation* of involuntary separation from the Service; in certain limited situations an opportunity for rehabilitation is available. The IRC further recommends the *mandatory initiation* of involuntary separation from the Service for certain other categories of substantiated instances of misconduct.

Rationale for this Change: The Gap between Experience & Reports of Sexual Harassment in the Military

In FY20, DoD reported 1,781 complaints of sexual harassment from the Services and the National Guard Bureau (NGB) (984 formal complaints, 765 informal complaints, and 32 anonymous complaints).[27] The 2018 Workplace and Gender Relations Survey of Active Duty Members (WGRA)[28] revealed that an estimated 9.2 percent, or nearly one in 10 Service members, experienced sexual harassment in 2018 (24.2 percent of women and 6.3 percent of men).[29] Data from the 2018 WGRA estimate that a total of 116,300 Service members indicated experiencing sexual harassment in the past year. If DoD reported 1,781 complaints, this means there is about a 1.5 percent reporting rate amongst those Service members who experience sexual harassment.[30]

These numbers were replicated, though on a much smaller scale, by the FHIRC. The FHIRC found that incidents of sexual assault and sexual harassment at Fort Hood are significantly underreported.[31] Data from a survey conducted by the FHIRC with 31,612 respondents revealed that 2,625 Soldiers (or 8 percent) observed a situation in the last twelve months they believed was sexual harassment. In FY19, Fort Hood had 36 formal and informal complaints of sexual harassment.[32] The titanic delta between experience rates and reporting rates begs to be addressed.

More, there appears to be an inverse relationship between the number of substantiated findings for sexual harassment allegations investigated using the formal complaint process versus those resolved using the informal complaint process.[33] Of those that require additional oversight, some version of a procedure for investigation, and reporting requirements (formal) there is a 61 percent substantiation

---

27 DoD SAPRO. (2021). Appendix F: Sexual Harassment Assessment. *Fiscal Year 2020 Annual Report on Sexual Assault in the Military*, 4-5. https://www.sapr.mil/sites/default/files/Appendix_F_Sexual_Harassment_Assessment_FY2020.pdf

28 Conducted by the DoD Office of People Analytics as part of congressionally mandated gender relations surveys of active duty members. See, Title 10 U.S. Code Section 481.

29 Breslin, R., Davis, E., Hylton, K., Hill, A., Klauberg, W., Petusky, M., & Klahr, A. (2019). *2018 Workplace and Gender Relations Survey of Active Duty Members: Overview Report*. Report No. 2019-027. Alexandria, VA: Office of People Analytics, 43. https://apps.dtic.mil/sti/citations/AD1072334

30 The reporting rate included Active Duty, Reserve, and National Guard while the WGRA only included the Active Duty component. There is likely an even lower reporting rate when adding in the total force.

31 Fort Hood Independent Review Committee. (2020). *Report of the Fort Hood Independent Review Committee*, 43. https://www.army.mil/e2/downloads/rv7/forthoodreview/2020-12-03_FHIRC_report_redacted.pdf

32 Ibid.

33 DoD SAPRO. (2021). Appendix F: Sexual Harassment Assessment. *Fiscal Year 2020 Annual Report on Sexual Assault in the Military*, 5. https://www.sapr.mil/sites/default/files/Appendix_F_Sexual_Harassment_Assessment_FY2020.pdf

rate and a 35 percent unsubstantiation rate; while those addressed within the unit at the lowest level (informal) have a 32 percent substantiation rate and a 61 percent unsubstantiation rate.[34] These data support, in the words of Justice Louis Brandeis, "sunlight is said to be the best of disinfectants."[35]

Current Process for Reporting and Resolving Sexual Harassment and Other Equal Opportunity Complaints

Service members are not covered by the protections of Title VII of the Civil Rights Act of 1964 (Pub. L. 88-352), which means they cannot take legal action to stop harassment or get restitution for harassment from their employer. Nor can they simply quit their job; in fact, doing so is a criminal offense.[36] They are therefore left to work within the closed system(s) created for them by DoD and/or their Service. At present, a Service member who believes they have been sexually harassed, discriminated against, bullied, hazed, retaliated against or the victim of reprisal can make an anonymous[37] complaint, an informal[38] complaint, or a formal[39] complaint.[40] Any Service member may also make use of the Inspector General complaint line for Senior Official Misconduct. Service members may contact their appropriate Congressperson for assistance. In some instances, an Article 138, UCMJ complaint made directly against a Service member's commanding officer may also be appropriate.[41] Finally, Service members may choose to leave the military, but only when their enlistment or obligation has ended.

---

34 Ibid.

35 While it can be argued that lower level allegations are those that account for informal complaints, there is no data to support this. And evidence supports that for those complaints that were substantiated a similar percentage of adverse action was taken; including a greater number of cases where criminal charges were initiated. Source: Id, 11.

36 Both desertion under Article 85, UCMJ and Absence Without Leave (AWOL) under Article 86, UCMJ are punishable by confinement and a punitive discharge. *Manual for Courts-Martial, United States* (2019 ed.) (*MCM*), pt IV, ¶¶ 10,11.

37 An allegation received by a commanding officer or supervisor, regardless of the means of transmission, from an unknown or unidentified source, alleging harassment. The individual is not required to divulge any personally identifiable information. Source: DoD SAPRO. (2021). Appendix F: Sexual Harassment Assessment. *Fiscal Year 2020 Annual Report on Sexual Assault in the Military*, 3. https://www.sapr.mil/sites/default/files/Appendix_F_Sexual_Harassment_Assessment_FY2020.pdf

38 An allegation, made either orally or in writing, that is not submitted as a formal complaint through the office designated to receive harassment complaints. The allegation may be submitted to a person in a position of authority within the Service member's organization or outside of the Service member's organization. Such complaints may be resolved at the lowest level through intervention by the first-line supervisor, using alternative dispute resolution techniques such as informal mediation. Source: Ibid.

39 An allegation submitted in writing to the staff designated to receive such complaints in the Military Department operating instructions and regulations, or an informal complaint, which the commanding officer or other person in charge of the organization determines warrants an investigation. Some complainants may request the allegations of sexual harassment be addressed and resolved informally. Source: Ibid.

40 DoD. (2020). *DoDI 1020.03, Harassment Prevention and Response in the Armed Forces*. https://www.esd.whs.mil/Portals/54/Documents/DD/issuances/dodi/102003p.PDF?ver=DAAzonEUeFb8kUWRbT9Epw%3D%3D

41 If a Service member believes they have been wronged by their commanding officer, they may seek redress from that commanding officer. If the redress is refused, the Service member may forward the complaint to the officer exercising General Court-Martial jurisdiction over that commanding officer for review. Source: Article 138, UCMJ, 10 U.S.C. § 938.

Barriers to reporting sexual assault and sexual harassment exist in all communities, but the unique environment of the military exacerbates those barriers. The 2018 WGRA informs what some of these unique military barriers are. For Service members who indicated experiencing sexual harassment, they reported experiencing negative actions for bringing their complaints to light. Some of those negative actions were being encouraged to drop the matter, and being treated worse by their co-workers, avoided, or even blamed for the problem.[42] Importantly, men are significantly less likely to report sexual harassment and gender discrimination.[43]

Additionally, satisfaction with the process for resolving sexual harassment complaints ranged between 31 and 39 percent.[44] Paradoxically, it is the chain of command, and ultimately the commander who is both responsible for the command climate that tolerates or condones sexual harassment, retaliation, and ostracism and who investigates and adjudicates sexual harassment and other discriminatory complaints from within the unit. Sexual harassment and other gender-based discrimination should not be an additional burden that women have to bear in order to serve their Country. Being mocked or ridiculed or otherwise having one's achievements debased to something earned not solely on merit and grit cannot be another weight added to the female rucksack. The primary consequences of sexual harassment are plain and obvious, and while DoD has repeatedly addressed the impact on force readiness and the corrosive effect on unit cohesion, the secondary and tertiary consequences of sexual harassment have not been addressed with equal measure.[45,46]

Service members who have experienced sexual assault and sexual harassment are more likely to leave the military early and suffer negative health outcomes as a result of their experiences.[47] The 2014 RAND study showed that among those who indicated they had been sexually harassed, the odds of separating were 1.7 times greater than those who indicated they were not sexually harassed.[48] It was estimated that out of 117,000 Service members who appeared to have experienced sexual harassment in FY14, 28,200 separated from the military within 28 months.[49] These separations are costly on many

---

[42] Breslin, R., Davis, E., Hylton, K., Hill, A., Klauberg, W., Petusky, M., & Klahr, A. (2019). *2018 Workplace and Gender Relations Survey of Active Duty Members: Overview Report*. Report No. 2019-027. Alexandria, VA: Office of People Analytics, 49. https://apps.dtic.mil/sti/citations/AD1072334

[43] Id, 48-50.

[44] Id, 50.

[45] DoD SAPRO. (2021). Appendix F: Sexual Harassment Assessment. *Fiscal Year 2020 Annual Report on Sexual Assault in the Military*, 1. https://www.sapr.mil/sites/default/files/Appendix_F_Sexual_Harassment_Assessment_FY2020.pdf

[46] DoD. (2020). *DoDI 1020.03, Harassment Prevention and Response in the Armed Forces*. https://www.esd.whs.mil/Portals/54/Documents/DD/issuances/dodi/102003p.PDF?ver=DAAzonEUeFb8kUWRbT9Epw%3D%3D

[47] Morral, A.R., Matthews, M., Cefalu, M. Schell, T.L., Cottrell, L. (2021). *Effects of Sexual Assault and Sexual Harassment on Separation from the U.S. Military; Findings from the 2014 RAND Military Workplace Study.* Santa Monica, CA: RAND Corporation, 5. https://www.rand.org/pubs/research_reports/RR870z10.html

[48] Id, 19.

[49] Even accounting for other characteristics associated with separation, RAND estimated 8,000 more separations of sexually harassed persons than would be predicted had they not experienced the harassment. Source: Id, 20.

fronts. For the military, there are unanticipated personnel and manpower year losses and premature recruitment and training costs.[50] For the Service member, they are losing immediate compensation that is often higher than in comparable civilian sector positions, bonuses, and potentially considerable postretirement compensation.[51] In addition to separating, those who experience sexual harassment while in the military have been shown to suffer a number of adverse health consequences.[52]

The most common method for making allegations of sexual harassment, harassment, or discrimination is through the use of the anonymous, informal, or formal complaint process called the Military Equal Opportunity Complaint Program. While one of the goals of DoD Instruction (DoDI) 1020.03 was to establish a comprehensive, DoD-wide harassment prevention and response program,[53] each Service handles the investigation and adjudication of sexual harassment complaints differently. It is therefore the case that similarly situated individuals have vastly different experiences

The IRC is mindful that the Total Force is made up of uniformed Service members and upwards of 900,000 civilian federal employees.[54] The IRC is also mindful that its charter limited it to addressing change within the uniformed Services. It would be myopic not to mention that sexual assault and sexual harassment affect the civilian workforce as well. To that end, the experts highlight the Government Accountability Office (GAO) report to Congressional committees on sexual harassment and assault for DoD civilians and the nineteen recommendations included therein.[55]

The Role of Command in Addressing Sexual Harassment

In general, DoD promotes the use of the chain of command and resolution at the lowest level. If an allegation of harassment is accepted for review, then the commander will appoint an available Investigating Officer (IO) to conduct the investigation. Depending on the Service branch, the IO may or may not be in the victim and/or accused's chain of command. Furthermore, the IO does not necessarily have any training on conducting investigations or any unique training on sexual harassment, discrimination, or trauma-informed techniques. Once the IO has finished and he or she makes findings and recommendations (subject to a legal review), those findings go back to the commander. It is the commander who determines whether the allegations should be substantiated. Stated differently, even if the IO makes a finding that sexual harassment occurred, the commander has the discretion to disapprove the finding(s). If there is a substantiated finding of harassment, the

[50] Id, 23-24.
[51] Ibid.
[52] Id, 5.
[53] DoD SAPRO. (2021). Appendix F: Sexual Harassment Assessment. *Fiscal Year 2020 Annual Report on Sexual Assault in the Military*, 2. https://www.sapr.mil/sites/default/files/Appendix_F_Sexual_Harassment_Assessment_FY2020.pdf
[54] Davidson, J. (2021, February 20). Most reports by civilians of sexual assault go unrecorded in Defense Department database. *The Washington Post.* https://www.washingtonpost.com/politics/defense-civilians-sexual-assault/2021/02/19/306c0150-729e-11eb-a4eb-44012a612cf9_story.html
[55] GAO. (2021). GAO-21-113 Sexual Harassment and Assault: Guidance Needed to Ensure Consistent Tracking, Response, and Training for DoD Civilians. https://www.gao.gov/products/gao-21-113

commander has complete discretion on how to adjudicate. This includes bringing criminal charges, nonjudicial punishment under Article 15, UCMJ, or other adverse administrative actions such as formal letters of reprimand or initiation of administrative separation from the Service.

The major takeaway from the IRC's conversations with victims of sexual harassment is that they do not trust the command to ensure that their complaints are properly investigated and acted upon. Further, they do not trust their command to protect them from negative consequences of reporting. These are the driving factors that lead the IRC to these recommendations. First, the experts believe that there is a gross underreporting of sexual harassment in the military as evidenced below. Second, they believe commanders are failing in their first duty, to "treat their subordinates with dignity and respect at all times and establish a command and organizational climate that emphasizes the duty of others to act in a similar manner toward their subordinates in accomplishing the unit mission."[56]

Implementation Considerations

Use of Independent, Well-Trained Investigators

In order to build faith in the reporting and investigation process, once an allegation of sexual harassment has been made, that process should be led by independent, well-trained investigators. This is because the investigation of sexual harassment allegations requires independent oversight in order to ensure accountability from outside the chain of command, similar to investigations of sexual assaults. However, unlike sexual assault investigations, the conduct involved in harassment complaints will most likely not involve a touching offense and therefore may not need the already scarce resources of the MCIOs in the Special Victim Investigation and Prosecution (SVIP) program. Recognizing that sexual harassment allegations require a competent investigator independent from the chain of command, the IRC considered several options.

One option is for sexual harassment allegations to be investigated by a representative from the Equal Opportunity Program. However, these individuals are mainly equipped to run the complaints process, and they lack the necessary training and skills to appropriately investigate a sexual harassment case. A second option is to utilize the cadre of uniformed and civilian police investigators employed by each Service. These police investigators can be leveraged to run these investigations as a part of the SVIP capability. This would provide additional manpower resources to address these very important investigations, ensure oversight of the investigations by the independent MCIO investigators, and ensure that the judge advocate community has visibility of all the conduct being investigated.

The IRC is mindful, however, that while all victims want the harassing behavior to stop, many may be reluctant to involve law enforcement. A supplemental solution, in the spirit of the "No Wrong Door"

---

[56] Department of the Army. (2020). Army Regulation 600-20: Army Command Policy. https://armypubs.army.mil/epubs/DR_pubs/DR_a/ARN30511-AR_600-20-002-WEB-3.pdf

approach[57], is to allow victims to report sexual harassment to a trained victim advocate, similar to how the Army SHARP program representatives are able to receive and assist with both sexual assault and sexual harassment. These trained victim advocates should be accessible, approachable, and knowledgeable. Victims should be able to make their initial report to these victim advocates who will discuss the reporting and investigation options with the victims. Based upon the gravity of the behavior and the preferences of the victim, the victim can choose to seek the assistance of the commander or file a formal report with the identified investigators to conduct a full investigation into the harassment.

To implement this recommendation, DoD should determine which body will serve as investigators for formal sexual harassment complaints, taking into account the comfort level of victims in talking to investigators and the capacity of each proposed group to understand and investigate sexual harassment cases.

If the victim chooses to file a formal report, it will be appropriately logged, investigated, and subject to a legal review. Nothing written here should be construed to prevent commanders from taking action necessary to protect the complainant.

Upon completion of the investigation, the investigator will make findings that substantiate or unsubstantiate a complaint. All substantiated findings will then be sent to the Special Victim Prosecutor for consideration of criminal charges. If criminal charges are not preferred by the Special Victim Prosecutor, the entire packet will be sent back to the first O-6 in the subject's chain of command for any other action deemed appropriate. This can include action under Article 15, UCMJ or any other adverse administrative action consistent with Recommendation 1.1: Creation of the Office of the Special Victim Prosecutor. Notwithstanding any adverse action taken by the commander, all substantiated findings of sexual harassment and other discriminatory behavior will result in the mandatory *initiation* of involuntary separation from the Service.

In certain limited situations, an opportunity for rehabilitation should be available. That is, for those cases that *do not* include instances of: *quid pro quo* (i.e., threats or attempts to influence another's career or job in exchange for sexual favors; rewards including bribes to influence favorably another's career in exchange for sexual favors); cases in which the rank differential between the subject and the victim is two or more grades (subject over victim) or the victim is in a technical or supervisory subordinate position to the subject; or unwanted physical contact of a sexual nature which, if charged as a violation of the UCMJ, could result in a punitive discharge, the subject is eligible to participate in a

[57] The "No Wrong Door" (NWD) approach is a person-centered approach to improving access to services and programs. At its most basic level, NWD refers to a system where a person who is seeking services from an organization will never encounter a "wrong door" to getting the care and support that they need. The NWD approach to victim care and services is recommended by the IRC's victim care and support experts.

rehabilitative/intervention program. The content of the behavior modification program will be evidence-based and utilize promising practices in the field of sexual violence prevention and risk reduction. Importantly, the content can be modified and enhanced based upon the findings and learnings of the Research Center envisioned as part of Recommendation 2.6. In the meantime, the college campus context provides promising models for offender rehabilitation, and the concept of required treatment as a condition of continued service has already been established and implemented in the substance abuse context.[58]

Successful completion of the program will require the active participation of the offender and a willingness to engage in individualized, psychosocial education. If the subject successfully completes this program to the satisfaction of the professionals who run the program, then his/her separation packet will be pulled from the separation process. Service members who fail to participate adequately in or to respond successfully to the program will be processed for separation. Further, if a subject has more than one substantiated instance of sexual harassment or discriminatory behavior in their career, they will not be eligible for the program and will be processed as if they did not meet eligibility criteria. Additionally, if another reason for involuntary separation exists, commanders have the discretion to proceed on those grounds. All actions stemming from a reported sexual harassment complaint or other discriminatory behavior complaint will be tracked and reported back to DoD as outlined in the *outcome metrics* section below. Additionally, this information will also be reported to the next superior officer in the chain of command who is authorized to convene a general court-martial.

Mandatory Initiation of Involuntary Separation

We further recommend the mandatory *initiation* of involuntary separation for Service members determined to have committed certain other offenses. An offense is determined to have been committed when there has been a court-martial conviction, nonjudicial punishment, civilian criminal trial conviction (domestic, not foreign), or the commander determines, based on a preponderance of the evidence or is in receipt of a substantiated finding from an investigator, that an offense was committed. These other offenses are those that are so detrimental to good order and discipline, mission readiness, and appropriate standards of performance and conduct that initiation of involuntary separation is required. The offenses include: supremacist or extremist conduct; hate based offenses; nonconsensual distribution or broadcasting of an intimate image that could be charged as a violation of or an attempt to violate the UCMJ or equivalent State Military Justice Code provision or State Criminal Code offense for members of the National Guard in Title 32 status; stalking; domestic violence; sexual misconduct including lewd and lascivious acts; rape; sexual assault; forcible sodomy; child pornography; incestuous relationships; or any sexual misconduct that could be charged as a violation of or an attempt to violate Articles 120, 120a, 120b, or 120c or equivalent criminal statute as a result of either misconduct due to commission of a serious offense or civilian conviction; or conduct of a substantially similar nature under Articles 133 or 134; or equivalent State Military Justice Code provision or State Criminal Code offenses for members of the National Guard in Title 32 status; violent misconduct that resulted in or had the potential to result in death or serious bodily injury

---

58 For reference, consider the Army Substance Abuse Program: AR 600-85.

including homicide, arson, armed robbery, assault with a deadly weapon; and acts or retaliation or reprisal.

This policy applies to members of the National Guard regardless of duty status. Notwithstanding the guidance provided above, the Chief of the NGB will implement Service policy and issue clarifying guidance, as necessary, that is applicable to the Army National Guard and Air National Guard.

Outcome Metrics

All actions stemming from a reported complaint, as described above, should be tracked and reported to OSD. Specifically, for each FY, the Military Departments and Services should report:

- The numbers of sexual harassment complaints and the number of complaints found to be substantiated or unsubstantiated;
- The numbers of investigations completed and pending;
- The number of actions taken by the Special Victim Prosecutor;
- The number of complaints sent back to the chain of command, and types of actions taken by the chain of command;
- The number of Service members who successfully complete the behavior modification program; and,
- The number of subjects involuntarily separated following substantiation of sexual harassment or other crimes as specified in the recommendation.

It is anticipated that thorough implementation of this recommendation will, over time, result in: decreased prevalence of sexual harassment as measured by the WGRA; increased reporting of sexual harassment and other discriminatory complaints; increases in Service members who report feeling satisfied with the sexual harassment process on the WGRA; and, decreases in Service members who report negative behaviors as a result of making sexual harassment and other discriminatory complaints. Finally, this recommendation seeks to achieve increased retention of Service members following experiencing sexual harassment or making a complaint of sexual harassment.

Recommendation 1.3: Judge-Ordered Military Protective Orders for Victims of Sexual Assault and Related Offenses

Victims of sexual assault, and related crimes, should be able to receive a judge-issued Military Protective Order (MPO) which complies with Full Faith and Credit Requirements, thus ensuring reciprocity with civilian law enforcement.

Rationale for this Change: Lack of Due Process Imperils Victims, is Unfair to Respondents

Multiple scoping sessions with victims, victim advocates, trial counsel, MCIOs, and SVCs/VLCs highlighted a consistent problem with the efficacy and enforceability of MPOs. Unlike Protective

Orders issued by states, tribes, or U.S. territories, MPOs do not currently provide due process and are therefore not afforded Full Faith and Credit by other jurisdictions as required under the Violence Against Women Act. Every state, tribe, and U.S. territory must enforce protective orders issued by other jurisdictions; however, that full faith and credit requirement only applies to protective orders that provide due process.[59]

Due process is a legal term which means that the Service member, the person against whom the protective order is sought, must be given reasonable notice and an opportunity to be heard.[60] The MPO's failure to be issued by a court or to provide due process results in two profound shortcomings: first, the MPO is not enforceable by civilian law enforcement officers; and second, the MPO does not preclude the respondent from purchasing or possessing a firearm.

This means that a victim with an MPO cannot receive protection off installation unless they also file for a civil protective order (CPO). Requiring a victim to apply for both a MPO and a CPO is overly burdensome and duplicative, and presents a clear safety risk.

Current Policy and Limits of Commander-Issued MPOs

When a Service member is accused of an offense, the Rules for Courts-Martial (RCM) allow an officer to impose "conditions on liberty," directing a person to do or refrain from doing specific acts before and during the disposition of an offense.[61] The military has formalized these orders with a standard DD Form 2873, which allows a commander to issue an MPO against a Service member under his or her command when the commander concludes that issuing the MPO is warranted in the best interest of good order and discipline. The MPO prohibits the Service member from assaulting, threatening, abusing, harassing, following, interfering with, or stalking the protected person. The commander can also use the MPO to prevent the Service member from initiating any contact or communication with the protected person directly or through a third party. Importantly, the MPO clarifies that communication is defined broadly and specifically includes electronic communication, including electronic communications or postings via the internet and social media. Finally, as with civilian issued protective orders, the commander can dictate the distance that the Service member must stay away from the protected person's home or workplace. The MPO remains in effect until the commander terminates the order.[62]

Currently, a unit commander can immediately issue a MPO against an active duty Service member under his or her command without the ability of the Service member to challenge it. While commander-issued MPOs can be a quick and simple method of pursuing good order and discipline

59 18 United States Code (U.S.C.), § 2265 (a), "Full faith and credit given to protection orders."

60 Ibid.

61 R.C.M. 304

62 18 U.S.C. § 1567 (a), "Duration of military protective orders."

and protecting victims, this efficiency comes at a cost. Although commanders are required to notify the local civilian authorities of the issuance of the MPO,[63] they are not enforceable by civilian law enforcement officers because they are not issued by a court and do not provide the subject Service member with due process. Consequently, if a victim has obtained an MPO against her abuser and the abuser comes to the victim's off-base home in violation of the MPO, the local police department cannot arrest the abuser for violating the MPO.[64] This leaves a significant gap in protections for victims which is particularly acute considering that the vast majority (64 percent) of Service members and their families live off-installation.[65]

Federal law generally prohibits individuals who are subject to a protective order from possessing firearms; however, that prohibition only applies if the individual received notice and an opportunity to participate in a hearing.[66] Since today's MPOs do not provide due-process, this prohibition does not apply. Since March 2020, commanders have been required to register MPOs with installation police so that they are entered into the National Crime Information Center Protective Order File.[67] Nonetheless, that registration is woefully inadequate because while the registration alerts authorities to the presence of an MPO, it does not prohibit the offender from purchasing or possessing a firearm.[68]

In the current system, the only way for a victim to receive a protective order that complies with due process is to apply for a civilian protective order in the jurisdiction where the victim lives. As a result, a victim must utilize and communicate with the military justice system for the court-martial proceeding while simultaneously utilizing and communicating with the civilian courts for the protective order process. Requiring a victim to participate in two separate, parallel legal processes is unduly burdensome, re-traumatizing, and potentially damaging to the outcome of the court-martial. The victim has to provide double the witness statements, testimonies, and interviews. Furthermore, that duplication may be detrimental to the military justice process because the sworn statements, testimony, and witness examination that the victim must separately provide during the civilian protective order

---

63 Ibid.

64 DoD. (2017, May 26). *DoDI 6400.06, Domestic Abuse Involving DoD Military and Certain Affiliated Personnel*. https://www.esd.whs.mil/Portals/54/Documents/DD/issuances/dodi/640006p.pdf

65 Blue Star Families. (2020). *2020 Military Family Lifestyle Survey Comprehensive Report,* 51. https://bluestarfam.org/wp-content/uploads/2021/03/BSF_MFLS_CompReport_FULL.pdf

66 18 U.S.C. § 922(g)(8), "Unlawful acts."

67 NDAA FY20, Section 543 amended section 1567(a) U.S.C. https://www.congress.gov/116/plaws/publ92/PLAW-116publ92.pdf

68 This recommendation will not alter the ability of military personnel who must be able to possess a firearm in their professional duties to do so. There is an "official use exemption" to the § 922(g)(8) prohibition that allows law enforcement and military personnel who are subject to a current protection order to possess their Service weapon while on duty. For the exemption to apply, the personnel must be authorized or required to receive or possess a duty weapon to perform their official duties. The authorization must be pursuant to federal, state or local statute, regulation, or official departmental policy. 18 U.S.C. § 925(a)(1). The official use exemption does not apply to any personal firearms.

process (where the victim will not have the benefit of the military's victim advocate nor special victim's counsel) could negatively impact the outcome of the court-martial. Any minor deviation in the victim's narrative, which naturally occurs when victims are forced to recount their experience numerous times to multiple individuals, can be used to impeach the victim and will negatively impact the court-martial.

Implementation of Judge-Ordered MPOs

Victims of sexual assault and related offenses should be allowed to apply for a Judge Ordered Military Protective Order (JMPO)[69] which complies with due process. Victims should be able to obtain this JMPO in addition to or in lieu of the currently existing, commander-issued MPO. While MPOs can be verbally or informally requested, a victim would draft the application for a JMPO with the assistance of a Family Advocacy Program (FAP) advocate, Sexual Assault Prevention and Response Victim Advocate (SAPR VA), Special Victim Counsel, or Special Victim Prosecutor.

The JMPO application would be submitted to a judge advocate serving as military magistrate for immediate review. If the magistrate finds that the information contained in the application for a JMPO meets the threshold requirements for issuance of the order, the magistrate will immediately issue a temporary ex-parte protective order and set a hearing date on the JMPO request. The Service member against whom the order is requested (i.e., the Respondent) would be served with notice of the issuance of the temporary ex parte order and the hearing date for the JMPO.

On the date of the hearing, the victim would be represented by the Special Victim's Counsel or other counsel, the Service member could be represented by defense counsel, and the application would be heard by a military judge. At that hearing, the standard burden of proof of Preponderance of the Evidence would apply, consistent with protective orders issued in every other state, tribe, or United States Territory.

If the military judge finds that violence, harassment, or threats have occurred, the judge will issue the JMPO. The duration of the JMPO will be set by the judge, but a standard order should be in effect for at least one year. If the Service member separates from the military, resulting in the military court no longer having jurisdiction over that individual, the military judge should send a copy of the JMPO to the civilian authorities in the jurisdiction where the victim resides to assist the victim in converting the JMPO to a civilian PO. In addition to ensuring that the JMPO procedure complies with due process, the wording of the JMPO should specifically include several additional improvements to the current MPO document and procedure. For example, the MPO currently prohibits the Respondent Service member from initiating any contact or communication, including electronic communications and social media, with the protected person directly or through a third party. The JMPO should also prohibit the Respondent from distributing any visual image of an intimate or sexual nature of the protected person.

---

69 These orders may also be referred to as Military Court Ordered Protective Orders, Court Ordered Protective Orders, or the like.

As with their civilian counterparts, the JMPO will prohibit the respondent from communicating with the victim (by any means, including through social media or electronic communications), going near the victim's home or work, or threatening or assaulting the victim. If the respondent violates the JMPO by engaging in behavior that qualifies as an enumerated offense in the UCMJ, such as assault, distributing a visual image of an intimate or sexual nature, stalking, etc., the respondent would be charged with *both* the underlying offense and the violation of the JMPO. If the respondent violates the protective order by engaging in conduct that would not constitute a criminal offense but for the JMPO, such as calling the victim on the phone or going to the victim's home, the respondent would be charged exclusively with violating the JMPO.

The major criticism of the recommendation to establish a JMPO that provides due process is that it would result in a vastly increased workload for the military justice system. The empirical evidence does not support that argument. For example, MPOs can currently be issued whenever a Service member is alleged to have committed sexual assault, stalking, domestic violence, child endangerment, or another offense. Furthermore, MPOs can be requested by a victim, a Sexual Assault Response Coordinator (SARC), SAPR VA, installation law enforcement, FAP clinician, or commander.[70, 71]

Despite this broad issuance ability and the relative ease with which an MPO can be ordered, the military does not issue an overwhelming number of MPOs. During FY20, the Army issued 2,625 MPOs, the Air Force issued 252, and the Navy/Marine Corps issued 2,288. In sum, the military is currently collectively issuing MPOs at the rate of approximately 5,000 per year. Even if every one of those victims also applied for a judge-issued MPO, the military justice practitioners with whom the Accountability experts consulted were confident this number is manageable. This recommendation supports and improves victim autonomy and safety because the victim, with the consultation and support of a SARC or SAPR VA, can determine whether to pursue a traditional commander-issued MPO and/or a JMPO. Additionally, the victim can request one or both of those orders immediately after an incident which causes the victim to feel unsafe and in need of protection.

Specifically, the JMPO can be, and likely will be, issued prior to any decisions regarding the preferral or referral of the underlying offense. Since the JMPO is heard and issued by a judge after a hearing on the merits of the application, it is fully enforceable both on-base and off-base, regardless of the final disposition of the underlying offense. This recommendation offers a seamless process for the victim, who only has to utilize and coordinate with one justice system to obtain both a fully enforceable protective order and to assist in the court-martial of the offender. The victim will be able to utilize the same SARC, SAPR VA, and SVC/VLC throughout both the protective order and military justice proceedings. This continuity similarly benefits the offender and the military as well, because all proceedings utilize in-house military personnel and venues, resulting in increased fairness and efficiency. In particular, fairness to the Service member is increased because the member is provided

---

[70] DoD. (2017, May 26). *DoDI 6400.06, Domestic Abuse Involving DoD Military and Certain Affiliated Personnel*. https://www.esd.whs.mil/Portals/54/Documents/DD/issuances/dodi/640006p.pdf

[71] DoD. (2020). *DoD Directive Form 2873: Military Protective Orders*. https://www.esd.whs.mil/Portals/54/Documents/DD/forms/dd/dd2873_2020.pdf

with due process by the military court where they are stationed rather than having to leave the installation and be heard by a civilian court.

During the Accountability team's comprehensive interviews and listening sessions, stakeholders reported that victims frequently declined to report their assault or harassment because of a strongly held perception that no good would come from reporting, but significant damage to their careers, reputations, and friendships would occur. In particular, these sessions clarified that neither victims nor perpetrators felt that MPOs in their current form are very effective or strictly enforced. The IRC heard from survivors and special victim counsel who reported that victims and abusers know that the MPO provides minimal protection in its current form. Survivors reported that even after obtaining an MPO, victims continue to be harassed and stalked by their abusers with relative impunity, especially if they live off installation.

Ideally, a formalized JMPO process will also result in ancillary benefits to victims and the military justice system. Most notably, given that the JMPO offers a real and tangible benefit to victims, the implementation of this recommendation will encourage more victims to report their assault or harassment. Increased reporting will in turn allow for early intervention and prevent abuse from escalating. Stakeholders also discussed the perceived unfairness of victims bearing the responsibility of requesting an expedited transfer to a new location and suffering the personal and career interruption of moving in order to get away from an abuser or harasser. Since the JMPO will provide due process, its issuance can be used by the military to consider requiring the abuser to change duty stations rather than placing this onus on the victim. Similarly, the provision of due process and a formal hearing will increase the overall gravitas of the protective order and allow imposition of more meaningful conditions on perpetrators. It will make the protective order process more protective of both the rights of the victim and the due process rights of the accused.

Outcome Metrics

The success of the implementation of this recommendation will be measured by several metrics. Special Victims Counsel and or victim's advocates will likely be the individuals who advise victims on the protective order opportunities that are available. These SVCs and advocates should capture that the information was provided and what decision victims made. Did victims choose to seek a JMPO, a MPO, both, or neither? Additionally, the military should monitor and report the number of MPOs and JMPOs granted.

All JMPOs will be required to be uploaded into NICS. If a prohibited individual seeks to purchase a firearm, NICS will contact the military law enforcement agency that submitted the JMPO information to alert them that the subject has attempted to purchase a firearm. It will be critical for the military to monitor the number of NICS alerts received. When a JMPO is violated off base, the local civilian law enforcement agency should immediately respond and arrest the perpetrator for Violation of a Protective Order. After the arrest, the local law enforcement agency will notify the military that a Service member is in custody. At that time, the military can assert jurisdiction over the case and take over the investigation and prosecution. The military should track the number of times that a civilian law enforcement agency responds to a JMPO.

The military should track the number of violations of JMPOs that occur and specifically how did the offender violate the order. Did the perpetrator engage in conduct that constitutes an independent enumerated offense in the UCMJ? Or did the perpetrator engage in conduct that would not be a crime absent the existence of the JMPO? The military should track the number of JMPO violations that occur and the outcome of those reports.

Importantly, the military should track victim satisfaction with the JMPO. This metric should include a detailed look at the process of obtaining a JMPO as well as any sacrifices or barriers that victims experienced in obtaining the order and trying to get the order enforced. Importantly, the military should assess whether the JMPO increased the victim's sense of safety after receiving it.[72]

Recommendation 1.4: Professionalize Career Billets for Military Justice Practitioners and Military Criminal Investigators

The Secretary of Defense should direct the Services to establish career litigation billets for prosecutors, defense counsel, special victim counsel, and military judges in the Services' JAG Corps,[73] and a career track for military criminal investigators in order to establish and reinforce confidence in the military justice system among Service members and the public, and to cultivate highly skilled and competent military justice practitioners.

Rationale for this Change: Lack of Experience is the Achilles' Heel of the Military Justice System

Historically, regardless of occupational specialty, military Service members are subject to continuous personnel rotations which contribute to an inexperienced military justice workforce with subpar qualifications to appropriately handle special victim cases. Outdated human resources practices tied to wartime operational needs of the Services cause unnecessary disruption to professional development, create instability among special victim capable professionals, and contribute to perpetual inexperience among military lawyers and criminal investigators. One Service's reassignment regulation claims the goal of permanent change of station moves is "to place the right Soldier at the right job, at the right time."[74] This philosophy, however, is incompatible with responding to, investigating, and

[72] Logan, T., & Walker, R. (2009). Civil Protective Order Outcomes: Violations and Perceptions of Effectiveness. *Journal of Interpersonal Violence*, 24(4), 675-692. doi:10.1177/0886260508317186

[73] Even though the Marine Corps does not have a JAG Corps, the Marine Corps has a cadre of Judge Advocates. Therefore, for ease of reference, throughout this section, when Service JAG Corps is mentioned, it is inclusive of Marine Corps Judge Advocates.

[74] Department of the Army. (2012). *Army Regulation 600-8-11, Personnel–General, Reassignment: 1–5. The personnel reassignment process*, 1. https://armypubs.army.mil/epubs/DR_pubs/DR_a/pdf/web/r600_8_11.pdf

prosecuting special victim crimes in the military. Instead, the military must finally commit to placing the right experts in the right billets right now – and permanently.

Highly trained practitioners with years of consistent, technical experience are a critical part of the solution to the military's sexual assault problem. Career litigators and investigators who specialize in special victim crimes will ameliorate the perception – and reality – that the military is ill equipped to investigate and prosecute these cases.

Lack of Career Litigation Billets in the Services' JAG Corps Perpetuates Lack of Expertise

Overall, the IRC found that military justice practitioners are hard-working, dedicated, and earnest. However, Service JAG Corps leadership – apart from the Navy[75] – do not allow for judge advocates who specialize in criminal litigation to stay in those positions for an entire career. This creates a lack of confidence in military lawyers by both Service members and the public. The Accountability experts found that resistance to change by senior leaders in the JAG Corps is historic and entrenched. With limited resources and missions requiring the development of both generalists and specialists in a large number of areas, judge advocate leaders have been reluctant to invest in career prosecutors and personnel necessary to have a deep, talented, and experienced cadre of military justice experts; experts who can only be grown through consecutive assignments across military justice billets.

After hearing from all forms of military practitioners – both past and present – as well as sexual assault victims who participated in the military justice court-martial system, it is breathtakingly apparent that the Service JAGs' refusal to allow talented practitioners to remain in career litigation billets harms victims and accused in special victim cases because those litigating special victim cases – largely through no fault of their own – do not possess the characteristics and skills that enable and improve efficiency and performance of their job which fosters institutional competence. This recommendation is complementary to Recommendation 1.1: Creation of the Office of the Special Victim Prosecutor, which provides for the independent reporting structure outside of the Services for these specialists and opportunities for professional growth that career litigators require.

> "Sexual assault cases are difficult to prosecute [and] require SEAL team caliber prosecutors."
>
> -Father of survivor, as told to the IRC in an interview

Nowhere was this sentiment more apparent than scoping sessions with judge advocates, former military judges, former court-martial panel members, and civilian HQEs assigned to assist military counsel. These individuals and groups of stakeholders unanimously reported that judge advocate competence in special victim cases is perpetually thwarted by high rates of turnover of personnel every one to two years. The father of a survivor who spoke with the IRC put it this way: "JAGs are given great responsibility early in their

[75] Navy JAG Instruction 1150.2E provides information and procedural guidance for the Navy Judge Advocate General's Corps MJLCT program and establishes guidelines for the selection, professional development, and detailing of Military Justice Litigation Qualified Officers.

careers and do a noble job, but they are generalists. They're required to be a Jack of All Trades which is important, but that also makes them a Master of None. We shouldn't be surprised at the astonishingly low conviction rates in the military. Sexual assault cases are difficult to prosecute as such, they should require SEAL team caliber prosecutors."

The impact on talent and quality of military litigators was palpable: these justice practitioners described junior prosecutor courtroom performance as ranging from "terrible" to "incompetent." However, in trials when seasoned special victim prosecutors participated as co-counsel to the more inexperienced and often junior counsel, the quality of government practice increased exponentially. The historic focus on generalists in the JAG Corps, however, does not allow current special victim prosecutors to perfect their craft without sacrificing their promotion potential. The military defense bar competence, in their estimation, was marginally better, but still fell victim to judge advocate career progression schemes. On the other hand, where civilian defense counsel was brought on the case to defend a Service member, one parent of a military sexual assault victim who watched the proceedings firsthand observed:

> "In my daughter's case, I was taken aback at how the civilian defense counsel ran circles around JAG prosecution. They absolutely cleaned JAG's clock. Later, I was stunned to learn the number of civilian firms that specialize in the defense of military members within military court proceedings. That's all they do, they don't even operate in civilian courtrooms. On their websites, they proudly display how they have trounced JAGs of all Service branches–and they have. They've identified this as an easy market–it's become a cottage industry."

Lack of Career Litigation Billets in the Services' JAG Corps Fuels Inexperience

Experience is the cornerstone of professional competence. The IRC found that there is a direct correlation between experienced, well-trained and specialized prosecutors and sexual assault victim satisfaction. Four years after the Judicial Proceedings Panel (JPP) on Sexual Assault in the Military issued its report examining training for prosecutors, defense counsel, and military judges,[76] the Services' JAG Corps (apart from the Navy) still have no uniform agreement on a requisite minimum level of experience for handling sexual assault cases. During 2016 site visits, military prosecutors told the JPP subcommittee that they were generally satisfied that they were receiving adequate and

[76] The NDAA for FY13 directed the JPP to assess trends in the training and experience levels of military trial counsel in adult sexual assault cases and the impact of those trends on the prosecution and adjudication of such cases. In order to assess the training and experience of adult sexual assault prosecutors, the JPP issued requests for information to the Services in February and December 2016. The JPP also heard testimony on the training and experience of prosecutors at a public meeting on May 13, 2016, during which the Panel heard from leaders of the Service JAG schools and members of the JAG Corps who litigate adult sexual assault crimes. In addition, the JPP Subcommittee spoke with prosecutors about their training and experience during site visits conducted during the summer of 2016 and reported this information to the JPP at a public meeting on March 10, 2017.

appropriate training, however, many remarked that the extensive training does not make up for their lack of in-court experience.

In response, some Services attempted to close the gap between training and repeated courtroom experience (e.g., Army Military Justice Redesign[77]), however, practitioners told the IRC that special victim prosecutors are no longer hand-picked and the Services so-called "specialization" programs have succumbed to traditional personnel requirements and rotations, which has not addressed the core problem: inexperience. One retired judge summed up what was obvious to the IRC: inexperience is the Achilles heel of JAG Corps litigators.

Between the three Accountability experts and the IRC's Senior Policy Advisor, all of whom are lawyers, there is greater than 100 years of experience in litigating and managing complex sexual assault cases – both on the prosecution and defense side. It has been the experience of these career professionals that military litigators with less than 2 years' experience are generally only capable of conducting simple direct examinations, handling less complex prosecution techniques, and acting in a support role for more experienced litigators. They are still developing trial skills and learning procedures, military rules of evidence, and administrative requirements. They have less training and need to work under close supervision. They are not ready for complex prosecutions involving sexual assault, traumatized victims, sexual assault forensic examination, and other forensic evidence. It is the rare trial counsel or defense counsel who is capable of handling such complex trials.

The IRC heard from both military justice practitioners and sexual assault victims that military prosecutors lacked fundamental knowledge of guiding principles of federal prosecution as well as the Crime Victim Rights Act (CVRA) and Article 6b of the UCMJ.[78] The CVRA affords victims several rights, including but not limited to:

- The right to be reasonably protected from the accused;
- The right to reasonable, accurate, and timely notice of any public court proceeding;
- The right not to be excluded from any such public court proceeding, unless the court, after receiving clear and convincing evidence, determines that testimony by the victim would be materially altered if the victim heard other testimony at that proceeding;
- The right to receive restitution;
- The reasonable right to confer with the attorney for the Government in the case;
- The right to proceedings free from unreasonable delay; and
- The right to be treated with fairness and with respect for the victim's dignity and privacy.

Many victims reported that the prosecutor handling their case rarely – if ever – allowed opportunity for conferral on their cases and delays were exceptionally long in the processing of their case, causing

[77] The Army's Military Justice Redesign is encapsulated in the allied business rules stemming from TJAG Policy Memorandum 19-01. The Redesign is intended to create greater expertise in litigation of both special victim and general crimes cases, however the program does not contemplate an experienced military prosecutor or special victim counsel staying in that billet for the rest of their career if they are appropriately qualified and desire to remain in that billet.

[78] 18 U.S.C. § 3771, "Crime victims' rights." The CVRA is analogous to Article 6b, UCMJ, 10 U.S.C. § 806b.

many victims to drop out of the process. Moreover, prosecutors do not explain the reason for the delay, which would greatly help the victim in an already stressful process. Seasoned military justice practitioners told the IRC that military prosecutors seem to believe the creation of SVCs/VLCs obviate their duty to comply with basic CVRA and Article 6b requirements, as detailed above. For crime victims in the military justice system, the message is simple: the military lawyers do not have the requisite experience to handle their cases.

The one Service leading the others in terms of growing competent and experienced litigators is the Navy. Established in 2007, the Navy's MJLCT provides a structure for developing and maintaining a cadre of judge advocates who specialize in court-martial litigation. The Annual Report of the Judge Advocate General of the Navy highlights the purpose for such a program: judge advocates who exhibit both an aptitude and a desire to further specialize in litigation may apply for inclusion in the MJLCT.[79] As the JPP report noted, "Once selected, MJLCT officers spend most of their career in litigation-related billets as trial counsel, defense counsel, and military judges."[80] This type of career track with dedicated litigation billets makes the most sense to the IRC, and should be the model across the Services for cultivating experienced litigators who can competently handle special victim cases and stay in that billet for a career if the individual is appropriately qualified, competent, and desires that course of action.

As mentioned in previous sections, sexual assault cases are complicated and obtaining convictions and justice for victims requires expertise at all levels of the investigation and prosecution. This is true in both the military and civilian justice systems. To better understand the advantages of shifting legal decisions in sexual assault cases from commanders to specialized prosecutors, the IRC compared military data on conviction rates and case processing with results from studies published by DOJ.

In reviewing the available research, several themes came to light:

- Jurisdictions with special victim prosecution programs achieve higher satisfaction among sexual assault victims, who are more likely to feel their cases were handled fairly, regardless of outcomes;[81]
- Jurisdictions with special victim prosecution programs tend to have higher conviction rates in sexual assault cases;[82] and,

---

[79] Joint Service Committee on Military Justice. (2020). *Reports of the Services on Military Justice for Fiscal Year 2019*, 25. https://jsc.defense.gov/Portals/99/Documents/Article%20146a%20Report%20-%20FY19%20-%20All%20Services.pdf?ver=2020-07-22-091702-650

[80] JPP. (2016). *Final Report, Chapter VI: on Training Prosecutors, Defense Counsel, and Military Judges*. https://jpp.whs.mil/Public/docs/03_Topic-Areas/10-Training_Exper_Attys/20160513/03_CSS_FinalReport_ChapterVI.pdf

[81] Klein, A.R. (2008). *Practical Implications of Current Domestic Violence Research Part II: Prosecution*. Washington, D.C.: U.S. Department of Justice, 2008, National Institute of Justice, NCJ 222320

[82] Ibid.

- Even without specialized units, civilian prosecutors have obtained higher conviction rates than their military counterparts in sexual assault cases.[83]

Research suggests[84] specialized prosecution programs work well on a number of levels, including victim satisfaction, increased prosecution and conviction rates, and more robust case dispositions.

The bottom line is that specialized prosecution units, especially if associated with specialized law enforcement units and courts, should increase special victim prosecutions and convictions, victim cooperation, satisfaction, and if dispositions are geared to defendant risk, safety.

Local, state, and federal civilian criminal justice offices usually have institutional career progression focusing on training, mentoring, and developing young practitioners, who eventually assume increasing levels of responsibility with experience. The JAG Corps are capable of similar professional development and sustainment of experience because the Services already allow uniformed personnel to specialize in career fields (e.g., aviation, medical, etc.). This specialization cultivates confidence, technical expertise, consistency, and institutional knowledge in those fields. The JAG Corps should be no different. Those litigators who possess the competence, experience, and desire to specialize should have the opportunity to appear before a selection board to remain in their profession as a career. This will increase both sexual assault victim satisfaction and conviction rates. The Secretary of Defense should direct the Services to establish formalized career tracks with litigation billets so that practitioners can remain in the military justice field without fear of getting passed over for promotion and to further professionalize the JAG Corps to effectively handle their one statutory mission: military justice.

Lack of Career Litigation Billets in the Services' JAG Corps Results in Attrition

The lack of career litigation billets creates an unnecessary attrition problem that makes no logical or financial sense for the military and the taxpayer. Since some of the JAG Corps do not allow prosecutors, defense counsel, victims legal counsel, and judges to stay in the litigation field as a career, some judge advocates who achieved technical competence and expertise in special victim case handling leave the military for jobs in District Attorney and United States Attorney's offices. After years of costly training and cumulative courtroom experience, the civilian sector is often the beneficiary of the fruits of the military's labor.

---

83 Morabito, M. S., Williams, L. M., Pattavina, A. (2019). *Decision making in sexual assault cases: replication research on sexual violence case attrition in the U.S.* (NCJ 252689). Washington, DC: U.S. Department of Justice, National Institute of Justice. https://www.ojp.gov/pdffiles1/nij/grants/252689.pdf

84 Klein, A. R. (2008). *Practical Implications of Current Domestic Violence Research Part II: Prosecution*. Washington, D.C.: U.S. Department of Justice, National Institute of Justice, NCJ 222320

Getting passed over for promotion was a consistent, resonant concern for judge advocates who desired to stay in the military justice field. Those who desire to make a career of litigation risk a price: non-selection for promotion due to the perception that skilled litigators are not generalized judge advocates and therefore have no potential to become a staff judge advocate. The Navy is leading the way on how to practically overcome this stigma. The Navy report[85] on their MJLCT Pilot Program explains specific precept language, which has been included in paygrade O-4, O-5, and O-6 promotion boards since establishment of the career track. The current precept language provides, "[s]ince 2007, the JAG Corps has maintained a separate career track for officers who specialized in prosecuting, defending, and judging criminal cases. After competitive selection by an administrative board, these officers spend significant portions of their careers in litigation-related billets." There are currently 13 O-6 or O-6 select career track designated officers out of 94 total O-6 or O-6 select Navy judge advocates on active duty. MJLCT officers regularly achieve the rank of O-6. These officers provide a breadth of experience throughout the ranks of the JAG Corps.

The IRC recommends the Secretary of Defense direct the Services' JAG Corps to adopt the Navy guidance in all promotion boards as a compliment to the implementation of the career litigation billets.

Lack of Career Billets in the Services' Military Criminal Investigative Organizations Breeds Inexperience

MCIOs have under-experienced criminal investigators working in overwhelmed and under-resourced offices which adversely affects the response to, and investigation of, special victim crimes. The IRC heard from MCIOs and had the benefit of the written findings and recommendations in the recent FHIRC report. Though Fort Hood was one installation inside one Service, it is apparent that criminal investigator inexperience is also the Achilles heel of MCIOs across the Services. Much like the JAG Corps, uniformed criminal investigators are subject to outdated personnel rotations that take practitioners out of special victim investigations just when they are starting to transition from apprentice to experienced investigator. The FHIRC made an overarching finding that the Fort Hood Criminal Investigation Division Office had various inefficiencies that adversely impacted its ability to accomplish the mission, including:

- Insufficient number of credentialed special agents on board to handle its caseload of complex sex crimes and death investigations;
- Agent inexperience;
- Agent over-assignment;
- Extremely long investigations; and

---

85 Kessmeier, C.L. (2021). Order Convening the FY-22 Promotion Selection Boards to Consider Staff Corps Officers on the Active-Duty List of the Navy for Permanent Promotion to the Grade of Captain. Department of Navy, 3-4. https://www.mynavyhr.navy.mil/Portals/55/Boards/Active%20Duty%20Officer/documents/FY22_Promotion_Board_Materials/FY22_AO6S_PSB_CONVENING_ORDER.pdf

- An office that was under-resourced.

The Fort Hood report shined a light on what this IRC continued to hear as a theme in both military prosecutions and investigations: experience in the investigation and prosecution of special victim cases matters. That 92 percent of the special agents assigned to the Fort Hood CID during FY19 were apprentices is representative of what this IRC heard from recent scoping sessions across the Services.[86] Scoping sessions with military justice practitioners across the Services aligned with the FHIRC's discovery that most special agents were reassigned after 26 months of investigative experience. Most relevant to this IRC's recommendation for career investigator billets was the following insight from the FHIRC regarding Army criminal investigators: "They are not ready for complex investigations involving deaths, traumatized victims, warrants and electronic and other forensic evidence."[87]

> "They [MCIOs] are not ready for complex investigations involving deaths, traumatized victims, warrants and electronic and other forensic evidence."
>
> -Fort Hood Independent Review Committee

Military sexual assault victims and the subjects of these complex investigations deserve to have experienced agents who can operate beyond investigatory checklists. The Fort Hood Report said what this IRC recommends: the time is now for career billets for military criminal investigators who are selected for their investigative acumen and sensitivity towards victims and who can specialize in special victim investigations as a career.

Outcome Metrics

Litigators and investigators who excel in both experience and technical competence should have the option of remaining in their desired billets without fear of getting passed over for promotion. Since special victim cases can be extremely difficult to handle both mentally and emotionally, lawyers and agents who need a break should always have the option of an off-ramp to another billet with a slower or different operational tempo. The metric of success for implementation of the Services professional career tracks with specialized billets for litigators and investigators is improved competency, greater level of experience, and higher rates of retention of these professionals within the military justice workforce.

---

86 An apprentice Agent is defined as an agent who has been at his first unit assignment less than a year and must receive mentorship and constant evaluation for suitability from a more experienced special agent. Upon successful completion of the year and the certification of his/her Special Agent in Charge, an apprentice becomes an accredited CID Special Agent.

87 Fort Hood Independent Review Committee. (2020). *Report of the Fort Hood Independent Review Committee*, 57-58. https://www.army.mil/e2/downloads/rv7/forthoodreview/2020-12-03_FHIRC_report_redacted.pdf

Recommendation 1.5: Judge-Alone Sentencing in all Noncapital General and Special Courts-Martial, Establishment of Sentencing Parameters, and Mandatory Restitution

To create uniformity that would reduce disparities in sentencing on rape and sexual assault cases, the Secretary of Defense should propose that Congress adopt the recommendations of the Military Justice Review Group (December 2015 report)[88] with respect to judge alone sentencing in all noncapital general and special courts-martial and establishment of sentencing parameters. To complement this change, the UCMJ should be amended to mirror the Mandatory Victims Restitution Act (MVRA) of 1996 to include victims of crimes tried by courts-martial.

Rationale for these Changes: Reducing Sentencing Disparity & Giving Victims Access to Restitution in the Military Justice System

The Military Justice Review Group provided a very helpful background with respect to the history of sentencing in the military after 1950. When the UCMJ was enacted in 1950, Congress provided the President with the authority to promulgate rules on sentencing under Article 36. In Article 56, Congress specifically authorized the President to determine the maximum punishments for violations of the UCMJ.[89] As originally enacted, the only offenses in the UCMJ that included mandatory minimum sentences were premeditated murder (life in prison); felony murder (life in prison) and spying (mandatory death).[90] In 1960, Congress enacted Article 58a to establish mandatory reductions for the enlisted grades as a collateral effect of a court-martial sentence, subject to exceptions in Service regulations.[91] In 1996, Congress enacted Article 58b to require mandatory forfeitures, if not adjudged at trial, during certain periods of confinement.[92] In 1997, Congress enacted Article 56a, to provide for the punishment of confinement for life without parole and restricted clemency authority for such sentences.[93] In 2013, Congress amended Article 56 to provide for mandatory punitive discharges for

[88] Military Justice Review Group. (2015). *Report of the Military Justice Review Group, Part I: UCMJ Recommendations*. https://www.jag.navy.mil/documents/NJS/MJRG_Report_PartI_22Dec15.pdf

[89] Act of May 5, 1950, Pub. L. No. 81-506, ch. 169, 64 Stat. 108.

[90] Ibid.

[91] Act of July 12, 1960, Pub. L. No. 86-633, 74 Stat. 468.

[92] NDAA FY 1997, Pub. L. No. 104-201, § 1068, 110 Stat. 2655 (1996).

[93] NDAA FY 1998, Pub. L. No. 105-85, §S 581-82, 1073(a)(9)-(11), 111 Stat. 1759, 1900 (1997). The limitations on clemency were passed in 2000 and are contained in Article 74.

rape and sexual assault.[94] There is no specific statutory requirement for restitution as part of court-martial practice, although restitution has been recognized as a valid term of a plea agreement since at least 1977.[95] When Congress enacted the MVRA of 1996, it did not specifically address victims of crimes tried by courts-martial.[96]

In light of the military's abysmal conviction rates for sexual assault offenses, when a military defendant is found guilty, punishment decisions are left predominantly to court-martial members who lack institutional expertise and are not provided with adequate sentencing guidelines to make meaningful and equitable punishment decisions. Military justice practitioners, victims, and advocates told us that disparities in sentencing – especially in the sexual assault context – are confusing and tend to re-traumatize victims participating in the military justice process. Likewise, defense counsel emphasized the deleterious effect of grossly disproportionate sentences on accused convicted of similar crimes.

Currently, military practice utilizes unitary sentencing in cases where court-martial members sit as fact finder, with the members adjudging a single sentence for the accused, regardless of the number of offenses for which the accused has been found guilty of committing.[97] If the accused has been found guilty of multiple offenses, the maximum authorized sentence is the sum of the maximum punishments for all offenses individually.[98] On the other hand, if an accused elects to be sentenced by a military judge, segmented sentencing is used. This requires the judge to fashion a sentence for each specification the accused was found guilty; and if there is more than one term of confinement, the judge determines if they shall run concurrently or consecutively.[99]

RCM 1002 provides the rule for sentence determination in courts-martial. The rule states that the sentence "is a matter within the discretion of the court-martial." Pursuant to this rule, except for the few offenses that have mandatory minimum sentences – which include premeditated murder and the sexual offenses described earlier – the court is free to arrive at a sentence anywhere from no punishment to the maximum established by the President under Article 56(a). The appropriate sentence for a defendant is generally within the discretion of the court-martial, and the court may adjudge any lawful sentence, from no punishment to the maximum established by the President. With a few exceptions, there are minimal constraints on the discretion of the sentencing authority in courts-martial.

It is clear that the current discretionary practice of sentencing accused anywhere between no punishment and the jurisdictional maximum of the court-martial is absurd. In this regard, the IRC agrees with the recommendations of the Military Justice Review Group, namely that military judge

---

94 NDAA FY14, Pub. L. No. 113–66, § 1705(a)(1), (2)(A), 127 Stat. 672 (2013). This amendment also provided for mandatory minimum sentences for convictions for rape and sexual assault of a child, forcible sodomy, and attempts of these offenses.

95 See United States v. Brown, 4 M.J. 654, 655 (A.C.M.R. 1977).

96 See 18 U.S.C. § 3663A, "Mandatory restitution to victims of certain crimes."

97 R.C.M. 1002(d)(1)

98 R.C.M. 1003(c)(1)(C)

99 R.C.M. 1002(d)(2); see also, Article 56(c)(2), UCMJ, 10 U.S.C. § 856

alone sentencing is appropriate for all sentencing, and that advisory sentencing parameters must be established.

A corollary change must be made with respect to restitution for crime victims. Presently, the MVRA of 1996 does not include victims of crimes tried by courts-martial. The IRC heard from several victim advocacy groups who expressed concern that the restitution is not available to victims participating in courts-martial. Instead, victims of military crimes must look to civilian courts for compensation for medical expenses, lost income, and damaged/destroyed property. Though the Military Justice Review Group recommended additional study of restitution in courts-martial in its 2015 recommendations, the JPP concluded in 2016 that some victims of sexual assault crimes committed by Service members lack adequate access to compensation. Accordingly, the Panel recommended that DoD establish and administer a uniform compensation program for such victims, but recommended against amending the UCMJ due to "substantial changes to the current system that would be required and the relatively few cases in which restitution would be needed."[100]

However, the JPP's recommendation is not consistent with what the IRC heard (the UCMJ can be easily amended, and there is an abundance of sexual assault victims seeking ways to become whole). Five years later, the JPP's observations and conclusions fall short of the concerns the experts heard – that victims are denied access to restitution by a technical impediment: that their perpetrator was tried by court-martial. Access to justice can no longer be delayed. In the year 2021 where federal law provides for mandatory restitution for certain crimes, and access to restitution for all crime victims, the UCMJ must be amended to closely mirror the MVRA to include victims who participate in the military justice system.

Disparities in Sentencing Data

The most recent sentencing data available to the IRC supports the recommendation that judge alone sentencing is the appropriate forum for adjudicating punishment at a court-martial. Not surprisingly, the likelihood of confinement as punishment in sexual assault cases was directly affected by the type of trial forum. The 2015 data highlight the disparity: military judges sentenced defendants to confinement in 83.7 percent of sexual assault convictions, while panels of military members sentenced a defendant to confinement only 63 percent of the time.[101] Astoundingly, victims of sexual assault offenses where members handled punishment saw their perpetrator walk freely out of court in 37 percent of all cases, despite a conviction. These data support the perspective of victims, accused, and military justice practitioners: the military must move to a judge alone sentencing scheme with parameters to hold those who commit sexual assault appropriately accountable for their crimes.

It is clear that the current discretionary practice of sentencing accused anywhere between no punishment and the jurisdictional maximum of the court-martial is absurd. That panel members with

---

[100]JPP. (2016). *Judicial Proceedings Panel Report on Restitution and Compensation for Military Adult Sexual Assault Crimes*, 22. https://papers.ssrn.com/sol3/papers.cfm?abstract_id=3066061

[101] JPP. (2017). *See Judicial Proceedings Panel Report on Statistical Data Regarding Military Adjudication of Sexual Assault Offenses for Fiscal Year 2015*, 72. https://papers.ssrn.com/sol3/papers.cfm?abstract_id=3066100

no legal experience are charged with meting out a sentence within these vast and wide guidelines should raise cause for concern. In this regard, the IRC agrees with the recommendations of the Military Justice Review Group, namely that military judge alone sentencing is appropriate for all sentencing, and that advisory sentencing parameters must be established. Establishment of sentencing parameters will also better inform the Department of Defense with respect to the collection of data on racial and ethnic disparities in military sentencing generally, and studies involving punishment of sexual offenses specifically with the goal of working toward a military justice system that is fair and just for everyone.[102]

Amending the UCMJ to add provisions that mirror the MVRA addresses concerns raised by several victims, victim advocacy groups, and victims legal counsel who said that victims were denied access to restitution simply by virtue of the case being tried by courts-martial. Though RCM 705(c)(2)(C) allows prosecutors to seek the accused's promise to provide restitution as a term of a pretrial agreement, the experts heard resoundingly that very few sexual assault cases resolve short of a trial. The IRC concluded that the restitution mechanism in this Rule is therefore ineffective for the majority of sexual assault victims. As a fix, the UCMJ should be amended to include new Articles 56a (addressing orders of restitution), 56b (addressing mandatory restitution to victims of certain crimes), and 56c (addressing procedures for issuance and enforcement of order of restitution). Understanding that some provisions of the MVRA are incongruous to military court-martial practice, the UCMJ should be amended as appropriately as possible to mirror the MVRA so that victims in the military justice system have the same access to restitution as victims in civilian courts.

The fact that the Services do not track the use of restitution in pretrial agreements adds insult to injury. The lack of data provides no meaningful discourse on the subject of making sexual assault victims whole in the military justice context. Restitution should be accessible to victims of sexual assault under the military justice system, and restitution data should be tracked accordingly. Understanding the JPP's concerns regarding the number of changes necessary to establish restitution under the UCMJ (see February 2016 report), the military can no longer ignore the fact that it is lagging behind its civilian counterparts when it comes to compensating sexual assault victims (as well as crime victims generally) in the military system.

---

102 Despite the current challenges with data collection in the Services, several recent studies have documented racial disparities in the administration of military justice. A May 2019 study by the U.S. GAO of all offenses under the UCMJ found that Black and Hispanic Service members were more likely than white Service members to be the subjects of recorded investigations in all of the Services and were more likely to be tried in general and special courts-martial in the Army, Navy, Marine Corps, and Air Force. An October 2020 report issued by the DAC-IPAD reviewed 1,904 cases documenting investigations of adult penetrative sexual offenses completed in fiscal year 2017. The FY17 data suggest that Black Service members are disproportionately affected by allegations of sexual offenses at the investigative stage. Both studies described how the limitations of the Services' data on race and ethnicity make it difficult to undertake meaningful comprehensive assessments. Source: GAO. (2019). Military Justice: DOD and the Coast Guard Need to Improve Their Capabilities to Assess Racial and Gender Disparities. https://www.gao.gov/assets/700/699380.pdf; Defense Advisory Committee on Investigation, Prosecution, and Defense of Sexual Assault in the Armed Forces. (2020). Report on Racial and Ethnic Data Relating to Disparities in the Investigation, Prosecution, and Conviction of Sexual Offenses in the Military. https://dacipad.whs.mil/images/Public/08-Reports/09_DACIPAD_RaceEthnicity_Report_20201215_Web_Final.pdf

Outcome Metrics

Markers of success for this recommendation include change in sentencing as a result of judge alone sentencing, and an increase in restitution for sexual assault victims in the military system.

Recommendation 1.6: Expedite Processing of Proposed Executive Orders Regarding Military Justice

The President should direct expedited processing of proposed Executive Orders regarding military justice, including establishing the elements of crimes enacted by Congress, such as the following crimes related to sexual assault:

- Article 117a: Wrongful broadcast or distribution of intimate visual images;
- Article 128b: Domestic Violence; and,
- Strangulation, under Article 128b.

This would also allow the enumeration of new offenses under Article 134, such as the offense of sexual harassment, and the publication of the figure of maximum punishments for those crimes. These Executive Orders implement changes to the UCMJ by making changes to the Manual for Courts-Martial, the seminal document for military justice practitioners.

Rationale for this Change: The Executive Branch Must do its Part to Promulgate Military Justice Reform

Justice requires the timely, effective, and efficient administration of the criminal process. The Manual for Courts-Martial's central role in the administration of military justice makes timely changes to the Manual imperative. The IRC therefore strongly recommends that the President direct the expeditious processing of proposed Executive Orders containing changes to the Manual for Courts-Martial.

Congress enacted the UCMJ, the keystone document in military justice, in 1951, and continues to amend it almost every year. The President implements the Code by issuing the Manual for Courts-Martial. The Manual includes the Rules for Courts-Martial, the Military Rules of Evidence, the elements of the Punitive Articles of the UCMJ, the Nonjudicial Punishment Procedure, and an appendix listing the Lesser Included Offenses for each punitive Article. Other Appendices to the Manual include a chart listing the maximum authorized punishments for each offense, analyses of the RCMs, Rules of Evidence, punitive Articles, and nonjudicial punishment procedure, and various forms essential to the administration of military justice. The importance of the Manual to the efficient, effective, and just administration of military justice, and thereby to assisting in maintaining good order and discipline, cannot be overstated.

Changes to the Manual are made by Executive Order. Changes are proposed when Congress amends the UCMJ, courts issue decisions requiring a Manual change, or internal reviews by DoD result in best practices requiring Manual changes. Often, Congressional amendments to the UCMJ have immediate effect or effective dates a relatively short time after enactment. Court decisions are effective immediately.

Historically, Presidents have signed Executive Orders amending the Manual in a timely manner. Unfortunately, sometimes they have not. In rare situations, Presidents have not signed a proposed Executive Order amending the Manual. In those situations, the Secretary of Defense includes the contents of that proposed Executive Order in the following year's proposed Executive Order. The last Executive Order on military justice signed by a President was on March 1, 2018, over three years ago.[103] That was the 25th such Executive Order signed in the preceding 35 years.

Implementation of this Change

DoD published a proposed Executive Order regarding military justice in the Federal Register for public comment on February 11, 2020. That proposed executive order implemented certain provisions in NDAAs for FY18, FY19, and FY20. A comprehensive Executive Order on military justice incorporating the 2020 proposal will be submitted for signature in 2021. Changes in the proposed Executive Order include establishing a new offense of sexual harassment, setting forth the elements of the offenses of domestic violence,[104] the wrongful broadcast or distribution of intimate visual images, and providing for their maximum punishments.

Expedited processing of these Executive Orders is essential to an efficient, effective, and just military justice system for all participants. The pending changes for Articles 128b, 117a, and 134 are especially meaningful for special victim crimes, as they disproportionately impact women and overlap with sexual assault and harassment.

In addition, the IRC strongly recommends that the pending Executive Order with respect to Article 128b should be updated to expand the definition of the elements of the crime of domestic violence to include dating partners, in addition to spouses and intimate partners, and should include the same definition of intimate partners that is provided in Article 130, UCMJ (stalking).[105]

Outcome Metrics

The metric of success for this recommendation is the number of days that pass between the date when DoD submits a proposed Executive Order for interagency coordination and the date the proposed

---

[103] Executive Order 13825. (2018). 2018 Amendments to the Manual for Courts-Martial, United States. https://www.govinfo.gov/content/pkg/FR-2018-03-08/pdf/2018-04860.pdf

[104] These offenses, including strangulation and wrongful broadcast or distribution of intimate visual images, were passed in the FY19 NDAA.

[105] This change would be consistent with the Violence Against Women Act. That definition should state: dating partner. The term "dating partner" refers to a person who is or has been in a social relationship of a romantic or intimate nature with the abuser, and where the existence of such a relationship shall be determined based on a consideration of— (A) the length of the relationship; (B) the type of relationship; and (C) the frequency of interaction between the persons involved in the relationship. 18 U.S.C. § 2266(10).

Executive Order is signed by the President. If fewer than 180 days pass between those dates, this recommendation has been successfully implemented.

Recommendation 1.7: Modify the UCMJ

The UCMJ should be modified in several key areas to increase uniformity, reliability and consistency of the military justice system, thus benefiting the victim, the alleged offender, and the command. Because sexual assault victims can experience re-victimization and trauma in the processing of their cases, and because a significant number of these victims have lost their trust in the military justice system, these recommended changes are uniquely important in sexual assault cases.

- 1.7 a: The Secretary of Defense should direct the DAC-IPAD to study Article 32 Preliminary Hearings;
- 1.7 b: The Secretary of Defense should direct the DAC-IPAD to study Article 34, Advice to Convening Authority Before Referral to Trial;
- 1.7 c: The UCMJ should be amended to establish a preponderance of the evidence standard for non-judicial punishment;
- 1.7 d: Article 25 of the UCMJ should be amended to establish random selection of panel members;
- 1.7 e: The Secretary of Defense should direct the Services to establish funding appropriate for defense counsel control of their own resources; and
- 1.7 f: Article 128b of the UCMJ should be amended to include dating violence.

Rationale for these Changes: Increase Uniformity, Reliability, and Consistency of the Military Justice System

The IRC is recommending two studies and several amendments to the UCMJ in order to increase uniformity, reliability, and consistency of the military justice system, thus benefiting the victim, the accused, and the command.

Recommendation 1.7 a: The Secretary of Defense Should Direct the DAC-IPAD to Study Article 32 Preliminary Hearings

Before a General Court-Martial can proceed, 10 U.S. Code § 832, requires that unless the accused waives this right, an Article 32 Preliminary Hearing must be held before referral of charges for trial by General Court-Martial. The Article 32 hearing is conducted by a hearing officer who determines whether or not there is probable cause to believe that the accused committed the charged offense. Currently, the decision of this Article 32 hearing is not binding on the GCMCA. The GCMCA can refer a case to a General Court-Martial even if the hearing officer at the Article 32 Preliminary Hearing determined that there was no probable cause to believe that the accused committed the charged offense(s) if the Staff Judge Advocate advises that there is probable cause.

Numerous stakeholders with significant military justice experience including defense counsel, trial counsel, and military judges agreed that it is not fair to the administration of justice for a GCMCA to proceed with a court-martial despite a no probable cause finding. This can be damaging to sexual assault victims, who often suffer through the process unaware that there is no chance of winning a conviction in their cases. At the same time, the IRC wants to ensure that provable, but difficult, cases are not prevented from proceeding due to the opinion of a solitary preliminary hearing officer, who may not have the military justice experience necessary to make such findings and credibility determinations.

To accommodate both of these concerns, the IRC is recommending that a study by conducted to determine if making the Article 32 hearing officer's no probable cause decision binding would promote justice, fairness, and efficiency. The IRC assumes that this will have some effect on the level of military justice experience expected of a preliminary hearing officer, and the study should include an assessment of whether military judges and military magistrates should be the Article 32 preliminary hearing officers.

Recommendation 1.7 b: The Secretary of Defense Should Direct the DAC-IPAD to Study Article 34, Advice to Convening Authority Before Referral to Trial

After the Article 32 Preliminary hearing is held, but before the GCMCA formally refers the case, the GCMCA must comply with the guidance outlined in Article 34.[106] This Article requires the staff judge advocate to certify the presence of several elements, including whether there is probable cause to believe that the accused committed the charged offense, before the convening authority can proceed with the referral of charges. Currently, Article 34 does not contain the standard language that governs other federal prosecutors. Specifically, the principles of federal prosecution require that in order to pursue a case, the prosecutor must believe that the admissible evidence will probably be sufficient to obtain and sustain a conviction (JM 9-27.220). This same threshold requirement should be included in Article 34 both as a matter of fundamental fairness and in the interest of the efficient administration of justice. Neither the victim nor the defendant benefits when the military pursues a case when there is no reasonable probability that the evidence will be sufficient to obtain or sustain a conviction. Furthermore, confidence and trust in the military justice system is undermined when cases are pursued when there is not reasonable chance of success.

It is important to emphasize that the proposed Article 34 language regarding the sufficiency of the evidence would be determined by the staff judge advocate, *not* by the preliminary hearing officer, judge, or any other party. Furthermore, the inclusion of this requirement should *not* inhibit prosecutors from pursuing difficult cases or prevent them from trying cases which do not have the benefit of corroborating evidence. A single witness who can testify to all the elements of the case, and who the trier of fact believes is credible, is sufficient to obtain and sustain a conviction. Lastly, it is important to note that at the time of the Article 34 decision, the prosecutor does *not* need to have in their possession all the evidence upon which they will rely at trial. Rather, the prosecutor must only have

[106] Article 34, UCMJ, 10 U.S.C. § 834.

a reasonable and good faith belief that the needed evidence will be available and admissible at the time of trial.

Recommendation 1.7 c: The UCMJ Should be Amended to Establish a Preponderance of the Evidence Standard for Non-judicial Punishment

Consistent with federal and state laws, the UCMJ clearly establishes that at a trial by court-martial, the burden of proving guilt is beyond a reasonable doubt. However, no standard burden of proof is articulated for the nonjudicial punishment authority to conclude that a Service member committed an alleged offense. The Services have inconsistent or no standard burden of proof.[107, 108, 109] It is mystifying a military that operates under a *Uniform* code can have such disparate treatment for its Service members. After all the available punishment is uniform, so too should the standard of proof necessary to impose said punishment. Nonjudicial punishment is not a criminal prosecution and is designed to provide commanders with essential and prompt means of maintaining good order and discipline and also promote positive behavior changes in Service members without the stigma of a court-martial conviction. Consequently, the burden of proof should be by a preponderance of the evidence. Far more sexual misconduct cases are handled by nonjudicial punishment than by trial, and this standard is consistent with the need for accountability in these cases.

Recommendation 1.7 d: Random Selection of Panel Members

Currently, the Court-Martial Convening Authority selects the panel from a pool of available members of the command and the convening authority has wide discretion in selecting the members of the jury pool.[110] In order to enhance the perception and reality of a fair and impartial panel, these members should be randomly selected, taking into account practical realities of location and availability.

---

[107] For the Army, the burden of proof at nonjudicial punishment proceedings is beyond a reasonable doubt. Source: Department of the Army. (2020). *Army Regulation 27-10, Legal Services, Military Justice*, 9. https://armypubs.army.mil/epubs/DR_pubs/DR_a/ARN31271-AR_27-10-001-WEB-2.pdf

[108] For the Navy and the Marine Corps, the burden of proof is the preponderance of the evidence. Source: Naval Justice School. (2015). *USN/USMC Commander's Quick Reference Legal Handbook*, 32. https://www.hqmc.marines.mil/Portals/135/Docs/JAM/Quickman%20Jan%2015.pdf

[109] For the Air Force, there is no stated burden of proof at an Article 15 proceeding; however, Commanders should be aware that the Airman could turn it down and demand a trial by Court-Martial, at which the standard of proof is beyond a reasonable doubt. This leaves the burden of proof somewhat undefined and up to the Commander's interpretation. Source: Department of the Air Force. (2021). *Air Force Instruction 51-202, Nonjudicial Punishment*, 18. https://static.e-publishing.af.mil/production/1/af_ja/publication/afi51-202/afi51-202.pdf

[110] Military case law is replete with examples of unlawful command influence, including with the selection of panel members. See United States v. Riesbeck, 77 M.J. 154 (CAAF 2018) "The salient facts paint a clear picture of court stacking based on gender in an atmosphere of external pressure to achieve specific results in sexual assault cases. Against that backdrop, purposefully selecting a panel that is seventy percent female, most of whom are victim advocates, from a roster of officers that was only twenty percent female and a pool of enlisted that was only thirteen percent female, smacks of a panel that was 'hand-picked' by or for the government."

Recommendation 1.7 e: The Secretary of Defense Should Direct the Services to Establish Funding Appropriate for Defense Counsel Control of their Own Resources

Stakeholders consistently report that defense counsel do not have timely or reliable access to resources that are necessary for the fair administration of justice. Specific concerns relate to funding for defense investigators, expert witnesses, and counsel travel. Currently, defense counsel must request authority to engage investigators and experts from the convening authority via the trial counsel, with sufficient justification to support the request. This forces the defense counsel to reveal part of its pretrial preparation and strategy to the government prosecutor. Ensuring that defense counsel have adequate resources for the proper defense of charged Service members without revealing pretrial preparation to the government prosecutor will increase fairness in military justice and reduce the number and success of appeals based on ineffective assistance of counsel or an inadequately resourced defense. The Accountability experts expect it will also reduce time spent litigating motions on compelling the aforementioned.

Recommendation 1.7 f: Article 128b of the UCMJ Should be Amended to Include Dating Violence

Currently, an individual can only violate Article 128b Domestic Violence if the perpetrator commits an offense against a spouse, an intimate partner, or an immediate family member. Offenses against dating partners are not specifically included and the definition of intimate partner is not provided in the text of this statute. Therefore, Article 128b Domestic Violence should be amended to include a spouse, an intimate partner, *a dating partner* or an immediate family member of that person. The term "intimate partner" should have the same meaning given to that term in article 130 of the Uniform Code of Military Justice and the definition of dating partner should state:

- Dating partner. The term "dating partner" refers to a person who is or has been in a social relationship of a romantic or intimate nature with the abuser, and where the existence of such a relationship shall be determined based on a consideration of— (A) the length of the relationship; (B) the type of relationship; and (C) the frequency of interaction between the persons involved in the relationship.[111]

Outcome Metrics

Recommendations 1.7 a and b are studies and therefore would not have an associated indicator of successful implementation. Recommendations 1.7 c and 1.7 d could be measured by victim

---

[111] 18 U.S.C. § 2266(10); see also, 34 U.S.C. § 12291(a)(9).

perceptions of fairness (desired state being an increase) in the Military Justice Experience Survey.[112] Recommendation 1.7 e can be tracked by checking the Services' compliance with such a change.

Recommendation 1.8: Study Caseloads to Attain the Optimum Timeline for the Military Justice Process

In order to reduce the overly long military justice process timeline to a level deemed satisfactory, the Secretary of Defense should direct a study to identify the length of time to process military justice cases that will encourage reporting and victims remaining in the process until completion. Once this timeline is established, the Secretary should direct a study to determine optimum caseloads per participant in the military justice process to achieve that timeline. A manpower management and fiscal analysis of the additional billets and budget necessary to achieve those caseloads should follow. Finally, the Secretary should work with Congress to obtain the necessary resources. Driving down the military justice timeline could be instrumental in increasing the reporting of sexual assault cases and increasing the number of cases that are tried by court-martial.

Rationale for this Change: The Processing of Sexual Assault Cases Are Unduly Long

DoD has long recognized that the military justice process takes too long to complete. Speedy trial rules to protect the Constitutional rights of the accused have been implemented, but they take effect only after charges have been preferred and have many exceptions. The Services have imposed timeline goals on various parts of the process with little effect. For example, the Army established a goal of no more than 14 days for judge advocates to issue opinions to Army Criminal Investigation Division agents regarding whether there was probable cause to believe that the suspect committed the crime being investigated, but the Fort Hood investigation revealed that this goal was often missed.

MCIOs have implemented case processing goals, but based on average case processing times thus allowing the relatively simple, easily resolved cases to mask the length of time that the more complex, difficult cases take. DoD laboratories have timeline goals as well, but investigators too frequently complete all other leads in a case only to sit waiting for laboratory results. Even taken together, these efforts have not reduced the timeline significantly. In the Accountability experts' opinion, the common missing element is adequate consideration of caseload.

During information gathering sessions, many victims, advocates, MCIOs, and trial and defense counsel stated that the lengthy timeline was a primary reason for the non-reporting of serious sexual assaults. They also said that in those cases where reports were made, the lengthy timeline was a

---

[112] Namrow, N., De Silva, S., Severance, L., Klahr, A., & Davis, L. (2018). *2016-2017 Military Investigation and Justice Experience Survey*. Alexandria, VA: Office of People Analytics. https://www.sapr.mil/public/docs/reports/FY17_Annual/Annex_3_2016-2017_Military_Investigation_and_Justice_Survey.pdf

primary reason given by victims for dropping out of the military justice process. To say that the lengthy military justice timeline adversely affects the search for accountability in serious sexual harassment and sexual assault cases is an understatement.

The prolonged military justice process also adversely affects the accused. When an allegation of misconduct is made, the Services take steps to freeze the personnel status of the accused. Orders to a new billet may be canceled, selection to attend an important career school may be withheld, and a promotion may be postponed. Not everything can be replaced as if it never occurred in those cases where no action is taken on the allegation, a not infrequent result.

An inescapable fact of criminal case processing is that the larger the caseload that participants (be they investigators, judge advocates, or victim advocates) carry, the longer it takes to get to pending actions and often to get an action done (due to interruptions from other cases). It is imperative to reduce the caseload of those involved in the military justice process in order to prevent the length of the timeline from being a reason to fail to report sexual assault or to drop out of a pending investigation of sexual assault.

The IRC recommends that the Secretary of Defense direct a study to identify the length of time to process military justice cases, from start to finish, that will encourage crime reporting and victims remaining in the process until completion of their cases. This timeline goal should be used primarily for the purpose of this study and to assess whether the additional billets approved as a result prove sufficient to meet the timeline goal. This timeline goal should not be used to assess performance of those involved in the military justice process because variations in the facts and conditions of each case make a timeline goal an exceptionally poor tool for measuring performance.

Implementation Considerations

Once this timeline goal is established, the Secretary should direct a study to determine optimum caseloads for every category of personnel who participate in the military justice process to achieve that timeline. Categories of personnel whose optimum caseload might be assessed during the study include criminal investigators of different levels and expertise, their administrative support personnel, laboratory personnel including those who perform the scientific tests and those who support them (factoring in time lost for investigative and trial preparation and testimony), defense counsel, trial counsel, SVC/VLC, SVPs and ASVPs, military judges and military magistrates, and SARCs and SAPR VAs.

It is likely that DoD currently does not have sufficient billets to maintain the optimum caseloads while meeting the timeline goal. A manpower management and fiscal analysis of the additional billets and budget necessary to achieve those caseloads should follow. Finally, the Secretary should work with Congress to obtain the necessary resources because driving down the military justice timeline will be instrumental in increasing the reporting of sexual assault cases and increasing the number of cases that are tried by court-martial.

Outcome Metrics

The first metric for success is the average case processing timeline for military justice cases; if the average timeline is equal to or less than the timeline goal established by the recommended study, the first metric for success has been achieved.

The second metric for success is the number of Unrestricted Reports of special victim cases reported per year. If the number of Unrestricted Reports increases compared to the previous year, the second metric for success has been achieved.

The third and final metric for success is the number of cases that have to be dismissed because the victim decides to stop cooperating in the military justice process. If the number of cases that have to be dismissed for this reason decreases compared to the previous year, the third metric for success has been achieved.

Conclusion

Junior enlisted Service members have lost trust in their commanders' commitment to ending sexual harassment and sexual assault. Regaining that trust is essential because commanders remain the key to stopping the continuum of sexual harm. Commanders can best regain that trust by focusing on actions squarely within their area of expertise: prevention, command climate, and care and support for victims of these crimes. Special Victim Prosecutors can assist in that effort by becoming responsible for actions squarely within their area of expertise: deciding whether there is sufficient evidence to charge a Service member in sexual harassment and sexual assault cases, and whether there is sufficient evidence in those cases to warrant trial by court-martial. Matching expertise with function provides the best opportunity for the Department to stop sexual harassment and sexual assault.

The challenge of stopping sexual harassment and sexual assault in the military is daunting, but achievable. Success starts with restoring junior enlisted Service members' trust in their commanders. These recommendations seek to help restore that broken trust.

The Gordian knot of sexual assault and sexual harassment in the military can't be untied or cut with one change. Rather, it takes a whole-of-body approach where prevention, climate and culture, accountability, and victim care and support work cooperatively. The IRC believes these recommended changes will facilitate this comprehensive solution by creating a new weapon system for commanders that strategically targets the problem.

Equipping the Force and Empowering Prevention: Recommendations to Prevent Sexual Harassment and Sexual Assault in the U.S. Military

Independent Review Commission on Sexual Assault in the Military

Contents

List of Figures

Acknowledgements

The Prevention experts on the Independent Review Commission (IRC) would like to honor and acknowledge the determination and leadership of survivors; those that work daily to advocate, heal, and support them; and individuals dedicated to eliminating sexual harassment and sexual assault. The findings and recommendations in this report are offered as the Commission's undeniable commitment to ending sexual harassment and sexual assault in the military. The Prevention experts worked to capture the experiences of survivors, advocates, prevention personnel, bystanders, and leaders from across the Department of Defense (DoD) to better understand the current gaps and strengths specific to prevention within the military. This report would not be possible without the candid feedback from prevention experts and leaders within the Office of the Secretary of Defense (OSD), subject matter expert (SMEs) from the Services (i.e., the United States (U.S.) Army, Navy, Marine Corps and Air Force), National Guard, and consultative group members who contributed professional insights and reflected a desire to eliminate sexual harassment and sexual assault.

Background

On February 26, 2021, the Secretary of Defense ordered the establishment of an IRC to conduct an independent assessment of DoD efforts against sexual harassment and sexual assault. The IRC officially began its work on March 24, 2021 and was charged with forming recommendations across four lines of effort: accountability; prevention; climate and culture; and victim care and support.

This report is issued by the highly qualified experts leading the Prevention line of effort. The Prevention experts were charged with the following tasks:

- Conduct a comprehensive assessment of ongoing prevention efforts to determine where gaps may exist and where additional resources may be needed; and
- Develop recommendations to achieve an enduring, Department-wide prevention infrastructure in which leaders are equipped with the data, people, resources, policy, and tools that the Military Departments and Services need to stop sexual assault and other readiness-detracting behaviors before they occur.

The success of the prevention recommendations is interdependent with proposals from other lines of effort focusing on offender accountability, climate and culture, and victim services and care. This appendix outlines recommendations to achieve the effective prevention of sexual assault and harassment in the military, such as equipping leaders with prevention science competencies and establishing a workforce to assess and implement strategies to prevent sexual assault and sexual harassment from occurring in the first place. In contrast, the culture and climate experts focused on the broader culture changes that encompass prevention and response but also extend beyond sexual assault, such as setting the conditions to change values, beliefs, and assumptions related to sexual harassment and the continuum of harm.

Collectively, the IRC's recommendations will present a comprehensive view of the problem and offer targeted solutions to build trust and restore confidence in the military's ability to prevent and respond to sexual assault and sexual harassment.

Introduction

> "Each year, the Services are losing 16,000 manpower years prematurely as a result of separations associated with sexual assault and sexual harassment."
>
> -2021 RAND Report

Sexual harassment and sexual assault are preventable, yet they continue to directly impact thousands of Service members in the U.S. military, disrupting mission readiness and eroding trust and cohesion between Service members and their leaders and peers. These incidents have a variety of negative consequences on those involved, including adverse psychological and physical health effects.[1] In addition to the significant human toll, sexual assault and harassment have costly operational consequences. RAND recently reported that the military prematurely loses at least 16,000 manpower years subsequent to sexual harassment and sexual assault in a single year.[2, 3] Exposure to sexual assault doubles the odds that a Service member separates from the military in the ensuing 28 months. Follow-on studies of these individuals show that their separations were disproportionately voluntary—that is, Service members were not discharged for problem behaviors or other failures.

Getting prevention "right" is integral to readiness: stopping harmful behaviors before they start is key to maintaining good order and discipline. For over a decade, the Department has invested significant resources into policies and actions to respond to sexual assault when incidents occur. Despite this increased attention, DoD is not moving the needle[4] by preventing perpetration and victimization of sexual harassment or sexual assault. Although Congress, DoD, and the general public have focused on the need for offender accountability and justice for victims, equal attention is needed on preventing incidents in the first place. A more deliberate, comprehensive

---

[1] Basile, K.C., & Smith, S.G. (2011). Sexual violence victimization of women: prevalence, characteristics, and the role of public health and prevention. *American Journal of Lifestyle Medicine, 5*(5), 407-417. https://doi.org/10.1177%2F1559827611409512

[2] Morral, A.R., Matthews, M., Cefalu, M., Schell, T.L., & Cottrell, L. (2021). *Effects of Sexual Assault and Sexual Harassment on Separation from the U.S. Military: Findings from the 2014 RAND Military Workplace Study*. Santa Monica, CA: RAND Corporation. https://www.rand.org/pubs/research_reports/RR870z10.html

[3] "At least 8,000 Service members chose to separate, rather than re-enlist, for reasons associated with sexual harassment. Re-enlistment periods are typically at least two years in length, so these separations likely deprived the military of at least 16,000 person-years of service." Source: RAND. (2021). *Effects of Sexual Assault and Sexual Harassment on Separation from the U.S. Military*. Santa Monica, CA: RAND Corporation, 24. https://www.rand.org/pubs/research_reports/RR870z10.html

[4] Ryan, M. (2021, May 6). 'We haven't moved the need' on sexual assault in the military, general says. *The Washington Post*. https://www.washingtonpost.com/national-security/military-sexual-assault/2021/05/06/a8f51a7c-ae98-11eb-8109-f8ba1ea2eeab_story.html

prioritization of sexual harassment and sexual assault prevention is required to establish and sustain a safer, healthier, and more resilient force.

This report addresses how prevention strategies can and should be tailored to the military environment. The military is a rank-based, hierarchical organization, and this unique structure of authority must be leveraged to successfully prevent sexual harassment, sexual assault, and the larger continuum of harm.[5] Leaders—both enlisted and officer—need to clearly understand their roles and responsibilities in prevention and how to implement effective strategies to prevent sexual violence.[6] DoD and the Services frequently cite a commitment to "prevention", yet leaders often struggle to define and understand their role in preventing sexual violence, and often confuse sexual assault response and awareness (e.g., training on reporting, conducting awareness campaigns) with prevention. Examples include teal pancake breakfasts,[7] dance contests,[8] and golf tournaments[9] to raise awareness of the SAPR program on base. Although these activities are well meaning, they may trivialize the seriousness of the issue, and alienate Service members who have experienced sexual assault. The time and dedication it takes to plan these events is admirable—but the Services need clear guidance to understand that prevention is a discrete skill set rooted in social science and public health. The following recommendations highlight the need for the military to incorporate the public-health approach to prevention using research-based policies, programs, and practices.

List of Recommendations

The IRC believes that DoD can advance prevention by equipping leaders and Service members with tailored prevention knowledge and skills; establishing a dedicated prevention workforce; prioritizing and investing in prevention research (including research on perpetration); providing high-risk populations with individualized support; and implementing research-based[10] community-level prevention strategies.

---

[5] The continuum of harm refers to a range of interconnected, inappropriate behaviors (e.g., sexist jokes, hazing, cyber bullying), that are connected to the occurrence of sexual assault and that support an environment that tolerates these behaviors. Source: Breslin, R.A., Klahr, A., & Neria, A. (2020). *The Continuum of Harm: Examining the Correlates of Sexual Assault Victimization*. Executive Note 2020-093. Alexandria, VA: Office of People Analytics.

[6] Sexual violence is sexual activity when consent is not obtained or not freely given. It is connected to other forms of violence and causes serious health and economic consequences. Source: Centers for Disease Control and Prevention. (2019). *Preventing Sexual Violence*. https://www.cdc.gov/violenceprevention/pdf/sv-factsheet.pdf

[7] Szoldra, P. (2021, April 14). *Army unit urges soldiers to 'be a hero, eat a pancake' for sexual assault*. Task & Purpose. https://taskandpurpose.com/news/army-sexual-assault-awareness-teal-pancakes-hero/

[8] Marine Corps Community Services. (2015*). The Sexual Assault Prevention Innovation Award Winner Did What?* https://usmc-mccs.org/articles/the-sexual-assault-prevention-innovation-award-winner-did-what/

[9] Levering, L. (2021, April 29). *It Takes a Team: Fort Gordon observes Sexual Assault Awareness and Prevention Month.* https://www.army.mil/article/245735/it_takes_a_team_fort_gordon_observes_sexual_assault_awareness_and_prevention_month

[10] Prevention activities selected based on research evidence that they have shown promise in evaluations to decrease the behavior of interest for a specific population or that the activity affected one or more contributing factors to the behavior of interest in settings similar to those being considered for the activity and that positive effects were sustained over time. Source: DoD. (2020). *DoD Instruction (DoDI) 6400.09: DoD Policy on Integrated Primary Prevention of Self-Directed Harm*

For recommendations requiring legislation, implementation will likely occur no earlier than October 1, 2023. For prevention recommendations that do not require legislation, but require DoD action, the IRC recommends immediate review and approval. Importantly, implementation of these recommendations should align with and complement the February 26th, 2021 Secretary of Defense immediate actions memo.[11]

2.1 Equip all leaders with prevention competencies and evaluate their performance.

2.1 a The Office of the Under Secretary of Defense for Personnel and Readiness (USD(P&R)) define the competencies leaders must have to oversee prevention.

2.1 b The Services and National Guard Bureau (NGB) develop and hold leaders appropriately accountable for prevention.

2.1 c The Services and NGB equip all leaders to develop and deliver informed prevention messages in formal and informal settings.

2.2 Establish a dedicated primary prevention workforce.

2.2 a USD(P&R) develop a model for a dedicated and capable prevention workforce.

2.2 b USD(P&R) develop a professional credential for the prevention workforce.

2.2 c The Services determine the optimum full-time prevention workforce, and equip all echelons of active duty, reserve, and guard organizations.

2.3 Implement community-level prevention strategies unique to Service members' environments.

2.3 a The Services and the NGB should resource and implement prevention strategies at organizational and community levels.

2.3 b USD(P&R) identify a non-clinical OSD-level Office of Primary Responsibility for alcohol policy and develop relevant policy guidance and oversight.

2.4 Modernize prevention education and skill-building to reflect today's generation of Service members.

2.5 Identify and actively support Service members with the most effective prevention interventions.

2.5 a The Services and the NGB should institute a pilot program to link Service members with resources and support.

2.5 b The Services and the NGB should employ virtual platforms to provide support to all Service members.

2.6 Create a state-of-the-art DoD prevention research capability.

---

and Prohibited Abuse or Harm, 30. https://www.esd.whs.mil/Portals/54/Documents/DD/issuances/dodi/640009p.pdf?ver=2020-09-11-104936-223

[11] DoD. (2021, February 26). *Immediate Actions to Counter Sexual Assault and Harassment and the Establishment of a 90-day Independent Review Commission on Sexual Assault in the Military.* https://media.defense.gov/2021/Feb/26/2002590163/-1/-1/0/APPROVAL-OF-MEMO-DIRECTING-IMMEDIATE-ACTIONS-TO-COUNTER-SEXUAL-ASSAULT-AND-HARASSMENT.PDF

2.6 a DoD establish a dedicated Research Center for the primary prevention of interpersonal and self-directed violence.

2.6 b USD(P&R), the Services, and the NGB continually review and update all policies that unnecessarily restrict data collection on important populations of Service members.

2.6 c Secretary of Defense immediately authorize operational testing of the Air Force Compatibility Assessment with a cross-Service pre-accession sample, allowing for important research and intervention development.

2.6 d USD(P&R) commission research on gender and masculinities to develop effective social marketing strategies to facilitate primary prevention efforts.

2.7 Establish a comprehensive National Guard primary prevention strategy.

2.7 a NGB develop Army National and Air National Guard prevention strategies aligned with DoD's Prevention Plan of Action (PPoA), based on the National Guard's unique construct and missions.

2.7 b USD(P&R) should submit legislative proposal providing authorization and funding for the NGB to conduct recurring National Guard unit inspections and staff assistance visits for prevention oversight and assistance.

2.8 Update DoD's prevention strategy to include approved IRC recommendations.

Scope of this Report and Key Definitions

Defining Primary Prevention

Many individuals mistakenly believe that prevention is "awareness" of sexual assault or sexual harassment (e.g., organizing a SAPR fun run). However, awareness and outreach efforts, while important in their own right, do *not* work as comprehensive prevention. Prevention is central to the field of public health, which groups prevention interventions into three levels based on when an intervention occurs: primary, secondary, and tertiary prevention. **Primary prevention is the focus of this report** and refers to what can be done *before* incidents occur to prevent initial perpetration or victimization.[12, 13] Figure 1. illustrates the levels of prevention interventions.[14, 15]

---

[12] DoD. (2020). *DoDI 6400.09: DoD Policy on Integrated Primary Prevention of Self-Directed Harm and Prohibited Abuse or Harm.* https://www.esd.whs.mil/Portals/54/Documents/DD/issuances/dodi/640009p.pdf?ver=2020-09-11-104936-223

[13] Primary prevention can include improving physical environments in barracks and installations, teaching basic sexual education and developing healthy communication skills for sexual activities, and strengthening and enforcing policies that prohibit hazing, stalking, and harassment, and increasing knowledge about military culture and violence prevention.

[14] Secondary prevention includes what can be done after an incident occurs to support the victim and combat the short-term consequences of trauma. For example, advocates at every installation are available to provide immediate counseling. Sexual Assault Response Coordinators (SARC) and Sexual Assault Prevention and Response Victim Advocates (SAPR VA) function as immediate resources for victims.

[15] Tertiary prevention refers to the long-term responses after an incident occurs to cope with the lasting consequences of violence and/or offender treatment interventions. This prevention includes on-going counseling, as well as consistent enforcement and consequences for the perpetrator.

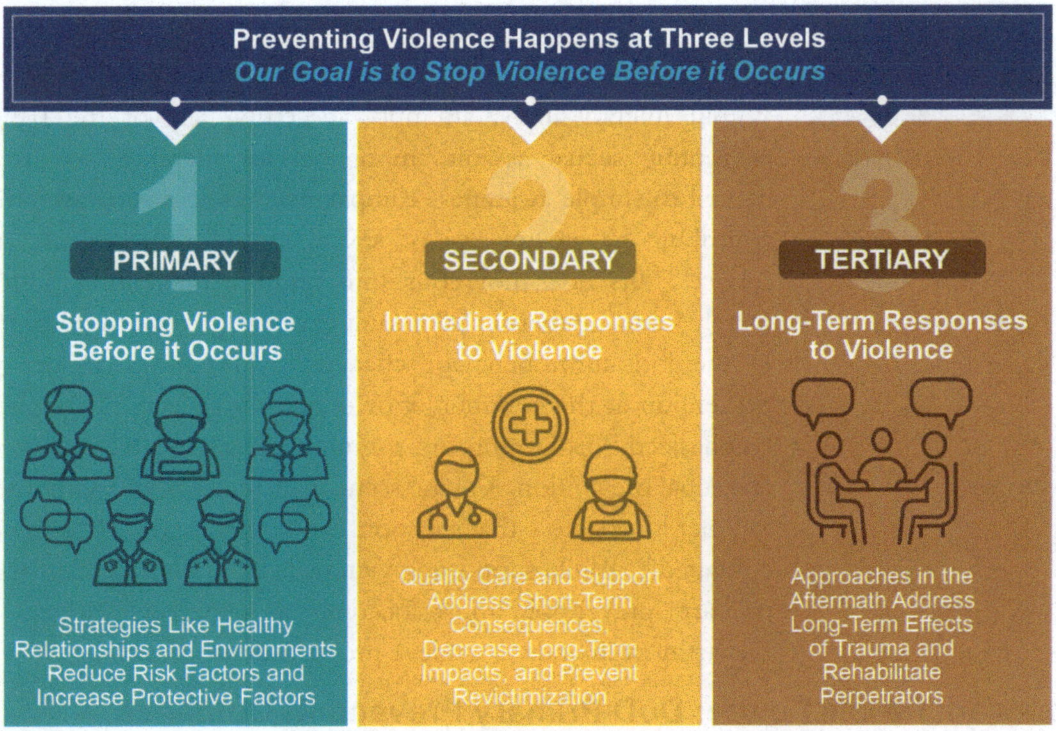

Figure 1. Three Levels of Prevention

While this report centers on the primary prevention of sexual harassment and sexual assault, the IRC believes that nesting these prevention activities within a larger, more comprehensive violence prevention effort will be key to eliminating incidents of sexual harassment and sexual assault in the future. Cross-cutting primary prevention should address all forms of interpersonal and self-directed violence, which encompasses intimate and non-intimate partner sexual assault, domestic violence, child maltreatment, suicide, workplace violence prevention.[16,17]

[16] The term interpersonal and self-directed violence is broader than sexual harassment and sexual assault which only address the sexual continuum of harm and sexual violence. The military should address sexual assault and harassment prevention activities within larger efforts that include interpersonal and self-directed violence due to the shared risk and protective factors and intervention strategies.

[17] DoD. (2020). *DoDI 6400.09: DoD Policy on Integrated Primary Prevention of Self-Directed Harm and Prohibited Abuse or Harm.* https://www.esd.whs.mil/Portals/54/Documents/DD/issuances/dodi/640009p.pdf?ver=2020-09-11-104936-223

Primary Prevention in the Military

> "Giving someone a water bottle with the hotline number is too late—that's response, not prevention. They tend to get conflated."
>
> -SARC, as told to the IRC in a listening session

Within military units, attempts at getting left of the bang[18] and preventing sexual assault among Service members are frequently limited to simple awareness campaigns. While raising awareness can contribute to greater use of sexual assault response and support services, this does not constitute primary prevention. Moreover, merely knowing that sexual assault exists as a problem does not result in the long-term behavior changes required to conduct primary prevention at the community or organization level.[19] As one SARC emphasized, "Educating the community on available resources does not equal prevention. Giving someone a water bottle with the hotline number is too late—that's response, not prevention. They tend to get conflated." While supporting victims is an enduring effort for DoD, primary prevention must become a significant priority if the Department intends to achieve prevention progress.[20]

A Framework for the Future: DoD Primary Prevention Guidance

In 2019, the USD(P&R) created the PPoA framework to provide comprehensive strategic guidance for prevention efforts at each echelon of the military environment.[21] This framework identifies the key military stakeholders and resources that make up the system needed to improve prevention efforts and it lays the foundation for concrete action to address sexual assault prevention in the military environment.[22] The prevention process includes understanding the problem and its contributing factors, developing an approach that targets these factors and engages Service members, implementing the approach with fidelity in supportive climates, and evaluating the approach. The combination of these elements (i.e., executing the prevention process in an optimized prevention system) is necessary to decrease sexual assault and sustain reductions over time.

In 2020, the Department issued DoDI 6400.09, DoD Policy on the Integrated Primary Prevention of Self-Directed Harm and Prohibited Abuse or Harm.[23] This policy directs prevention as a promising

---

[18] This phrase was repeated by various leaders and Service members during the IRC's information gathering sessions as military slang or the catch-all term for primary prevention.

[19] Basile, K.C., DeGue, S., Jones, K., Freire, K., Dills, J., Smith, S.G., Raiford, J.L. (2016). *STOP SV: A Technical Package to Prevent Sexual Violence*. National Center for Injury Prevention, Control, Centers for Disease Control and Prevention. https://www.cdc.gov/violenceprevention/pdf/SV-Prevention-Technical-Package.pdf

[20] DoD SAPRO. (2020). *Fiscal Year 2019 Annual Report on Sexual Assault in the Military*. https://www.sapr.mil/sites/default/files/DOD_Annual_Report_on_Sexual_Assault_In_The_Military_FY2019_Consolidated.pdf

[21] DoD. (2019). *Prevention Plan of Action*. https://www.sapr.mil/sites/default/files/PPoA_Final.pdf

[22] One consistent shortcoming of the PPoA is its systematic adoption across all levels of the military. While Service headquarters staff (e.g., resilience or personnel policy experts at the Services' headquarters level) have taken steps to implement the PPoA, their efforts have not trickled down to the operational or tactical levels.

[23] DoD. (2020). *DoDI 6400.09: DoD Policy on Integrated Primary Prevention of Self-Directed Harm and Prohibited Abuse or Harm*. https://www.esd.whs.mil/Portals/54/Documents/DD/issuances/dodi/640009p.pdf?ver=2020-09-11-104936-223

emerging effort to integrate core aspects of primary prevention across a range of harmful behaviors, including sexual harassment, sexual assault, suicide, domestic abuse, child abuse, and problematic sexual behavior in children and youth.[24] In addition, the DoD Prevention Collaboration Forum[25] was recently established to ensure that prevention remains a critical, long-standing policy and programmatic priority for the Department.[26]

These policies and new collaborations, while heartening, are only the beginning of the process needed to cement primary prevention into everyday military activities. Work at the Department level has yet to permeate down to every military installation and Service location. Additionally, primary prevention requires an enduring DoD research capability to provide evidence of what works and what does not work to reduce sexual harassment and sexual assault. With the appropriate authorities and resources, the Department has the opportunity to set the standard as a leader and a pioneer in preventing sexual violence and the continuum of harm.

Methodology

The IRC's Prevention experts conducted a series of data gathering efforts and information session engagements across the Department and Services. The prevention working group—comprised of Senior Executive Service/General and Flag Officer level prevention leaders and SMEs from each Service—met regularly to discuss the current state of prevention efforts in the military. Discussions included: Service implementation of the DoD PPoA; research efforts and policy updates; public health expertise across the enterprise; prevention training and development strengths and gaps; military leadership competencies and support for prevention efforts; and other topics. The Prevention experts also reviewed literature for existing sexual assault prevention requirements and best practices, including all sexual assault prevention National Defense Authorization Act (NDAA) requirements from Fiscal Year (FY) 2015 (FY15) to FY21, and reports from the DoD Office of People Analytics (OPA), DoD Government Accountability Office, RAND, and the Centers for Disease Control and Prevention (CDC).

The Prevention experts held more than a dozen stakeholder meetings with internal and external organizations and agencies, including but not limited to: USD(P&R) Manpower and Reserve Affairs (Accessions, Readiness, and Promotions Policy), OPA, CDC, Office for Diversity, Equity, and Inclusion (ODEI), Defense Equal Opportunity Management Institute (DEOMI), OSD Cost Assessment and Program Evaluation and Comptroller, Office of General Counsel, the Defense

---

[24] Generally, "integrated" or "cross-cutting" prevention efforts refer to strategies that address multiple forms of violence at once. For example, women's unemployment or underemployment is a risk factor for sexual harassment, sexual assault, child abuse, and domestic violence. Providing financial support and employment opportunities to women is an example of a cross-cutting prevention approach.

[25] DoD. (2020, Feb 26). *Prevention Collaboration Forum Charter*.

[26] The IRC supports the work of the DoD Prevention Collaboration Forum. In line with its prescribed role in DoDI 6400.09, the PCF is an appropriate body to provide oversight and accountability for the prevention recommendations outlined in this report.

Personnel and Security Research Center, and others. The Prevention experts also attended the numerous survivor sessions, research sessions, and briefings hosted by the IRC.

After initial engagements with the working group and stakeholders, the Prevention experts determined that further information was required to understand existing prevention progress and barriers at the operational and tactical levels across the military. They proceeded to launch an enterprise-wide information gathering effort, comprised of small group discussions with officers and enlisted personnel of all ranks from across the Services and National Guard. In total, the Prevention experts conducted 43 virtual information gathering sessions with commanders, SAPR personnel, Service Prevention experts, and Service members across the military. Figure 2 depicts this approach:

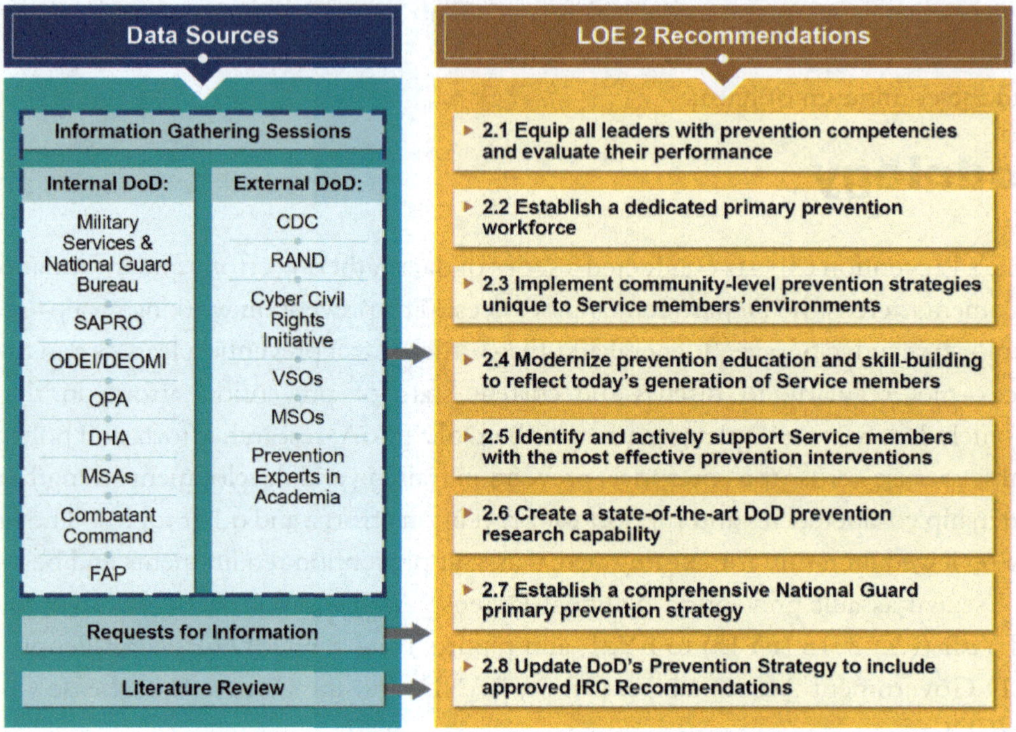

Figure 2. Prevention Line of Effort Methodology[27]

The information gathering sessions included respondents from across the Air Force, Army, Marine Corps, Navy and National Guard. Within each Service, the Prevention experts targeted three separate echelons or levels of military personnel:

- **Strategic-level** information gathering sessions included combatant commander and Vice Service Chief-level and their senior enlisted advisors, as well as leaders and experts in sexual assault prevention, diversity and inclusion, and public health at Service-level Headquarters.

---

[27] In addition to the offices already defined above in the preceding text, the IRC met with: The Defense Health Agency (DHA), Veteran Service Organizations (VSOs), Military Service Organizations (MSOs), and the DoD Family Advocacy Program (FAP).

- **Operational-level** information gathering sessions included commanders, mid-grade officers, senior enlisted advisors, and relevant military/civilian policy/program managers at the Major Command level.
- **Tactical-level** information gathering sessions included installation commanders, senior enlisted advisors, installation prevention practitioners, Service members (various ranks), and accessions professionals.[28]

Before the sessions, the Prevention experts prepared separate lists of probing questions for personnel who were responsible for conducting sexual assault prevention, commanders, accessions instructors, and enlisted personnel, respectively.[29] Sessions were conducted as non-attributional to add to the candor of participants.[30]

Information session transcripts and notes were analyzed for major themes. The following key topics emerged and informed the recommendations outlined in this report:

- Current implementation of the DoD PPoA;
- "Unfunded mandates" (un-resourced requirements);
- Importance of cross-cutting primary prevention efforts;
- Tensions between sexual assault response versus prevention responsibilities in the SAPR workforce;
- Content, dosage, and delivery of existing SAPR training;
- Challenges evaluating prevention efforts;
- Social and cultural practices that contribute to sexual assault prior to military service (e.g., lack of basic sex education in U.S. high schools); and,
- Unique challenges for the National Guard.

Recommendation 2.1: Equip All Leaders with Prevention Competencies and Evaluate Their Performance

Leaders are critical to the health and performance of organizations. Commanders, in particular, are the center of gravity for prevention in units, as they have unique and considerable authorities, responsibilities, and opportunities to affect people's lives and their organizational missions. Many leaders want to support primary prevention efforts, but lack the requisite competencies (knowledge, skills, and attitudes) to do so. The Department should develop leaders with distinct prevention

---

28 Accessions professionals include personnel such as instructors at schoolhouses and drill sergeants at initial military training (i.e., boot camp).

29 The sessions on average contained two to five participants and varied from 30 to 90 minutes in length. Sessions were deliberately semi-structured and informal, allowing for candid thoughts and opinions from participants. Respondents were asked to answer three broad questions: 1) what works, 2) what does not work, and 3) what is missing in sexual harassment and sexual assault prevention efforts and why?

30 Overall, the prevention experts conducted 14 sessions with strategic level personnel, 8 sessions with operational-level personnel, and 21 sessions with tactical-level personnel.

competencies, provide them specific prevention expectations aligned with their roles and responsibilities, and routinely assess their ability to lead prevention of sexual harassment, sexual assault, and related forms of violence.

- 2.1 a: USD(P&R) should define the competencies leaders must have to oversee prevention;
- 2.1 b: The Services and NGB should develop and hold leaders appropriately accountable for prevention; and,
- 2.1 c: The Services and NGB should equip all leaders to develop and deliver informed prevention messages in formal and informal settings.

Rationale for these Changes: Leaders do not Understand Primary Prevention

Prevention practitioners, sexual assault response personnel, and Service members across DoD agreed that, "a lot of leaders *want* to lead prevention, they just don't know how." Leaders do not have the specific knowledge, skills, and attitudes to effectively oversee the prevention of sexual harassment, and sexual assault. Senior leaders and commanders in particular must address prevention across many different domains and levels, as shown in Figure 3.

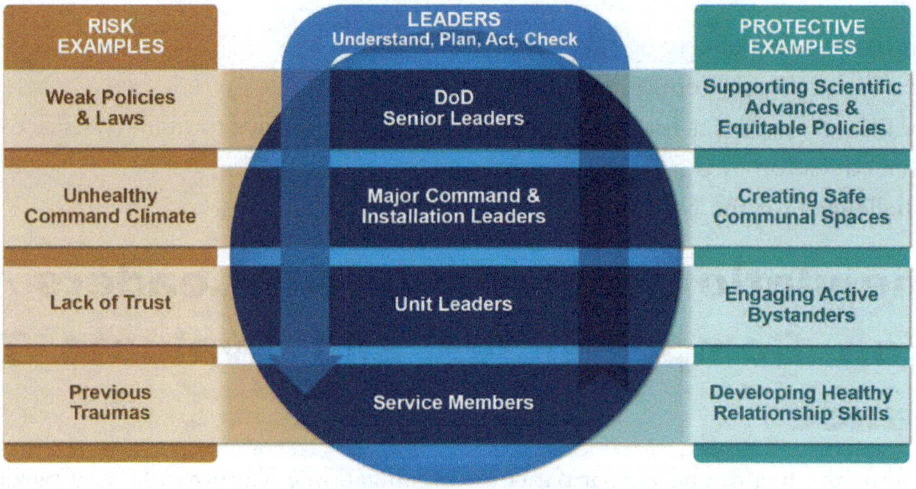

Figure 3. Military Social Ecological Model

This socio-ecological model represents the dynamic interrelations between different levels of the military's unique authority structure and highlights specific roles and responsibilities for leaders. Figure 3 depicts a small sample of risk and protective factors across the four distinct domains. Leaders should understand risk and protective factors that apply to their population and then nest these factors into a larger prevention strategy in their unit, installation, or Service branch. Risk factors may be reduced through intervention or eliminated if under the leader's control. Example risk factors listed above include weak policies and laws at the DoD or Service-level; an unhealthy command climate at an installation-level, lack of trust at the unit-level, and previous traumas of victims and perpetrators at the individual-level.

In this example, weak policies and laws can have a permissive effect on violence; therefore, it is important for leaders to develop policies that strengthen prevention strategies. Unhealthy command climates can include a toxic command culture in which leaders at a variety of levels ignore or neglect cases of harassment and/or verbal, emotional, and physical abuse between Service members. This may trickle down to enlisted leaders creating sub-climates that create space for violence. The lack of trust between leaders, peers, and subordinates can create environments where individuals do not feel safe. Recent research on Service members also reveals that individuals with previous traumas may be more susceptible to future violence.[31]

Currently, the Department has not defined the essential competencies leaders across DoD require to understand these environmental considerations. Furthermore, without these clearly defined expectations, the Services and National Guard are not developing leaders with prevention competencies and evaluating their performance relative to their roles and responsibilities.

This recommendation addresses the current deficiency in leader development and discusses how to hold leaders appropriately accountable for prevention *before* sexual harassment and sexual assault occur. Equipping leaders with the requisite prevention competencies will empower them to accurately understand their environment, and subsequently implement and evaluate effective prevention strategies, ultimately reducing the prevalence of sexual violence.

Recommendation 2.1 a: USD(P&R) Should Define the Competencies Leaders Must have to Oversee Prevention

USD(P&R) should define the specific competencies (knowledge, skills, and attitudes) required to lead prevention at *all* levels of leadership. These competencies can include:

- Risk and protective factors within specific population
- Different levels of the social ecological model (e.g., individual level interventions versus community level interventions);
- Social bias and common stereotypes (e.g., gender discrimination);
- Emotional intelligence (self-awareness, self-regulation, relationship management skills);
- Key public health concepts such as cause/effect relationships and core elements of evidence-based policies, programs, and practices; and,
- Basic standards for implementation fidelity and evaluation of prevention policies, programs, and practices.

Leaders Too Frequently "Check the Block" When Doing Prevention

The IRC's information gathering sessions revealed that leaders either: 1) conflated primary prevention with sexual assault response, or 2) conceptualized primary prevention as "awareness" or "training." Many leaders "check the box" for prevention by signing "zero tolerance" policy letters or make general

[31] Office of People Analytics. (2019). *2018 WGRA: Dominance Analysis of Demographic Risk Factors for Sexual Assault, Survey Note*. OPA Report No. 2019-062.

statements about their support for preventing sexual assault. These methods, while acknowledging the problem of sexual assault, do not constitute primary prevention. Leading in prevention requires more than a one-time awareness campaign or simple statements of support. In the same way that leaders evaluate new environments to develop relevant strategies to win battles and wars, leaders urgently need to master specific prevention knowledge, skills, and attitudes in order to lead prevention activities.

Many sexual assault response personnel working alongside commanders mentioned the shortcomings of their leadership. One SARC commented, "The officer in charge of SHARP [Sexual Harassment and Assault Response and Prevention program] was kind of clueless…" This frustration with leaders was echoed across the Services by Service members and SAPR practitioners alike. Many SARCs and leaders admitted that bandwidth and leader attention for sexual assault was consumed by response requirements. Moreover, when leaders did give attention to prevention, they often used a variety of ad-hoc methods and tools to prevent sexual assault from occurring. However, these methods were not necessarily comprehensive or based on research.

Failures Occur When Leaders Lack Essential Skillsets

While many sexual assault investigation reports (e.g., the Fort Hood Report) accuse leaders of failing to prevent sexual assault *after* an incident, these reports neglect to mention that military leaders have never been deliberately equipped to lead prevention—nor are they held accountable before incidents. The Department and the public hear similar stories: that leaders are failing to lead or that the Services are not "doing enough" to reduce sexual assaults. However, until the military institutionalizes a deliberate, consistent approach to equipping leaders with specific prevention skillsets and evaluating them, it should not be surprising to see a repeat of leadership ignorance and neglect. The Fort Hood Independent Review Commission noted in its report, "during the review period, no Commanding General or subordinate echelon commander chose to intervene proactively and mitigate known risks of high crime, sexual assault and sexual harassment."[32] However, if leaders conflate prevention with response, or believe that "awareness" activities constitute prevention, they inherently lack the knowledge, skills, and attitudes to proactively intervene in the first place.

Recommendation 2.1 b: The Services and NGB Should Develop and Hold Leaders Appropriately Accountable for Prevention

The Services and the NGB should adopt and implement the DoD leader prevention competencies outlined in Recommendation 2.1 a. Subsequently, the Services and NGB should collaborate with government, academia, and industry for strategies to embed these competencies within officer and

---

[32] Fort Hood Independent Review Committee. (2020). Report of the Fort Hood Independent Review Committee. https://www.army.mil/e2/downloads/rv7/forthoodreview/2020-12-03_FHIRC_report_redacted.pdf

enlisted education and developmental forums.[33] They should also design methods for formally assessing the prevention competencies of officer and enlisted leaders in annual evaluations and promotions.[34] Leaders include all officers and enlisted Service members with supervisory duties.

Lack of Prevention Accountability is Widespread

When discussing the recently released Fort Hood Independent Review Committee report[35] in the information sessions, several Soldiers commented that the report was "not surprising." One officer admitted, "that could have been anywhere." This lack of oversight and accountability for leaders to play a role in sexual violence prevention is not unique to the Army. There is little to no deliberate leadership accountability for proactive primary prevention across the Services. In part, this is due to widely held misconceptions about prevention, such as accepting sexual assault as "inevitable," conflating prevention with response, or confusing prevention with "awareness" (See: Recommendation 2.1 a: USD(P&R) Should Define the Competencies Leaders Must have to Oversee Prevention).

> "Right now, it is easier to hold the commander accountable for an incident than the environment before the incident."
>
> -Senior Leader, as told to the IRC in a listening session

Leaders must be given the opportunity to master the requisite knowledge, skills, and attitudes to lead prevention, but once they do, they must also be held accountable. Put plainly: there must be consequences when leaders *fail* to engage in prevention activities (before sexual harassment or sexual assault occur). As one senior leader stated bluntly, "Right now, it is easier to hold the commander accountable for an incident than the environment before the incident." Sexual violence prevention competencies must be adopted into the existing talent management efforts and job performance evaluation systems. Currently, the Services do not deliberately provide leaders with prevention skillsets or systematically evaluate their related performance.

Lastly, the scope and extent of leader accountability must change as the leader's roles and responsibilities increase. As one SARC commented, "[Enlisted leadership] is where the rubber meets the road. If the lead petty officer hears derogatory comments all day or is aware of fraternization and favoritism and turns a blind eye, it sends a message to the team that it is endorsed." Several SAPR personnel advocated for holding enlisted leaders and junior officers accountable for addressing individual-level protective and risk factors, while holding senior leaders appropriately accountable for addressing risk and protective factors at the installation-level and above.

---

33 William M. (Mac) Thornberry National Defense Authorization Act for Fiscal Year 2021, Public Law No. 116-283, 534. (2021). https://www.congress.gov/116/bills/hr6395/BILLS-116hr6395enr.pdf

34 Sachdev, A. R., Grossman, R., & Burke-Smalley, L. A. (2019). Beyond "checking the box": Using accountability to promote the effectiveness of sexual misconduct training. *Industrial and Organizational Psychology*, *12*(1), 100-105.

35 Fort Hood Independent Review Committee. (2020). Report of the Fort Hood Independent Review Committee. https://www.army.mil/e2/downloads/rv7/forthoodreview/2020-12-03_FHIRC_report_redacted.pdf

Recommendation 2.1 c: The Services and NGB Should Equip All Leaders to Develop and Deliver Informed Prevention Messages in Formal and Informal Settings

The Services and the NGB should equip leaders with effective methods, messages, and tools to communicate about prevention. These messages must invite Service members from diverse backgrounds to be part of the solution to sexual harassment and sexual assault.[36] These messages should reinforce prevention knowledge development and skill building. Ensuring leaders have the skills necessary to deliver prevention messages will increase Service member buy-in for prevention at all levels and facilitate the sharing of on-the-spot prevention knowledge, skills, and attitudes.

This approach is intended to avoid some of the all too common communication methods that currently do not work. Methods such as one-size-fits-all PowerPoint briefings in large group settings (i.e., provided to hundreds of people at once)—often in the form of annual refresher trainings—do not meet community prevention needs.[37] Similarly, episodic "down-days" often do not have the intended effect, especially if the goals of the down days are not understood at the lowest levels. Instead, junior enlisted Service members in IRC discussions expressed a sincere desire to have authentic, small group discussions to explore key questions about consent, respectful workplace behavior, personal boundaries, and related prevention themes in scenario-based activities. Leaders must be prepared to lead and support these discussions within their units.

Leaders Need Better Communication Tools

Commanders are frequently unprepared and uncomfortable having conversations with Service members about healthy intimacy, and sexual activity.[38] Moreover, enlisted participants in information sessions made it clear that Service members are most comfortable discussing sexual activities and norms with peers and equals, not necessarily their commanders. This places a significant burden on lower level supervisors (e.g., junior noncommissioned officers and petty officers) to discuss consensual sex and healthy intimacy with their Service members. Higher-ranking leaders must have tools to empower their frontline supervisors to strategically engage Service members in these conversations.

Commanders in particular must also create an environment where it is easy to understand "what right looks and sounds like." As one prevention expert noted, "I think the biggest thing we need is support. Support from our senior leaders and commanders who are willing to have uncomfortable conversations and create an environment where it is safe to have those conversations." To this point, leaders must consider each audience's unique needs and have tools that inspire desired prevention

---

[36] See also: Recommendation 2.6 d for increasing research to support social marketing campaigns to improve prevention messaging.

[37] See Recommendation 2.4 for more information on prevention education and skill-building.

[38] As stated in Recommendation 2.4, this need to understand healthy sexual activity is very urgent due to the lack of consistent and effective sex education in K-12 schools in the U.S.

outcomes (e.g., tools to give to junior leaders to demonstrate how to stop homophobic and/or sexist comments).

Furthermore, junior leaders stressed that a lack of effective messaging about primary prevention by senior leaders—coupled with the challenges of juggling many overwhelming priorities and little to no prevention resources—constitute a significant barrier to leading and communicating about prevention. As one commander put it, "Yes, we need messaging from above that this is important, but we also need to know *how* to make it important. If everything is a priority, nothing is a priority."

Implementation Considerations

To implement this recommendation, USD(P&R) should collaborate with the public and private sectors to develop definitions for essential primary prevention competencies for leaders (i.e., knowledge, skills, and attitudes). DoD should also include associated policy and guidance for evaluation requirements and define generally expected performance and effectiveness outcomes.

Each Service and the National Guard have unique characteristics and should adapt and evaluate requirements in ways that best align with their Service members' leadership levels and unique settings and demands. Concurrently, the Services and NGB should provide leaders effective primary prevention communication tools, including messages and methods for delivering them, and evaluating effectiveness. The tools and methods should be provided in professional military education settings and focused heavily on impacting small group forums.

Outcome Metrics

The Services and NGB should provide USD(P&R) annual qualitative assessments of their approaches to developing and evaluating leader performance and effectiveness with primary prevention competencies. Ultimately, success of this recommendation will occur when prevention competencies are taught in leader professional military education, evaluated in annual performance reports, and a key consideration for promotion readiness. Evaluation of a leader's prevention skillsets includes assessing the leader's ability to use research-based approaches to:

- Understand their environment (reflected in strategic use of environmental assessments, e.g., the Defense Organizational Climate Survey/DEOCS);
- Develop and execute prevention strategies for their environment in conjunction with prevention experts (prevention experts could additionally submit evaluations of leaders); and,
- Evaluate and adapt their prevention strategies over time (reflected in Service member belief and attitude changes and eventual decreases in sexual harassment and sexual assault prevalence).

Recommendation 2.2: Establish a Dedicated Primary Prevention Workforce

In numerous engagements across all levels, there was general agreement that unfunded mandates have caused little progress in prevention, and one of the greatest deficits has been the near complete lack of a professional prevention workforce. Effective prevention of sexual harassment, sexual assault, and other forms of violence requires the time and dedication of full-time personnel with specific public health and behavioral social science expertise.[39] Prevention responsibilities should not be carried out as a collateral or additional duty. Building a primary prevention workforce capability will require long-term investments from Military Department leadership to empower the Services and National Guard.

- 2.2 a: USD(P&R) develop a model for a dedicated and capable prevention workforce;
- 2.2 b: USD(P&R) develop a professional credential for the prevention workforce; and,
- 2.2 c: The Services determine the optimum full-time prevention workforce and equip all echelons of active duty, reserve, and guard organizations.

Rationale for these Changes: Lack of a Critical Infrastructure Impedes Prevention Progress

Currently, the Services do not have an effective workforce model. They lack a systematic approach to recruiting, credentialing, promoting, and sustaining a professional workforce dedicated to primary prevention. Many military personnel currently engaged in primary prevention activities are double-hatted, or tasked as a collateral duty (i.e., simultaneously working sexual assault response), making prevention efforts inconsistent and under-resourced. Double-hatted personnel lack both the capability and capacity to perform requirements essential to preventing sexual harassment, sexual assault, and other forms of violence and abuse. This results in a significant lack of progress in prevention. It is also important to recognize that the overall DoD organizational structure would benefit from a holistic model that considers comprehensive integration of the prevention workforce from the strategic to the tactical level, including how individuals in different roles and responsibilities report to and align with the installation-level and headquarters-level personnel.

Recommendation 2.2 a: USD(P&R) Should Develop a Model for a Dedicated and Capable Prevention Workforce

Designing, hiring, and sustaining a new workforce should be done with a thoughtful strategy and detailed plans. USD(P&R) must develop a primary prevention workforce model that can then be adopted by the Services and the National Guard. This model must outline a workforce capable of:

---

[39] Songer, T., Stephens-Stidham, S., Peek-Asa, C., Bou-Saada, I., Hunter, W., Lindemer, K., & Runyan, C. (2009). Core competencies for injury and violence prevention. *American Journal of Public Health, 99*(4), 600–606. https://doi.org/10.2105/AJPH.2008.137331

continuously conducting research and analysis; advising commanders and leaders; designing and writing strategic and operational policies and programs; collaborating at the local level to integrate and analyze community-level data; and implementing and evaluating programs and activities.

In developing this model, USD(P&R) should provide the Services and NGB policies and guidance on workforce roles and responsibilities, as well as address how prevention practitioners will serve and advise all levels of military leaders and commanders. Due to the cross-cutting nature of the primary prevention mission—e.g., similar risk and protective factors of sexual violence, substance misuse, suicide, etc.—the oversight and responsibility for these areas should all be aligned within one Office of Primary Responsibility (OPR) focused solely on primary prevention, and reporting directly to the organization's senior leader at installation and higher headquarters levels. Specifically, the workforce model should formally integrate the following primary prevention functions:

- Sexual harassment;
- Sexual assault, including intimate partner and non-intimate partner;
- Family violence, including child abuse, domestic abuse/intimate partner violence;
- Suicide; and,
- Workplace violence.

This integration under one OPR reporting directly to the organization's senior leader would ensure more effective and efficient strategies, policy, programming, research and analysis, interventions, strategic communications, advocacy for resourcing, and ultimately drive faster primary prevention results.

A comprehensive workforce model will also help the Services and National Guard determine how to array and employ a workforce across diverse and disparate organizations, population sizes, and geographies, with differing cultures, missions, and risk and protective factors. DoD has an opportunity to pioneer an effective workforce that can provide comprehensive primary prevention across the Department's entire enterprise.

Prevention Workforce Roles and Responsibilities

Sexual harassment, sexual assault (intimate and non-intimate partner), family violence (child maltreatment and domestic abuse/intimate partner violence), workplace violence, and suicide all share common risk and protective factors.[40] An integrated OPR would enable the Services and NGB to overcome the existing barriers due the silos/stovepipes and fragmentation that inhibits communication, coordination, resourcing, evaluation, and strategies. Ultimately, this integration would enable more effective and efficient prioritization of primary prevention. An effective and cross-cutting primary prevention workforce will require:

---

40 Wilkins, N., Myers, L., Kuehl, T., Bauman, A., & Hertz, M. (2018). Connecting the dots: State health department approaches to addressing shared risk and protective factors across multiple forms of violence. *Journal of Public Health Management and Practice*, *24* (Suppl 1 Injury and Violence Prevention).

- Robust primary prevention research;
- Data collection and analysis for implementation and evaluation of prevention activities;
- Functional and community collaboration with stakeholders who can inform prevention, including but not limited to:
  - Sexual assault response program managers and coordinators
  - Family advocacy (response) program policymakers and personnel
  - Equal opportunity (EO) (response) policymakers and personnel
  - Military personnel policy (MPP) policymakers and associated personnel offices within each Service
  - Local stakeholders (e.g., police) at the installation-level
- Policy development within DoD and Service headquarters;
- Program management;
- Leadership advisement;
- Program and activity implementation and oversight; and,
- Continuous evaluation, adaptations, and communication.

Recommendation 2.2 b: USD(P&R) Should Develop a Prevention Credential

USD(P&R) should develop a professional primary prevention credential with associated knowledge development and skill building requirements for the workforce. A primary prevention credential specifically addresses the need to have a skilled, professional prevention workforce. Without a credentialing process, leaders and Service members will lack confidence in prevention practitioners' competencies, which has implications for future trust and confidence in all prevention efforts. The Services and National Guard need consistent quality standards for *every* level of the enterprise, from small field units to Service headquarters. As part of the professional requirements for the prevention workforce, continuing education and professional development should also be built into the career-cycle of a prevention practitioner such that competencies and scientific expertise increase over time.

Prevention staff will need varying basic qualifications and backgrounds in public health, statistics, and other forms of behavioral social science in order to effectively address protective and risk factors at all levels of the social-ecological model. Specific competencies should include such subjects as understanding evidence and research-based prevention, behavior change theory, prevention planning, implementation, evaluation, systems thinking, capacity building, and violence prevention within the military context. DoD should also consider developing a feedback mechanism for leaders and commanders to provide input to USD(P&R) focused on continually improving the quality of the credential.

Currently, there is no standardized prevention credential across the Services, although professionalization of a prevention workforce is an aspect of the PPoA. Many individuals presently attempting to conduct prevention are neither trained nor certified in prevention. For many response personnel, prevention duties are secondary to other job responsibilities. The field of primary prevention is significantly different from response. These fields require distinct areas of knowledge and skills. A workforce that can execute prevention activities will require separate education and training apart from response and cannot be retrofitted or repurposed from a victim response workforce. Doing so would not only be a disservice to victims, whose care and support should be the sole focus of response personnel, but also fundamentally will not move the needle on prevention.

The only Service with a sizable violence prevention capability is the Air Force.[41,42] The Air Force has Violence Prevention Integrators (VPI) working on bases to prevent sexual violence. However, the majority of the VPIs at the tactical level were not provided the necessary expertise and resources to conduct primary prevention. Some VPIs had limited knowledge of basic prevention principles, but in-depth public health expertise on violence prevention almost exclusively existed at the Service headquarters level and within the Military Service Academies. This "gap" in public health expertise has many second and third order effects across the Services. For example, in some of the information gathering sessions, the VPIs and accessions instructors held some common misconceptions about sexual assault prevention. Figure 4 includes these misconceptions.

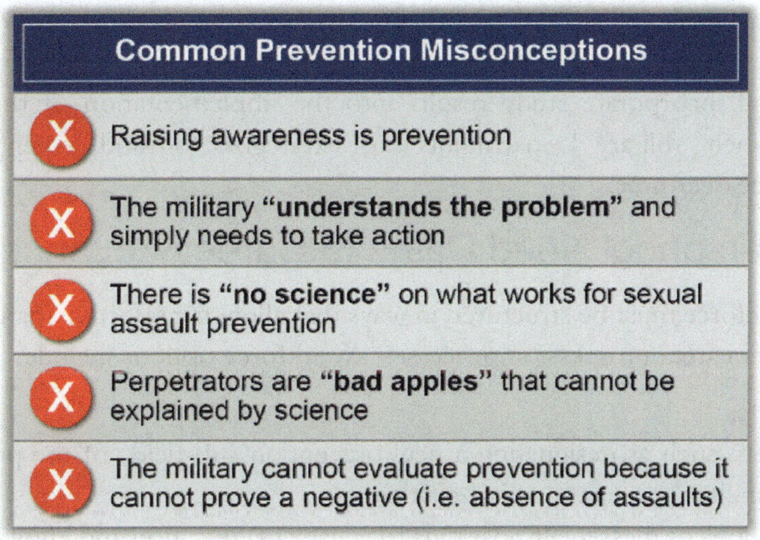

Figure 4. Prevention Misconceptions

These misconceptions truly jeopardize and undermine prevention efforts. A dedicated, credentialed prevention workforce is necessary to counter these myths and ensure prevention efforts receive attention and buy-in from Service members and senior leaders.

---

[41] The Marine Corps Embedded Preventive Behavioral Health Capability (EPBHC) personnel are also prevention practitioners, but their numbers are very small. Despite information gathering sessions with the Marine Corps, the IRC was unable to obtain specific information on the EPBHC personnel's roles and responsibilities.

[42] U.S. Air Force. (2019, January 25). *Air Force Instruction 90-5001: Integrated Resilience.* https://static.e-publishing.af.mil/production/1/af_a1/publication/afi90-5001/afi90-5001.pdf

Recommendation 2.2 c: The Services Should Determine the Optimum Full-time Prevention Workforce, and Equip All Echelons of Active Duty, Reserve, and Guard Organizations

The Services should develop their optimum prevention workforce to address current and future primary prevention needs. Once DoD completes and distributes the primary prevention workforce model, the Services must conduct a manpower study to determine how to effectively tailor and implement the workforce model to meet the needs of their Service. A thorough manpower management and fiscal analysis will determine the specific capability and capacity required at various levels (e.g., strategic, operational, and tactical), while taking into account any unique mission circumstances, such as organizations with members who live in remote or disparate locations, or who have extremely limited contact time with military communities, and so forth.

The Services should avoid one-size-fits-all solutions for the prevention workforce. Prevention needs will vary by Service, installation, and unit. For example, one prevention expert may provide sufficient oversight for several small or low-risk installations, whereas several prevention experts may be required to oversee a large, high-risk installation. After the Services successfully conduct the manpower study and incorporate study results into the implementation of the DoD prevention workforce model, each Military Department must strategize to fund, equip, and sustain their prevention workforce over time.

Prevention Personnel Need Paths to Career Advancement

The prevention workforce must be structured in ways that allow for effective management, retention, promotion, and other career progression processes. Workforce options include:

- Civilian billets;
- Military billets, such as designating a new prevention sub-fields of the public health and/or psychology military occupational specialties;
- Communications or messenger positions to engage in education and knowledge dissemination (civilian or military); and,
- Non-professional prevention opportunities for Service members (working under prevention experts).

The IRC recommends the Services and NGB consider military personnel (e.g., public health career field), to address the benefits of leveraging a pre-existing model for military career-field education, certifications, development, and progression, flexibility in assignability and deployability, etc., as well as civilian, or hybrid solutions for an enduring workforce. All options should be considered when constructing the prevention workforce to allow for creative solutions and effective management of competence and expertise. Ideally, individuals with less experience and expertise will work under the supervision of those with more experience and expertise.[43] As the prevention workforce matures, individuals should be able to promote to more advanced and challenging positions. Violence prevention practitioners should not be forced into "dead-end" jobs with no options for upward mobility or career choices.

Hiring prevention experts for installation and headquarters staff may prove challenging. As one prevention SME succinctly stated, "recruiting top-level academics to apply for government jobs is difficult. A more systematic approach to hiring population-based public health, social psychologists, sociologists, and behavioral health professionals would be beneficial." Special attention should be given when hiring academic personnel. However, not every unit will need a violence prevention practitioner with a Ph.D. in public health. As another SME noted, a prevention workforce requires the creation of a number of different roles and responsibilities. Each of these roles needs to be defined in scope and associated with specific competencies for a prevention workforce to be successful.

The Workforce Must be Adapted to Serve the National Guard's Unique Community

Additionally, National Guard members noted the unique challenges regarding prevention with a part-time, collateral duty, geographically disparate workforce. Not only do collateral duty SARC personnel lack the time to execute evidence-based prevention, they also lack knowledge about risk factors specific to the National Guard because Soldiers and Airmen are "so scattered." Moreover, a level of frustration exists within the National Guard that, unlike active duty, a lack of ample time exists to "enhance the movement of prevention." The evolution of prevention in the National Guard includes a full-time prevention workforce with requisite competencies as well as sustained collaborative relationships within local communities serving National Guardsman. Similar to their active duty counterparts, prevention expertise is concentrated at the HQ level and does not filter down to the installation or tactical level (arguably, where these skills are most needed).

Implementation Considerations

The Services and NGB should complete gathering and submitting workforce data to OSD by 1 October 2021, in response to the Secretary of Defense's Immediate Actions Memo. Senior leaders in the Services should also immediately begin communicating "why" the workforce is required and specifically articulate the roles and responsibilities of prevention professionals. USD(P&R) should use the workforce data and collaborate with public and private organizations to develop a comprehensive primary prevention workforce model by the end of calendar year 2021. USD(P&R) should also establish the most relevant credential program to standardize a common base of education and experience within the Services' and National Guard's prevention workforce.

---

[43] Several VPIs in the Air Force told the IRC that they do not report to a manager or job leader who is more skilled and/or more experienced at violence prevention than themselves. Instead, their work is evaluated by military commanders and/or other unit staff who may or may not know anything at all about public health or violence prevention interventions. While prevention experts will need to advise commanders, they also need oversight and guidance from prevention practitioners with more experience and expertise than themselves.

The DoD workforce model should inform the Services' follow-on manpower studies, which should be completed in six months. These manpower studies should consider unique Service and National Guard dynamics and various personnel options including military, civilian, or hybrid solutions. Ultimately, the Services should focus on ensuring programming the workforce for FY24.

Importantly, resourcing for the workforce cannot simply ebb and flow with every change of leadership or administration. Therefore, the Secretary of Defense should propose that Congress adopt legislation which establishes a prevention workforce and appropriates funds that can only be used to establish and maintain that workforce.

Outcome Metrics

Outcome metrics for this recommendation should include completion of a unique workforce model and credential. Other measures should include a comprehensive manpower study and the acquisition of a full-time dedicated workforce, programmed in FY24. To promote accountability for the prevention workforce, the Defense Advisory Committee for the Prevention of Sexual Misconduct (DAC-PSM) should be established, as called for in the FY20 NDAA.[44] A fully-appointed DAC-PSM could report to Congress regularly on prevention workforce policies, programs, and practices across the military.

Recommendation 2.3: Implement Community-level Prevention Strategies Unique to Service Members' Environments

Military environments vary tremendously depending on geographic location, deployment status, Service, and other factors. For example, the various risk and protective factors for a young, male Sailor deployed on a submarine are very different from the various risk and protective factors for a female Lieutenant in the Marine Corps serving her first tour in Okinawa, Japan. Similarly, different locations—particularly international locations—may sell cheap, accessible alcohol irrespective of Service member age. The communities surrounding military installations may endorse beliefs and values (e.g., rape myths, racism) at odds with the DoD values of inclusion and respect.[45]

[44] In order to formally establish the Committee, DoD prepared a Charter and Membership Balance Plan and appointed a Designated Federal Officer in 2020. With those in place, the DoD formally established the DAC-PSM on November 30, 2020. Per the NDAA, the Secretary of Defense can appoint up to 20 members of the Committee representing expertise in prevention research and implementation science, drawn from institutions of higher education, public health officials, non-profits, and academia. In 2020, DoD started the process to nominate an initial class of 10 members, allowing for growth as additional expertise requirements were identified. However, those nomination efforts were halted on Jan 30, 2021 when the Secretary of Defense called for a zero-based review of DoD's advisory committees.

[45] Service members can also hold attitudes and beliefs at odds with the DoD values of inclusion and respect.

Military leaders must implement community-level prevention strategies by reducing risk and increasing protective factors unique to Service members' environments. Tracking and changing the social and physical environment (e.g., better local onboarding practices for incoming recruits, mapping where Service members feel unsafe and/or isolated) can create lasting and meaningful change over time.[46] Training the local bar, restaurant, and/or nightclub staff to recognize sexually aggressive behavior and intervene can lower the risk of sexual assault.[47] Advocating for better military family housing and stronger job security for military spouses can reduce intimate partner and family violence.[48] These "community-level" interventions and strategies require dedication, collaboration, and long-term planning. This recommendation highlights the need for leaders and prevention practitioners to introduce tailored, location-specific interventions to reduce the risk of sexual harassment and sexual assault across the Services.

- 2.3 a: The Services and the NGB should resource and implement prevention strategies at organizational and community levels; and,
- 2.3 b: USD(P&R) identify a non-clinical OSD-level Office of Primary Responsibility for alcohol policy and develop relevant policy guidance and oversight.

Rationale for these Changes: Existing Military Prevention Activities are too Individualistic

As discussed in Recommendation 2.1, information gathering sessions revealed that many leaders mistakenly conflated prevention with response. Partially due to this conflation,[49] leaders often implemented prevention strategies *only* at the individual-level, such as protecting potential victims instead of scrutinizing the ingrained social attitudes, beliefs, and norms that perpetuate unhealthy climates (e.g., male entitlement, male control of all social and dating spaces).

Pursuing primary prevention at the individual-level—i.e., targeting *individual* leaders and Service members—is not enough to reduce sexual violence. The military must create community-level prevention strategies that address the unique risk and protective factors in different social and physical environments.[50] Communities can be physical (e.g., an installation), virtual (e.g., class alumni forum

---

[46] Hirsch, J.S., & Khan, S. (2020). *Sexual citizens: A landmark study of sex, power, and assault on campus*. WW Norton & Company.

[47] Powers, R.A., & Leili, J. (2018). Bar training for active bystanders: Evaluation of a community-based bystander intervention program. *Violence Against Women*, *24*(13), 1614-1634. https://doi.org/10.1177/1077801217741219

[48] Basile, K.C., DeGue, S., Jones, K., Freire, K., Dills, J., Smith, S.G., & Raiford, J.L. (2016). *STOP SV: A technical package to prevent sexual violence*. National Center for Injury Prevention, Control, Centers for Disease Control and Prevention. https://www.cdc.gov/violenceprevention/pdf/SV-Prevention-Technical-Package.pdf

[49] When leaders spend time reviewing cases of sexual assault and engaging in response efforts, they tend to focus their attention on individual victims and individual perpetrators, as opposed to community-level risk and protective factors.

[50] A community can be defined as "a group of people with diverse characteristics who are linked by social ties, share common perspectives, and engage in joint action in geographical locations or settings." Source. MacQueen, K. M., McLellan, E., Metzger, D. S., Kegeles, S., Strauss, R. P., Scotti, R., & Trotter, R. T. (2001). What is community? An evidence-based definition for participatory public health. *American Journal of Public Health*, *91*(12), 1929-1938. https://pubmed.ncbi.nlm.nih.gov/11726368/

of an academy), or some combination therein (e.g., a sports team with an active Facebook group). From a public health perspective, communities are important because they often have unique social norms, beliefs, obligations, and customs.[51] Similarly, physical environments can vary in their security, lighting, housing quality, walkability, local crime rate, etc.[52] These factors can interact in dangerous or helpful ways.

Leaders must understand communities—and other social units and social processes *larger* than the individual—to effectively prevent sexual harassment and sexual assault. In the military context, this could include teams, social cliques or groups, networks of families, military units (e.g., battalion, boat), and the broader communities in which these smaller groups are embedded. Only when leaders successfully shift their analytic focus and "see" their larger environment will important community-level risk and protective factors be addressed.

Recommendation 2.3 a: The Services and the NGB Should Resource and Implement Prevention Strategies at Organizational and Community Levels

The CDC STOP Sexual Violence technical package (2016) outlines five strategies and a variety of specific approaches leaders and prevention practitioners can adapt for use in diverse military communities.[53] While *all* strategies should be considered for effective prevention,[54] recommendation 2.3.a highlights the importance of creating protective environments and promoting healthy social norms specific to military communities. Additionally, this recommendation will require collaboration with partners, such as the CDC, Department of Education, other government agencies, academia, and/or industry to ensure that the military can evaluate and assess the impact of their community-level prevention strategies both in the short and long-term.[55]

During one tactical information gathering session, an officer lamented that preventing sexual assault is almost impossible because leaders "cannot" identify individual offenders before they commit the crime. He commented, "The red-flags are individual. So, while one offender might present this red flag, another offender won't…most really good sexual offenders are not going to show any red flags

---

[51] Lin, J., & Mele, C. (Eds.). (2012). *The urban sociology reader*. Routledge.

[52] Richards, T. B., Croner, C. M., Rushton, G., Brown, C. K., & Fowler, L. (1999). Information technology: Geographic information systems and public health: Mapping the future. *Public health reports, 114*(4), 359.

[53] These strategies include: 1) promoting social norms that protect against violence, 2) teaching skills to prevent sexual violence, 3) providing opportunities to empower and support girls and women, 4) creating protective environments, and 5) supporting victims/survivors of sexual assault. Source: Basile, K. C., DeGue, S., Jones, K., Freire, K., Dills, J., Smith, S. G., & Raiford, J. L. (2016). *STOP SV: A technical package to prevent sexual violence*. National Center for Injury Prevention, Control, Centers for Disease Control and Prevention. https://www.cdc.gov/violenceprevention/pdf/SV-Prevention-Technical-Package.pdf

[54] Teaching skills to prevent sexual violence is addressed by Recommendations 2.4.a and 2.4.b while supporting victims is address by the victim care and support line of effort.

[55] See also: Recommendation 2.6 on primary prevention research activities. The new DoD Prevention Research Center can assist and aid the Services in their evaluation efforts.

at all."[56] This remark echoes a sense of helplessness expressed by other leaders when trying to "get left of the bang" and stop sexual assault before it occurs. Yet this sense of helplessness demonstrates that leaders do not understand the problem. Addressing risk and protective factors for individual perpetrators *can* and must be done,[57] but the following community-level prevention topics must also be a focus:

- Widely shared ideas about gender and sexuality, e.g., beliefs that men "should" be sexually aggressive while women "should" be sexually submissive[58];
- Popular drinking habits;
- Safety/risks of communal gathering spaces;
- Formal or informal organizational policies that promote and/or discourage reporting of sexual harassment and assault; and,
- Existing social practices and norms governing the communities where Service members work, live, and engage in sexual activity.[59]

Two evidence-based community prevention strategies are prioritized in this recommendation: 1) promoting healthy social norms and 2) creating protective environments. These community-level strategies fill a current gap in the military's prevention efforts.

1) Engaging the Community through Promoting Healthy Social Norms

The CDC STOP Sexual Violence technical package highlights that "restrictive gender norms, i.e., rigid ideas about the appropriate roles and behavior of men and women, can serve to support or condone violent behavior in intimate and other relationships."[60] Moreover, research demonstrates that, "communities adhering to restrictive and harmful social norms are more likely to perpetrate physical, sexual, and emotional violence against women."[61] Leaders embedded at Service headquarters can use this knowledge to identify high-risk bases or posts (e.g., high rates of gender discrimination, hostile

---

[56] While patterns across types of offenders/perpetrators are still being discovered, sexual violence perpetration is fast-growing literature with valid research findings. For examples, see: Greathouse, S.M., Saunders, J.M., Matthews, M., Keller, K.M., & Miller, L.L. (2015). *A review of the literature on sexual assault perpetrator characteristics and behaviors.* RAND Corporation. Stander, V.A., Thomsen, C.J., Merrill, L.L., & Milner, J.S. (2018). Longitudinal prediction of sexual harassment and sexual assault by male enlisted Navy personnel. *Military Psychology*, *30*(3), 229-239. https://doi.org/10.1037/mil0000171

[57] Recommendation 2.6.c addresses the need for research on perpetration.

[58] Crawford, M., & Popp, D. (2003). Sexual double standards: A review and methodological critique of two decades of research. *Journal of sex research*, *40*(1), 13-26. https://doi.org/10.1080/00224490309552163

[59] Armstrong, E.A., Hamilton, L., & Sweeney, B. (2006). Sexual assault on campus: A multilevel, integrative approach to party rape. *Social Problems*, *53*(4), 483-499. https://doi.org/10.1525/sp.2006.53.4.483

[60] Basile, K. C., DeGue, S., Jones, K., Freire, K., Dills, J., Smith, S. G., & Raiford, J. L. (2016). *STOP SV: A technical package to prevent sexual violence*. National Center for Injury Prevention, Control, Centers for Disease Control and Prevention, 15. https://www.cdc.gov/violenceprevention/pdf/SV-Prevention-Technical-Package.pdf

[61] Ibid.

workplace environments, sexually harassing behaviors, etc.).[62] Occupations with very high percentages of men (<95 percent) have a reputation for being "more toxic for female Service members" than occupations with higher percentages of women.[63] Leaders at the installation-level can use this knowledge to identify high risk social groups within their community.

Leaders should be particularly conscious of unhealthy social norms within their community.[64] For example, some social groups may consider certain sexual activities (e.g., premarital sex, casual sex, multiple partners, etc.), normal and appropriate for *men*, but immoral and inappropriate for *women*. Gendered double standards often pressure men into pursuing sexual conquests while simultaneously hindering women from voicing their sexual needs and boundaries.[65] Leaders can also target different military occupations (e.g., Infantry culture, Pilot culture) have different social norms and gender ratios, and therefore have different risk and protective factors associated with their groups.[66] Leaders should carefully consider how to promote healthy social norms within different groups when developing a tailored, comprehensive primary prevention strategy for their community.

2) Engaging the Community by Creating Protective Environments

Promoting healthy social norms targets a specific aspect of the environment, namely, the local culture of the community and the various sub-cultures of different social groups within the community. However, other prevention approaches use alternative methods to alter the physical and social environment to increase protective factors and reduce risk factors.[67] Such approaches include changing physical spaces, altering laws and policies, and adopting different institutional practices. Importantly, many of these approaches do not involve changing deeply entrenched belief systems. These are "easy wins" that are often low cost and relatively simple to implement.

---

[62] Harris, R. J., McDonald, D. P., & Sparks, C. S. (2018). Sexual harassment in the military: Individual experiences, demographics, and organizational contexts. *Armed Forces & Society*, *44*(1), 25-43. https://doi.org/10.1177%2F0095327X16687069

[63] Breslin, R., Davis, E., Hylton, K., Hill, A., Klauberg, W., Petusky, M., & Klahr, A. (2019). *2018 Workplace and Gender Relations Survey of Active Duty Members: Overview Report*. Report No. 2019-027. Alexandria, VA: Office of People Analytics, 19. https://apps.dtic.mil/sti/citations/AD1072334

[64] Additionally, leaders should be reflexive and identify their own biases when addressing gender norms in military communities. For example, male leaders with stay-at-home wives may have more rigid ideas about gender about gender-appropriate roles and behaviors than female leaders or leaders with spouses actively employed in the labor force. Source: Kroska, A., & Elman, C. (2009). Change in attitudes about employed mothers: Exposure, interests, and gender ideology discrepancies. *Social Science Research*, *38*(2), 366-382. https://doi.org/10.1016/j.ssresearch.2008.12.004

[65] Unhealthy social norms—like "slut-shaming" sexually active women but applauding sexually active men—can lead to sexual harassment and sexual assault. Source: Endendijk, J.J., van Baar, A.L., & Deković, M. (2020). He is a stud, she is a slut! A meta-analysis on the continued existence of sexual double standards. *Personality and Social Psychology Review*, *24*(2), 163-190. https://doi.org/10.1177/1088868319891310

[66] Occupations and spaces that are highly male dominated (<10 percent women) may be more likely to have incidents of sexual harassment and sexual assault. Source: Pershing, J. L. (2006). Men and women's experiences with hazing in a male-dominated elite military institution. *Men and Masculinities*, *8*(4), 470-492. https://doi.org/10.1177%2F1097184X05277411

[67] DeKeseredy, W. S., Donnermeyer, J. F., & Schwartz, M. D. (2009). Toward a gendered second generation CPTED for preventing woman abuse in rural communities. *Security Journal*, *22*(3), 178-189. https://doi.org/10.1057/sj.2009.3

- Changing physical spaces to improve safety:
  - "Hot spot" mapping, i.e., identifying areas of buildings and spaces that are unsafe and in need of additional security, locks, cameras, or surveillance[68]
  - Creating well-lit areas, enhancing visibility, restricting access to buildings to specific personnel[69]
  - Removing dilapidated, old, or insecure housing and barracks
  - Training local bar and restaurant staff how to identify and intervene in cases of sexual harassment
- Altering laws and policies:
  - Creating simple and easy-to-use procedures for reporting incidents of stalking, sexual harassment, and unwanted attention[70]
  - Making policies that restrict Service members' movement into high-risk spaces and/or policies that encourage Service member activity in protective or communal spaces[71]
  - Legislating and approving laws and policies prohibiting or restricting the use or availability of alcohol
- Adopting better institutional practices:
  - More thorough onboarding procedures for Service members reporting to a new installation or location
  - Working with local police and women's shelters to understand local civilian risk and protective factors
  - Better methods of "letting off steam" and coping with stress that do not involve alcohol, such as recreational hobbies and fitness activities
  - Stronger leadership transitions (i.e., warm hand-offs, leadership transition period) that enable prevention programs and practices to be sustained across changes in command

Recommendation 2.3 b: USD(P&R) Should Identify a Non-clinical OSD-level Office of Primary Responsibility for Alcohol Policy and Develop Relevant Policy Guidance and Oversight

Currently, oversight for alcohol prevention within DoD is through Health Affairs, which provides a clinical/medical framework for alcohol abuse detection and treatment. Treatment of those with substance use disorder is important but does not address overconsumption or prevention of problem

---

[68] Weinborn, C., Ariel, B., Sherman, L.W., & O' Dwyer, E. (2017). Hotspots vs. harmspots: Shifting the focus from counts to harm in the criminology of place. *Applied Geography*, *86*, 226-244. https://doi.org/10.1016/j.apgeog.2017.06.009

[69] Cozens, P., & Love, T. (2015). A review and current status of crime prevention through environmental design (CPTED). *Journal of Planning Literature*, *30*(4), 393-412. https://doi.org/10.1177%2F0885412215595440

[70] Chamberlain, L.J., Crowley, M., Tope, D., & Hodson, R. (2008). Sexual harassment in organizational context. *Work and Occupations*, *35*(3), 262-295. https://doi.org/10.1177%2F0730888408322008

[71] Mustaine, E. E., & Tewksbury, R. (2002). Sexual assault of college women: A feminist interpretation of a routine activities analysis. *Criminal Justice Review*, *27*(1), 89-123. https://doi.org/10.1177/073401680202700106

drinking and associated behaviors. This recommendation requires that USD(P&R) begin to investigate alcohol policy, density, and availability across installations and Services. A need exists to identify a non-clinical Office of Primary Responsibility that can provide a public health perspective and an evidence-based policy approach to prevent alcohol overconsumption. Alcohol use creates a risk for sexual violence that may not reach the threshold for substance abuse yet may be effectively treated through evidence-based community-level alcohol policies. Addressing alcohol pricing and alcohol outlet density on and near military installations is an important part of a comprehensive, cross-cutting approach to sexual violence prevention.[72]

Correlation is Not Causation: The Role of Alcohol in Sexual Assault is Poorly Understood

Alcohol, by itself, does not cause sexual assault or sexual harassment to occur. In the 2018 Workplace Gender Relations Survey of Active Duty Members (WGRA), 52 percent of female survivors and 62 percent of male survivors reported *not* drinking at the time of their incidents. Which is to say, less than half of sexual assaults in the military involve alcohol.[73] Leaders must avoid blaming victims for sexual assault incidents regardless of alcohol use (e.g., chastising victims for drinking). In general, leaders should be cautious making assumptions about the connection between alcohol and sexual assault as current research on the topic is still evolving. In the last decade, civilian research examining alcohol use and sexual assault has shifted from examining victims' use of alcohol to perpetrators' use of alcohol.[74] The emerging literature on perpetration finds that "men who drink heavily in general and in dating and sexual situations commit more sexual assaults and more severe sexual assaults than other men."[75] This can be at least partially attributed to the fact that heavy drinking is a risk factor for many other forms of violence.[76] Some research has shown that heavy drinking serves an important habit or ritual for men who drink together to reaffirm bonds and social ties.[77] However, these male

[72] Lippy, C., & DeGue, S. (2016). Exploring alcohol policy approaches to prevent sexual violence perpetration. *Trauma, Violence, & Abuse, 17*(1), 26-42. https://doi.org/10.1177/1524838014557291

[73] Breslin, R., Davis, E., Hylton, K., Hill, A., Klauberg, W., Petusky, M., & Klahr, A. (2019). 2018 Workplace and Gender Relations Survey of Active Duty Members: Overview Report. Report No. 2019-027. Alexandria, VA: Office of People Analytics. https://apps.dtic.mil/sti/citations/AD1072334

[74] For example, see: Testa, M. & Cleveland, M.J. (2017). Does alcohol contribute to college men's sexual assault perpetration? Between-and within-person effects over five semesters. *Journal of Studies on Alcohol and Drugs, 78*(1), 5–13. https://doi.org/10.15288/jsad.2017.78.5

[75] Abbey, A., Wegner, R., Woerner, J., Pegram, S. E., & Pierce, J. (2014). Review of survey and experimental research that examines the relationship between alcohol consumption and men's sexual aggression perpetration. *Trauma, Violence & Abuse, 15*(4), 265–282. https://doi.org/10.1177/1524838014521031

[76] Cleveland, M.J., Testa, M., Hone, L.S.E. (2019). Examining the roles of heavy episodic drinking, drinking venues, and sociosexuality in college men's sexual aggression. *Journal of Studies on Alcohol and Drugs 80*(2), 177-185. https://doi.org/10.15288/jsad.2019.80.177

[77] West, L. A. (2001). Negotiating masculinities in American drinking subcultures. *The Journal of Men's Studies*, 9(3), 371-392. https://doi.org/10.3149/jms.0903.371

drinking rituals can encourage high-risk taking behaviors and impulsivity, delinquency, and social norms condoning forceful or violent sex.[78]

In short, heavy alcohol use may help "point" leaders and prevention practitioners towards the high-risk groups and high-risk individuals. However, there is a great deal more to know about how perpetrators opportunistically use alcohol for themselves and for victims to create risky situations.[79] Better alcohol policy oversight at the DoD level will allow the military to gain a deeper understanding of the problem and simultaneously address the problem with evidence-based policy guidance.

Broader Implications of Alcohol Use in the Military

Across the force, most Service members do not self-identify as heavy drinkers.[80] However, a significant proportion (about 10 percent) report dangerous levels of alcohol use. The 2018 DoD Health Related Behaviors Survey (HRBS) asked Service members about their perceptions of alcohol culture in the military—that is, whether respondents found it hard to "fit in" with their command if they did not drink, believed that drinking was part of being in one's unit, believed that everyone was encouraged to drink at social events, or believed that leaders were tolerant of drunkenness when personnel were off-duty.[81] Altogether, 28.2 percent of Service members agreed with at least one of these statements that military culture supports drinking. Thus, prevention and intervention efforts must take steps to shift the culture away from excessive use.

Moreover, limiting alcohol availability and density[82] may have important implications for suicide and intimate partner violence. Alcohol misuse and alcohol use disorders "are one of the main risk factors for suicidal behavior (i.e., death by suicide and suicide attempts)."[83] Alcohol is also a main risk factor for domestic violence and intimate partner violence.[84] In short, targeting alcohol use and misuse is a crucial component enabling primary prevention of *all* forms of sexual violence.

---

[78] Bushman, B.J., Bonacci, A.M., Van Dijk, M., & Baumeister, R.F. (2003). Narcissism, sexual refusal, and aggression: Testing a narcissistic reactance model of sexual coercion. *Journal of Personality and Social Psychology*, *84*(5), 1027. https://doi.org/10.1037/0022-3514.84.5.1027

[79] Johnson, S. A. (2017). Intoxicated perpetrators of sexual assault & rape know what they are doing despite intoxication: What the literature has to say. *Journal of Forensic Sciences & Criminal Investigation*, *1*(4). https://juniperpublishers.com/jfsci/pdf/JFSCI.MS.ID.555570.pdf

[80] Breslin, R., Davis, E., Hylton, K., Hill, A., Klauberg, W., Petusky, M., & Klahr, A. (2019). 2018 Workplace and Gender Relations Survey of Active Duty Members: Overview Report. Report No. 2019-027. Alexandria, VA: Office of People Analytics, 5. https://apps.dtic.mil/sti/citations/AD1072334

[81] DoD. (2018). *Department of Defense Health Related Behaviors Survey (HRBS): Results for the Active Component*. RAND Corporation. https://www.rand.org/pubs/research_briefs/RB10126.html

[82] This effort may need to involve civilian authorities such as local governments. Alcohol outlets near military installations are common and not under the control of DoD.

[83] Borges, G., Bagge, C., Cherpitel, C.J., Conner, K., Orozco, R., & Rossow, I. (2017). A meta-analysis of acute alcohol use and the risk of suicide attempt. *Psychological Medicine*, *47*(5), 949-957. https://doi.org/10.1017/S0033291716002841

[84] Results from four studies which investigated neighborhood-level alcohol outlet density and physical and sexual domestic violence victimization and perpetration showed that alcohol outlet density was associated with perpetration of physical domestic violence among women and with victimization and perpetration of physical domestic violence among men.

Implementation Considerations

USD(P&R) should ensure the Services and NGB have the most effective environmental assessment tool to aid community-level evaluation efforts to track progress relative to protective environments.[85] With the appropriate implementation and evaluation tools, the Services and National Guard should have their installations conduct recurring community-needs assessments and should use existing infrastructure to facilitate community-level approaches such as current military community forums and/or sponsorship programs.

Identifying an OPR for alcohol policy at the DoD level will ensure that the Services have the tools and technical assistance to implement DoDI 6400.09. USD(P&R) should develop a plan within six months, outlining establishment of a non-clinical office of primary responsibility for alcohol policy; including defining roles and responsibilities, authorities, resourcing, policy, and program standards, etc.[86] Implementation of this recommendation also includes collaborating with the Services and NGB to determine immediate and long-term research, policy, and program opportunities for alcohol policy (e.g. studies for alcohol density, marketing, pricing; how alcohol use and or abuse impacts perpetrators, victims, bystanders, etc.).

Outcome Metrics

Important metrics include:

- The proliferation and quality of military community forums to assist with creation, implementation, and evaluation of prevention;
- The quality of evidence-based community-level interventions (e.g., sponsorship programs; the use of promoting healthy social norms, and creating protective environments); and,
- Outcomes associated with implementation of relevant policies, such as: reduction in alcohol intoxication, alcohol-involved sexual violence, alcohol outlet density, and alcohol pricing incentives.

Recommendation 2.4: Modernize Prevention Education and Skill-building to Reflect Today's Generation of Service Members

The Services should modernize the content, delivery, and dosage of prevention knowledge and skill-building across the life-cycle development of Service members. Prevention messaging, practices, and

Research has also found that higher alcohol prices are associated with lower rates of domestic violence victimization in communities.

[85] The NGB for example has invested heavily in advanced analytics/machine learning model that leverages publicly available data (e.g., social determinants of health) and DoD aggregate data to determine risk and protective factors unique to a geographic area. This helps to inform decision making based on objective data.

[86] DoDI 6400.09, Section 4.4., "Substance Use" states: "DoD integrated primary prevention policies and programs will prevent substance misuse and abuse by working with community partners on responsible alcohol use."

programs must be tailored for the setting, prior traumas, current level knowledge, and be culturally competent for diverse populations. Some Service members enter the military with very limited sexual education or understanding of consent and healthy relationships. This lack of exposure and education for many Service members means that prevention topics are not universally understood across the DoD enterprise.

Rationale for this Change: Current Training is Out-dated & Out-of-Touch

The current method of developing prevention knowledge and building prevention skills for Service members is insufficient. In fact, information gathering sessions revealed the content, dosage, and delivery have all contributed to a dearth of prevention knowledge and skills across the military. The one-size-fits-all approach used to conduct annual training has not contributed to a growth in primary prevention knowledge and skills, but rather an exhaustion and exasperation with the topic.[87] Instead of repeating definitions of consent and/or telling individual Service members, "Don't Rape," effective prevention knowledge and skills must target audiences…for example, some audiences would receive content such as basic sexual education knowledge and respecting healthy relationship boundaries.

To achieve success with prevention, Services must increase the uptake and retention of essential knowledge and skills for the prevention of sexual violence and the continuum of harm. This requires prioritized attention on the content (i.e., curriculum/material), delivery (i.e., methods used to impart knowledge and or skills), and dosage (i.e., frequency and timing of knowledge development or skill building). Figure 5 describes the optimal content, delivery, and dosage of prevention learning activities.

[87] The quality of current sexual harassment and sexual assault prevention training can vary widely across the Services. Moreover, existing SAPR trainings—which in theory should incorporate prevention—are heavily response-focused with limited content on primary prevention.

Requirement	Description
Content	• Content should incorporate **current public health science** on online dating, sexting, and hookup culture, **real world examples** to facilitate case-based learning, and **evidence-informed interventions**. • A holistic strength-based approach is needed to prioritize sexual assault prevention within healthy relationship and healthy masculinity education. • Content should be **tailored to the experience, skill, and knowledge-level of the individual**. A Service member with minimal sexual education knowledge or with a history of childhood sexual abuse will have different training and skill needs. Likewise, a Service member in his or her fifth deployment will need different skills than a newly deployed Service member.
Delivery	• **New technologies and techniques** should be used to tailor the delivery of knowledge development and skill-building to meet Service members' needs, rather than presenting a "one-size-fits-all" approach. • **Small group discussions can be productive** for understanding basic prevention topics while online or self-paced courses can ensure privacy and confidentiality for highly sensitive topics (e.g., previous traumas)
Dosage	• Education content should be **front-loaded for junior officers and enlisted personnel** to build skills and increase knowledge with appropriate dosages to sustain transformation in the field as these members move into leadership positions while avoiding training fatigue. • **Adult learning principles** should be incorporated to ensure knowledge is retained. Adult learning principles engage learners through shorter, case-based, bidirectional skill building sessions throughout the year.

Figure 5. Content, Delivery, and Dosage Requirements to Build Prevention Knowledge

Annual Training Requirements Do Not Build Primary Prevention Skills

Current sexual assault prevention and response trainings are redundant and unengaging.[88] Annual training requirements and standard lectures do not build primary prevention skills or change behavior related to sexual assault and sexual harassment prevention in the military. As one Service member stated, "We have these SHARP classes all the time, it's still the same, same, same, over and over and over again…I fall asleep with the rest of the Soldiers."

Similar themes emerged during other information gathering sessions. One Service member commented, "We need to get rid of battalion-sized briefs…." Battalion-sized briefs are not going to train, or they might train [Service members] on information [SARC, DoD Safe Helpline, etc.], but they are not going to teach Soldiers how to be human beings."

Some Service Members Lack Basic Sexual Education Knowledge

Some Service members enter the military with very limited sexual education, while others begin their time in service with more experience and nuanced knowledge. As one prevention expert explained,

[88] DoD SAPRO. (2020). *Fiscal Year 2019 Annual Report on Sexual Assault in the Military*. https://www.sapr.mil/sites/default/files/DOD_Annual_Report_on_Sexual_Assault_In_The_Military_FY2019_Consolidated.pdf

"The amount of human healthy sexuality and sexual health education that they received is so varied from state to state. Some have come to us with nothing." According to the CDC, only 41.3 percent of U.S. schools teach curricula based on the National Sex Education Standards.[89,90,91] As a foundation for sexual violence primary prevention, basic education on sexuality, relationships, and sexual health is needed across the force, including instruction on topics such as common sexual scenarios, sexual entitlement, boundaries, and consent.

Methods of communicating about sex and intimacy should also be addressed in basic sexual education. Specifically, Service members must understand that communication will vary across the domains of work, home, and personal life.[92] Effective communication in one sphere (e.g., work) will not make for effective communication in another sphere (e.g., private life). As one Service member explained, "We work in an environment where toxic masculinity traits are valued. Where the person who is extra driven, doesn't take no for an answer – that person is valued. But those same traits don't make for a good partner or friend." Service members must grasp that social-emotional intelligence—e.g., checking in with one's partner and "taking no" for an answer—is a critical skill for preventing sexual assault.

Service Members Want SAPR Training that is Relatable

In 2019, DoD focus group participants said that prevention training should be more relatable and tailored to Service members' needs and developmental stage, using small group discussions to make the content more engaging for Service members. The IRC heard the same comments from Service members during their information gathering sessions. One SARC emphasized, "Give real life scenarios" that grab Service members' attention. Another SARC added, "Sailors like real life stories," i.e., narratives of events that could actually happen to them during their time in the military. A consistent theme was the need to make sexual assault prevention training content relevant for everyone, using real-life examples from local or recent events.

Information sessions revealed that there is also a present gap between current training topics and Service members' questions and concerns around sex. As one Service member explained, "it's not just drinking and or dating advice. We have a lot of Soldiers who just want to go out and meet someone for the night or just do something for a one-time thing." In short, education like marital advice or how to remain in long-term monogamous relationships will not resonate with 18-year-old

---

[89] CDC. (2016). *Results from the School Health Policies and Practices Study*. https://www.cdc.gov/healthyyouth/data/shpps/pdf/shpps-results_2016.pdf.

[90] The goal of the National Sex Education Standards (NSES) is to provide clear, consistent, and straightforward guidance on the essential, minimum, core content and skills needed for sex education that is age-appropriate for students in grades K–12 to be effective. Source: Future of Sex Education. (2020). *National Sex Education Standards: Core Content and Skills, K-12 (Second Edition)*, 7. http://www.advocatesforyouth.org/wp-content/uploads/2020/05/NSES-2020-web.pdf

[91] NSES consists of seven topic areas: Consent and Healthy Relationships, Anatomy and Physiology, Puberty & Adolescent Sexual Development, Gender Identity and Expression, Sexual Orientation and Identity, Sexual Health, and Interpersonal Violence. Source: Ibid.

[92] This may be particularly challenging for Service members whose work, home, and personal lives overlap or intertwine, particularly in a deployed environment.

Service members more interested in short-term, or one-off sexual encounters. Online dating poses additional challenges not captured in current SAPR trainings. As one Service member noted, "The thing about Tinder is, it's portrayed as a site for you to meet someone for a hookup, so we're again where someone [online] might think that I'm meeting someone [for sex]...but how do you identify whether or not someone is saying yes or no? Like, 'cause nobody's gonna to say, 'Hey, yes, let's go out and have sex.' It's not just that cut and dry...I don't know if 4-stars and 3-stars are paying attention to that kind of dating platform." Indeed, several SAPR program managers highlighted a "generation gap" between senior leaders and incoming Service members. Young adults entering the military are likely more sexually adventurous and/or sexually open to new experiences than older leaders who—more often than not—are married with children.

Service members need better guidance on social media, texting communication (e.g., sexting), and support identifying negative behaviors and language over texting to help them navigate the modern dating world in a healthy and respectful manner. As one Service member said, "we need the do's and don'ts for using Tinder." Different educational content is needed for every stage of a Service member's life cycle in the military, from flirting, online dating, casual sex, relationship-building, intimacy, communication, and beyond.

Current Training is Not Effectively Delivered, Nor Appropriately Dosed

Civilian literature also shows the long-term positive effects of small group education programs on preventing adolescent dating violence.[93] While the military's current "one-size-fits-all" approach to prevention knowledge is not effective, the IRC heard several instances of promising small-group prevention programs across the Services. For example, the Air Force is currently exploring tailored training approaches that initially gauge an Airman's level of knowledge and then provide the right "level" of education to build upon that knowledge. In short, someone with little to no knowledge receives the bare basics, while someone with more in-depth knowledge receives more complex concepts and ideas. In another example, a Marine Corps program featured small group discussions where Service members of all ranks participated out of uniform and shared a wide variety of personal experiences. Evaluation feedback from these discussions was very positive.

While the Services have begun to do away with standardized PowerPoint lectures, there has been little education for SAPR personnel on *how* to teach prevention education. For example, one senior leader noted, "We've gone away from the PowerPoint...you know what we've always gotten back is, hey, we hate PowerPoint. Don't do PowerPoint, so the guidance that we provided to leaders is stop doing PowerPoint, but we've never come back and said, here's what right?" In short, critiques of current trainings are useful, but ultimately the Services need actionable guidance on what *works* regarding prevention education, instead of lectures on what "not" to do. Prevention training should be front-

---

[93] Foshee, V., Bauman, K., Ennett, S., Linder, G., Benefield, T., & Suchindran, C. (2004). Assessing the long-term effects of the safe dates program and a booster in preventing and reducing adolescent dating violence victimization and perpetration. *American Journal of Public Health*, *94*(4), 619–624. https://doi.org/10.2105/ajph.94.4.619

loaded for junior officers and enlisted personnel to build skills and increase knowledge—building from the "ground up"—with appropriate dosages to sustain transformation in the field as these members move into leadership positions.

An important way to increase primary prevention skills and change behaviors related to sexual assault is to introduce adult learning theory principles. Educational theory has also evolved over the last two decades, increasing the knowledge base on adult learning optimization. Sessions with prevention experts in the Services relayed that existing prevention efforts in the military do not apply the well-established Principles of Effective Prevention Programs.[94,95] These general principles gleaned from effective interventions may help military prevention personnel plan and implement more effective programs.

Implementation Considerations

The Services and NGB should collaborate with public and private organizations focused on cutting edge solutions to modernize the content, delivery, and dosage of prevention knowledge development and skill building. Also, injecting DoD evidence-based best practices into prevention curricula would enable the Services and NGB to provide Service members the most effective and efficient learning experiences across their life cycle of development.[96]

Delivering more personalized education experience will require increased resources, such as the cost of people being away more from day-to-day mission responsibilities, the cost of technology, and the cost of sustaining multiple versions of programs, to name a few. DoD should consider pursuing and scaling up the Air Force research project, "Personalized Training for Optimal Acquisition and Sustainment of Performance," focused on leveraging machine learning to determine the personalized uptake and retention of information.[97]

Additionally, the Services and National Guard should stop doing what is not working. First, the Services and Guard need to identify ineffective trainings. Trainings that create frustration, boredom, and antagonism often do more harm than good. While implementing evidence-based approaches may be time and resource-consuming and challenging at first, they are well worth the effort to build prevention knowledge and skills over time.

---

[94] Nation, M., Crusto, C., Wandersman, A., Kumpfer, K.L., Seybolt, D., Morrissey-Kane, E., & Davino, K. (2003). What works in prevention: Principles of effective prevention programs. *American Psychologist*, *58*(6-7), 449–456. https://doi.org/10.1037/0003-066x.58.6-7.449

[95] The nine characteristics consistently associated with effective prevention programs include that programs were comprehensive, included varied teaching methods, provided sufficient dosage, were theory driven, provided opportunities for positive relationships, were appropriately timed, were socio-culturally relevant, included outcome evaluation, and involved well-trained staff.

[96] See Recommendation 2.6 on DoD prevention research.

[97] See Jastrzembski, T.S., Walsh, M., Krusmark, M., Kardong-Edgren, S., Oermann, M., Dufour, K., & Stefanidis, D. (2017, January 1). Personalizing training to acquire and sustain competence through use of a cognitive model. In *International conference on augmented cognition*: 148-161. Springer, Cham.

Outcome Metrics

Key metrics include:

- Shifts in attitudes towards prevention education (e.g., focus groups show that Service members are neutral or positive towards prevention education instead of openly hostile or negative to prevention education);
- Increase knowledge of consent, healthy and respectful relationships, and sexual health;
- Increased skills related to communication, respectful relationships, conflict resolution, consent, and bystander intervention;
- Reduced risk factors associated with perpetration, including adherence to traditional gender roles, hostility toward women, and male endorsement of aggression;
- Reduced prevalence across the spectrum of sexual violence and the continuum of harm; and,
- Percentage of prevention programs/activities with/without scientific basis.

Recommendation 2.5: Identify and Actively Support Service Members with the Most Effective Prevention Interventions

In addition to community-level interventions (see Recommendation 2.3), effective primary prevention also must involve targeted strategies and interventions at the individual-level. Recommendation 2.5 a requires the Services test and evaluate individual-level interventions for individuals who may be at higher risk of sexual violence, such as individuals with exposure to trauma during childhood. Recommendation 2.5 b outlines another individual-level intervention: creating additional online resources and virtual platforms promoting Service member connectivity and sense of inclusion.

- 2.5 a: The Services and the NGB should institute a pilot program to link Service members with resources and support and,
- 2.5 b: The Services and the NGB should employ virtual platforms to provide support to all Service members.

Rationale for these Changes: High-Risk Service Members Need Support

Given that individuals with Adverse Childhood Experiences (ACEs)[98] may face higher future adverse outcomes (including sexual assault), this recommendation addresses the importance of bolstering protective factors by offering voluntary behavioral health and wellness resources to Service members, as a preventative measure. Early assessments can enable connecting Service members with the support they need as they begin their careers. Additionally, virtual platforms can provide accessible,

---

[98] Centers for Disease Control and Prevention. (2021, April 6). *Preventing Adverse Childhood Experiences.* https://www.cdc.gov/violenceprevention/aces/fastfact.html

anonymous support to help Service members connect to community members as well as referral services.

Recommendation 2.5. a: The Services and NGB Should Institute a Pilot Program to Link Service Members with Resources and Support

Adverse childhood experiences (ACEs) can range from sexual abuse within the family, to household dysfunction, such as living in a household with substance misuse, mental health, or instability due to parental separation or incarceration; or witnessing violence in the home or community. Such traumas can lead to long-term health consequences like self-harm, violence to others, and victimization.[99]

However, evidence has shown that potential negative outcomes due to ACEs can be mitigated or prevented by identification and interventions. This recommendation is about assessing ACEs and coupling it with a deeper understanding of social determinants of health (i.e., environmental conditions where people work, live, and play that affect a range of quality-of-life outcomes and risks) to connect Service members with care and services. This can decrease the likelihood of future adverse outcomes (including sexual assault) and increase the likelihood of a successful career, improved health outcomes, and safer communities. Civilian studies of ACEs demonstrate how traumas are linked to chronic health problems, substance misuse, and mental health problems as well as other mission detracting behaviors.

The Services should implement a pilot program that proactively assesses new Service members for pre-existing risk factors such as prior trauma exposure and social determinants of health and provides preventative support to at-risk Service members.[100] Such information must be used only as an assessment tool to connect Service members with needed resources, not as a diagnostic measure. This assessment is only intended to empower Service members to successfully continue serving in their careers, by bolstering protective factors. Long-term impact of trauma exposure such as ACEs can be successfully decreased, but this needs to be done in a thoughtful and concerted manner.

About 61 percent of adults surveyed across 25 states reported that they had experienced at least one type of ACE, and nearly 1 in 6 reported they had experienced four or more types of ACEs.[101] Multiple

---

[99] Nelson, C.A., Bhutta, Z.A., Harris, N.B., Danese, A., & Samara, M. (2020). Adversity in childhood is linked to mental and physical health throughout life. *BMJ*, *371*, m3048.

[100] Social determinants of health (SDOH) have a major impact on people's health, well-being, and quality of life. Examples of SDOH include: (1) Safe housing, transportation, and neighborhoods, (2) Racism, discrimination, and violence, (3) Education, job opportunities, and income, (4) Access to nutritious foods and physical activity opportunities. (5) Polluted air and water and (6) Language and literacy skills. SDOH also contribute to wide health disparities and inequities. Source: Department of Health and Human Services. (n.d.). *Social Determinants of Health.* https://health.gov/healthypeople/objectives-and-data/social-determinants-health

[101] Centers for Disease Control and Prevention. (2021, April 6). *Preventing Adverse Childhood Experiences*. https://www.cdc.gov/violenceprevention/aces/fastfact.html

studies have found that Service members have a significantly higher prevalence of ACEs compared to those without military service.

Assessments May Address Current Needs of Incoming Recruits

In information gathering sessions with accessions instructors, drill sergeants and officers explained that *many* incoming recruits have histories of prior trauma. As part of basic training, recruits receive an in-depth SAPR class including the definitions of sexual assault and sexual harassment. As one drill instructor explained, new recruits often recognize trauma from their past when they hear this information. The instructors further explained that, after that "light-bulb" moment, recruits are frequently distraught, upset, and in need of support. However, drill sergeants have limited means to support their recruits in that moment of basic training. One sergeant noted that she explicitly tells her recruits, "Don't tell us because we are obligated to immediately report it." While this may sound callous, she explained to the IRC that reporting prior-to-service incidents usually triggered an unhelpful and long bureaucratic process for the recruit.

Instead of reporting prior-to-service incidents to the drill sergeants, recruits call the SAPR hotline. As one instructor noted, "After that in-depth class [we] have a line of recruits out at the office wanting to make a call to the SAPR hotline." In short, the military needs a systematic method of dealing with Service members' previous traumas—one that connects incoming Service members with genuine care and support.

Recommendation 2.5 b: The Services and NGB Should Employ Virtual Platforms to Provide Support to all Service Members

The Services and NGB should employ virtual platforms to provide support to all Service members, including those with prior trauma exposure or case management needs. These platforms should be created with the goals of increasing Service members' sense of belonging, connectedness, and inclusion as well as referral and support for mental health, substance misuse, and trauma to prevent and reduce sexual harassment and assault. In alignment with the IRC's Victim Care and Support effort, Recommendation 2.5 b seeks to leverage mobile applications and improved online content for Service members seeking help and community.

Virtual Platforms Provide Accessible, Anonymous Support

Today's military is younger and more tech savvy than ever, with about 46 percent of Active Duty Service members being 25 years or younger.[102] This recommendation aims to build upon the existent technologies and platforms available to Service members to create more online communities. Telehealth availability for behavioral health (including victim advocacy for sexual assault) was enabled across the Services in various installations and through diverse platforms as providers adapted to the

[102] DoD. (2018). *2018 Demographics Profile of the Military Community.* https://download.militaryonesource.mil/1238/MOS/Reports/2018-demographics-report.pdf

COVID-19 pandemic. These services, however, are not consistently available across the force. Providing the technology (e.g. professionally issued devices) to installation service providers, is critical.

The military already has several examples of impactful mobile applications that have enhanced readiness.[103] In one such example, an Air Force Reserve unit rolled out a mobile application to several squadrons across the Reserve base. The app was designed to maximize Unit Training Assembly (UTA) preparedness. Reservists often only enter military installations once a month and maximum preparedness is a huge priority for commanders. The mobile app solution prioritized communicating news and training, sharing important documents, assigning and managing tasks, and delivering lifesaving help and resources. The pilot resulted in a marked increase in the consumption of information and compliance with assigned tasks. The app also saw substantial growth over the pilot lifetime, which lead to consistent increases in productivity that drastically improved UTA preparedness.

Another example of a successful application is the Kinetic Virtual Resilience Center (VRC), developed by Deskless Workers, which allows for content that fits the needs of each installation community. The VRC is built to help Service members and their families with the difficulties and stresses of military life including family assistance, mental health, childcare, suicide prevention, sexual assault and more. The Kinetic app also helps SARC's distribute content to base members on sexual assault prevention, detection, and response. These successful cases of applications demonstrate that virtual platforms work and should be leveraged more often in primary prevention efforts.[104]

Implementation Considerations

Recommendation 2.5 a: Pilot Program to Link Service Members with Resources & Support

Information about individuals collected under this program should not be shared with any other military or civilian agencies or institutions and should be used only to provide voluntary support services for individuals. All reporting, including aggregate reports, should not include any personally identifying information about participants. If the Secretary of Defense determines that a privilege covering this information should be established to ensure the necessary protections, the Secretary should draft and propose such a privilege.

The New Mexico Army National Guard (NMANG) is one of the three state National Guards that implemented a proactive case management pilot program. Although evidence is still preliminary and

---

[103] The Air Force is also studying implementation of a tailored tablet-and classroom instruction-based program previously tested at Air Force Basic Training and now being implemented and tested at the Air Force Academy.

[104] Telehealth availability for behavioral health (including victim advocacy for sexual assault) was enabled across the Services in various installations and through diverse platforms as providers adapted to the COVID-19 pandemic. These services, however, are not consistently available across the force. Providing the technology (e.g., professionally issued devices) to installation service providers is critical).

small in sample size, the initial screening, performing follow-up phone calls or surveys, and the provision of immediate resources may reduce the number of Service members who become future clinical cases. The NMANG found that the best parameters for identifying at-risk Service members and predicting future clinical cases are Service members that have a high number of ACEs and test highly on the Global Appraisal of Individual Needs-Short Screener (GAIN-SS).[105] Using these parameters in a broad risk model, the NMANG flagged 66 percent of all recruits as being at risk and accurately predicted 75 percent of Soldiers and Airmen who required more intensive management, with no adverse outcomes from participation.

Recommendation 2.5 b: Enable Virtual Support Platforms

To implement this policy, Services and NGB should develop and disseminate policy and guidance that outlines and directs operationalizing a pilot to link Service members to resources. Policy considerations should address the required workforce and resources, administration of the assessment, and data and records management. Policy should also provide guidance for collaborative relationships that may provide additional capabilities to support individuals that require assistance with substance use counselors, recovery programs, etc.

The Services should consult with the DoD Office of General Counsel to ensure policies and precautionary measures for implementation of the intake assessment. Also, the IRC recommends each Service collaborate with NGB for lessons learned and to tailor and implement pilots; and should re-evaluate progress within one year based on referrals, retention, and improvements in functioning measured on standardized quality of life assessments.

The Services and NGB should also support research, development, evaluation, adoption, and dissemination of virtual platforms that increase Service members' protective factors and decrease risk factors (e.g. increase a sense of belonging, connectedness, and inclusion, and/or provide referral and support services for mental health, substance misuse, and trauma).

Outcome Metrics

Some of the metrics to assess the success of implementing this recommendation are:

- Achievement of pilot linking Service members to resources;
- Evaluations of negative outcomes associated specifically with the assessment;
- Quality of life in follow-on assessments; and,
- Measures of connectedness and belonging from virtual platforms.

---

[105] Dennis, M., Feeney, T., Stevens, L., & Bedoya, L. (2008). *Global Appraisal of Individual Needs–Short Screener (GAIN-SS): Administration and Scoring Manual Version 2.0.3.* https://dpi.wi.gov/sites/default/files/imce/sspw/pdf/gainssmanual.pdf

Recommendation 2.6: Create a State-of-the-Art DoD Prevention Research Capability

The current state of DoD's primary prevention research underscores the need for the Department to develop a Research Center capability with the authority and responsibility for development, execution, and oversight of a robust strategic research agenda. Under the umbrella of this research, this recommendation also recognizes that the removal of policy barriers and restrictions (e.g., restrictions preventing research on sexual assault perpetration) would increase opportunities for achieving necessary research to inform decision-making across the Department.

- 2.6 a: DoD establish a dedicated Research Center for the primary prevention of sexual harassment, sexual assault and other forms of interpersonal and self-directed violence;
- 2.6 b: USD(P&R), the Services, and the NGB continually review and update all policies that unnecessarily restrict data collection on important populations of Service members;
- 2.6 c: The Secretary of Defense immediately authorize operational testing of the Air Force Compatibility Assessment with a cross-Service pre-accession sample, allowing for important research and intervention development; and,
- 2.6 d: USD(P&R) should commission research on gender and masculinities to develop effective social marketing strategies to facilitate primary prevention efforts.

Rationale for these Changes: Research is Necessary to Know What Works

Current DoD research on sexual harassment and sexual assault is diffused and poorly disseminated, leading to limited returns on research investments. As a result, decision makers lack research-informed prevention solutions. Moreover, the implementation and impact of policies are largely unknown, and the majority of prevention practices are either untested or ineffective. Failure to disseminate research findings across agencies has resulted in duplication of research efforts over time. Epidemiological studies, conducted to build knowledge and fully understand the causal processes that lead to sexual violence, are at times inaccessible or unavailable to military practitioners.

Without a robust research infrastructure supporting new data and analysis efforts, and recurring reviews and removal of policy barriers, the Department and the Services will continue to struggle to know what "works" in prevention. As one commander stressed, "We don't really have a good assessment tool to see ourselves. It's really important to see down to the small unit level if we have issues, right?" Which is to say, the Services lack the research and data capabilities necessary to evaluate whether their prevention programs and policies result in the intended effect of reducing sexual harassment and sexual assault. Without evaluation—made possible by research—prevention progress cannot be "seen" by commanders and leaders.

Recommendation 2.6 a: DoD Establish a Dedicated Research Center for the Primary Prevention of Interpersonal and Self-directed Violence

An entirely new DoD Research Center capability, singularly dedicated to prevention, would adopt innovative methodologies from diverse academic fields (e.g., not only public health but behavioral economics, sociology, psychology, anthropology, etc.) to gain a deeper understanding of prevention science in the military context. The Center would address the cross-cutting nature of primary prevention, not only incorporating sexual harassment and sexual assault but also suicide, substance misuse, and intimate partner violence.[106] The Center would also incorporate research on secondary and tertiary prevention to fill gaps in knowledge on response processes and systems.[107] Additionally, this capability would help overcome the lack of data on perpetration, victimization, risk and protective factors specific to the military population; provide a system that builds foundational primary prevention knowledge for the Services' use; support rigorous evaluations of Service-level prevention activities, and ensure consistent and reliable resourcing.

Limited Data from Perpetrators and Units of Analysis Larger than the Individual

Over the last ten years, the existing portfolio of DoD-funded research has been limited in scope because research has been driven primarily by external factors, such as Congressional mandates which are heavily response-focused. Studies rely heavily on administrative records for usage of victim services and self-report surveys assessing victimization. Limited data from perpetrators, leaders, peers, and units of analysis larger than the individual (e.g., teams, squads, wings, boats, ships, brigades, communities, installations, etc.) limits the current understanding of the full spectrum of sexual assault prevention. Moreover, there is little to no research on sexual harassment prevention within the Department.[108, 109]

The Need for Transparency and Sharing of Research Results

Additionally, results from current research efforts in the Services are not shared across the enterprise. Results from "applied" studies—testing a particular practice or intervention—usually conducted at

---

[106] The Center would provide the foundation knowledge, data, and analytics relevant for the effective oversight and implementation of DoDI 6400.09.

[107] For examples of gaps in sexual harassment and sexual assault response research, see the current DoD SAPR Research Agenda. Source: DoD SAPRO. (2020). *FY21-FY25 Research Agenda.* https://www.sapr.mil/sites/default/files/public/docs/research/FY21-25_DoD_SAPR_Research_Agenda_FINAL.pdf

[108] In addition, the majority of research does not capture social trends and processes occurring at the interactional, team, unit, community, or organizational levels.

[109] In 2020, the DoD published the first ever DoD Sexual Assault Prevention and Response Research Agenda which identifies ten research priorities. The agenda guides and informs SAPR research across the Department but is not directive in nature or enforceable. Additionally, although the various forms of sexual violence share common risk and protective factors, the current research agenda is not integrated (e.g., inclusive of suicide, substance misuse), and therefore misses important opportunities to discover or test cross-cutting interventions.

the Service or installation-level, are not shared upwards to headquarters or Department level researchers. This bifurcation results in problematic "silos" of research: academic, public-health research at higher echelons of the military on the one hand, and, intuitive "guesses" at best practices by commanders and SARCs/VPIs at lower echelons of the military on the other hand. This lack of transparency produces a variety of military prevention policies, programs, and practices in disparate places and at various stages of development with little to no evaluation framework across the Services.

Advancing Capabilities and Processes

The new Prevention Research Center would support consolidation of required approvals for violence prevention research; while streamlining and expediting potentially lengthy processes such as Institutional Review Boards (IRB), survey control numbering, and Office of Management and Budget (OMB) requirements. As one SME explained to the IRC, "We have limited analytics and data, we have human research protection programs…we have the IRB, the process will take 18 months to get a survey or focus group, through that process." Institutional Review Boards—intended to protect human subjects during research processes—often follow regulations and strict guidelines designed for the medical testing of drugs and pharmaceuticals. Following common practices in academia, social science research (e.g., surveys, interviews, etc.), should undergo different, more expedited approvals.

Lastly, a DoD Prevention Research Center would also provide the infrastructure and oversight capability to sustain many of the other larger recommendations offered in this paper, including leadership competencies, a credentialed prevention workforce, and more modernized prevention education.

Recommendation 2.6 b: USD(P&R), the Services, and NGB Should Continually Review and Update All Policies that Unnecessarily Restrict Data Collection on Important Populations of Service Members

Removal of restrictive policies on sensitive data collection can advance primary prevention of sexual assault and sexual harassment in the military across numerous important populations. Gay and bisexual men in the military experience sexual assault at a rate nine times higher than heterosexual men. Lesbian and bisexual Service women are sexually assaulted at double the rate of heterosexual Service women.[110] Prevention research on these important populations must not be restricted.

Urgency of Research on Perpetration

Existing legal concerns within the Department have limited the types of questions and inquiries available for research. Distinct causal processes drive victimization versus perpetration. To date, the

---

[110] Morral, A.R. & Schell, T.L. (2021). Sexual Assault of Sexual Minorities in the U.S. Military. Santa Monica, CA: RAND Corporation. https://www.rand.org/pubs/research_reports/RRA1390-1.html

Department has exclusively focused on victimization.[111] However, without complementary research on perpetration—and the unique risk and protective factors that lead to perpetration—the military only has half of the total information needed to paint the full picture of how and why sexual assault occurs in the military. As a result, the impact of prevention activities in military communities, particularly activities aimed at reducing perpetration, remains relatively unknown.

Research for Specific Populations

Sexual minorities in the military face higher risks of sexual harassment and sexual assault than heterosexual individuals.[112] To date, a policy memo from 2011[113] restricts Service-level research on these populations, requiring all research entities to receive DoD approval for LGBTQ+ data collection.[114] While intended to protect the privacy of Service members who faced discharge during Don't Ask, Don't Tell, this bureaucratic hurdle remains an obstacle for prevention experts and other researchers who wish to study the unique risks and experiences of LGBTQ+ Service members.

Service-level research institutions are also wary of having data on Service members' sexuality, gender identity, or transgender status. Depending on the Administration—specifically, the governing party's policies toward LGBTQ+ individuals—the Services do not want to be forced to report names of such individuals if requested. However, legal protections could be made to restrict the use of such data. Moreover, anonymous surveys automatically provide such protections while still enabling research on these specific populations.

Recommendation 2.6 c: The Secretary of Defense Should Immediately Authorize Operational Testing of the Air Force Compatibility Assessment with a Cross-Service Pre-Accession Sample, Allowing for Important Research and Intervention Development

An accessions compatibility instrument administered prior to Military Service entry could provide DoD an understanding of the nature, magnitude, risk, and protective factors for Service members who perpetrate behaviors on the continuum of harm against other Service members, civilians, and

---

111 The need to gather data on perpetration was emphasized in many IRC working group meetings as an urgent research gap for the Department and the Services.

112 According to the 2018 WGRA, lesbian, gay, and bisexual (LGB) Service members face an increased risk of sexual harm and sexual violence. Among LGB women, an estimated 9.0 percent experienced sexual assault in 2018—a significant increase from 6.3 percent of LGB women in 2016. Among LGB men, an estimated 3.7 percent experienced sexual assault in 2018—about the same rate as observed in 2016—compared to 0.4 percent of non-LGB Service men.

113 USD(P&R). (2011, January 28). *Memorandum for the Secretaries of the Military Departments: Repeal of Don't Ask Don't Tell and Future Impact on Policy*. Department of Defense. https://archive.defense.gov/home/features/2010/0610_dadt/USD-PR-DADT_28Jan11.pdf

114 To clarify, DoD currently collects data on gender (excluding transgender or non-binary Service members) and sexual orientation. This recommendation seeks to enable and encourage research on LGBTQ+ Service members at the Service-branch level (e.g., Department of the Army, Department of the Navy, and research institutions aligned with the Services).

family members. The Air Force Compatibility Assessment (AFCA) is already in development and simply needs approval from senior leaders. The IRC recommends DoD authorize testing AFCA as a pilot with a cross-Service pre-accession sample to better understand the characteristics of new accessions for two key purposes: 1) to inform the future development of an evidence-based accessions instrument; and, 2) to inform DoD and the Services about risk factors among the military population, to guide the selection, adaptation, or development of prevention approaches.

How Much Perpetration Risk is the Department Accessing Daily?

The most effective way to prevent victimization is to prevent perpetration. However, the Department lacks sufficient data to make evidence-based decisions in this domain. Currently, the military does not know how much perpetration risk the Department is assuming every day someone joins the military. Legal and methodological barriers prevent a full picture understanding of perpetration in a military context. Legislation could more appropriately address these issues.

> "The military does not know how much perpetration risk the Department is assuming every day someone joins the military."
>
> - Former Commander & Prevention Expert

Currently, the Department relies on victims' reports of perpetrator characteristics or data from suspected and/or convicted offenders. This paints an incomplete picture of the behaviors, attitudes, and beliefs that create risk for sexual harassment and sexual assault, particularly in the military context. The Department would increase its understanding of modifiable risk and protective factors for offenders, which would inform targeted intervention and rehabilitation efforts. While challenges exist with conducting this sensitive research, the cost of failing to stop problematic lower level behaviors (e.g., bullying, non-touching sexual harassment offenses) is too high to ignore.[115] The IRC fully understands the Department's legal concerns in using any compatibility instruments as grounds for exclusion to the military without further due diligence.[116] Legal concerns regarding privacy can be addressed by anonymity, confidentiality of survey data, and other industry standards for research protections that DoD currently leverages when gathering data on illicit or sensitive behaviors.

---

[115] These lower-level behaviors often escalate to produce more violent behaviors over time (e.g., sexual assault).

[116] Legal concerns regarding privacy can be addressed by anonymity, confidentiality of survey data, and other industry standards for research protections that DoD currently leverages when gathering data on illicit or sensitive behaviors.

Recommendation 2.6 d: USD(P&R) Should Commission Research on Gender and Masculinities to Develop Effective Social Marketing Strategies to Facilitate Primary Prevention Efforts

Social marketing has been established by the CDC as an effective model for behavioral change on key public health issues.[117,118] While traditional social marketing efforts have targeted health, environmental protection, and public safety concerns (e.g., condom-use, breastfeeding, wearing seatbelts), new social marketing techniques can be developed to reduce sexual harassment and sexual assault in specific populations. Importantly, social marketing ensures that all forms of sexual harassment and sexual assault communications and messaging are credible and convincing to their audience.[119] Social marketing strategies help frame new behaviors in ways that "make sense" and engage the targeted population. Different populations will require different communication and messaging approaches. Furthermore, social marketing strategies will enrich the knowledge development and skill-building activities outlined in Recommendation 2.4.

All social marketing techniques must emerge directly from robust communication and behavioral social science research. The new DoD Prevention Research Center will have the capacity to conduct the research required to develop different social marketing strategies, which the Services can then adapt and adopt for use. Researchers have already identified specific gaps in prevention within the military environment, including but not limited to:

- Healthy masculinities and culturally competent bystander intervention tactics;
- Perpetrator characteristics and patterns of behavior (see Recommendation 2.6 c);
- Hierarchies of masculinities as they relate to sexual violence, including problematic definitions of strength (e.g., strength defined as domination of others, including sexual domination), and the use of violence as a viable method to solve everyday problems; and,
- Social influencers within Service members' social networks (e.g., how social influencers promote and spread rape myths).

Researching these topics may be a time-consuming process, yet essential to building the knowledge foundation necessary to gaining Service member buy-in and allyship for prevention across Services

---

[117] CDC. (2021). *Building Our Understanding: Social Marketing on a Dime, Using Social Media to Do More with Less*. https://www.cdc.gov/nccdphp/dch/programs/healthycommunitiesprogram/tools/pdf/social_marketing.pdf

[118] CDC Division of Nutrition, Physical Activity, and Obesity. (2021). *Strategy 8. Social Marketing*. https://www.cdc.gov/breastfeeding/pdf/strategy8-social-marketing.pdf

[119] Information gathering sessions with prevention experts revealed an urgent need for "credible messengers" when delivering sexual harassment and sexual assault prevention information. For example, a feminine woman who has never served in the military and who has a degree in social work may be *less* persuasive in engaging male Service members about prevention than an athletic, male Marine veteran who served 20 years before getting his degree in public health. Social marketing efforts should study the demographics of the messengers and educators to determine which individuals are most persuasive and effective with different audiences.

and paygrades. Implementation of well-intentioned but ineffective messaging can be immensely detrimental to prevention efforts.

Existing SHARP/SAPR Awareness Efforts May Not be Effective with Some Men

The IRC's discussions with junior enlisted Service members revealed a persistent "disconnect" between SAPR efforts (prevention or response) and Service members. As one SARC stated, "Marines join the Marine Corps to shoot guns and blow stuff up. So, the whole touchy-feely advocacy stuff isn't necessarily in their wheelhouse." Any messaging that is too "touchy-feely" will fall flat with most of the military population.[120] As another SARC commented, "The Army has—and this is what right looks like—info-commercials. All the Soldiers make fun of those. The messaging, versus the actual in practice behavior, there is a disconnect."

The Services have already invested in programs that use innovative messaging and methods to educate Service members on prevention topics like healthy masculinity, sexual boundaries, and gender. Programs such as We End Violence, Unnamed Conspirator, Can I Kiss You, and Sex Signals have been fielded to some Service members in recent years.[121] Such programs are often research-based but originally designed for civilians—and have not yet been tested or evaluated on military audiences. Which is to say, the appetite exists across the Services for effective, persuasive sexual harassment and sexual assault prevention messaging tools, but these tools have not yet been developed. Instead, current military messaging on sexual assault and sexual harassment can actually harm prevention efforts. Worrisomely, a growing body of research indicates that some men who hold hostile attitudes towards women may endorse increased sexual aggression after exposure to anti-violence messaging. These findings speak volumes about the critical need for additional research in military settings.[122]

Ineffective messaging also impacts the prevention and response workforce and their ability to perform their job. As one SARC explained, "They say, 'Oh, you're making the Marines soft. You're trying to be the Care Bears of the Marine Corps.' So, framing the conversation as, 'This is how we make the Marines healthy and more ready' is what we do. We get more buy-in this way." Indeed, connecting sexual assault prevention to military readiness is a key communication strategy that DoD frequently

---

[120] In 2016, the Canadian Armed Forces launched operation "HONOUR" to address sexual assault and sexual harassment of women in the military. However, the operation did not receive buy-in from the troops, who relabeled the effort Operation "Hop on Her." In short, it is crucial that prevention efforts resonate and "make sense" to their audience before they can be successful. Source: Taber, N. (2020). The Canadian Armed Forces: Battling between Operation HONOUR and Operation Hop on Her. *Critical Military Studies*, 6(1), 19–40.

[121] The IRC distributed a request for information to the Services, asking for examples of programs that target or engage men in SAPR and healthy masculinity. The final list included over 50 educational and awareness programs already in use in varying degrees in different Services and installations. These efforts have been largely recent (i.e., in the last three years). Participants in such programs often include the existing SAPR workforce, and—to a lesser extent—Service members. However, many of these programs were initially designed for civilian populations and/or facilitated by civilians with limited experience in military settings. There is a need to test and validate the use of such programs in the military environment.

[122] Malamuth, N. M., Huppin, M., & Linz, D. (2018). Sexual assault interventions may be doing more harm than good with high-risk males. *Aggression and Violent Behavior*, *41*, 20-24. https://doi.org/10.1016/j.avb.2018.05.010

uses in its policy and personnel messaging. Little is known, however, about the effectiveness of this message.

Lastly, some male Service members expressed anger and fear about false accusations of sexual harassment and sexual assault. While empirical findings demonstrate that false accusations of sexual assault are rare (approximately 2 percent of cases),[123] prevention messaging must take this "fear" of being accused into account when communicating with male Service members.[124] Given the significance of these challenges, the military needs a deeper understanding of Service member belief systems, sustained by long-term research and social marketing strategies, to reduce men's resistance to sexual violence prevention messaging.

Implementation Considerations

Recommendation 2.6 a: Establish a Primary Prevention Research Center

USD(P&R) should immediately establish a new consolidated research center with a portfolio solely dedicated to primary prevention of sexual violence and the continuum of harm. The research center would require the authority to develop and enforce a comprehensive prevention research agenda and should be incorporated in the Violence Prevention Cell, reporting directly to the Office of Force Resiliency to ensure a cross-cutting research portfolio.[125] The agenda should be created by a DoD Prevention Research Working Group and formally coordination with the Services. The majority of the OSD, Military Departments, and NGB funded research for sexual violence and the continuum of harm should be aligned with the DoD Prevention Research Agenda.

Concurrent with the recommendation to establish stable funding to support the creation and maintenance of a primary prevention workforce, similarly consistent funding is needed to establish and maintain the dedicated research center. Primary prevention requires a relentless commitment to learning and improving. Therefore, the Secretary of Defense should propose that Congress adopt legislation which establishes unique, recurring congressional funding that will ensure unabated actionable research aligned with the DoD Research Agenda. This funding should provide a more enduring capability that provides consistency through changes in leadership and administrations

The Services should also consider a consolidated Office of Primary Responsibility with the authority, responsibilities, and resources to prioritize and oversee primary prevention research for their Service.

---

123 DoD SAPRO. (2020). Appendix B: Statistical Section. *Fiscal Year 2019 Annual Report on Sexual Assault in the Military*. https://www.sapr.mil/sites/default/files/DOD_Annual_Report_on_Sexual_Assault_In_The_Military_FY2019_Consolidated.pdf

124 Lisak, D., Gardinier, L., Nicksa, S.C., & Cote, A.M. (2010). False allegations of sexual assault: An analysis of ten years of reported cases. *Violence against women*, *16*(12), 1318-1334.

125 DoD's Office of Force Resiliency (OFR) can leverage the Prevention Collaboration Forum and the newly instated OFR Violence Prevention Cell to develop the Center.

Recommendation 2.6 b: Immediate Policy Recommendation

As a part of this implementation, USD(P&R) should immediately rescind DoD's 2011 Don't Ask Don't Tell Memorandum to allow research regarding important DoD populations and ensure the DoD Research Center has the authorities and resources to conduct future reviews and address research barriers caused by policies.

Recommendation 2.6 c: Accessions Compatibility Study

DoD should use the Air Force Compatibility Assessment as a pre-accession instrument, as it has already had an Independent Review which identified potential ways to address legal concerns. An acceptability study should be completed within 9 months and longitudinal feedback should be completed in 3-5 years (including concurrently determining potential interventions). Importantly, the Services should collaborate with the DoD Office of General Counsel to ensure policies and precautionary measures are developed to avoid any unintended consequences (e.g., confidentiality concerns, legal issues, etc.).

Recommendation 2.6 d: Social Marketing

USD(P&R), via the DoD Prevention Research Center, should collaborate with the public and private sectors to create a comprehensive, contemporary or updated social marketing campaign that normalizes the education connected to healthy masculinity and its role in preventing all forms of sexual harassment and assault.

Outcome Metrics

One of the most important outcomes for this recommendation is establishment of a consolidated DoD Primary Prevention Research Center with appropriate authorities and resources to achieve full operational capability in FY24. Other important measures include:

- A new cross-cutting, enforceable annual research agenda;
- Completion of an acceptability study for an accessions compatibility instrument within nine months and a longitudinal study in three to five years, using the Air Force Compatibility Assessment; and,
- An effective social marketing campaign that normalizes the education connected to healthy masculinity.

Recommendation 2.7: Establish a Comprehensive National Guard Primary Prevention Strategy

The National Guard serves key roles in the defense of the nation, at home and globally. The dual state-federal mission of the National Guard places unique requirements on National Guard personnel to carry out their missions in the 50 states, the Commonwealth of Puerto Rico, the District of Columbia, the Virgin Islands, and Guam. To be successful in conducting its diverse missions and simultaneously preventing sexual harassment and sexual assault, the National Guard should also implement a comprehensive primary prevention strategy. This strategy should entail all of the PPoA's system components, including human leadership, a prevention workforce, collaborative relationships, as well as prevention-specific data, policy, and resources. The system would execute the prevention processes outlined in DoD's PPoA.

- 2.7 a: NGB develop Army National and Air National Guard prevention strategies aligned with DoD's PPoA, based on the National Guard's unique construct and missions; and,
- 2.7 b: USD(P&R) submit legislative proposal providing authorization and funding for the NGB to conduct recurring National Guard unit inspections and staff assistance visits for prevention oversight and assistance

Rationale for these Changes: The National Guard Faces Unique Challenges

The National Guard shares many of the challenges faced by the Title 10 active component, while also facing exclusive Title 32 challenges.[126] Challenges include: less unit contact time, pressure to accomplish similar requirements with less duty time, unit personnel who live in geographically distant and disparate communities (with differing risk and protective factors), and unit sizes with differing, limited, or a complete lack of resources. These challenges impact the prevalence and prevention of sexual assault and the continuum of harm. Of significant note, States and territories do not have preexisting prevention strategies and resources to execute prevention activities and evaluate their implementation. Importantly, the NGB does not possess the authority to regulate each state's National Guard, which can limit its ability to provide oversight and hold leaders and organizations accountable for prevention. The complex governing system of Title 10 and Title 32 authorities make prevention oversight and accountability highly convoluted, stalling necessary change and progress.

Recommendation 2.7 a: NGB Should Develop Army National and Air National Guard Prevention Strategies Aligned with DoD's PPoA, Based on the National Guard's Unique Construct and Missions

DoD's PPoA intends to "advance prevention by establishing the expectations for a comprehensive prevention process and prevention system, as well as specific actions the Department, Services, and NGB will take to realize effective prevention in every military community."[127] As SMEs emphasized, "the PPoA indicates the need for a full-time prevention workforce which creates a challenge for the

---

[126] A National Guard member may be mobilized for active Service under Title 10 or Title 32 of the United States Code. When mobilized (or activated) under Title 10, a Service member is directed by the president to report for active duty in an official capacity. Activation under Title 32 means that a National Guard member's state governor has been directed by the president to mobilize the National Guard in that state. Under Title 32, the Service member would perform on active duty under state control, but with pay and benefits provided by the federal government. Source: Absher, J. (2021). *What's the Difference Between Title 10 and Title 32 Mobilization Orders?* Military.com. https://www.military.com/benefits/reserve-and-guard-benefits/whats-difference-between-title-10-and-title-32-mobilization-orders.html

[127] DoD. (2019). *Prevention Plan of Action*. https://www.sapr.mil/sites/default/files/PPoA_Final.pdf

National Guard due to resource limitations." Moreover, "policies at the highest-level need to explicitly state that a dedicated full-time prevention workforce is required, to mandate the direction of manning authorizations and resourcing for these critical positions as well as including the mandatory verbiage to which commanders are held to for prioritization."

Consistent feedback from participants during the information sessions emphasized that the challenging nature of the National Guard structure exacerbated the already difficult task of preventing sexual harassment and sexual assault. The Army National and Air National Guard must fully resource prevention requirements, including a prevention workforce, leadership requirements, and education and skill-building, and relevant research to uniquely address the National Guard's organizational construct and culture.

Part-time Resources Do Not Meet the Needs of a Low-contact Time, Geographically Distant and Disparate, Dual State-federal Mission Workforce

National Guard participants in information sessions stressed the need for a full-time, equipped, and resourced prevention workforce at all echelons. As one participant simply stated, "We need to put our money where our mouth is in terms of staff and resources if we want to tackle [sexual assault prevention]." When developing prevention strategies and policies at the state and federal level, the question, "Is this something the National Guard can accomplish?" is extremely relevant if the Department is serious about addressing the National Guard's part-time, geographically distant and disparate, and dual state-federal workforce. Creative solutions will be necessary to design an effective National Guard prevention workforce.

Recommendation 2.7 b: USD(P&R) Should Submit a Legislative Proposal Providing Authorization and Funding for the NGB to Conduct Recurring National Guard Unit Inspections and Staff Assistance Visits for Prevention Oversight and Assistance

While Recommendation 2.7 addresses complete implementation of a comprehensive primary prevention strategy, this recommendation acknowledges the need to evaluate the National Guard's prevention strategy execution through continuous oversight. With respect to the adage, "inspect what you expect," a comprehensive oversight program should provide the NGB with the confidence that units across the National Guard have the resources they require and are implementing the prevention strategy in the most effective manner.

Implementation Considerations

Recommendation 2.7 a: Primary Prevention Strategy

To implement this recommendation, the National Guard's prevention strategy should clearly articulate the prevention mission, and outline the required requirements, resources, and expected outcomes. In the near-term, the National Guard should continue working to resource prevention workforce capabilities aligned with OSD's efforts to develop the workforce model and the Services manpower study efforts.

Recommendation 2.7 b: Inspections and Staff Assistance Visits

USD(P&R) should draft and submit proposed legislation to ensure NGB has the necessary authorities and resources to inspect and assist National Guard units. The National Guard should also develop, disseminate, and implement policies, programs, and practices governing inspections and Staff Assistance Visits. Lastly, the National Guard should create a recurring schedule that ensures sufficient continuous oversight for 54 states and territories.

Outcome Metrics

One metric should be the completion of policies and guidance for the NGB's prevention strategy and also for the inspection and staff assistance visit requirements. Another important measure should be derived from a follow-up self-assessment compared to the one directed by OSD in 2020; as well as analysis from recurring surveys measuring attitude and behavior changes related to sexual violence and the continuum of harm.

Recommendation 2.8: Update DoD's Prevention Strategy to Include Approved IRC Recommendations

USD(P&R) should update the Department's prevention strategy, including the DoD PPoA, to incorporate the IRC's prevention recommendations taken for action by the Department.

Rationale for this Change: An Opportunity for Enduring Contributions to the Department's Strategy

The IRC acknowledges the primary prevention foundation the Department is building[128] and does not want the recommendations to supplant or overshadow most of those efforts. Instead, the IRC prevention recommendations build on and, in many cases, extend and accelerate existing requirements

[128] However, sexual assault prevention efforts are more evolved within the Department than sexual harassment prevention efforts. The re-issued PPoA should explicitly outline sexual harassment prevention and address the operational requirements necessary to support sexual harassment prevention strategies, within the context of the continuum of sexual harm.

found in the PPoA and other strategy documents. To ensure that all approved IRC recommendations are implemented in the context of current policy rather than in addition to or in place of it, the IRC recommends that DoD revise and reissue relevant documents to ensure a cohesive and comprehensive implementation of the recommendations.

Implementation Considerations

The PPoA should be revised and updated in light of the IRC recommendations and reissued within 120 days. The Prevention Collaboration Forum, and the recently established Violence Prevention Cell,[129] should be leveraged to ensure that adjustments made to the PPoA are cross-cutting and integrative in nature, spanning sexual harassment and all forms of interpersonal and self-directed violence, not just sexual assault.[130] The implementation period should be adjusted as needed. OSD and the Military Departments should complete a review of other relevant policies and strategies within six months to identify additional documents that may need to be revised, updated, and reissued. Changes should be made within 6 months.

Outcome Metrics

Success of this recommendation will occur when the PPoA and other relevant policy documents reflect the accepted IRC recommendations as intended (e.g., not diminished).

Conclusion

It is more urgent than ever to prevent sexual harassment, sexual assault, and other forms of violence in the military. These acts are not inevitable and can be prevented. However, significant progress hinges on leaders who are equipped to lead primary prevention, guided by a dedicated workforce of prevention professionals, and empowered with evidence-based prevention strategies from robust research capabilities.

Although it is clear to the IRC that leaders at every level are the center of gravity for prevention, and leaders across the DoD enterprise convey a desire to prevent sexual harassment and sexual assault, they and the Service members who follow them consistently highlight DoD has not provided them specific skillsets to effectively lead prevention. As one Service member commented, "If leaders had the skills and were leading prevention, we wouldn't be having this conversation about sexual harassment and sexual assault."

Moreover, while leaders lack important skillsets, it is also clear they are not guided by a capable workforce, nor empowered by the relevant research, policies, and programs they need to succeed with primary prevention. There is not a credentialed workforce of prevention professionals who have the

---

129 The Office of Force Resiliency Violence Prevention Cell was established on March 25, 2021, to align with the Prevention Collaboration Forum and support its activities, develop and monitor integrated policy, and synchronize efforts towards a more rigorous DoD prevention model.

130 Simply stated, these recommendations must not be siloed or assigned to a single DoD office.

necessary expertise to leverage research, analytics, strategy development, implementation, and evaluation to effectively support the military's prevention efforts. Across the Department, the important mission of primary prevention has been predominately fulfilled by individuals whose primary duties are sexual assault response, a problem exacerbated by response personnel's lack of prevention development and resourcing. Additionally, Service members at risk for trauma should be identified and supported early to prevent sexual assault and sexual harassment.

These recommendations underscore the bottom-line that getting primary prevention right requires deep investments. Building the prevention infrastructure necessary to ensure the growth of comprehensive, evidence-based prevention strategies will take time, money, and expertise. However, without an infrastructure to support prevention activities—i.e., the relevant research, workforce, and leader capabilities—the military will continue to lack the capability and capacity to "move the needle" to reduce sexual harassment, sexual assault, and other forms of violence.

The Imperative of Leadership in the War Against Sexual Assault: Recommendations for Climate & Culture

Independent Review Commission on Sexual Assault in the Military

Contents

List of Figures

Acknowledgements

The Climate and Culture line of effort of the Independent Review Commission (IRC) sincerely thanks everyone they consulted during their review, including the dedicated experts who patiently answered their questions, and the many uniformed Service members who authentically shared their challenges, needs, and expectations. To all the survivors with whom the experts spoke—the IRC heard you and is thankful that you took the time to share painful, emotional experiences so that the Services might do better going forward. Finally, the Climate and Culture experts are grateful for the Service subject matter experts (SME) and consultative group for their expertise and guidance throughout the 90-Day commission.

Introduction

As former commanders, the Climate and Culture experts leaned into their 80 years of collective experience entrenched in a culture that has encouraged, turned a blind eye to, or undermined efforts to prevent sexual violence.[1, 2] The combination of their experiences, discussions with experts at the enterprise level, interactions with junior Service members, and academic research has shown that policies and programs developed to tackle the problem to-date have failed. Why? After decades of applying Band-Aids to fix a broken culture, these efforts have done little but maintain the status quo because too many leaders—at all echelons of the enterprise—continue to believe that sexual violence is a distraction from the military's core warfighting mission, and therefore not something it must take seriously. To this point, the November 2020 review of the command climate at Fort Hood, Texas found that leaders treated sexual violence as a "perfunctory task, not a priority."[3]

"We the chain of command, we the generals and colonels, the captains and so on, we have lost the trust and confidence of those subordinates in our ability to deal with sexual assault. So we need to make a change."

-Chairman Milley

[1] Sexual violence refers to sexual activity when consent is not obtained or not given freely. Anyone can experience sexual violence. The person can be, but is not limited to, a friend, intimate partner, coworker, neighbor, or family member. Source: Basile, K., Smith, S., Breiding, M., Black, M., & Mahendra, R. (2014). Sexual Violence Surveillance: Uniform Definitions and recommended Data Elements, Version 2.0. Centers for Disease Control and Prevention (CDC), National Center for Injury Prevention and Control. https://www.cdc.gov/violenceprevention/pdf/sv_surveillance_definitionsl-2009-a.pdf

[2] In the Army, processing of sexual harassment complaints follow the same procedures as outlined for equal opportunity complaints. In contrast, charges of sexual violence are to be processed through legal/ law enforcement channels. Source: Department of the Army. (2008). *AR 600–20*. https://dacowits.defense.gov/Portals/48/Documents/Reports/2011/Documents/DACOWITS%20September%202011%20Committee%20Meeting/09%20Army%20Sexual%20Harassment%20Policy.pdf

[3] The Fort Hood Independent Review Committee. (2020). *Report of the Fort Hood Independent Review Committee,* 18. https://www.army.mil/e2/downloads/rv7/forthoodreview/2020-12-03_FHIRC_report_redacted.pdf

This is not to say some leaders have not tried to make an impact in this space. Since 2010, there have been more than 10 Department of Defense (DoD) Inspector General (IG) engagements to review and improve prevention and assault.[4] In addition, since 2012, there have been:

- Over 50 Secretary of Defense directed initiatives to improve prevention and response;
- Over 150 Congressional provisions operationalized related to sexual assault;
- Over 200 recommendations from government panels and task forces assessed for applicability to the sexual assault prevention and response (SAPR) mission space; and,
- Over 60 Government Accountability Office (GAO) sexual assault related recommendations assessed to measure prevention and response efforts and to inform future programming.[5]

More than a decade ago, the DoD Sexual Assault Prevention and Response Office (SAPRO) Director explained that changing attitudes, behaviors, and beliefs related to sexual assault would take between eight and ten years to achieve, and that they had begun to see those changes occur.[6] In those intervening 11 years, however, DoD estimates[7] that roughly 135,000 active duty Service members (65,400 women and 69,600 men)[8] have been sexually assaulted and about 509,000 active duty Service members (223,000 women and 286,000 men) have experienced sexual harassment.[9] These hundreds

---

[4] DoD SAPRO. (n.d.). Policy and Strategy. https://www.sapr.mil/sites/default/files/Policy%20and%20Strategy%20Overview%20Slicksheet_Reference_0.pdf

[5] Ibid.

[6] Isikoff, M. (2011). *Lawsuit Claims Pentagon Ignored Military Rape Victims*. NBC. https://www.nbcbayarea.com/news/politics/did_pentagon_turn_blind_eye_to_rape_victims_/1909120/

[7] DoD estimates the number of Service members who have been sexually assaulted and sexually harassed in the 12 months prior to survey administration, which the Department has administered every two years since 2010. Sexual harassment figures for 2014 were estimated based on the proportion of those who indicated an experience of sexual harassment on the RMWS multiplied by the active duty end-strength that year. Sexual harassment data were not available for men in 2006.

[8] These figures do not represent incidents that could have occurred during years that DoD did not conduct a survey. In addition, this number does not necessarily represent unique Service members (i.e., some Service members may have experienced sexual assault and/or sexual harassment in separate survey years), nor does it account for Service members who recorded several incidents within the same survey period.

[9] Breslin, R., Davis, E., Hylton, K., Hill, A., Klauberg, W., Petusky, M., & Klahr, A. (2019). *2018 Workplace and Gender Relations Survey of Active Duty Members: Overview Report.* Report (No. 2019-027). Alexandria, VA: Office of People Analytics. https://apps.dtic.mil/sti/citations/AD1072334; Davis, L., Grifka, A., Williams, K., Coffey, M., Van Winkle, E. P., & Hurley, M. (2017). *2016 Workplace and Gender Relations Survey of Active Duty Members: Overview Report.* (No. 2016-050). Alexandria, VA: DMDC. https://apps.dtic.mil/dtic/tr/fulltext/u2/1032638.pdf; Morral, A. R., Gore, K. L., & Schell, T. L. (2015). *Sexual Assault and Sexual Harassment in the U.S. Military: Volume 1. Design of the 2014 RAND Military Workplace Study*. Santa Monica, CA: RAND National Defense Research Institute. https://www.rand.org/content/dam/rand/pubs/research_reports/RR800/RR870z2 1/RAND_RR870z2-1.pdf; Defense Manpower Data Center. (2013). *2012 Workplace and Gender Relations Survey of Active Duty Members: Tabulation Volume* (No. 2012-065). Arlington, VA: DMDC. https://sapr.mil/public/docs/research/WGR_ActiveDuty_2012_Report.pdf; Rock, L., Lipari, R.N., Cook, P.J., & Hale, A.D. (2011). *2010 Workplace and Gender Relations Survey of Active Duty Members: Overview Report of Sexual Assault* (No. 2010-025). Arlington, VA: DMDC. https://sapr.mil/public/docs/research/DMDC_2010_WGRA_Overview_Report_of_Sexual_Assault.pdf; Lipari, R.N., Cook, P.J., Rock, L., & Matos, K. (2007). *2006 Gender Relations Survey of Active Duty Members* (No. 2007-022). Arlington, VA: DMDC. https://sapr.mil/public/docs/research/DMDC_2010_

of thousands of Service members who experienced sexual harm are clear evidence that culture has not changed, and that leaders have failed to "move the needle," as Chairman Milley recently acknowledged.[10]

The IRC's recommendations for climate and culture echo the following basic principle from the Fort Hood Independent Review Commission (FHIRC).[11]

"Where there is respect for the value, purpose and contributions of all soldiers, no matter their gender, the environment will not tolerate sexual assault or sexual harassment in any form."

- Fort Hood Independent Review Committee

Trust in Leadership is Broken

The DoD Instruction (DoDI) that governs the military's SAPR program highlights a close examination of units' climate and culture as central to accomplishing the goal of a culture free of sexual assault.[12] The DoDI states:

- "Scrutinize more closely the organization's climate and culture for contributing factors [in order to accomplish the goal of] a culture free of sexual assault, through an environment of prevention, education and training, response capability, victim support, reporting procedures, and appropriate accountability that enhances the safety and well-being of all persons covered."

The military will only achieve this goal through an emphasis on transparency and ownership at all levels of leadership, which is the linchpin in eliminating sexual violence. Unfortunately, change has been slow, due to the perpetuation of harmful gender stereotypes, widespread cultural norms of victim blaming[13] and rape myth acceptance, and hostility and exclusion that extends to multiple vulnerable populations within the force. All of the above are elements of a toxic climate that is the sole responsibility of the commander to fix.[14]

_Overview_Report_of_Sexual_Assault.pdf

10 Ryan, M., & Lamothe, D. (2021). *'We haven't moved the needle' on Sexual Assault in the Military, General Says*. The Washington Post. https://www.washingtonpost.com/national-security/military-sexual-assault/2021/05/06/a8f51a7c-ae98-11eb-8109-f8ba1ea2eeab_story.html

11 The Fort Hood Independent Review Committee. (2020, November 6). Report of the Fort Hood Independent Review Committee, 115. https://www.army.mil/e2/downloads/rv7/forthoodreview/2020-12-03_FHIRC_report_redacted.pdf

12 DoD. (2021). *DoDI 6495.02, Volume 1: Sexual Assault Prevention and Response: Program Procedures*. https://www.esd.whs.mil/Portals/54/Documents/DD/issuances/dodi/649502_vol1.PDF

13 Britzky, H. (2021, March 18). The truth about false sexual assault reports in the military. *Task and Purpose*. https://taskandpurpose.com/news/truth-about-false-sexual-assault-reports/

14 Ryan, M. & Lamothe, D. (2021). *'We haven't moved the needle' on Sexual Assault in the Military, General Says*. The Washington Post. https://www.washingtonpost.com/national-security/military-sexual-assault/2021/05/06/a8f51a7c-ae98-11eb-8109-f8ba1ea2eeab_story.html

Until leaders embrace that responsibility and prioritize a safe and respectful workplace for all who serve, the enterprise will fail to recruit and retain a diverse and talented force.[15] The American public is noticing this problem. Last summer, following the deaths of two Service women—PFC Vanessa Guillen and Airman 1st Class Natasha Aposhian—the National Hispanic Caucus of State Legislators wrote a letter to the Secretary of the Army and Secretary of the Air Force, stating, "Enlisted women—especially enlisted women of color, have more to fear from those with whom they serve than from this nation's enemies."[16]

"Enlisted women—especially enlisted women of color, have more to fear from those with whom they serve than from this nation's enemies."

-National Hispanic Caucus of State Legislators

Today's multi-domain battlefield requires the military to tap into the nation's brightest, most creative thinkers and planners who "may not fit traditional perceptions of what it means to be a warrior but who may have the critical skills for 21st Century combat."[17] A force that continuously degrades half of society's talent pool is destined to fail at readiness. The military must ensure that sexual violence is not an occupational hazard or the price of Service.

Trust is broken across the force between junior enlisted Service members and the senior leaders who command them. This was highlighted at Fort Hood and more recently at an Army Cohesion Assessment Team Pilot visit. Perhaps most importantly, interview responses make it quite clear that Platoon, Company, and Battalion leaders and Non-Commissioned Officers (NCOs) fundamentally and uniformly continue to see sexual assault and sexual harassment as peripheral to unit dynamics–unrelated to improving the climate of their units, organizational trust-building, and promotion of unit cohesiveness/esprit de corps. The IRC's interviews with junior enlisted members across the Services echo these findings.

For the military to move forward, urgent steps must be taken to signal to Service members that inclusivity and equitable, respectful treatment of all who serve is the priority of all Command Teams. There needs to be a line of demarcation that says, as of today, the force will work together from top to bottom and shift the culture to be protective of all Service members.

---

[15] Morral, A.R., Matthews, M., Cefalu, M., Schell, T.L., & Cottrell, L. (2021). *Effects of Sexual Assault and Sexual Harassment on Separation from the U.S. Military: Findings from the 2014 RAND Military Workplace Study*. Santa Monica, CA: RAND Corporation. https://www.rand.org/pubs/research_reports/RR870z10.html

[16] Thayer, R.L. (2020, July 10). *Hispanic state lawmakers call for review following deaths of airman at Grand Forks, soldier at Fort Hood.* Stars and Stripes. https://www.stripes.com/news/us/hispanic-state-lawmakers-call-for-review-following-deaths-of-airman-at-grand-forks-soldier-at-fort-hood-1.637062

[17] Klein, M.A. & Gallus, J. (2018). The Readiness Imperative for reducing sexual violence in the US Armed Forces: Respect and Professionalism as the foundation for change. *Military Psychology*, *30*(3): 264-269.

Changing Climate and Shifting Culture in the Military

An organization's culture consists of shared beliefs and values established by leaders and communicated and reinforced down the chain. Culture is set at the top and guides the specific and implied values of the organization. This broad set of values, practices, beliefs, and language binds individuals to that institution. In the military, culture is defined by DoD and Service core values. When an organization has a strong culture, three conditions are met: employees know how top management expects them to respond in any given situation; employees believe that the expected response is the right one; and, employees know they will be rewarded for demonstrating the organization's values.[18, 19]

There may be no institution more defined by its core values than the United States (U.S.) military. At its best, these values define the military's cultural norms and create a shared sense of identity throughout the force. DoD and the Services have failed to move the needle on sexual violence in part because they have been unable to effectively tie the issue to the military's core values. The military must move away from a culture in which Service members who harm their battle buddies—but who happen to be top performers—are not seen as liabilities or risks to good order and discipline. This mindset comes at the expense of unit safety and cohesion, and victims are made to be the problem.[20] The Services must engender positive, proactive, and meaningful actions that combat sexual harm as part of their core values.

Command climate is the action of implementing Service culture. It is the intersection of individual perceptions, behaviors, and attitudes at the unit level. In the military, climate "lives" at the lowest levels—at the squad or platoon; on the deck plate; or the flight line; or in the office where Service members work together. Climate issues, therefore, are most critically handled by middle management, at the brigade and below. A shift in climate regarding sexual violence is only possible when officer and enlisted leaders at these levels have the knowledge, skills, and ability to implement such a shift, and clearly understand *what* shift in climate is required. In order for this to happen, significant investments must be made in educating these leaders, equipping them with the requisite knowledge, skills, and abilities, and incentivizing them to make changing the climate regarding sexual violence a priority. Leaders must also stress that everyone, at every rank, has a role to play in fostering a safe and healthy climate.

---

[18] A pragmatic way to put this model into practice is to frame it as four distinct steps: diagnose, name, and validate the culture of the organization; reframe the cultural narrative; role-model and communicate cultural change; and reinforce a new belief system.

[19] SHRM. (2021). *Understanding and Developing Organizational Culture*. https://www.shrm.org/resourcesandtools/tools-and-samples/toolkits/pages/understandinganddevelopingorganizationalculture.aspx

[20] Sadler, A., Lindsay, D., Hunter, S., & Day, D. (2018). The Impact of Leadership on sexual harassment and assault in the military. *Military Psychology, 30*(1): 1-12.

The example set by leaders dictates the proper way to behave, because how leaders are seen to live those values and model "what right looks like" shapes subordinates' perceptions, behaviors, and understanding. Culture shift[21] occurs when an individual at the lowest level can effectively communicate the senior leaders' intent. For the military to effectively tackle the problem of sexual violence, that answer to the question "why should I care?" should be a resounding, "because the safety of one, impacts the safety of all." Commanders and leaders of all echelons, and Service members of all ranks, must commit to applying the ethos of "leave no man behind" to support survivors of sexual harassment and sexual assault.

Outdated Social Norms Contribute to a Culture of Hostility toward Service Women

Although the military has become increasingly diverse, women make up less than 18 percent of the total force, and less than 30 percent of the force identifies as some racial minority.[22] With these dynamics, many women who serve report being treated differently than their male counterparts. When women are considered "less than" by their male peers or leaders, unit climates are breeding grounds[23] for gender discrimination, sexual harassment, and sexual assault. Women disproportionately bear the burden as victims of these readiness detracting behaviors and abuses. For example, 1 in 4 Service women who responded to the Workplace and Gender Relations Survey of Active Duty Members (WGRA) shared they had been sexually harassed in the military (compared to 1 in 10 men).[24] Although men outnumber women in the force at a ratio of roughly 4 to 1, over the past decade, DoD estimates similar numbers of women and men have been the victim of sexual assault.[25]

---

[21] Organizational culture change has been analyzed using Kotter's organizational change model in a wide range of industries for the last 40 years. For the purposes of this analysis, culture shift can be summarized by three phases: "unfreezing" the beliefs in an organization; "change" through role-modeling and setting new behaviors and beliefs; and "refreezing" the organization to lock in a new culture. A pragmatic way to put this model into practice for military sexual assault is to frame it as three distinct steps: diagnose the culture of the organization through the IRC; communicate recommendations that reflect the new culture, and reinforce a new belief system through policy and structural changes. Source: Deloitte. (2016, November). *Culture shift: Changing beliefs, behaviors, and outcomes*. CFO Insights. https://www2.deloitte.com/us/en/pages/finance/articles/cfo-insights-culture-shift-beliefs-behaviors-outcomes.html

[22] Of Total Force members in 2018 (i.e., Active Duty, Reserve, and Guard members from all Military Services), 82 percent identify as male and 71 percent identify as White. Source: Military One Source. (2019). *2018 Demographics: Profile of the Military Community*. https://download.militaryonesource.mil/12038/MOS/Reports/2018-demographics-report.pdf, pp. 6-7.

[23] Flood, M. & Pease, B. (2009). Factors Influencing Attitudes to Violence Against Women. *Trauma, Violence & Abuse, 10*(2), 125-142. www.jstor.org/stable/26636200

[24] Breslin, R., Davis, E., Hylton, K., Hill, A., Klauberg, W., Petusky, M., & Klahr, A. (2019). *2018 Workplace and Gender Relations Survey of Active Duty Members: Overview Report*. Report (No. 2019-027). Alexandria, VA: Office of People Analytics. https://apps.dtic.mil/sti/citations/AD1072334

[25] Ibid. Calculations based on point estimates from the 2006 Gender Relations survey, 2010, 2016, and 2018 iterations of the WGRA, and the 2014 RAND Military Workplace Study. When these point estimates are combined, DoD estimates show that roughly 135,000 active duty Service members (65,400 women and 69,600 men) were sexually assaulted.

Sexual violence is an outgrowth of lingering "subcultures of misogyny," as recently described by the Commandant of the Marine Corps.[26] Too often, unit cohesion is built around the shared identity of the majority of its members.[27] Approximately 1 in 6 soldiers; 1 in 5 sailors; 1 in 12 Marines; and 1 in 5 Airmen are women.[28] With these gender ratios dominating the force, that shared identity is a narrow version of manhood, which further isolates women, LGBTQ+ troops, and Service members from communities of color from being seen as earning their place as part of the team, advancing in rank, and ultimately, being seen as belonging.[29, 30] This "othering" dynamic is especially concerning given that research shows men are more likely than women to view victims as "deserving" or blameworthy for an assault, as well as more likely to exonerate perpetrators.[31,32]

Reinforcing women's roles as outsiders, male bonding within a unit often consists of sexist comments with the intent to entertain their male peers at the expense of women in the unit, or humiliate them, or both. This aspect of male culture also exists in the civilian population,[33] but it is uniquely harmful in the military, where Service members must entrust their lives and their safety with one another. Examples of hostile language and behavior indicative of a toxic command climate can be seen in Figure 1, which was informed by the IRC's scoping discussions with Military Serving Organizations, Veteran Serving Organizations, and discussions with junior enlisted personnel.

---

[26] Senate Armed Services Committee. (2020, March 5). Statement of the Honorable Thomas B. Modly Acting Secretary of the Navy, Admiral Michael M. Gilday, Chief of Naval Operations, and General David H. Berger, Commandant of the U.S. Marine Corps on Fiscal Year 2021 Department of the Navy Budget before the Senate Armed Services Committee. https://www.armed-services.senate.gov/imo/media/doc/Modly--Gilday--Berger_03-05-20.pdf

[27] Morris, M. (1996). By Force of Arms: Rape, War, and Military Culture. *Duke Law Journal, 45*(4): 651-781. https://scholarship.law.duke.edu/dlj/vol45/iss4/1/

[28] Military One Source. (2020). *2019 Demographics: Profile of the Military Community*, 13-72. https://download.militaryonesource.mil/12038/MOS/Reports/2019-demographics-report.pdf

[29] Archer, E. M. (2013). The power of gendered stereotypes in the U.S. Marine Corps. *Armed Forces & Society, 39*(2), 359-391. https://doi.org/10.1023/A:1025164221364.

[30] Boyce, L. A., & Herd, A. M. (2003). The relationship between gender role stereotypes and requisite military leadership characteristics. *Sex Roles, 49*(7): 365-378.

[31] Angelone, D.J., Cantor, N., Marcantonio, T., & Joppa, M. (2021). Does Sexism Mediate the Gender and Rape Myth Acceptance Relationship? *Violence Against Women, 27*(6-7): 748-765.

[32] Viki, G. T., Abrams, D., & Masser, B. (2004). Evaluating Stranger and Acquaintance Rape: The Role of Benevolent Sexism in Perpetrator Blame and Recommended Sentence Length. *Law and Human Behavior, 28*(3): 295-303. https://doi.org/10.1023/B:LAHU.0000029140.72880.69.

[33] McLaughlin, H., Uggen, C., & Blackstone, A. (2012). Sexual Harassment, Workplace Authority and the Paradox of Power. *American Sociological Review, 77*(4): 625-647.

Examples of Hostile Language and Behavior Indicative of Toxic Command Climates

Bounties	Bounties and bets may be placed on who "gets" to the new Service member first with intention to haze and harass that person.
Phase Sharking	Service members may view the new person entering their unit as a potential sexual conquest, and compete to "win."
Contests for "Wins"	Service members may attempt to acquire nude or semi-nude pictures of the new person.
Recall Roster	Service members may obtain the new person's phone number from the recall roster and misuse it for unintended purposes such as cyber stalking and/or sending inappropriate pictures and messages.

Figure 1. Examples of Hostile Language and Behavior Indicative of a Toxic Command Climate

Despite the phased integration of women into various military career fields and combat arms,[34] contingents of resentment towards women and a belief in a double standard persist across the force. Comments from a May 2021 survey[35] of more than 1,000 women in Army special operations demonstrate the depth of these biases.[36] The report on survey results by U.S. Army Special Operations Command[37] reveals that many women "work harder to be seen as equals", while 46 percent of men in special operations believe women are held to a lower standard. In addition to ill-fitting body armor sending women the message "you don't belong," 20 percent of women note experiencing sexual harassment (with 71 percent of these women also stating they don't feel comfortable reporting it).

Even with so few women reporting harassment[38] (or sexual assault),[39] some Service members (men and women) subscribe to common rape myths, like believing in high numbers of false reporting[40] and the "weaponization" of SAPR/Sexual Harassment and Assault Response and Prevention (SHARP).

---

[34] Robles, J. (2018). Gender Integration into Combat Arms. *NCO Journal*. Army University Press. https://www.armyupress.army.mil/Journals/NCO-Journal/Archives/2018/July/Gender-Integration/

[35] Britzky, H. (2021, May 21). 'Stop the social experiment'—New Survey Spotlights Bias Against Women in Army Special Ops. *Task and Purpose*. https://taskandpurpose.com/news/army-special-operations-women-survey/

[36] Ibid.

[37] Ibid.

[38] DoD SAPRO. (2021). Appendix F: Sexual Harassment Assessment. *Fiscal Year 2020 Annual Report on Sexual Assault in the Military*. https://www.sapr.mil/sites/default/files/Appendix_F_Sexual_Harassment_Assessment_FY2020.pdf

[39] DoD SAPRO. (2021). Appendix C: Metrics and Non-Metrics on Sexual Assault. *Fiscal Year 2020 Annual Report on Sexual Assault in the Military*. https://www.sapr.mil/sites/default/files/Appendix_C_Metrics_and_NonMetrics_on_Sexual_Assault_FY2020.pdf

[40] In 2020, 33 out of 3,358 sexual assault cases were not taken for action due to allegations determined to be "false or baseless." Source: DoD SAPRO. (2021). Appendix B: Statistical Data on Sexual Assault. *Fiscal Year 2020 Annual Report on Sexual Assault in the Military*.

As one male officer states in the Army report,[41] "I am afraid that if I fail a female who fails to meet the standards, she can end my career by claiming SHARP."[42]

Hostility Extends to Other Vulnerable Populations within the Force

As others have rightly observed, "our military is a reflection of our own society."[43] In addition to sexism, entrenched social norms, such as racism, homophobia, and transphobia, exist among the military population. Like rigid views on gender, harmful attitudes and beliefs towards racial and ethnic minorities, and LGBTQ+ individuals develop early in life.[44] The military has a unique duty—and opportunity—to inculcate alternative values of inclusion and equity in the accessions and initial entry process. Leaders must also set a tone of dignity and respect for all on day one upon taking command of a new unit, at every duty station, and as a part of every training with their troops. All Service members deserve to be treated equally with dignity and respect. Addressing climate and culture in the prevention of sexual assault and sexual harassment cannot take place without a holistic effort to combat racism, homophobia, and transphobia.[45]

Racial disparities in the military justice system are inherently tied to sexual harassment and sexual assault.[46] In parallel with the civilian justice system, the unequal treatment of communities of color, particularly Black Service members, may create additional complexities impacting victims' decisions whether to report harassment, assault or abuse.[47] These disparities can result in distrust amongst Black Service members, and there are unseen consequences when a victim does not trust the system. If Service members from underrepresented populations fear reprisal, lack confidence that the system will treat them fairly, and do not feel their service is valued when compared to those in the majority,

---

[41] Britzky, H. (2021, May 21). 'Stop the social experiment'—New Survey Spotlights Bias Against Women in Army Special Ops. *Task and Purpose*. https://taskandpurpose.com/news/army-special-operations-women-survey/

[42] This sentiment is consistent with comments the IRC heard directly from junior enlisted Service members in its site visits to installations in the U.S., and virtual meetings with outside the continental U.S (OCONUS) junior enlisted (across all Services).

[43] Shinkman, P.D. (2021, April 20). How the Military Attempts to Right Racial Wrongs. *U.S. News*. https://www.usnews.com/news/national-news/articles/2021-04-20/military-racism-george-floyd-and-new-attempts-at-change-air-force-chief-gen-brown-discusses-the-future-of-the-armed-forces

[44] Basile, K.C., DeGue, S., Jones, K., Freire, K., Dills, J., Smith, S.G., & Raiford, J.L. (2016). *Stop Sexual Violence: A Technical Package to Prevent Sexual Violence*. CDC: Division of Violence Prevention, National Center for Injury Prevention and Control. https://www.cdc.gov/violenceprevention/pdf/sv-prevention-technical-package.pdf

[45] There are additional sub-categories of Service members who may be uniquely vulnerable to maltreatment and abuse, including immigrants serving as they seek citizenship, and anyone in the recruitment pipeline (due to power of recruiters and military training personnel).

[46] Cronk, T.M. (2020). *Top Legal Officers Address Racial Disparity in Military Justice*. Defense.gov. https://www.usnews.com/news/national-news/articles/2021-04-20/military-racism-george-floyd-and-new-attempts-at-change-air-force-chief-gen-brown-discusses-the-future-of-the-armed-forces

[47] Prevalence of sexual violence, among the civilian population, is disproportionately high for women of color, particularly Black women, and American Indian/Alaska Native women. Source: CDC. (2012). *National Intimate Partner and Sexual Violence Survey: 2010 Summary Report*. https://www.cdc.gov/violenceprevention/pdf/NISVS_Report2010-a.pdf. Although DoD sexual assault and harassment prevalence data from the WGRA do not show a similar disproportionate impact, the IRC notes that racial/ethnic minority women may experience both racial harassment and gender-based violence simultaneously, perhaps making both more difficult to detect or report.

then their experiences and decision-making when it comes to reporting sexual harassment or sexual assault will be affected.

The death of PFC LaVena Johnson exemplifies these connections.[48] On a deployment to Iraq in 2005, 19-year-old PFC Johnson was found dead in her tent. Although the Army ruled her death a suicide, her family and friends, and many outside stakeholders, believe the case is unresolved, as her remains showed evidence of rape and battery. Many believe that part of the reason she has not received justice is because she is Black.

Training often misses the opportunity to teach Service members how to discuss intersectionality. To correct this, leaders must learn to be comfortable with having uncomfortable conversations. Intersectional biases and discriminations contribute to instances of harassment and assault – especially in communities most impacted.

In the battle against sexual violence in the military, there can be no middle ground.

Leaders must understand that the experience of sexual harm is not divorced from victims' multilayered identities. This embrace of intersectionality is critical, because victims of sexual harassment and sexual assault can experience these harms differently, in connection with their gender, sexual orientation or gender identity, race, or ethnicity.[49] For example, new data from RAND shows that just 12 percent of Service members identify as "other than heterosexual", but account for 43 percent of sexual assaults in the military.[50] Approximately 1 in 3 Black Service members report experiencing past-year racial/ethnic harassment.[51] Command climates with "zero tolerance" for sexual violence go hand-in-hand with a commitment to addressing racial discrimination and anti-LGBTQ+ attitudes and beliefs.

Leaders are either "all in" for a culture free from sexual harassment and sexual assault or allow for a culture of impunity to persist. In the development of the recommendations that follow, we called on the imperative of leaders to lead at all costs. Fostering a climate free from sexual violence and other harmful attitudes and beliefs is challenging, but not impossible, with the right leaders in command.

---

[48] Leonard, M.D. (2015, July 19). 10 Years Later, a Soldier's Family Still Grieves and Questions the Army's Version of her Death. *St. Louis Public Radio*. https://news.stlpublicradio.org/government-politics-issues/2015-07-19/10-years-later-a-soldiers-family-still-grieves-and-questions-the-armys-version-of-her-death

[49] Given that victims of sexual assault, sexual harassment, and other special victim crimes may be targeted because of who they are, the IRC's Accountability line of effort recommends that designated independent special victim prosecutors have disposition authority not only for sexual assault, but also for bullying, hazing, and bias or hate crimes on the basis of the victim's gender, sex, race, ethnicity, color, religion, national origin, sexual orientation, gender identity, or disability.

[50] Morral, A.R. & Schell, T.L. (2021). *Sexual Assault of Sexual Minorities in the U.S. Military*. Santa Monica, CA: RAND Corporation. https://www.rand.org/pubs/research_reports/RRA1390-1.html

[51] Daniel, S., Claros, A.Y., Namrow, N., Siebel, M., Campbell, A., McGrath, D., & Klahr, A. (2019). *2017 Workplace and Equal Opportunity Survey of Active Duty Members: Executive Report*. Report (No. 2018-023). Alexandria, VA: Office of People Analytics. https://taskandpurpose.com/app/uploads/2021/01/27/2017-Workplace-and-Equal-Opportunity-Survey-Report.pdf

List of Recommendations

3.1 The Office of the Under Secretary of Defense for Personnel and Readiness (USD(P&R)) should codify in policy and direct the development and implementation of metrics related to sexual harassment and sexual assault as part of readiness tracking and reporting.

3.2 USD(P&R) should direct the Services to educate the force about sexual harassment and sexual assault within the context of the Services' core values.

3.3 DoD must fully execute on the principle that addressing sexual harassment and sexual assault in the 21st century requires engaging with the cyber domain.

3.3 a Collect data to measure the problem of cyberharassment (and related harms).

3.3 b Educate leaders on cyberharassment and technology-facilitated sexual harassment and sexual assault.

3.3 c Hold Service members accountable who engage in cyberharassment and other forms of technology-facilitated sexual harassment and sexual assault.

3.4 DoD should ensure that there is an internal focus on sexual violence across the force in implementing the 2017 National Women, Peace, and Security Act.

3.4 a Elevate and standardize the gender advisor workforce.

3.4 b Use qualitative data as part of indicators for Defense Objective One of the WPS Strategic Framework.

3.4 c Integrate a gender analysis into the military's planning & operational frameworks.

3.4 d Review and revise PME & DoD schoolhouse curricula to mainstream WPS priorities.

3.4 e Congress should support and codify into legislation DoD's inclusion of Personnel & Readiness in WPS implementation.

3.5 Use qualitative data to select, develop, and evaluate the right leaders for command positions.

3.5 a Use qualitative data to select and develop the right leaders.

3.5 b Include a meaningful narrative section in performance evaluations for officers and NCOs.

3.6 Building a climate for the reduction of sexual harassment and sexual assault as a fundamental leader development requirement.

3.7 USD(P&R) should undertake a series of enhancements to the climate survey process to ensure that timely, actionable data can be used to improve unit climate on sexual harassment and assault.

3.7 a USD(P&R) should develop a standardized "pulse survey" tool that would enable unit-level commanders to collect real-time climate data on sexual harassment and sexual assault from Service members in their units between required administrations of the Defense Organizational Climate Survey (DEOCS).

3.7 b The Secretary of Defense should direct the Services to develop a formal system to release climate survey data at the unit level and initiate and evaluate corrective action plans.

3.7 c USD(P&R) should accelerate efforts to develop a validated "Climate Benchmark" to measure healthy and unhealthy climate at the unit level.

3.7 d Assess whether current DoD policies and EO workforce have capacity to help commanders resolve climate issues.

3.8 The Services should publish the nature and results of all disciplinary actions related to sexual misconduct and disseminate this information to troops periodically.

Methodology

The IRC's Climate and Culture experts leveraged their combined 80+ years of experience serving in the U.S. military towards the development of a process to gather information and meet with stakeholders that would ultimately shape their recommendations. In addition to holding regular discussions with the Service representatives serving as SMEs to this line of effort, the Climate and Culture team interviewed more than seventy individuals including: commanders and command teams at the O3-O5 and E7-E9 levels; SMEs in organizational psychology; international military experts from the Five Eyes countries; and, personnel leading and implementing promising cultural change initiatives across OSD (e.g., the Office of Force Resiliency). Of particular importance for this group was meeting with the commanders from each Service and the Joint Staff assigned to the Climate and Culture consultative team.

Recommendation 3.1: USD(P&R) Should Codify Metrics Related to Sexual Harassment and Sexual Assault as part of Readiness Tracking and Reporting

Unit readiness is the key to military effectiveness. It is widely known that "what does not get measured, does not get done." DoD and the Military Services and Departments have long referred to sexual assault and sexual harassment as "readiness issues," but neither DoD policy (DoDI 7730.66), Joint Staff instruction (CJCSI 3401.02B), nor Service directives require metrics related to sexual violence to be "rolled up" the chain of command within their readiness reports.

Instances of sexual violence reduce a unit's combat effectiveness and overall operational readiness and must receive the appropriate level of attention from commanders. Yet in hearing from hundreds of survivors of sexual assault, the IRC often heard that commanders simply do not treat instances of sexual violence with the same level of time or attention that they treat a broken vehicle.

The Office of the Secretary of Defense (OSD) USD(P&R) should codify in policy and direct the development and implementation of metrics related to sexual violence as part of readiness tracking and reporting. Readiness metrics should include availability of fully qualified response personnel, victim care and services availability (e.g., forensic exams, ongoing expedited transfers), number of military protective orders (MPOs) issued against unit members, and other measures specific to the unit's capabilities to respond to instances of sexual assault. Care should be taken to ensure the privacy and confidentiality of victims and protect the rights of accused Service members subject to courts-martial, disciplinary actions, or MPOs, in collecting and reporting relevant data points.

Rationale for this Change: Sexual Violence Harms Readiness

Current Readiness Policies

DoDI 7730.66[52] establishes the Defense Readiness Reporting System (DRRS) to collect, report, submit, display, and share readiness data among stakeholders across the Department. This standardized reporting process allows Service Chiefs and Department policy officials oversight to ensure that units are resourced and ready to respond when the Nation needs them. Joint Staff Instruction 3401.02B[53] provides the requirements for unit reporting and the calculations for determining unit readiness.

This policy defines readiness as the degree to which a unit possesses the required resources to undertake the full wartime missions for which it is organized or designed. To this end, the Services have the delegated authority to determine the specific metrics on which units are required to report. Within and across the Services, specific requirements vary by unit type (as different units have vastly different equipment requirements); however, reporting generally fell into four broad categories:

- Administrative and Medical Readiness;
- Equipment Condition;
- Personnel Training Status; and,
- Supply Availability.

A unit's overall readiness is measured by a "C" score, which represents the status of the selected unit resources measured against the resources required to undertake the wartime missions for which the

[52] DoD. (2011). DoDI 7730.66: Guidance for the Defense Readiness Reporting System (DRRS). https://www.esd.whs.mil/Portals/54/Documents/DD/issuances/dodi/773066p.pdf
[53] Join Staff. (2011). CJCSI 3401.02B. https://www.jcs.mil/Portals/36/Documents/Doctrine/training/cjcsi3401_02b.pdf?ver=2017-12-29-171240-350

unit is organized or designed. Commanders are also held accountable for correcting the deficiencies identified and are expected to dedicate the time and resources required to do so.

Sexual Violence Impacts Readiness

Instances of sexual violence in a unit do not only impact the readiness of the individual who has been harmed but degrade the unit's ability to function as a team. When both the victim and perpetrator are part of the same unit, the harm to combat readiness is magnified.[54] In these cases, the unit can experience internal divisions and disruptions to good order and discipline that undermine training and readiness.[55, 56] Further, Service members who engage in harassing behavior, are abusive towards others, or are found to have perpetrated sexual assault are a liability to commanders as they risk the safety of the unit.

Implementation Considerations

To elevate the importance of combatting sexual violence, and to ensure that appropriate time and resources are allocated, metrics must be captured across three dimensions.

Status of Workforce

In order to be ready to support victims, unit readiness scores must include an assessment of whether a particular unit has the right composition of people for these roles, and that these personnel are up to date on training and qualifications. Just as a unit is not ready if they do not have the personnel with the given core competencies for warfighting, a unit is not ready if they do not have their victim support personnel.

Ability to Provide Necessary Response Activities

Ensuring that units have the ability to provide the needed care for survivors is a key aspect of readiness. This includes, but is not limited to: the ability of a unit to collect DNA evidence for a Sexual Assault Medical Forensic Exam in a deployed environment; the ability of a unit to provide timely access to victim advocacy; and the ability of Service member in a unit to quickly access special victims' counsel.

Status of Unit Personnel

Instances of sexual harm disrupt unit activities. Readiness indicators must also include individuals undergoing or awaiting nonjudicial punishment, court martial, or other adverse administrative action for perpetrating sexual violence, as well as those who have to move units. These actions impact the makeup of a unit – and require additional resources to compensate for deficiencies.

Some units across the Services engage in readiness tracking for staffing, training and provisioning of Sexual Assault Response Coordinators and SAPR Victim Advocates, but this practice is ad-hoc and

---

54 Klein, M., & Gallus, J. A. (2018). The readiness imperative for reducing sexual violence in the US armed forces: Respect and professionalism as the foundation for change. *Military Psychology, 30*(3): 264-269.

55 Wood, E. J. (2010). Rape is not inevitable in war. *Yale Journal of International Affairs, 5*: 161.

56 Lyall, J. (2020). Divided Armies: Inequality and Battlefield Performance in Modern Warn. *Princeton University Press.*

command-specific. Including metrics in the categories above will help ensure that units receive the resources they need to combat sexual violence and incentivize commanders to prioritize the time needed to address it. Per DoDI 7730.66 and Chairman of the Joint Chiefs of Staff Instruction (CJSCI) 3401.02B, higher level commanders–up to and including the Joint Chiefs–are charged with using DRRS reporting to identify which units require additional resources in order to meet their main warfighting missions. Whether it is downed aircraft or broken vehicles, ineffective personal training, or medical issues, units that have deficiencies in their operations reports receive resources to correct their deficiencies. Including instances of sexual harm in these reports will help ensure that deficiencies are addressed as early as possible.

Finally, an additional benefit of including sexual harm in operational reporting is that operations officers–those responsible for the tracking and reporting of DRRS tracking–are quite often the individuals selected for command.[57] Readiness tracking is done in the operations sections of units. This will elevate sexual harm to a primary area of concern for commanders. Including sexual harm in readiness reporting will also expose future commanders earlier in their career to the importance of preventing harm on operational readiness and help ensure that we are promoting leaders who take the issue seriously. The operations section of units is also the "owner" of a unit's time and focus. Tracking sexual harm as part of readiness reporting will ensure that it is prioritized by unit leaders.

Outcome Metrics

The first outcome of this recommendation should be a revision of CJSCI 3401.02B to include tracking of sexual harm in its calculation of operational readiness (known as the C-level). This would codify sexual harm as a key part of readiness. The second outcome would be an increase in reporting of these issues in DRRS, which would allow for this specific readiness metric to be tracked over time. The third outcome should be an increase in resources to the most impacted units, and more meaningful input for commander's rating forms.

Recommendation 3.2: USD(P&R) Should Direct the Services to Educate the Force About Sexual Harassment and Sexual Assault within the Context of the Services' Core Values

Beginning with recruitment, reinforced in basic training, and expanded upon in Professional Military Education (PME), Service members should comprehend and be able to apply key concepts, such as—but not limited to—consent and respect, within a framework of desired and honorable behavior. This core values framework may reflect Service unique cultures but should explain and reinforce the links between the prevention of sexual harassment and sexual assault and their relation to improvements in military readiness. Commensurate with rank and position, Service members should be able to

[57] The Climate and Culture line of effort consultative team indicated that most of the leaders selected for O-5 command had served as an operations officer. According to senior leaders in the Air Force, this assignment "is a key leadership development requirement for our future commanders."

demonstrate how their behavior and example contribute to a healthy unit climate where all can serve with dignity and respect.

Rationale for this Change: Sexual Violence is Incompatible with Service Values

Sexual harm is a continuum and can exist across many domains. Behaviors across the continuum are counter to the core values to which the Services subscribe.

Service	Values
Army	Loyalty, Duty, Respect, Selfless Service, Honor, Integrity, Personal Courage
Navy	Honor, Courage, Commitment
Air Force	Integrity First, Service before Self, and Excellence in All We Do
Marine Corps	Honor, Courage, Commitment

Figure 2. Military Service Values

Learning to embody these values is a primary means by which civilians are inculcated into military Service culture. Since the inception of the all-volunteer force, the Military Services have been using an appeal to their values to recruit and retain individuals.[58, 59, 60] Through the use of these values, the military Services focus on "training out" behaviors that are present in civilian life and "training in" specific actions in order to create a sense of comradery and forge the bonds necessary to do the work expected of them.[61] For example, learning and becoming habituated to the custom of the military salute is instilled in every Service member upon entry. Sexual violence should also be included in this education and appeal to Service values. Treating your fellow Service member with dignity and respect should be integral to a Marine, Sailor, Airman, Guardian, or Soldier's identity.

Living values is the touchstone of a military career. As Secretary of Defense Austin noted in his Commencement Address at the U.S. Military Academy, "the values you uphold are the values that hold you up."[62] The Services' core values thus provide a guide to living in such a way as to combat sexual harm.[63]

---

[58] Woodward, R. (2000). Warrior heroes and little green men: Soldiers, military training, and the construction of rural masculinities. *Rural Sociology*, *65*(4), 640-657.

[59] Bachman, J.G., Sigelman, L., & Diamond, G. (1987). Self-selection, socialization, and distinctive military values: Attitudes of high school seniors. *Armed Forces & Society*, *13*(2): 169-187.

[60] Ricks, T.E. (2007). *Making the Corps* (2nd ed.). Simon & Schuster.

[61] Hunter, K. (2018). Warrior Culture: Ancient Roots, New Meaning. In K.H. Thomas & D.L. Albright (Eds.). *Bulletproofing the Psyche: Preventing Mental Health Problems in Our Military and Veterans* (29-44). Praeger.

[62] DoD. (2021). *Secretary of Defense Austin Remarks for the U.S. Military Academy Graduation Ceremony (As Delivered)*. Defense.gov. https://www.defense.gov/Newsroom/Transcripts/Transcript/Article/2628547/secretary-of-defense-austin-remarks-for-the-us-military-academy-graduation-cere/

[63] Evidence from our NATO allies shows how including combatting sexual harassment and assault into core values can meaningfully change culture. A 2017 study of the German military found that making "respect for the whole person" a key part of core values training created a more human-centered approach to leadership and reduced the number of incidences

In addition to using a framework of core values, the Services must ensure that the continuum of harm is addressed in all educational materials. Sexual harm does not start with assault. Sexual harassment and sexual assault have similar underlying individual and community-level (climate-related) risk factors.[64] To create a culture where individual Service members are able to serve with dignity and respect, behaviors must be addressed as early as possible.

Implementation Considerations

In April 2021, DoD SAPRO released a new policy instruction (DoDI 6495.02, Volume 2) to set standards for the Services' sexual assault training and education.[65] This new policy critically sets a requirement for training and education across the military career cycle to promote Service core values "to reinforce social norms that prevent assault", starting with accession education.[66] The IRC recommends this specific focus on core values in the Services' prevention education, particularly in the early stages of the military career cycle, be evaluated and reviewed as a part of future SAPRO policy compliance.[67]

This is a welcome development, as the Services note that while education and training on sexual violence is presently included in basic training and annual refreshers, the focus is on what actions one *should not* do rather than focus on values as a positive guide for proactive behavior.[68] Using the core values to discuss the continuum of sexual harm should make clear that harassing behaviors are inconsistent with living a life of "honor," nor can one claim to possess "courage" while watching a teammate suffer sexual harassment. Punitive measures alone do not change culture; instead, they must be complemented by proactive practices that demonstrate positive behavior and reinforce positive norms.[69]

---

of harassment within units. Source: Leonhard, N. (2017). Towards a new German military identity? Change and continuity of military representations of self and other(s) in Germany. *Critical Military Studies, 5*(4), 304-321. https://www.tandfonline.com/doi/abs/10.1080/23337486.2017.1385586

64 OPA. (2020. December 14). Contextual Risk Factors Associated with Sexual Assault and Sexual Harassment, Army briefing.

65 DoD. (2021). *DoDI 6495.02, Volume 2: Sexual Assault Prevention and Response: Education and Training.* https://www.esd.whs.mil/Portals/54/Documents/DD/issuances/dodi/649502_vol2p.PDF?ver=x0Y2PHILAnffN3xcghUPbg%3D%3D

66 The new instruction requires content regarding Service core values in the context of preventing sexual assault for: accessions education and training; initial entry training and education; pre-command training; annual refreshers; and PME.

67 DoD Instruction 6495.02, Volume 2. (2021, April 9). *Sexual Assault Prevention and Response: Education and Training*: 6-7.
https://www.esd.whs.mil/Portals/54/Documents/DD/issuances/dodi/649502_vol2p.PDF?ver=x0Y2PHILAnffN3xcghUPbg%3d%3d

68 In speaking with the Service senior leaders on its Consultative Team, the experts were informed that the general climate around prevention and awareness training on sexual violence is one of behavior avoidance; this approach does not equip Service members with knowledge of prosocial, honorable behavior.

69 Hunter, K. (2018). Warrior Culture: Ancient Roots, New Meaning. Bulletproofing the Psyche: Preventing Mental Health Problems in Our Military and Veterans: 29-44.

As the Services begin to implement the new policy requirements related to core values, particular attention must be paid to loyalty. In the military, loyalty can be easily mistaught (and misunderstood) as being loyal to the institution at all costs, even when it means accepting the bad behavior of individuals; for example, minimizing the widespread harms inflicted by sexual violence as the result of "a few bad apples." This misapplication of loyalty is a contributing factor to toxic environments; instead, loyalty must be presented as a collective value, in which the safety of one affects the wellbeing of all, promoting a more positive climate and a greater likelihood that people will watch out for each other.[70]

Outcome Metrics

Shifts in climate and culture occur slowly. Over time, however, the IRC would expect to see evidence of success from this approach to prevention education through increased reporting of sexual harassment initially, and lower prevalence of sexual harassment and sexual assault in the long run. An initial increase in reports of harassment will be indicative of more people reporting harmful behavior sooner. The initial increase in reports is also evidence of a culture that understands that this behavior is not tolerable. While it will take time, the combined efforts of educating across the continuum of harm, incorporation into core values, and swift punishment as appropriate will lead to lower prevalence rates overall. The WGRA as well as pulse surveys will provide the data for showing success in this metric.

More immediately, the first metric for success of this recommendation will be evidence that the Services have complied with the new policy requirements to frame sexual assault prevention in the context of core values. As the IRC is recommending the full continuum of sexual harm (to include both sexual assault and sexual violence) be taught through core values across the military career cycle, future iterations of the training policy should reflect this approach.

Recommendation 3.3: Addressing Sexual Harassment and Sexual Assault in the 21st Century Requires DoD to Engage with the Cyber Domain

Addressing sexual violence in today's force requires a targeted response to cyberharassment and all forms of technology-facilitated abuse.[71] To do so, DoD must commit to collecting data to measure

---

[70] Dagless, J.W. (2018). Toxic leadership in the military. *In The Leadership Hubris Epidemic*, 93-135. Palgrave Macmillan, Cham.

[71] Technology-facilitated abuse includes specific behaviors or crimes under the UCMJ, such as:
Article 117a, nonconsensual distribution of intimate digital images and Article 130 stalking. Additionally, technology-facilitated abuse describes forms of harmful behavior or interpersonal violence that are communicated through social media, or other internet-based platforms/applications. For example, retaliation for reporting a sexual assault can take place online by posting a derogatory comment or even a threat to someone's social media page. Similarly, a Military Protective Order can be violated via electronic communications if the subject contacts the victim through electronic means, i.e., email, chat, messenger, or other social media application.

the scope of the problem, including the cyber domain in all education and training on sexual violence, and holding Service members accountable who engage in harmful or criminal behavior through technology.

- 3.3 a: Collect data to measure the problem of cyberharassment (and related harms);
- 3.3 b: Educate leaders on cyberharassment and technology-facilitated abuse; and,
- 3.3 c: Hold Service members appropriately accountable who engage in cyberharassment and other forms of technology-facilitated abuse.

Rationale for these Changes: DoD Lacks a Systematic Approach to Combatting Cyberharassment

The fluidity between what constitutes "real life" and what takes place over the internet has specific consequences for the military's ability to maintain good order and discipline.

The online environment and the pervasive nature of social media have fundamentally changed the way that individuals interact with one another, blurring the line between the virtual and physical worlds. This is especially true for people between the ages of 17 and 24,[72] who spend more than nine hours per day consuming social media content—sharing images, chatting with friends, and posting content.[73] These trends are significantly concentrated among the military population, with nearly half (46 percent) of the active duty members, and over half (52 percent) of active duty enlisted Service members, age 25 and younger.[74] More than any generation before them, today's and tomorrow's Service members are (and will be) accustomed to technology as a fundamental part of their personal and professional lives.[75] Social media, in particular, is seen by many young people as a natural extension of their "real world" experiences, and attest to being and are online "almost constantly."[76]

---

[72] This is the same age cohort of women shown to be most targeted by nonconsensual pornography in the general population; in the military, this age bracket of women and men is at highest risk of experiencing or perpetrating sexual assault. Sources: https://datasociety.net/pubs/oh/Nonconsensual_Image_Sharing_2016.pdf and https://www.sapr.mil/sites/default/files/DoD_Annual_Report_on_Sexual_Assault_in_the_Military.pdf

[73] Hunter, K. & Journe, E. (2021). All Women in the Kitchen and Other Dangerous Tropes: Online Misogyny as a National Security Threat. *Journal of Advanced Military Studies*, *12*(1), 57-85.

[74] Military One Source. (2020). 2019 Demographics: Profile of the Military Community. https://download.militaryonesource.mil/12038/MOS/Reports/2019-demographics-report.pdf, 8 and 36.

[75] These changes have been rapid. In 2002, approximately 15 percent of young people reported developing relationships online. By 2019 it was over 60 percent. Source: Yunarti, S., Wijayanti, S., & Savitri, N. (2018). *Teen vulnerability in online relationships based on development needs for friendships and a search for identity*. https://doi.org/10.31227/osf.io/5tche.

[76] Research shows that 45 percent of 13 to 17-year old's say they are online almost constantly. Source: https://www.pewresearch.org/social-trends/2020/05/14/on-the-cusp-of-adulthood-and-facing-an-uncertain-future-what-we-know-about-gen-z-so-far-2/.

Young people (most junior enlisted Service members) are more likely to view the online environment as "flat" and that everyone they are "friends" with are of similar importance. These dynamics have specific meaning in the military, in which relationships and rank are formalized, because hierarchies are broken down in the digital space.[77] For example, when more senior Service members "friend" their subordinates on social media, it can impact unit climate. The chain of command becomes muddied, as it may be hard to distinguish an online comment from a "friend" from an order. There is also evidence that some senior Service members abuse this lack of clarity to exploit more junior Service members.[78]

> Among active duty women, 30 percent who have experienced sexual harassment indicate the harassment took place online, on social media or by other electronic means.
>
> -2018 DoD Workplace and Gender Relations survey of Active Duty Service Members

At the same time, the senior leaders who are charged with promoting a safe and respectful climate may lack an understanding of how social media platforms (and other technologies) are used by younger Service members. Their relationship to technology[79] stands in stark contrast to those they command, as they are, on average, much older than junior enlisted personnel.[80] Senior leaders' limited digital literacy hinders their ability to detect and fully grasp the impact (and harm) of certain online behaviors. For example, testifying before Congress in the wake of the Marines United scandal, General Neller, then-Commandant of the Marine Corps, reluctantly admitted he "didn't have a good answer" for how to hold the offenders accountable.[81]

This is especially concerning because the online environment has made it easier for individuals to engage in behavior across the spectrum of harm. Sharing sexually explicit content without someone's

---

[77] Kesharwani, A. (2020). Do (how) digital natives adopt a new technology differently than digital immigrants? A longitudinal study. *Information & Management*, *57*(2): 103-170.

[78] Hunter, K. & Journe, E. (2021). All Women in the Kitchen and Other Dangerous Tropes: Online Misogyny as a National Security Threat. *Journal of Advanced Military Studies*, *12*(1): 57-85.

[79] Those who have grown up using online technology are more likely to see the online environment as a personal space, where relationships formed and information shared are the same as in the in-person environment; while those who saw the creation and adoption of online communication during their lifetime use technology for communication, yet are less likely to share personal details of their life.
Source: Kesharwani, A. (2020). Do (how) digital natives adopt a new technology differently than digital immigrants? A longitudinal study. *Information & Management, 57*(2), 103-170.

[80] The average age for Active Duty enlisted personnel is 26.9 years, and the average age for Active Duty officers is 34.4 years with approximately 1 in 4 active duty officers aged 41 and older (born 1980 or earlier). Source: Military One Source. (2020). *2019 Demographics: Profile of the Military Community.* https://download.militaryonesource.mil/12038/MOS/Reports/2019-demographics-report.pdf, iv.

[81] At the March 14, 2017 Senate Armed Services Committee hearing, Senator Gillibrand asked, "Who has been held accountable?" "I don't have a good answer for you," Neller answered. "That's a lame answer, but ma'am, that's the best I can tell you right now." Source: March, J.K. (2017, March 16). The Rise And Fall (And Rise) Of 'Marines United.' *Task and Purpose.* https://taskandpurpose.com/news/rise-fall-rise-marines-united/

consent (or to which a former intimate partner may have previously consented) is increasingly common. Disturbingly, perpetrators of sexual harm are often rewarded for sharing pictures of their conquests with "likes" and reposts of their content (as was the case with Marines United,[82] and several other similar events[83] since then).[84,85]

Commanders need to grapple with the cyber domain in order to set and maintain a tone of inclusion, dignity, and respect. Cyberharassment contributes to hostile work environments and is, for some victims, the primary means by which they experience abuse.[86] DoD's own surveys indicate that one-third of victims who report experiencing sexual assault felt they had been the target of retaliation through online ostracism or maltreatment.[87, 88]

Although the online environment offers new avenues through which perpetrators can inflict harm, and in many ways shields bad actors through a cover of anonymity,[89] the military must make accountability for offenders a priority. Without a systematic approach to detect prevalence, nor a commitment to mainstreaming the cyber domain in all training and education on sexual violence, DoD's approach will continue to be ineffective and piecemeal. Despite the presence of social media policies by the Services,[90] these bad behaviors persist. This has created a culture of impunity around

---

[82] In 2017, the Marines United scandal unfolded after a whistleblower, a former Marine, made public the existence of a 30,000-member-strong Facebook group of Marines that circulated thousands of nude images of female Service members, ex-girlfriends, and wives, without their knowledge or consent.

Source: https://www.cnas.org/publications/commentary/confronting-digital-misogyny-why-the-militarys-metoo-moment-must-tackle-cyberharassment

[83] Liautaud, A. (2018). *Exclusive: The Pentagon hasn't stopped the military's revenge porn problem*. Vice. https://www.vice.com/en/article/pamxk7/exclusive-the-pentagon-hasnt-stopped-the-militarys-revenge-porn-problem

[84] Dodge, A. (2016). Digitizing rape culture: Online sexual violence and the power of the digital photograph. *Crime, Media, Culture, 12*(1), 65-82.

[85] In addition, an industry has emerged focused on repairing individuals' reputation online after they are subject to humiliation. Many of the people these firms sell Services to are women Service members because they have more incentives to keep their reputation solid and feel hopeless that the military will do anything to punish offenders. Source: Bartow, A. (2009). Internet defamation as profit center: The monetization of online harassment. *Harvard Journal of Law & Gender, 32*, 383-429. https://scholars.unh.edu/cgi/viewcontent.cgi?article=1296&context=law_facpub

[86] Breslin, R., Davis, E., Hylton, K., Hill, A., Klauberg, W., Petusky, M., Klahr, A. (2019). *2018 Workplace and Gender Relations Survey of Active Duty Members: Overview Report*. Report (No. 2019-027). Alexandria, VA: Office of People Analytics. https://apps.dtic.mil/sti/citations/AD1072334

[87] DoD SAPRO. (2017). *Fiscal Year 2016 Annual Report on Sexual Assault in the Military*. https://sapr.mil/public/docs/reports/FY16_Annual/FY16_SAPRO_Annual_Report.pdf

[88] The survey defined 'ostracism' as involves improper exclusion from social acceptance; 'maltreatment' is defined as includes actions committed against a reporter of sexual assault by someone that may include physical or psychological force or threat of force. Online retaliation took place through Facebook, Twitter, Yik Yak, and/or Snapchat.

[89] Pittaro, M.L. (2007). Cyber stalking: An analysis of online harassment and intimidation. *International Journal of Cyber Criminology, 1*(2): 180-197.

[90] These policies include the Army Regulation 600-20, Office of the Chief of Naval Operations Instruction 5300.13, Marine Corps Order 5354.1E, and Air Force Instruction 36-2710.

online behavior.[91] The following recommendations will help DoD and the Services build a comprehensive approach to addressing sexual harm in the online environment.

Recommendation 3.3 a: Collect Data to Measure the Problem of Cyberharassment (and Related Harms)

USD(P&R) should direct the Office of People Analytics (OPA) to develop a systematic approach to tracking prevalence of cyberharassment and technology-facilitated abuse. The most recent data for online sexual violence in the military come from the 2019 WGRA, which revealed that 30 percent of active duty women and 17 percent of active duty men who experienced sexual harassment stated that it happened on social media or other forms of electronic communication.[92] These numbers are troubling, largely because cyberharassment is more prone to underreporting[93] than harassment in the physical world. This is particularly true in instances where individuals do not trust that the system will meaningfully address their case.[94]

DoD and the Services lack the ability to track the prevalence of cyberharassment, online stalking and retaliation, and other technology-facilitated abuse, such as the non-consensual distribution of intimate digital images. While some information about online sexual violence has been gathered through questions in the Workplace and Gender Relations surveys and the DEOCS, the information to-date has not been collected with the intent to compare across data sets, detect how many Service members have experienced this form of abuse, nor track trends in victimization and perpetration over time.[95]

Without a systematic, targeted approach to collecting data on harassing and harmful behaviors in the cyber domain, DoD and the Service will lack information critical to informing prevention measures. Further, the digital landscape can change drastically in two years, emphasizing the importance of regular survey data, not only through prevalence measures in WGRA, but also in DEOCS, or a new

---

[91] DoD SAPRO. (2021). Appendix F: Sexual Harassment Assessment. *Fiscal Year 2020 Annual Report on Sexual Assault in the Military*. https://www.sapr.mil/sites/default/files/Appendix_F_Sexual_Harassment_Assessment_FY2020.pdf

[92] Breslin, R., Davis, E., Hylton, K., Hill, A., Klauberg, W., Petusky, M., Klahr, A. (2019). *2018 Workplace and Gender Relations Survey of Active Duty Members: Overview Report.* Report (No. 2019-027). Alexandria, VA: Office of People Analytics, 48. https://apps.dtic.mil/sti/citations/AD1072334

[93] Ahlgrim, B. & Terrance, C. (2021). Perceptions of Cyberstalking: Impact of Perpetrator Gender and Cyberstalker/Victim Relationship. *Journal of Interpersonal Violence, 36*(7-8).

[94] Galloway, R. (2017). *Underreporting of Cyberbullying and Reasons Why* (Master's thesis, Regent University).

[95] DoD began collecting information about online sexual violence in 2016, with a special focus group survey on social media in the 2016 WGRA. Since 2018, the WGRA has asked Service members if their worst experience of sexual harassment (and/or gender discrimination) occurred "online on social media or via other electronic communications." However, this was not a prevalence rate (only a lower bound), since with this question the Service member is only describing the "one worst situation" they experienced. The *WGR* now also includes the option, "Showed or threatened to show private images, photos, or videos of you to others" as a response to survey questions about retaliation following sexual assault. The *2019 Active Duty Focus Groups (MSGR)* also revealed social media, dating apps, and sharing explicit images as emergent themes.

pulse survey. This information would provide a critically missing tool for commanders to fix climate issues related to online harassment and sexual violence promulgated through technology.

To fill this important gap,[96] the IRC recommends that OPA conduct a review of all relevant surveys[97] on sexual harassment, sexual assault, and climate, to identify inefficiencies and develop a comprehensive approach to measuring the prevalence of cyberharassment, online stalking and retaliation, and other technology-facilitated abuse, such as the non-consensual distribution of intimate digital images. Based on this review, future iterations of the identified DoD surveys should include a new prevalence metric for cyberharassment and related harm, which should be complemented by qualitative measures of technology-facilitated abuse in iterations of the Service Academy Gender Relations (SAGR) Focus Groups.[98]

Recommendation 3.3 b: Educate Leaders on Cyberharassment and Technology-facilitated Sexual Harassment and Sexual Assault

The Secretary of Defense should direct the Services to ensure that the cyber domain is included in PME[99] related to sexual violence. Senior leaders and commanders who, unlike today's junior enlisted personnel, did not grow up with the internet and social media, require specific knowledge and skills to be able to model professional online behavior for their troops, as well as better detect abusive, sexual violence. The Military Services should develop a learning module to develop digital literacy for commanders at the upper echelons who may lack awareness and understanding of social media and how technology platforms can be exploited to bully, harass, and intimidate fellow users.

Bridging this gap is essential for ensuring that commanders develop the appropriate knowledge to understand how the cyber environment shapes their unit cultures and empower them to take the appropriate actions to address and correct it.

---

96 Given the IRC's findings on lack of trust in command among Service members, we can conclude that the prevalence is much higher. Rebuilding trust in the system will require meaningful and swift action to hold perpetrators accountable.

97 This includes the WGRA, Workplace Gender Relations Survey of Reserve Component Members (WGRR), and the Service Academy Gender Relations Survey (SAGR).

98 Barry, A., Hill, A., Petusky, M., Klauberg. W., Davis, L., & Klahr, A. (2020). *2019 Service Academy Gender Relations Focus Groups Overview Report*. OPA Report No. 2019-068. https://www.sapr.mil/sites/default/files/Appendix_G_OPA_2019_Service_Academy%20_Gender_Relations_Focus_Groups-Overview_Report.pdf

99 PME refers to the professional training, development, and schooling of military personnel. It encompasses many schools, universities, and training programs designed to foster leadership in military Service members. It is at the parochial learning level that future military leaders will learn how to foster healthy command climates.

Recommendation 3.3 c: Hold Service Members Appropriately Accountable Who Engage in Cyberharassment and Other Forms of Technology-Facilitated Sexual Harassment and Sexual Assault

The Military Services must commit to holding Service members accountable who engage in cyberharassment, the nonconsensual distribution of intimate visual images, or other crimes or violence perpetrated through technology, and providing remedies to victims. Commanders and military justice practitioners must treat cyberharassment and technology-facilitated sexual violence as they do all other crimes and harmful behaviors.[100]

While DoD and the Services address the online environment in their harassment policies[101, 102, 103], accountability remains scarce. One of the reasons that accountability remains low is that reporting of cyber activities is difficult. As part of ensuring that the cyber domain is adequately included in efforts to combat sexual harm, there must be a simplified and streamlined way for users to report instances they encounter online.

Service members who experience cyberharassment, the nonconsensual distribution of intimate visual images, or other technology-facilitated abuse should be able to easily report to a trained, specialized professional independent of the chain of command. Several of the IRC's Accountability recommendations (See: Appendix B) enhance access to justice for victims and strengthen the military justice response to those who engage in abusive online behaviors—many of which are specific crimes under the UCMJ.[104]

Outcome Metrics

Outcome metrics for this suite of recommendations largely depend on DoD's adoption of updates to surveys. Questions related to the online environment should be included in the DEOCS, WGRA, and other datasets, as determined by OPA, as well as included in the development of a future pulse survey tool (See: Recommendation 3.7 a: USD(P&R) Should Develop a Standardized "Pulse Survey" Tool that would Enable Unit-level Commanders to Collect Real-time Climate Data on Sexual Harassment and Sexual Assault from Service Members in their Units between Required Administrations of the DEOCS). This will enable DoD to measure and track prevalence of

---

[100] Citron, D. (2014, October 17). Cops Don't Take Harassment of Women Seriously—Especially Online. *Time.com.* https://time.com/3513763/anita-sarkeesian-hate-crimes/

[101] Harassment can be oral, written, or physical. Harassment can occur in person, through electronic communications, including social media; and through wrongful broadcast or distribution of intimate visual images and other forms of communication.

[102] U.S. Marine Corps. (2021). *2021 Social Media Handbook.* https://www.marines.mil/Portals/1/Docs/2021USMCSocialMediaHanbook.pdf?ver=vdVBkAYIQohHSc2KKyViKQ%3d%3d&timestamp=1610492306183

[103] DoD. (2020). *DoDI 1020.03: Harassment Prevention and Response in the Armed Forces.* https://www.esd.whs.mil/Portals/54/Documents/DD/issuances/dodi/102003p.PDF?ver=DAAzonEUeFb8kUWRbT9Epw%3D%3D

[104] U.S. Congress. (1958). United States Code: Uniform Code of Military Justice, 10 U.S.C. § 917a: Art. 117a. Wrongful broadcast or distribution of intimate visual images. https://www.law.cornell.edu/uscode/text/10/917a

cyberharassment and technology-related abuse. The incorporation of digital literacy training for commanders on the nature of the online environment and its impact on unit climate (as a part of PME) should better equip leaders to detect misconduct among their troops and hold Service members appropriately accountable over time.

Recommendation 3.4: Ensure that there is an Internal Focus on Sexual Violence Across the Force in DoD Implementation of the 2017 National Women, Peace, and Security Act

Sexual violence is a leading barrier to women's meaningful participation in the military—within our own ranks, as well as in our allied forces. DoD should build on the 2020 WPS Strategic Framework and Implementation Plan (SFIP) to ensure an internal focus on preventing gender discrimination, and guarantee that sexual violence is fully integrated into future policy and operations on women, peace, and security.[105]

- 3.4 a: Elevate and standardize the gender advisor workforce;
- 3.4 b: Use qualitative data as part of indicators for Defense Objective One of the WPS Strategic Framework;
- 3.4 c: Integrate a gender analysis into the military's planning & operational frameworks;
- 3.4 d: Review and revise PME & DoD schoolhouse curricula to mainstream WPS priorities; and,
- 3.4 e: Congress should support and codify into legislation DoD's inclusion of Personnel & Readiness in WPS Implementation.

Rationale for these Changes: Sexual Violence is a Leading Barrier to Women's Meaningful Participation in the Military

The WPS Act of 2017 promotes women's meaningful inclusion and participation in defense, diplomacy, and global security to prevent, mitigate, and resolve violent conflict. This law ensures that the U.S. Government is integrating a gender perspective[106] across all of its diplomatic, development and defense-related activities. The Act recognizes that in order for the U.S. to effectively argue that partner nations support women's meaningful participation within the defense and security sectors, we must set an example for the rest of the world by ensuring that our own military serves as a model of

[105] DoD. (2020). *Women, Peace, and Security Strategic Framework and Implementation Plan.* ://media.defense.gov/2020/Jun/11/2002314428/-1/-1/1/WOMEN_PEACE_SECURITY_STRATEGIC_FRAMEWORK_IMPLEMENTATION_PLAN.PDF

[106] Gender analysis is the systematic gathering and examination of information on gender differences and on social relations between men and women in order to identify and understand inequities based on gender. Source: Office of the NATO Security General's Special Representative for Women, Peace and Security. (2019). *Concepts and Definitions.* https://www.nato.int/nato_static_fl2014/assets/pdf/pdf_2019_07/20190709_1907-wps-glossary.pdf

diversity and inclusion. In fact, the Act stipulates that the U.S., "should be a global leader in promoting the meaningful participation of women."[107]

The Act requires a government-wide strategy on WPS and a specific implementation plan from DoD. To satisfy these requirements, the Department developed the DoD WPS SFIP. The SFIP details the Department's roles and responsibilities for implementing the WPS Strategy and establishes WPS Defense Objectives. The very first of these overarching, long-term Defense Objectives states:

- Defense Objective One. The Department of Defense exemplifies a diverse organization that allows for women's meaningful participation across the development, management, and employment of the Joint Force.[108]

Despite these commitments, implementation of WPS within DoD (and throughout the U.S. government)[109] has primarily focused on how women are faring abroad, divorced from a recognition of gender inequities at home. This external gaze has meant that, while the Combatant Commands work to incorporate a gender lens in their operations, or encourage allied militaries to promote women in their own security forces, the U.S. military continues to struggle with the retention[110] and advancement of women in the force. This is particularly troubling because experiencing sexual harassment or sexual assault is a leading reason women leave the military. Service women who experience sexual harm are more than twice as likely to separate from Service as those who did not.[111] The U.S. is not positioned to credibly promote the meaningful inclusion of women in partner nations, or ensure the security and safety of women abroad, when women within our own ranks are suffering.

---

[107] DoD. (2017). *Women, Peace, and Security Act of 2017.* https://uscode.house.gov/statutes/pl/115/68.pdf

[108] DoD. (2020). *Women, Peace, and Security Strategic Framework and Implementation Plan.* https://media.defense.gov/2020/Jun/11/2002314428/-1/-1/1/WOMEN_PEACE_SECURITY_STRATEGIC_FRAMEWORK_IMPLEMENTATION_PLAN.PDF

[109] The 2017 National WPS Act tasks not only DoD, but also the State Department, and the Department for Homeland Security, to implement women, peace, and security priorities throughout their policies, including the development of a strategy for WPS for each agency.

[110] The IRC is encouraged by recent, ongoing efforts by DoD to better understand the impacts of sexual harassment and sexual assault on military readiness, retention, and resilience. Several research efforts within OPA can provide insight to military leaders and commanders on the extent to which the career trajectories of Service members who experience these violent and harmful events differ from their peers. Work is underway to examine a variety of career outcomes over a 5-year period for active duty members who experienced sexual harassment and/or sexual assault, including differences for those who reported the experience. The career outcomes currently being analyzed include separations, characterization of service among those that separated, promotions, demotions, and security clearance actions. The main objective of this study is to identify whether different career trajectories exist for those who did or did not experience sexual harassment and/or sexual assault as a means to assess potential readiness impacts of such experiences on the all-volunteer force. Continued research in this area is imperative. By demonstrating the ways in which sexual assault and sexual harassment have real implications for the readiness, resilience, and retention of the all-volunteer force, military leaders and commanders will understand the critical importance of not only the prevention of those experiences, but also the response to incidents that do occur.

[111] Morral, A.R., Matthews, M., Cefalu, M, Schell, T.L., Cottrell. L. (2021). Effects of Sexual Assault and Sexual Harassment on Separation from the U.S. Military: Findings from the 2014 RAND Military Workplace Study. Santa Monica, CA: RAND Corporation. https://www.rand.org/pubs/research_reports/RR870z10.html

The U.S. must recognize the connective tissue between WPS principles and improving conditions for women within our own military in order to achieve our overall national security objectives.

Recommendation 3.4 a: Elevate and Standardize the Gender Advisor Workforce

The Secretary of Defense should direct the DoD components, to include the Services and the Combatant Commands, to standardize the gender advisor workforce, elevate this role into a full-time, billeted, and resourced position, and ensure this workforce is equipped and trained with core knowledge on DoD and Service-level policies pertaining to sexual assault, sexual harassment, and domestic abuse.

The use of gender advisors in military operations has become increasingly common since the passage of UN Resolution 1320 in September 2000.[112] A key rationale for the establishment of the NATO gender advisor program was to protect civilians (with an emphasis on women and children) from sexual harm during conflict or stability operations.[113] Nonetheless, the successful employment of gender advisors has been demonstrated to reduce sexual violence perpetrated not only against civilians in foreign conflict zones, but also blue-on-blue offenses. Evidence from our allies suggests that adopting a gender mainstreaming approach to issues like sexual violence within their forces can lower the risk for sexual harm.[114]

Although funding was provisioned by Congress for WPS implementation, the U.S. military does not currently have a standardized gender advisor program, nor are gender advisors a full-time, billeted, and resourced uniform position.[115] Further, commanders are not given training on how to use gender advisors or the benefit that they can bring to military operations. The result is that gender advisors are often ignored or dismissed by commanders.[116] While gender advisors are available to Combatant Commanders, individuals are assigned on an ad-hoc basis and as a temporary or collateral duty. Without a permanent position, these specialists can be pulled out of gender advisor assignments to

---

[112] United Nations Security Council. (2020, September 15). *Resolution 1320 (2000)*. Adopted by the Security Council at its 4197th meeting. https://digitallibrary.un.org/record/422493?ln=en

[113] NATO Allied Command Transformation. (2021). *HQ Office of the Gender Advisor*. https://www.act.nato.int/gender-advisor

[114] Norway, a leader in fully adopting gender perspectives into its integrated force, has seen continual decline in sexual assault within its military since it adopted a comprehensive gender mainstreaming program. Source: Lucero, G. (2018). From sex objects to sisters-in-arms: Reducing military sexual assault through integrated basic training and housing. *Duke Journal of Gender Law & Policy 26*(1), 1-21. https://scholarship.law.duke.edu/cgi/viewcontent.cgi?article=1332&context=djglp.

[115] The FY21 National Defense Authorization Act (NDAA) provides funding for the DoD and the Services to implement the 2017 WPS Act. DoD. (2021). FY21 NDAA. https://www.govinfo.gov/content/pkg/BILLS-116hr6395enr/pdf/BILLS-116hr6395enr.pdf

[116] Trogus, N. (2021). Bridging the Gap Towards a Gendered Perspective in Security Force Advising. National Defense University. [Thesis].

return to their previous roles, resulting in the loss of knowledge and a missed opportunity to build skills. Standardizing the workforce will ensure that the knowledge base is retained.

Gender advisors in the U.S. Military should be established at the battalion (or equivalent) and above level.[117] They should report to the commander and have a strong liaison relationship with operations and logistics. In addition to their external focus, gender advisors should receive training so that they are familiar with the key risk and protective factors for sexual violence relevant to the safety of Service members. Their role in the operations and planning sections of units will further elevate the importance of combatting sexual harm. While gender advisors primarily serve an external-facing WPS role, it is critical that these personnel have a basic understanding of P&R policies[118] specific to promoting climates of dignity, safety, and respect for all who serve. Conversely, gender advisors should also be connected with the relevant P&R points of contact at their Gender Advisors at Combatant Commands who should in turn understand the overlap and connection with WPS.

Recommendation 3.4 b: Use Qualitative Data as Part of Indicators for Defense Objective One of the WPS Strategic Framework

Comprehensive implementation of the WPS has the potential to drive culture change; however, solely tracking quantitative indicators of that implementation is insufficient to measure progress. While increasing the number of women in the Services is an important first step to drive and sustain institutional change, the climate for women as they are integrated across the force is equally significant to measure.[119, 120, 121, 122, 123, 124, 125]

---

[117] The FY21 NDAA provides funding for the Services to implement the 2017 WPS Act. The Services are currently in process of doing so. A revision to the WPS 100 and 200 syllabi to include an understanding of internal policies around sexual violence would be simple and effective. This training is currently administered at the joint level and should stay as such.

[118] Policies under the authority of DoD USD(P&R), including the policies for SAPR, domestic abuse/intimate partner violence (Family Advocacy Program), and sexual harassment (ODEI).

[119] Evidence shows that achieving a critical threshold in the number of women–approximately 30 percent—is needed for the impact of gender integration to take hold and be sustained. Source: Rosen, J. (2017). Gender quotas for women in national politics: A comparative analysis across development thresholds. *Social Science Research*, *66,* 82-101.

[120] Beckwith, K., & Cowell-Meyers, K. (2007). Sheer Numbers: Critical Representation Thresholds and Women's Political Representation. *Perspectives on Politics*, *5*(3), 553-65.

[121] Wroblewski, A. (2019). Women in Higher Education Management: Agents for Cultural and Structural Change? *Social Sciences*, *8* (6), 172.

[122] Hyrynsalmi, S.M. (2019). *The underrepresentation of women in the software industry: thoughts from career-changing women*. IEEE/ACM 2nd International Workshop on Gender Equality in Software Engineering (GE), 1-4.

[123] Glass, C. & Cook, A. (2018). Do women leaders promote positive change? Analyzing the effect of gender on business practices and diversity initiatives. *Human Resource Management, 57*(4), 823-837.

[124] Seierstad, C., Warner-Søderholm, G., Torchia, M., & Huse, M. (2017). Increasing the number of women on boards: The role of actors and processes. *Journal of Business Ethics, 141*(2), 289-315.

[125] Hunter, K. (2019). Shoulder to Shoulder Yet Worlds Apart: Variations in Women's Integration in the Militaries of France, Norway and the United States. [Unpublished Dissertation]. *Josef Korbel School of International Studies*.

> "We're working to make a more inclusive, diverse and safe force, and that will translate to what we do overseas. It impacts our credibility in carrying that message."
>
> -Service Gender Advisor, as told to the IRC in a listening session

Implementation of the 2017 WPS Act provides an opportunity to better understand the scope of sexual harassment and sexual assault on women's meaningful participation in the force, and to enhance strategies to mitigate it. The IRC recommends DoD add qualitative indicators, such as insights from the Military Service and Gender Relations Focus Groups, and OPA's forthcoming study on career outcomes for Service members who experience sexual violence,[126] to its existing set of WPS indicators for Defense Objective One. It is encouraging to see that the FY21 WPS SFIP Indicators for Defense Objective One have expanded to include the addition of incidence and prevalence of sexual assault, sexual harassment, and reports of domestic abuse; this is critical starting point that will be augmented with qualitative data.

Additionally, the Services should explore convening focus groups related to gender discrimination, sexual harassment and sexual assault as part of their reporting on WPS implementation. For example, the recent U.S. Army Special Operations Command[127] report on Women in Special Operations is a model for the type of qualitative feedback that will help identify what steps need to be taken to better facilitate women's inclusion and advancement in the force.

Recommendation 3.4 c: Integrate a Gender Analysis into the Military's Planning & Operational Frameworks

DoD should direct all components, including the Services and Combatant Commands, to integrate a gender analysis into planning and operational frameworks to ensure they holistically incorporate diverse perspectives (including gender, race, religion, sexual orientation and gender identity) and contain a focus on preventing sexual harm to Service members.

Although the impact of sexual harassment and sexual assault are wide-ranging, it tends to be seen as peripheral from the military's warfighting mission, and therefore relegated to a low priority for commanders, excluded from the key tenants of operational design.[128] In reality, sexual violence is an operational issue, and must be elevated and addressed as such.

---

[126] DoD collects a variety of survey and administrative data that can be leveraged to understand the impacts of sexual harassment and sexual assault on military readiness, retention, and resilience. Several research efforts within OPA can provide insight to military leaders and commanders on the extent to which the career trajectories of Service members who experience these violent and harmful events differ from their peers.

[127] Britzky, H. (2021, March 18). The truth about false sexual assault reports in the military. *Task and Purpose*. https://taskandpurpose.com/news/truth-about-false-sexual-assault-reports/

[128] Haynie, J.G., & Hunter, K. (2020). *War Through a Gender Lens.* Responsible Statecraft. https://responsiblestatecraft.org/2020/01/10/war-through-a-gender-lens/

The failure to consider diverse perspectives, specifically gender, not only impedes the inclusion of all Service members, it can also impact the success of military operations. The consequences of such a failure were keenly demonstrated during the 2018 Talisman Saber exercise. During this training exercise, U.S. forces were focused exclusively on kinetic operations and unaware of the rapes occurring in displaced persons camps and the harms occurring to their own Service members, compromising the success of the overall mission.[129] Though just an exercise, this scenario revealed how unprepared the U.S. is to handle situations outside of "traditional" security issues.

The importance of military commanders' views in shaping operational design cannot be overstated. Surveys of U.S. commanders revealed that they saw sexual assault as a "trivial" matter when compared to their primary operational focus. This perceived lack of urgency results in a culture that accepts sexual harm[130] as inevitable.[131]

Revising the planning process will signal to the force that addressing sexual violence is essential, and lead to a culture where the safety and wellbeing of all Service members is seen as an essential part of security and operations.

Recommendation 3.4 d: Review and Revise PME & DoD Schoolhouse Curricula to Mainstream WPS Priorities

The Secretary of Defense and the Services should conduct a review of all curricula, period of instructions, and training and education guidance across DoD Schoolhouses[132] and PME institutions to ensure WPS principles are mainstreamed throughout.[133] The schoolhouses are a Service member's first introduction to their roles in the military. Shifting climate and steering cultural change is a long-term project, and will require continued, intentional efforts to mainstream gender perspectives across military education and training.

To aid this shift, WPS principles must be integrated throughout curriculum and guidance across DoD schoolhouses and PME institutions. Service members must be introduced to this framing early, and have it reinforced often. Consistently integrating and mainstreaming a gender perspective in all

---

[129] Holt-Ivry, O. (2018). *Mind the Gender Capability Gap*. Defense One. https://www.defenseone.com/ideas/2018/07/gender-capability-gap/149477/.

[130] Sexual harm is used interchangeably throughout this report with sexual violence, to collectively refer to the continuum of harm that includes sexual harassment and sexual assault.

[131] Wood, E. J. & Toppelberg, N. (2017). The persistence of sexual assault within the US military. *Journal of Peace Research, 54*(5): 620-633.

[132] Several continuing education schoolhouses exist within DoD and the Services. Examples include the National War College, the College of Information and Cyberspace, the College of International Security Affairs, the Eisenhower School, and the Joint Forces Staff College.

[133] These principles include: (1) Women are more prepared and increasingly able to participate in efforts that promote stable and lasting peace; (2) Women and girls are safer, better protected, and have equal access to government and private-assistance programs, including from the U.S., international partners, and host nations; and (3) the U.S. and partner governments have improved institutionalization and capacity to ensure WPS efforts are sustainable and long-lasting. Source: USAID. (2021). *Implementation of the U.S. Strategy on Women, Peace, and Security*. https://www.usaid.gov/women-peace-and-security

learning tools regarding military operations will elevate sexual violence as a primary security concern and ensure that necessary resources are provided. Modified and newly developed curriculum and guidance should seek to educate and increase awareness of how diverse perspectives and gender equality enhance military effectiveness and also benefit the safety and welfare of Service members. Starting with initial education and reinforcing these ideas throughout a Service member's educational journey will further promote the concept that combatting sexual violence is a key aspect of the warfighting mission.

Recommendation 3.4 e: Congress should Support and Codify into Legislation DoD's Inclusion of Personnel & Readiness in WPS Implementation

The DoD is making strides on operationalizing WPS and recognizing the inherent ties between the treatment of Service women within the force, and success in carrying the message of women's meaningful participation in the militaries of partner nations. This commitment was evident in speaking with each of the Services' WPS leads and the OSD Policy team responsible for implementing the 2017 WPS Act.

Going beyond its Congressional mandate,[134] DoD is working towards meaningfully employing WPS tools not only to promote external military effectiveness, but also to ensure that the U.S. military is truly a place where diverse perspectives are considered, and all people can serve with dignity and respect. In order to fully codify the benefits of implementation, the IRC recommends that Congress work in concert with DoD leaders to codify the clear connections between external operations and internal readiness.[135]

Outcome Metrics

The IRC is making several concrete recommendations which should be monitored for compliance. Outcome metrics include:

- The number and level of gender advisors established across the Services' Combatant Commands.

---

[134] The 2017 WPS Act required, "the Secretary of Defense shall ensure that relevant personnel receive training, as appropriate, in the following areas: (1) Training in conflict prevention, peace processes, mitigation, resolution, and security initiatives that specifically addresses the importance of meaningful participation by women, (2) Gender considerations and meaningful participation by women, including training regarding (A) international human rights law and international, humanitarian law, as relevant; and (B) protecting civilians from violence, exploitation, and trafficking in persons, (3) Effective strategies and best practices for ensuring meaningful participation by women. Of note, none of these provisions specify a requirement for DoD to address the condition and safety of women within the U.S. military.

[135] The IRC notes these connections are not exclusive to DoD. USAID, DHS, and the State Department must all work to ensure the safety of their workforce, and that they have meaningful access to victim services and remedies for sexual violence in the workplace, including while on diplomatic missions or in delivering aid. See, for example: Hansler, J. (2020). *Democrats introduce legislation to strengthen anti-sexual harassment protocols at State Department.* CNN. https://www.cnn.com/2020/09/30/politics/shape-act-state-department/index.html

- A revised WPS syllabi which reflects an internal focus on P&R policies, ensuring awareness of the ties between external operations and internal readiness.
- The inclusion of qualitative measurements adopted by DoD in future iterations of indicators for Defense Objective One of the WPS Strategic Framework and Implementation Plan, to better assess the military's success in creating a diverse organization that allows for women's meaningful participation across the development, management, and employment of the Joint Force.
- The number of components, including Services and Combatant Commands, that develop planning and operational frameworks which integrate a gender analysis and a focus on preventing sexual harm to Service members.
- A revision of Joint Publication 05,[136] the document which provides the foundation for military planning and the basis for the Services' doctrine on operational design, to include an internal focus on the safety of Service members from sexual harm and an emphasis on the need to consider diverse perspectives in the planning process.
- A review and revision of all curriculum and training materials to ensure that these documents consistently reference and incorporate WPS principles and tie back to the established SFIP Indicators.

Recommendation 3.5: Use Qualitative Data to Select, Develop, and Evaluate the Right Leaders for Command Positions

Courageous, compassionate, and competent military leaders are an essential component to eradicating sexual harassment, sexual assault, and the unacceptable behaviors that fuel these devastating crimes. Selecting and developing leaders with the appropriate emotional intelligence and moral courage to create a healthy military climate and culture is critical to building trust among Service members and the American public. Using qualitative data to select and develop the right leaders will ensure that those responsible for the care of our nation's Service members will adhere to the rule of law, moral standards, and best practices.

- 3.5 a: The Secretary of Defense should direct the Services to use qualitative feedback and in-person interviews in the selection of Command Teams at the O5 and E8 levels to identify leaders who are not upholding Service values, as well as to recognize and advance transformative leaders; and,
- 3.5 b: The Secretary of Defense should direct the Services to revise their performance evaluation policies for Officers and Noncommissioned Officers to include a comprehensive narrative section related to unit climate and handling of sexual harassment and sexual assault cases.

---

136 Joint Chiefs of Staff. (2020). *Joint Planning: Joint Publication 5-0.* https://fas.org/irp/doddir/dod/jp5_0.pdf

Rationale for these Changes: Selecting and Developing the Right Leaders to Create a Healthy Military Climate and Culture is Critical to Building Trust Among Service Members

For decades, sexual harassment and sexual assault have continued to plague the military while many senior leaders continue to "check the block" on prevention and response programmatic levels but are completely disconnected from what Service members are actually experiencing on the ground. Only after "major" incidents do senior leaders seem to take notice of the insidious problem created by a culture that has tolerated deviant behaviors that lead to sexual harassment and assault: Tailhook (1991),[137] Aberdeen (1996), the Air Force Academy scandal (2003),[138] the Air Force Basic Training scandal (2009-2012),[139] and the sexual harassment and murder of Vanessa Guillen at Fort Hood (2020).[140] In the wake of these incidents, it is apparent that leaders at all levels of command failed to create a culture of dignity and respect. Developing qualitative data to ensure the right military leaders are at the helm is a crucial step to tackling the sexual harassment and assault problem in the military.

Recommendation 3.5 a: Use Qualitative Data to Select and Develop the Right Leaders

The Secretary of Defense should direct the Services to use qualitative feedback and in person interviews in the selection of Command Teams at the O-5[141] and E-8[142] paygrades to identify leaders who are not upholding Service values nor placing a high priority on prevention of sexual assault/sexual harassment and victim care as well as to recognize and advance transformative leaders. Command Teams at the O-5 and E-8 levels have a critical role in the military organizational structure across the Enterprise. These mid-level commanders and NCOs are responsible for multiple companies of junior Service members and can have the most impact on the climate and culture of a unit. Officers at the O-5 level have the power to adjudicate Field Grade Article 15s—a powerful tool that can be used to correct and punish unwanted behaviors that can lead to sexual harassment and assault before the behaviors become more serious. The E-8 NCOs complement their O-5 counterparts by enforcing standards from the top down.

---

137 Winerip, M. (2013, May 13). Revisiting the Military's Talihook Scandal. *The New York Times*. https://www.nytimes.com/2013/05/13/booming/revisiting-the-militarys-tailhook-scandal-video.html

138 Schmitt, E. & Moss, M. (2003, March 7). Air Force Academy Investigated 54 Sexual Assaults in 10 Years. *The New York Times*. https://www.nytimes.com/2003/03/07/us/air-force-academy-investigated-54-sexual-assaults-in-10-years.html

139 Lawrence, C. (2012). 31 victims identified in widening Air Force sex scandal. *CNN*. https://www.cnn.com/2012/06/28/justice/texas-air-force-scandal/index.html

140 Horton, A. (2021, April 30). Army punishes more Fort Hood leaders after Vanessa Guillén's killing reveals command failures. *The Washington Post*. https://www.washingtonpost.com/national-security/2021/04/30/vanessa-guillen-report-ft-hood/

141 O-5 signifies a mid-grade officer, referred to as "Lieutenant Colonel" in the Army, Marine Corps, and Air Force and "Commander" in the Navy.

142 E-8 designates a senior enlisted member, referred to as Master Sergeant or First Sergeant in the Army and Marine Corps, Senior Master Sergeant or First Sergeant in the Air Force, and Senior Chief Petty Officer in the Navy. E-8s operate as commanders' senior advisers for enlisted matters.

Having the right type of leaders at the mid-command level is critical in the context of sexual harassment and sexual assault. These leaders set the tone and example for what is right and what is wrong. Junior Service members look to these leaders as role models as they progress in their own military careers. Only those leaders who uphold Service values, place prevention of sexual harassment and sexual assault as the highest priority, and appropriately respond to and care for victims of these crimes, should wear the mantle of command. In-person interviews and qualitative feedback will help ensure the right leaders are selected for this especially important responsibility.

Qualitative interviews must screen for values and opinions around diversity, equity, inclusivity, and belonging and the importance leaders attribute to maintaining a unit climate that does not tolerate sexual assault and sexual harassment. Research shows that including such measures will allow the Military Services and NGB, "to capitalize on the talents of those high in interpersonal competence and identify those whose lack of social acumen, [which] may prove detrimental" to unit climates, as well as promote leaders with the "emotional intelligence and sensitivity required" to appropriately handle sexual assault and sexual harassment issues.[143]

Leaders are the Key to a Healthy or Unhealthy Command Climate

Leaders' actions or inactions create direct consequences that impact risk of sexual violence. In order to shift culture and move to acceptance of healthy social norms, the right leaders must be in the command positions. As one Senior Enlisted Advisor told the IRC, military leaders "should never walk past anything." If leaders see or hear something that must be corrected, it should be addressed on the spot. This is the constant drumbeat that engaged supervisors must be sounding in order to maintain a healthy climate.

One of the five factors that enhance the likelihood that sexual harassment will occur is uninformed leadership "that lacks the intentionality and focus to take the bold and aggressive measures needed to reduce and eliminate sexual harassment."[144] Leadership engagement therefore is the number one preventive factor in reducing sexual harassment and stopping the progression of unacceptable, negative behaviors along the continuum of harm. The FHIRC report clearly identified what can happen when leaders do not make safety and welfare of their personnel a priority: a command climate permissive of sexual harassment and sexual assault.[145]

It is too often the case that NCOs or officers tolerate unacceptable comments or behaviors that lead to an unhealthy command climate. In a study of active duty Service women, 24 percent of NCOs did nothing when sexually demeaning comments were made toward women whom they were responsible

143 Klein, M., & Gallus, J.A. (2018). The readiness imperative for reducing sexual violence in the US armed forces: Respect and professionalism as the foundation for change. *Military Psychology*, *30*(3): 264-269.

144 National Academies of Medicine. (2018). *Annual Report*. https://nam.edu/wp-content/uploads/2019/05/National-Academy-of-Medicine-2018-Annual-Report.pdf

145 The Fort Hood Independent Review Committee. (2020, November 6). *Report of the Fort Hood Independent Review Committee*, iii. https://www.army.mil/e2/downloads/rv7/forthoodreview/2020-12-03_FHIRC_report_redacted.pdf

for and 40 percent did not do anything about deviant sexual activity in barracks that they knew about.[146] These surveys underscore what the FHIRC highlighted about this leadership neglect phenomenon: the negative consequences that come from leaders walking past unhealthy unit culture, which is allowed to then harden and set.[147]

Actions Taken	DoD Women	DoD Men
They were encouraged to drop the issue	49%	52%
Someone talked to the person(s) to ask them to change their behavior	47%	40%
Their coworkers treated them worse, avoided them, or blamed them for the problem	44%	35%
The person they told took no action	36%	43%
The rules on harassment were explained to everyone	41%	43%
The person(s) stopped their upsetting behavior	31%	24%

Figure 3. Top Actions Taken as a Result of Reporting/Filing a Sexual Harassment Complaint[148]

More disturbing, however, are survey data from FY18 represented in Figure 3. Data indicate that about half of those who reported unwanted behavior were "encouraged to drop the issue" and in more than one-third of the cases "the person they told took no action."[149] This goes beyond leaders walking past or ignoring unhealthy climate behaviors. This data, as reflected in the chart below, suggests unit members feel unable to report incidents of unhealthy unit behavior because someone in command is actively trying to deter them from officially reporting the incident.

However, there are indications that some military leaders are taking action to respond to sexual harassment in the workplace; in FY18, 47 percent of women and 40 percent of men who experienced sexual harassment reported that someone talked to the offender to ask them to change their behavior."[150] This kind of involvement by leadership is necessary to the health and welfare of units, and should be encouraged and uplifted as part of the selection process for Command Teams.

---

146 Sadler, A., Mengeling, M., Booth, B., O'Sea, A., & Torner, J. (2017). The Relationship between the U.S. Military Officer Leadership Behaviors and Risk of Sexual Assault in Reserve, National Guard and Active Component Servicewomen in Nondeployed Locations. *American Journal of Public Health*, *107*(1): 147-155.

147 The Fort Hood Independent Review Committee. (2020, November 6). *Report of the Fort Hood Independent Review Committee*, 114. https://www.army.mil/e2/downloads/rv7/forthoodreview/2020-12-03_FHIRC_report_redacted.pdf

148 Breslin, R., Davis, E., Hylton, K., Hill, A., Klauberg, W., Petusky, M., Klahr, A. (2019). *2018 Workplace and Gender Relations Survey of Active Duty Members: Overview Report*. Report (No. 2019-027). Alexandria, VA: Office of People Analytics, 50. https://apps.dtic.mil/sti/citations/AD1072334

149 Breslin, R., Davis, E., Hylton, K., Hill, A., Klauberg, W., Petusky, M., Klahr, A. (2019). *2018 Workplace and Gender Relations Survey of Active Duty Members: Overview Report*. Report (No. 2019-027). Alexandria, VA: Office of People Analytics, 50. https://apps.dtic.mil/sti/citations/AD1072334

150 Ibid.

The IRC is encouraged by several emerging programs in some Services. For example, the Battalion Commander Assessment Program (BCAP) and the Colonels Command Assessment Program (CCAP) currently being used by the Army show promise in weeding out toxic leaders. BCAP is the Army's program to determine an officer's fitness for command and strategic leadership potential.[151,152] Service SMEs also told the Climate and Culture experts that the Navy is in the midst of piloting the Navy Command Leadership Assessment and Selection Program, which uses 360-degree feedback for all prospective Commanding Officers (COs), Executive Officers (XOs), and Senior Enlisted Leaders (SEL). Two peers, two subordinates, and two senior reviewers at a minimum are engaged for feedback with a goal of at least 10 responses. The feedback is then provided to the perspective CO/XO/SELs at the Naval Leadership and Ethics Center in Newport Rhode Island where all are required to attend before assuming their leadership roles. The IRC supports the Services to continue to develop these meaningful approaches to leader selection.

Recommendation 3.5 b: Include a Meaningful Narrative Section in Performance Evaluations for Officers and NCOs

The Secretary of Defense should direct the Services to revise their performance evaluation policies for Officers and NCOs to include a comprehensive narrative section related to the Service member's unit climate and handling of harassment and assault cases. Policies should set clear guidelines for categorizing performance in this area. Command climate assessments must be more than a "check the box" exercise[153] — these evaluations provide an opportunity for a meaningful conversation around development and upholding Service values. Leaders must be held accountable for their organizational climate, specific to sexual harassment and sexual assault through the performance evaluation system.[154] Current performance evaluation instructions across the force discuss all these items but leave very little room on the actual forms to sufficiently cover the topics. Figure 4 details these instructions.

---

[151] BCAP has become a requirement for officers competing for battalion command opportunities and consists of a four-day assessment conducted at Fort Knox, Kentucky. Each candidate is assessed on physical fitness, verbal and written communications, and through cognitive and non-cognitive assessments with the program culminating in a double-blind panel interview with senior Army officers. In conjunction with the Centralized Selection List process, the BCAP results help ensure that the Army is selecting the best qualified officers for command.

[152] Denton, C.J. (2021). *BCAP: The Battalion Command Assessment Program. Army.mil.* https://www.army.mil/article/243040/bcap_the_battalion_command_assessment_program

[153] This section of an evaluation should be narrative with specific actions taken to improve climate. It should specifically address what is going well and what needs improvement. Specific guidance should be given on how to rate a Service member as meets, exceeds, significantly exceeds, progressing or does not meet. This should not be entirely subjective. DoD's OFR should be consulted to provide examples of actions and behaviors that represent each category. Specific behaviors should then be incorporated into the narrative section of the report. The Navy has made some progress in this area with an actual section for climate and descriptors of how to categorize actions, however, there is no narrative section.

[154] Sadler, A.G., Lindsay, D.R., Hunter, S.T., & Day, D.V. (2018). The impact of leadership on sexual harassment and sexual assault in the military. *Military Psychology, 30*(3), 252-263. https://doi.org/10.1080/08995605.2017.1422948

Service	Command Selection Directive	Description
Army	Army Directive 2013-20	Mandated that support forms include goals and objectives relevant to eliminating sexual harassment and assault and promoting a culture of dignity and respect. Raters were then to comment on significant positive actions as well as any negative information.
Navy	Bureau of Naval Personnel Instruction 1610.10E	To achieve high marks in areas of the performance evaluations, Sailors must demonstrate how they have cultivated or maintained command climates where improper discrimination of any kind, sexual harassment, sexual assault, hazing, and other inappropriate conduct is not tolerated; where all hands are treated with dignity and respect; and where professionalism is the norm.
Air Force	Air Force Instruction 36-2406	It is mandatory for raters to include expectations for contributing to a healthy organizational climate for airmen up to the grade of Senior Airman. Raters must also ensure that NCOs and officers are accountable for creating a healthy organizational climate. Raters must ensure that every Commander knows he(she) is responsible for, and will be held accountable for, ensuring their unit has a healthy command climate.
Marine Corps	Marine Corps Order 1610.7A	Commanders are evaluated on their ability to set a command climate that is non-permissive of misconduct, to include: sexual assault, sexual harassment, hazing, discrimination, retaliation, and social media/internet misconduct.

Figure 4. Current Performance Evaluation Instructions by Service

Subordinate feedback should be incorporated into all performance evaluations for Command Teams and all development plans for both officers and NCOs to identify Service members who are not upholding Service values nor placing a high priority on the safety and welfare of their teammates. The IRC further recommends that a mechanism to obtain command climate feedback via exit interviews with departing Service members be developed. Feedback here is particularly meaningful as departing Service members are in position to comment on climate and care for personnel without fear of retaliation.

The IRC heard from survivors of sexual assault who described command climates that permitted harmful behaviors indicative of a culture of sexual harassment and assault with little to no accountability for those in charge. Survivors consistently reported experiences of permissive counter-professional environments with no expectation that these behaviors would be addressed and corrected.

One way of both addressing and correcting poor command climates is through performance evaluation systems. Evaluations matter to leaders hoping to rise through the ranks. If one has to be held directly accountable for performance in the area of unit climate and appropriate handling of sexual harassment and assault cases, it follows that leaders who want to get promoted will take notice. Leaders cannot fake a healthy command climate. Those subordinate to the command team are in the best position to hold their leaders accountable for upholding Service values. As such, performance evaluations should include subordinate feedback along with a detailed narrative of how the command is creating a healthy and professional climate in the unit.

The use of qualitative feedback and in-person interviews can help screen out toxic leaders while identifying effective leaders who will not tolerate unhealthy command climates. Proactively identifying potential leaders with attributes like excellent interpersonal competence and high social emotional intelligence (also known as "non-cognitive capabilities") allows the Services to select leaders who can—and will—break the hardened and set toxic cultures that have been allowed to persist from command to command. Conversely, using in-person interviews and qualitative feedback in military leadership selection processes can help identify those whose lack of social acumen may continue to fuel the so-called leadership neglect phenomenon which the Fort Hood IRC identified.[155,156] This selection paradigm is especially important given the discretion and sensitivity required to properly address sexual harassment, sexual assault, and related concerns impacting Service members under a commander's care.

Civilian Best Practices – 360-Degree Feedback

The military lags behind the best practice in the civilian work force which uses peer and subordinate feedback both for promotion and development purposes, commonly known as 360-degree feedback.[157] The 360-degree feedback is a process through which feedback from an employee's subordinates, colleagues, and supervisor(s), as well as a self-evaluation by the employee themselves is gathered.[158] The 360-degree feedback is so named because it solicits feedback regarding an employee's behavior from a variety of points of view (subordinate, lateral, and supervisory).

This system of performance evaluation can be contrasted with the military's "downward feedback" approach.[159, 160] Without "upward feedback"–feedback delivered to supervisory or management by subordinates–leaders' neglect of climate and culture will continue to persist. These 360-degree feedback tools highlight discrepancies across stakeholder groups making it easier to identify leaders who need improvement before they advance further in their careers.[161]

---

155 This phenomenon was reinforced through the IRC's discussions with junior enlisted personnel and survivors.

156 The Fort Hood Independent Review Committee. (2020, November 6). *Report of the Fort Hood Independent Review Committee*, 114. https://www.army.mil/e2/downloads/rv7/forthoodreview/2020-12-03_FHIRC_report_redacted.pdf

157 Hazucha, J.F., Hezlett, S.A., & Schneider, R.J. (1993). The Impact of 360-Degree Feedback on Management Skills Development. *Human Resource Management*. https://onlinelibrary.wiley.com/doi/abs/10.1002/hrm.3930320210

158 Such feedback can also include, when relevant, feedback from external sources who interact with the employee, such as customers and suppliers or other interested stakeholders.

159 McGregor, J. (2013, April 16). *Turning the tables on a top-down military culture*. The Washington Post. https://www.washingtonpost.com/national/on-leadership/2013/04/16/7dbd802a-a6ad-11e2-8302-3c7e0ea97057_story.html

160 This approach includes receiving traditional feedback on work behavior and performance delivered to subordinates by supervisory or management employees only.

161 Leaders must have tangible ways to reinforce a positive command climate, monitor compliance, and correct those leaders who are walking past behaviors unbecoming of Service members. The use of Service-wide, uniformed 360-degree feedback evaluations will provide key indicators for commanders. This analysis must be performed routinely and should be included on all commander's performance evaluations. The criteria can be as simple as "Would you work for or with this person again?" or "Does this person support the Service Values?"

Several studies[162,163] indicate that the use of 360-degree feedback helps to improve employee performance because it helps the evaluated see different perspectives of their performance.[164] Additional studies show that 360-degree feedback may be predictive of future performance.[165]

Ideally, 360-degree feedback should be used to "ask peers and direct reports the extent to which an employee 'lives' the organizations values."[166] This type of feedback system can—and should—have positive outcome metrics in the military, thereby facilitating the selection of the right leaders, who can reverse the toxic climates that were allowed to harden and set from previous commands.

Pilot Programs Underway in Support of this Recommendation

The Services use fragmented forms of 360-degree feedback in numerous ways. For example, Army and Navy are piloting 360-degree feedback to select senior commanders. While promising, the IRC recommends adapting this type of feedback as a development tool for O-2 through O-4s and E-6 through E-7s across all Services. This would be particularly important in the development of soft skills and emotional intelligence in the context of preventing and responding to sexual harassment and sexual assault.

At one time, the Army had the most extensive 360 assessment program for all officers. The rated officer would pick and choose superiors, peers, and subordinates. During their information gathering stage, the Climate and Culture line of effort learned that this program was discontinued a few years ago by the issuance of Army Directive 2018-07, which gave commanders the full authority, while making prudent risk informed decisions, "to simplify, reduce, or eliminate those tasks which are not combat related."[167] This same Directive also eliminated the requirement for a Command Climate Survey at the 6 month point of a command assignment.[168]

The Marine Corps and Air Force do not use or have 360-degree feedback pilot programs. The Marine Corps has a traditional mentorship program, but no evaluation system wherein feedback is solicited from leaders, peers, and subordinates to evaluate perspective leaders' command style. The Air Force

---

162 London, M., & Wohlers, A.J. (1991). Agreement between subordinate and self-ratings in upward feedback. *Personnel Psychology, 44*(2), 375–390. https://doi.org/10.1111/j.1744-6570.1991.tb00964.x

163 Walker, A. & Smither, J.W. (1999). A Five-Year Study of Upward Feedback: What Managers do with their Results Matter. *Personnel Psychology, 52*: 393-423.

164 In a 5-year study, no improvement in overall rater scores was found from the 1st year to the 2nd, but scores rose with each passing year from 2nd to 4th. Reilly et al. (1996) found that performance increased between the 1st and 2nd administrations and sustained this improvement 2 years later.

165 Maylett, T.M., & Riboldi, J. (2007, September). Using 360° Feedback to Predict Performance. *Training + Development, 61:* 48–52. https://www.researchgate.net/publication/293399871_Using_360_feedback_to_predict_performance

166 Culwell, A. (2018). *How leaders can strengthen their organizations culture*. Stanford Social Innovation Review.

167 Department of the Army. (2018). *Army Directive 2018-07 (Prioritizing Efforts-Readiness and Lethality)*. https://www.army.mil/e2/downloads/rv7/leaders/ad_2018_07_prioritizing_efforts_readiness_and_lethality.pdf

168 Office of the Secretary of the Army. (2018, October 26). *Army secretary releases reduction requirement memos to improve readiness.* https://www.army.mil/article/207160/army_secretary_releases_reduction_requirement_memos_to_improve_readiness

uses some principles of 360-degree feedback for General Officers and some command courses, but on the whole, the Service relies on traditional "top down" evaluation systems.[169]

Outcome Metrics

A marker of success for this recommendation would be for all Services to revise their policies listed in Figure 4 and adopt new Commander selection programs. In addition, positive trending DEOCS results indicating an increase in trust of leadership at the O5 and O6 level would also demonstrate success.

Commanders must have tangible ways to reinforce positive command climates, monitor compliance, and correct those leaders who are walking past behaviors unbecoming of Service members. The use of Service-wide, uniformed 360-degree feedback evaluations will provide key indicators for commanders. This analysis must be performed routinely and should be included on all commander's performance evaluations. The criteria can be as simple as "Would you work for or with this person again?" or "Does this person support the Service Values?"

Recommendation 3.6: Building a Climate for the Reduction of Sexual Harassment and Sexual Assault as a Fundamental Leader Development Requirement

The Secretary of Defense should direct the Services to establish "Building a Climate for the Reduction of Sexual Harassment and Sexual Assault" as a fundamental leader development requirement within all PME and pre-Command courses. PME should also include examples of "lessons learned" to uplift best practices in leadership in the area of sexual violence.

Leaders must be taught how to build a climate where every Service member is treated with dignity and respect in an environment free from sexual harassment and sexual assault. The best proving ground for teaching and training is PME.

PME across the Services should therefore prepare to integrate the concept of "Building a Climate for the Reduction of Sexual Violence" into all curricula with focus on five key areas: (1) addressing cultural norms that allow sexual harassment to be tolerated; (2) emphasizing appropriate unit culture for leaders who serve in units where there are fewer women; (3) incorporating unconscious bias training for leaders at all levels; (4) training scenarios that give commanders clear examples around uncomfortable climate issues, and (5) lessons learned to uplift innovative or exemplary efforts in addressing the climate around sexual harassment and sexual assault across the Services.

---

169 Based on information provided by the Services in the Climate and Culture consultative team.

Rationale for this Change: Leaders Must be Taught How to Build a Climate Where Every Service Member is Treated with Dignity and Respect

Leaders need to be supported in developing some of the "softer but critical skills" needed for building positive climates, such as acknowledging mistakes, actively listening, and treating others fairly.[170] PME and pre-command courses should teach attendees to listen, and to practice empathy in order to adequately prepare them to lead discussions around difficult topics as they seek to improve climate. Leaders must also be trained to have the moral courage not to ignore behavior they see as harmful or deleterious to unit health. These behaviors must be addressed on the spot and stopped immediately.

PME Should Teach Leaders to be Aware of and Address the Cultural Norms that Allow Sexual Harassment to be Tolerated

DoD needs to train leaders at all levels regarding sexual assault and sexual harassment, so they take this on as a focused leadership challenge and proactively work to end a culture of permissive behavior that perpetrates negative and unhealthy climates. This education program of instruction should be developed at the DoD level, implemented across all PME, and rolled into the prevention competency program as recommended by the Prevention line of effort.[171]

Current teaching programs in the military suggest men should be cautious of forging relationships with women, to the point that women—even in the same unit—are viewed as "other" versus part of the same military community. This can lead to isolation which is a further risk factor for sexual assault and sexual harassment. Worse still, societal norms that permit harassment of those viewed as "other" are magnified and endorsed within the male power structures of the military. For example, the IRC heard from enlisted personnel about men making sexist comments for the entertainment of the men around them, and the sense that women feel silenced and unable to speak up against these behaviors, as they may be perceived as threatening the "traditional" male-dominated ecosystem some men in the Services seek to preserve. Policies have set left and right limits for behavior but if left unchecked, outdated norms will continue to drive behavior.[172]

PME Should Emphasize Appropriate Unit Culture for Leaders Who Serve in Units Where There are Fewer Women

In the Reserve component, men in units where women accounted for less than 10 percent of their military coworkers were more likely to endorse sexist beliefs than men in units with a higher

---

[170] Klein, M. & Gallus, J. (2017). The Readiness Imperative for reducing sexual violence in the US Armed Forces: Respect and Professionalism as the foundation for change. *Military Psychology, 30*(3), 264-269.

[171] IRC recommendation 2.1. Equip all leaders with prevention competencies and evaluate their performance.

[172] Klein, M. & Gallus, J. (2017). The Readiness Imperative for reducing sexual violence in the US Armed Forces: Respect and Professionalism as the foundation for change. *Military Psychology, 30*(3), 264-269.

percentage of women.[173] The Climate and Culture experts also learned that combat arms units with a low density of women had greater command climate issues, as reported in the FHIRC report, and during a RAND briefing to the IRC. These findings suggest that leaders of certain occupational specialties, as well as those commanding units that have lower percentages of women, may especially benefit from PME that emphasizes the need to dispel common rape myths (like false reporting), as well as challenge outdated gender stereotypes.[174]

PME Across the Services Must Incorporate Unconscious Bias Training for Leaders at All Levels

Generally speaking, gender bias is the tendency to prefer one gender over another, either explicitly or implicitly.[175, 176] Gender bias exists in workforces everywhere, but can be particularly acute in the military, particularly in units with very few women. Take the perspective of a woman in a special operations unit: "Men are accepted as they are, and have to prove themselves worthless in the unit whereas women are expected to be worthless, and have to prove themselves worthy."[177] Education on implicit gender bias for leaders is critical. According to research in the *Harvard Business Review*, the "single most important trait generating a sense of inclusiveness is a leader's visible awareness of bias."[178]

Unconscious bias training should not only address gender bias, but also incorporate lessons on racial and ethnic bias, as well as bias against LGBTQ+ Service members. This education is a critical component of changing the climate and culture of the military to be more cohesive and inclusive of all Service members.

---

[173] Breslin, R., Klahr, A., Hylton, K., Petusky, M., White, A., & Tercha, J. (2020). *2019 Workplace and Gender Relations Survey of Reserve Component Members: Overview Report.* DoD Office of People Analytics, Report No. 2020-054, xii. https://www.sapr.mil/sites/default/files/16_Annex_2_2019_Workplace_and_Gender_Relations_Survey_of_Reserve_Component_Members_Overview_Report.pdf

[174] Breslin, R., Klahr, A., Hylton, K., Petusky, M., White, A., & Tercha, J. (2020). *2019 Workplace and Gender Relations Survey of Reserve Component Members: Overview Report*. DoD Office of People Analytics, Report No. 2020-054. https://www.sapr.mil/sites/default/files/16_Annex_2_2019_Workplace_and_Gender_Relations_Survey_of_Reserve_Component_Members_Overview_Report.pdf

[175] Dunham, C.R. (2017). Third Generation Discrimination: The Ripple Effects of Gender Bias in the Workplace. *Akron Law Review.* https://papers.ssrn.com/sol3/papers.cfm?abstract_id=3019163

[176] It is a form of unconscious bias, or implicit bias, which occurs when one individual unconsciously attributes certain attitudes and stereotypes to another person or group of people. These ascribed behaviors affect how the individual understands and engages with others.

[177] Britzky, H. (2021, May 21). 'Stop the social experiment' — New Survey Spotlights Bias Against Women in Army Special Ops. *Task and Purpose*. https://taskandpurpose.com/news/army-special-operations-women-survey/

[178] Bourke, J. & Titus, A. (2020). The Key to Inclusive Leadership. *Harvard Business Review*. https://hbr.org/2020/03/the-key-to-inclusive-leadership

Scenarios that Give Commanders Ideas and Illustrations Around Uncomfortable Climate Issues Should be Covered as Part of PME and Updated in Unit Climate Handbooks

A Climate Handbook is essentially a how-to guide for leaders on improving and maintaining a positive unit climate. It contains multiple scenarios for dealing with interpersonal conflict, leader development, unit stressors, and other behaviors and issues which can disrupt the working environment or a Service member's performance. While the DEOCS can identify issues, it does not give guidance on the resolution of those issues. The Climate Handbook helps a leader assess climate, develop a plan for improvement and then execute that plan. While providing excellent advice in a number of areas, the handbooks that exist currently do not confront topics such as racism, sexism, or discrimination against LGBTQ+ Service members. These Handbooks therefore need to be revised and should become part of curriculum for all PME.

Leaders need to be coached on how to model the correct behaviors when they encounter harassment and how to create a more mission focused environment verses one that focuses on individuals. Following requests from the Climate and Culture SMEs, the IRC found no scenarios on climate and sexual assault and sexual harassment in any of the Service's Climate and Culture Handbooks (Army and Marines) or Memo (Air Force). The Army has one page that highlights how a negative climate can contribute to sexual harassment and sexual assault but gives no advice or scenarios on how that occurs or what to fix. This was surprising given statutory training requirements for new commanders related to prevention that include: "How to foster a command climate that does not tolerate sexual assault, encourages persons assigned to the command to prevent potential incidents of sexual assault, and encourages victims of sexual assault to report any incident of sexual assault."[179]

Implementation Considerations

Include Lessons Learned to Highlight Innovative Leadership and Climate-related Practices Across the Services

The Climate and Culture experts also identified at least three successful programs that can be incorporated into PME to generate discussion around uncomfortable unit climate issues. During discussions with the U.S. Military Academy Course Director, the experts learned about a pilot program on Relational Character, which teaches cadets how to have informed conversations around uncomfortable subjects. The goal of this program is to establish positive norms around gender, sexuality, and violence. Cadet confidence in facilitating conversations increased significantly, and their comments were universally positive in saying, "Everyone should take this training."

---

[179] U.S. Congress, House Committed on the Armed Service. (2013). National Defense Authorization Act for Fiscal Year 2013; Report of the Committee on Armed Services, House of Representatives on H.R. 4310 together with dissenting views (including cost estimate of the Congressional Budget Office). Washington: U.S. Government Publishing Office. https://www.congress.gov/112/plaws/publ239/PLAW-112publ239.pdf

The IRC also learned that units across Army FORSCOM conduct a "foundational day" once a month which provides opportunities for small group discussions around issues such as sexual assault and sexual harassment, and other climate conversations. The IRC heard that these unit level trainings have been well received especially by junior soldiers who appreciate the time to broach tough conversations.

Finally, promising practices for improving unit climate can also come from our allies. For example, the Canadian Ministry of Defense is engaging survivors through a "Restorative Engagement" program to gather lessons learned. Survivors of sexual assault are speaking with future and current leaders and sharing their stories to affect culture change regarding the way the Canadian military responds to these harms. Canada calls this a "learning, planning, action approach."[180]

Recommendation 3.7: USD(P&R) Should Undertake a Series of Enhancements to the Climate Survey Process

Several actions are needed to improve the command climate survey process to ensure that data is timely, actionable, and useful for commanders:

- 3.7 a: USD(P&R) should develop a standardized "pulse survey" tool that would enable unit-level commanders to collect real-time climate data on sexual harassment and sexual assault from Service members in their units between required administrations of the DEOCS;
- 3.7 b: The Secretary of Defense should direct the Services to develop a formal system to release climate survey data at the unit level and initiate and evaluate corrective action plans;
- 3.7 c: USD(P&R) should accelerate efforts to develop a validated "Climate Benchmark" to measure healthy and unhealthy climate at the unit level; and,
- 3.7 d: Assess whether current DoD policies and EO workforce have capacity to help commanders resolve climate issues.

Rationale for these Changes: Climate Surveys Should Provide Leaders with the Timely Data They Need to Foster a Climate Free of Sexual Harassment and Assault

A climate survey is a checkup of the unit. This process is meant to reveal indicators of positive and negative unit climates and assist commanders in addressing concerns. This system should help commanders become more aware, empathetic leaders who can remedy negative environments. As early as 2014, data gathered by the RAND corporation showed there was an extreme risk of sexual harassment and assault for Service members at Fort Hood, yet several iterations of command teams

[180] Government of Canada. (2021). *Restorative Engagement*. https://www.canada.ca/en/department-national-defence/services/benefits-military/health-support/sexual-misconduct-response/restorative-engagement.html

came and went without addressing the ticking time bomb.[181] Climate is too important of an issue to not have dedicated oversight at echelons above the installation chain of command.

The FY13 National Defense Authorization Act mandated that unit commanders conduct a climate survey within 120 days of assuming command and annually thereafter for the purposes of preventing and responding to sexual assault.[182] To comply, the Department expanded the existing DEOCS to include sexual assault prevention and response[183]. Today, the DEOCS serves as a commander's tool to assess 19 protective and risk factors that can impact a unit's climate and ability to achieve its mission. The survey includes over 100 questions assessing leadership, cohesion, morale, inclusion, and sexually harassing behaviors, among other factors. A new DEOCS platform launched in July 2020 and the survey was revised in January 2021 to include more comprehensive indicators of climate. The Climate and Culture experts identified the need for additional improvements in the climate survey process specifically for sexual harassment and assault, including more simplified and timely surveys, targeted assistance for command in remedying negative climates, and the development of a climate benchmark.

Recommendation 3.7 a: USD(P&R) Should Develop a Standardized "Pulse Survey" Tool that would Enable Unit-level Commanders to Collect Real-time Climate Data on Sexual Harassment and Sexual Assault from Service Members in their Units between Required Administrations of the DEOCS

Climate lives at the lower levels, making it essential for unit commanders to have readily available data that can help identify immediate problems. This pulse survey is not meant to replace the DEOCS, but rather to supplement it as a new means for leaders to conduct "spot checks" with an on-the-ground look for timely action specific to sexual harassment and sexual assault. The pulse survey should be conducted between required administrations of the DEOCS.

The DEOCS is a complex tool that requires commanders to understand the relationship between risk and protective factors and how they interact to affect climate across the board. In this mix, climate specifically related to sexual harassment can get lost. The new DEOCS (DEOCS 5.0) includes a short

---

[181] The Fort Hood Independent Review Committee. (2020, November 6). *Report of the Fort Hood Independent Review Committee.* https://www.army.mil/e2/downloads/rv7/forthoodreview/2020-12-03_FHIRC_report_redacted.pdf

[182] U.S. Congress, House Committed on the Armed Service. (2013). National Defense Authorization Act for Fiscal Year 2013: Report of the Committee on Armed Services, House of Representatives on H.R. 4310 together with dissenting views (including cost estimate of the Congressional Budget Office). Washington: U.S. Government Publishing Office. https://www.congress.gov/112/plaws/publ239/PLAW-112publ239.pdf

[183] The DEOCS is a confidential, command-requested organization development survey that measures cross-cutting risk and protective factors to help DoD leadership and unit/organization leaders gain an understanding of problematic behaviors in their organization. Source: DoD. (2020). *DEOCS: Frequently Asked Questions.* https://www.defenseculture.mil/Portals/90/Documents/A2S/OPA-DEOCS-Survey_Admins_FAQs-20201230.pdf?ver=duUEjU3taRCECammowSlzA%3D%3D

form section on sexual harassment as part of the larger survey. In contrast, during information gathering sessions, the Climate and Culture experts learned that the Army is currently trying to field a pulse survey to timely monitor sexual harassment and gender discrimination. The survey is ten questions and requires no more than five minutes to complete. The FHIRC also conducted a twenty-question electronic survey that took respondents five minutes or less to complete and covered sexual assault, sexual harassment, retaliation, knowledge of SHARP basics, equal treatment, confidence in leadership, and safety.[184]

The DEOCS also takes a limited approach to identifying how unit climate affects the *reporting* of sexual assault. The standardized DEOCS survey includes questions to measure sexual harassment as a potential risk factor for sexual assault, but questions about the response to sexual assault are optional for commanders. A RAND report on Organizational Characteristics Associated with Risk of Sexual Assault and Sexual Harassment in the U.S. Army notes this problem, stating while the DEOCS routinely measures sexual harassment risk, it "does not assess sexual assault risk in a comprehensive way" and thus would require additional surveys specific to sexual assault risk and, relatedly, sexual assault reporting climate.[185]

The use of the DEOCS as a climate indicator for sexual harassment has been hampered by delays in data release to the installation level. The Climate and Culture experts heard numerous reports of frustration with these delays. OPA has addressed these delays, making DEOCS results available to commanders within 72 hours of the survey, but the perception that these data are not available is widespread.[186] Along with timely results, OPA has developed a new interactive commander dashboard that includes a broad picture of risks and protective factors in their organizations. Sexually harassing behaviors is one of a number of indicators of poor climate.

The IRC is mindful that many DEOCS improvements are still in the preliminary stages and need more time to succeed. At the same time, commanders need focused tools to develop meaningful action plans around sexual harassment and assault. A pulse survey will help accomplish these goals.

---

184 The Fort Hood Independent Review Committee. (2020, November 6). *Report of the Fort Hood Independent Review Committee,* 10. https://www.army.mil/e2/downloads/rv7/forthoodreview/2020-12-03_FHIRC_report_redacted.pdf

185 Matthews, M., Morral, A.R., Schell, T.L., Cefalu, M., Snoke, J., Briggs, R.J. (2021). *Organizational Characteristics Associate with Risk of Sexual Assault and Sexual Harassment in the U.S. Army*. Santa Monica, CA: RAND Corporation, 65.

186 The Department has recognized this and working to address it by developing a Commander's Dashboard to allow command to see their results much quicker.

Recommendation 3.7 b: The Secretary of Defense Should Direct the Services to Develop a Formal System to Release Climate Survey Data at the Unit Level and Initiate and Evaluate Corrective Action Plans, Including Clear Guidance on Metrics Requiring Action

The Climate and Culture experts note that the priority given to climate should be as great as routine issues like maintenance and training. This includes greater transparency of survey data and a formal evaluation system for tracking improvements. Currently there is no forcing function beyond the next level of supervision to publish and evaluate a formal action plan after a new commander receives their initial 90-day[187] DEOCS. Given that there is no mandated follow up beyond the next level commander, addressing climate issues easily falls off a busy priority list. This "next level up" system also provides the opportunity for negative reports to be dismissed or ignored.

OPA encourages commanders to share results with their organization, but there is no requirement to do so. Sharing results acknowledges issues that exist and sets the expectation that unit leaders will work together to solve concerns. Creating a feedback loop and "authentic, transparent communication about the steps an organization is taking will go a long way toward helping members know leadership is serious about change."[188] Not surprisingly, publishing results could also reduce survey fatigue, as Service members will see their comments being heard and acted upon.

Steps towards transparency and accountability include publishing climate survey results to all unit members and the chain of command in a timely manner; releasing an action plan to the entire unit and brief updates quarterly as part of operations/training plan briefings; and linking action plans to the Services' Climate Handbooks.[189] Commanders should also request additional training and coaching as part of the unit's existing development plan. Commanders should be evaluated on executing their actions plans, including what help they sought and what initiatives were put in place.

The Climate and Culture experts further recommend that DoD establish clear metrics for DEOCS that require commander action. Currently, these points of action are left up to the Services. The only

---

[187] For the National Guard, Coast Guard, and Reserves, the DEOCS is administered within 180 days of a new command.

[188] Moran, G. (2019, March 8). *How to Rebuild Trust in a Toxic Workplace*. Fast Company. https://www.fastcompany.com/90314680/how-to-rebuild-trust-in-a-toxic-workplace

[189] Department of the Army. (2020). *Army Command Policy, AR 600-20*. https://armypubs.army.mil/epubs/DR_pubs/DR_a/ARN30511-AR_600-20-002-WEB-3.pdf; Department of the Navy. (2017). *Navy Equal Opportunity Program, OPNAVINST 5354*. https://www.med.navy.mil/sites/nmcphc/health-promotion/womens-health/Documents/Policies_and_Instructions/Policies_and_Instructions_Naval_Equal_Opportunity_Program_Manual.pdf; Department of the Navy, Office of the Chief Naval Operations. (2018). *Command Resilience Team Guide (CRT) Supplement*. https://www.mynavyhr.navy.mil/Portals/55/Support/21stCenturySailor/Equal_Opportunity/CRT%20Guide.pdf?ver=hqz3d23YIjnwB0cW3vMnXw%3D%3D; Department of the Navy, Headquarters United States Marine Corps. (2021). *Prohibited Activities and Conduct Order, MCO 5354.1F*. https://www.marines.mil/Portals/1/Publications/MCO%205354.1F.pdf?ver=u8ycNd_hNCfPiCca6eAfSQ%3d%3d; Department of the Air Force. (2020, September 9). *Air Force Guidance Memorandum (AFGM) to Air Force Instruction (AFI) 36-2710, Equal Opportunity Program*.

current metric the experts were able to identify was the Air Force with a 49 percent negative response requiring follow-up. This means if only 48 percent of your unit said it was a miserable place to be, no action would be needed. The FHIRC report recommended that 60 percent favorable become the action threshold, but even that may be too high.

The experts are mindful that the Office of Force Resiliency (OFR) is currently conducting a pilot project to identify and address potential installations with unit climates that are promising, as well as those at-risk. This is anticipated to send a surge of support to work with the entire chain of command to fully identify and resource issues. In an environment with many pressing priorities, this will provide a failsafe to ensure that "Fort Hoods" can be addressed before they become a tragedy. Still, commanders need help addressing climate before it reaches this critical stage.

Recommendation 3.7 c: USD(P&R) Should Accelerate Efforts to Develop a Validated "Climate Benchmark" to Measure Healthy and Unhealthy Climate at the Unit Level

USD(P&R) should accelerate efforts to develop validated thresholds to measure healthy and unhealthy climate at the unit level.

A climate benchmark is essential for Command Team evaluations to objectively measure positive unit climate associated with positive outcomes. OFR and OPA are currently working on this project but need additional support and direction to work together to get this done. As one step, USD(P&R) should direct moving relevant OPA variables and data into DoD's enterprise-wide data system, Advana[190], on a timely and frequent interval. Advana allows DoD to synthesize several disparate data sources and standardize data elements across the Services in order to examine data at several integral levels, depending on users' needs. Dashboards in Advana that leverage real-time or near real-time data can provide the Services with immediate feedback to inform actionable mitigation strategies as problematic climate behaviors arise.

The Climate and Culture experts recommend that the climate benchmark also include actions commanders can take to address issues by recommending a plan for improvement. This plan should reflect positive climate knowledge, skills and attitudes tied to the values of each Service.

---

190 Advana, which stands for Advanced Enterprise Analytics, provides DoD with a central data platform aimed at standardizing data collection, synthesizing data sources, and providing real-time data updates across the Department. Source: Lin, G. (2021, April 7). *Meet Advana: How the Department of Defense Solved its Data Interoperability Challenges.* Government Technology Insider. https://governmenttechnologyinsider.com/meet-advana-how-the-department-of-defense-solved-its-data-interoperability-challenges/

Recommendation 3.7 d: Assess Whether Current DoD Policies and EO Workforce Have Capacity to Help Commanders Resolve Climate Issues

Through numerous briefing sessions, the IRC learned of a serious gap in the training and technical assistance available to the Services and to commanders to address climate issues related to sexual harassment and assault. DEOMI provided this assistance when it was responsible for administering DEOCS. In February 2018, OPA assumed the management and administration of the DEOCS,[191] but the responsibility for assisting the Services with follow up was not formally assigned to any DoD component. OPA has stepped in to offer some assistance but does not have the capacity to respond across the Services or to the needs of individual commanders. On a regular basis, these calls for help are turned away. Given the complexity of the DEOCS results and the need for specialized information about sexual harassment and assault, this lack of capacity is troubling. The need for assistance is ongoing, as reassessments may be needed as improvements are implemented.

At the Services level, the responsibility for assisting leaders with command climate assessments rests with the Military Equal Opportunity (MEO) specialists.[192] Despite several inquiries and briefings, the IRC did not receive enough information to determine the capacity of the MEOs to address climate issues related to sexual harassment. These individuals are often serving in these positions as collateral duty and may lack the specialized training that is necessary to advise commanders on sexual harassment.[193] The effectiveness of these policies, however, largely depends on having access to expert advice on issues that rise to the surface as problem areas. When sexual harassment is one of those areas, commanders need access to specialized expertise.

The Secretary of Defense should direct an assessment of ODEI, DMOC, DEOMI and the Service-level EO programs to identify whether current policies and the EO workforce meet the needs of commanders in addressing climate for sexual harassment and related climate issues. If gaps are identified, the Secretary should direct immediate actions to enhance training and technical assistance. The Secretary's review should include relevant components within DoD who carry some of this responsibility, as well as an assessment of the capacity of the Services EO programs to address sexual

---

[191] DoD. (2020, November 17). *DEOCS: Redesign 101*. https://www.defenseculture.mil/Portals/90/Documents/A2S/OPA-DEOCS-Redesign_101-20201118.pdf?ver=wnzUZBGX2NO18H3FnybAsg%3D%3D

[192] MEO specialists prepare and maintain equal opportunity case files, analyze pertinent data, develop relevant reports, assess education program activities, counsel military personnel and civilian employees on policies, and provide recommendations and advice to leaders in resolving problems related to equal opportunity matters. Source: DoD. (2020). DoDI 1350.02: DoD Military Equal Opportunity Program. https://www.esd.whs.mil/Portals/54/Documents/DD/issuances/dodi/135002p.pdf

[193] AFI 36-2710, Equal Opportunity, Air Force Guidance Memorandum regarding the DEOCS update states, "In coordination with the unit commander, the installation Equal Opportunity Office will conduct a follow up meeting, six-months after the report close-out, with units whose report reflected below 49 percent of favorable results, except when a regularly scheduled Out and About has been conducted in the six months following the DEOCS. (T-1). Alternatively, commanders may appoint a unit member (in the grade of O-4 or above or civilian equivalent) to conduct this follow up. Upon completion of the Equal Opportunity Office six-month follow up, commanders will provide a six-month status report of the commander's action plan to next higher commander."

harassment and how well they collaborate with SAPR/SHARP experts when poor response to sexual assault is noted on the DEOCS.

Recommendation 3.8: The Services Should Publish the Nature and Results of All Disciplinary Actions Related to Sexual Misconduct

Rationale for this Change: Publishing Information will Promote Transparency and Rebuild Trust

The Services should publish the nature and results of all disciplinary actions[194] related to sexual harassment and sexual assault, without identifying the subject, victim or unit, to promote greater transparency and accountability. The Services should disseminate this information to troops periodically.

Similar to a recommendation from the FHIRC,[195] the Services should be required to make publicly available to the force a summary of all adverse actions for Service members held accountable for sexual harassment and sexual assault, including courts-martial and nonjudicial punishment.

Implementation Considerations

This information should be easily accessible and disseminated on a regular basis with updated content.[196] The Services can determine whether the information is best distributed at the installation level, or Service-wide.[197]

---

194 This includes: courts-martial and nonjudicial punishment.

195 The FHIRC recommended that, "the nature of the case and the results of all SHARP disciplinary actions should be published at least semiannually, without identifying the subject, victim or Unit, in order to deter future conduct and engender confidence in the SHARP response process," and to "publicly disseminate court-martial convictions for SHARP offenses." Source: The Fort Hood Independent Review Committee. (2020, November 6). *Report of the Fort Hood Independent Review Committee,* iv. https://www.army.mil/e2/downloads/rv7/forthoodreview/2020-12-03_FHIRC_report_redacted.pdf

196 Houmard, C. (2020, December 17). *What is the Teal Hash Report? 6 News looks at SHARP Program quarterly report*. https://www.kcentv.com/article/news/military-matters/what-is-the-teal-hash-report-6-news-looks-at-sharp-program-quarterly-report/500-e24c7215-de6e-4d90-b636-32a2256f1fd6

197 Gathering Lessons learned on other topics is a consistent Service practice. Each Service is required to have a capability to collect lessons learned and there are directives covering joint lessons learned as well. This is an example of the process from the Air Force. Most telling is the caption, "No culture change" and a "Lesson Not learned will be collected again." The Army gathers lessons learned on a variety of topics at the Combined Arms center at Ft Leavenworth. While a directive existed for the SHARP Academy to collect SHARP Lessons Learned, the climate and culture experts learned that this never came to fruition. In collaboration with the Naval Safety Center, CMC(SD) staff produces a series of Lessons Learned documents, providing examples and insights to a variety of mishap and risk experiences throughout the Marine Corps and the Navy. By doing so, readers are able to recognize the symptoms, causes, and effects of a number of hazards; making

Conclusion

Because leadership is at the heart of military culture and unit climate, these recommendations are set forth to target the developmental deficits, toxic environments, and ineffective leadership that, when eliminated, could prevent another 135,000 Service members[198] from experiencing sexual violence in the next decade—and beyond. As former commanders, the IRC's Climate and Culture experts know firsthand that the operational culture of the military thrives on a "lessons-learned" approach to planning. When it comes to sexual harassment and sexual assault, the IRC believes the following points can be leveraged into lessons-learned that inform best practices for climate and culture:

- Core values must apply to sexual assault.
- The cyber domain is now a permanent feature of today's climate and culture.
- Leaders need to be equipped with relevant skills and timely unit data.
- DoD and the Services can learn from best and promising practices from other militaries, and the civilian sector.
- Words matter—especially from leadership.

Taken together, the IRC's recommendations for climate and culture suggest innovative as well as evidence-informed ways to improve policies, procedures, and people. In the IRC's discussions with survivors and experts, one survivor noted the need for the military to shift its language surrounding sexual assault, similar to how the Force has made strides in talking about suicide. A desire for more impactful messaging was reiterated throughout the IRC's interactions. Service members recognized the importance of using the right terminology, stressing the most vital information, and a renewed emphasis on change. How DoD informs and influences the Force through these messages in all forms of media will have major implications going forward.

On a final note, the IRC suggests consideration of two implementation strategies could improve communication efforts and elevate messaging. The first is to revise the SAPRO website to address greater transparency of data, resources for stakeholders, and tools for leaders and other products in a user-friendly interface. The second is to host a high-level conference on improving climate and culture and emphasizing addressing sexual misconduct from the senior level down to the ground level. While SAPRO holds regular conferences, no Secretary of Defense has hosted a such an event to influence the Force and assess Service progress on sexual harassment and assault. The IRC is mindful that both these strategies require additional resources.

---

certain that those incidents don't occur in vain By leaning from these occurrences, Marines will be better able to avoid similar situations moving forward.

[198] These figures do not represent incidents that could have occurred during years that DoD did not conduct a survey. In addition, this number does not necessarily represent unique Service members (i.e., some Service members may have experienced sexual assault and/or sexual harassment in separate survey years), nor does it account for Service members who recorded several incidents within the same survey period.

The Commission's Climate and Culture experts challenge DoD and the Services to encourage highly engaged leadership that fosters an empathetic command climate, wherein all members of the team are valued, supported, and capable of supporting their fellow Service members.

Addendum A: IRC Accountability Recommendations Related to Technology-Facilitated Abuse

Recommendation 1.1 proposes sexual assault and other special victim cases be handled by designated independent judge advocates, who should replace commanders in deciding whether to charge a suspect with a crime (preferral), and whether that charge should be tried at court-martial (referral). The military justice system should anticipate and respond to cyberharassment, stalking and other technology-facilitated abuse. These offenses would qualify as Special Victims crimes and would be prosecuted by the Special Victims Prosecutor (SVP).

Recommendation 1.2 would require investigation of all sexual harassment (including cyberharassment) and other discriminatory allegations to be performed by an independent, well-trained body that is outside the chain of command. These allegations are subject to a legal review for consideration of criminal charges, which is important in the context of online harassment, since some types of cyberharassment and abuse can constitute a stand-alone offense under the UCMJ, such as 10 U.S. Code § 917a - Art. 117a, Wrongful broadcast or distribution of intimate visual images. Substantiated allegations not criminally charged should be referred back to the chain of command for consideration of nonjudicial punishment, as well as the mandatory initiation of involuntary separation.

Recommendation 1.3 would provide victims of sexual assault and related crimes the ability to receive an MPO issued by a military court, allowing it to be enforced outside the installation. The IRC has specified that MPOs must expressly prohibit the Respondent from utilizing technology to communicate with, stalk, or monitor the victim, and that cyberharassment and online abuse should be honored as grounds for the issuance of an MPO.

Recommendation 1.4 calls for the Military Services to adequately resource and train military justice professionals, including SVPs, Special Victims Counsel, and military criminal investigative organizations' personnel, to have the requisite expertise and skills to counsel, prosecute, and investigate special victim crimes. This will require an additional focus on understanding cyber-related crime, how to collect and evaluate digital evidence, and the dynamics of online abuse.

Honoring Our Duty to Survivors of Military Sexual Assault: Recommendations on Victim Care & Support

Independent Review Commission on Sexual Assault in the Military

Contents

Acknowledgements

The findings in this report are the result of extensive meetings, briefings, requests for information, and individual conversations. The Commission's Victim Care and Support experts relied heavily on the insights and knowledge of the Service and DoD representatives serving on their consultative team and as subject matter experts (SMEs). These representatives helped to explain Service policies, recall historical events, and connect the IRC with others to provide further detail. Current and former Sexual Assault Response Coordinators (SARCs) and Sexual Assault Prevention and Response Victim Advocates (SAPR VAs) offered keen and necessary insight to help the IRC understand the day-to-day challenges and rewards of ensuring the care and safety of survivors of sexual assault and harassment. Most of all, the Victim Care and Support experts want to thank the hundreds of survivors who took the time to share their experiences and unvarnished views of what improvements needed to be made. The resilience, courage, and tenacity they displayed were a daily inspiration. This report is for them.

Background

On February 26, 2021, the Secretary of Defense ordered the establishment of the Independent Review Commission to conduct an independent assessment of Department of Defense (DoD) efforts against sexual harassment and sexual assault. The IRC officially began its work on March 24, 2021 and was charged with forming recommendations across four lines of effort: accountability; prevention; climate and culture; and victim care and support.

This report is issued by the highly qualified experts (HQEs) leading the victim care and support line of effort. The Victim Care and Support experts were charged with the following tasks:

- Conduct a review of clinical and non-clinical victim services to ensure they are comprehensive, evidence-based, and available to all victims regardless of reporting status; and
- Develop recommendations on trauma-informed, victim-centered mental and physical health care.

The success of the victim care and support recommendations is interdependent with proposals from other lines of effort focusing on accountability, prevention, and climate and culture. Taken as a whole, the IRC's recommendations will present a comprehensive view of the problem, and offer targeted solutions for commanders of all ranks, the Services, and the Department to build trust and restore confidence in the military's ability to prevent and respond to sexual assault and sexual harassment.

Introduction

After hearing from victims,[1] speaking with Service members, and meeting with SAPR personnel across the Services, the IRC concluded that for many victims, the institutional response to sexual assault and sexual harassment only deepens their trauma. Survivors who spoke with the IRC shared experiences of:

- Victim-blaming;
- Commanders' unwillingness to give primacy to the unique needs of the survivor;
- Difficulty accessing needed care; and
- SAPR VAs and Special Victims Counsel who failed to provide regular updates on case status.

These, and many other inconsistencies—large and small—can combine to form an astonishing institutional betrayal.[2,3] Many survivors are forced to make the untenable choice to leave the military not as a result of their assault,[4] but rather due to their perception that the military fundamentally did not care about the harm they suffered. Multiple survivors with whom the IRC met revealed suicidal ideation or had attempted suicide in the aftermath of seeking help for their sexual assault.

The Department has a profound duty to support Service members who experience sexual assault and sexual harassment during their service to our country—but it is falling short. Given that approximately 20,000 active duty Service members experience sexual assault and sexual harassment in a given year,[5] it is imperative that the military provide them with adequate care and support so they can do more than just survive, but also heal and prosper—during their Service, and after the transition back to civilian life. The findings and analyses in this report highlight key reasons as to *why* and provides recommendations to aid DoD and the Services in making good on their promise to care for victims.

Access to care and delivery of services are inconsistent across the Services, National Guard Bureau (NGB), and the Reserves. The current SARC/SAPR VA workforce structure is fractured, inefficient, and under-resourced, and relies too heavily on personnel serving collateral (i.e., part-time) duty. Moreover, survivors' needs are not consistently prioritized, nor well understood by command, exacerbating barriers to recovery and reintegration. Finally, training for SARCs, SAPR VAs, leaders,

---

[1] The IRC uses the terms "victim" and "survivor" interchangeably throughout the report and recommendations.

[2] Monteith, L.L., Bahraini, N.H., Matarazzo, B.B., Soberay, K.A., & Smith, C.P. (2016). Perceptions of Institutional Betrayal Predict Suicidal Self-Directed Violence Among Veterans Exposed to Military Sexual Trauma. *Journal of Clinical Psychology*. doi:10.1002/jclp.22292

[3] Andresen, F.J., Monteith, L.L., Kugler, J., Cruz, R.A., & Blais, R.K. (2019). Institutional betrayal following military sexual trauma is associated with more severe depression and specific posttraumatic stress disorder symptom clusters. *Journal of Clinical Psychology, 75*(7), 1305-1319. doi:10.1002/jclp.22773

[4] Morral, A.R., Matthews, M., Cefalu, M., Schell, T.L., & Cottrell, L. (2021). *Effects of Sexual Assault and Sexual Harassment on Separation from the U.S. Military: Findings from the 2014 RAND Military Workplace Study*. Santa Monica, CA: RAND Corporation. https://www.rand.org/pubs/research_reports/RR870z10.html

[5] DoD SAPRO. (2021). *Fiscal Year 2020 Annual Report on Sexual Assault in the Military*, 5. https://www.sapr.mil/sites/default/files/DOD_Annual_Report_on_Sexual_Assault_in_the_Military_FY2020.pdf

and chaplains across the Services and NGB is inconsistent, and often lacks a skills-based approach that is victim-centered, trauma-informed, and culturally competent. The result is that the quality of care for survivors is not only different between—but also varies within—each of the Services.

List of Recommendations

The recommendations that follow stem from an awareness that victims of sexual assault and sexual harassment[6] carry a heavy burden when trying to obtain the care and support they need—a burden that should be minimized to the greatest extent possible.

The core philosophy underlying this suite of recommendations is simple: victim care and support must center the needs of the victim. Service members who have experienced sexual assault and sexual harassment have suffered a profound moral injury,[7] which must be acknowledged and redressed. The IRC has developed targeted proposals to enhance victim care and support in ways designed to maximize Service members' chances for full recovery and healing. The recommendations are based on the experts' observations and many discussions with survivors, as well as civilian best practices and promising programming from across the Services.

4.1 Optimize the victim care and support workforce.

4.1 a Move SARCs and SAPR VAs from the command reporting structure.

4.1 b Eliminate collateral duty for SARCs and SAPR VAs with exceptions for ships, submarines, and isolated installations that do not warrant full-time staff.

4.1 c Explore the co-location of SAPR and SHARP with other special victim services, such as the Family Advocacy Program (FAP), to improve coordination, collaboration, and consistency in victim support.

4.1 d Train more Independent Duty Corpsmen (IDCs) to be Sexual Assault Medical Forensic Examiners (SAMFEs), so patient care and evidence collection can be provided in deployed or isolated environments.

4.2 Expand victim service options to meet the needs of all survivors of sexual assault and harassment.

4.2 a Increase access to and visibility of civilian community-based care.

4.2 b Authorize Service members to access the full spectrum of Veterans Affairs (VA) services for conditions related to military sexual assault and harassment confidentially and without a referral.

---

[6] DoD policy refers to those who report sexual harassment as "complainants;" however, the IRC recognizes that the impact of harassment merits response and support if that is what the Service member wants. For this reason, the IRC refers to persons who have experienced sexual harassment as "victims" throughout the report.

[7] Wolfendale, J. (2021). *Military Sexual Assault is a Moral Injury*. War on the Rocks. https://warontherocks.com/2021/05/the-military-justice-improvement-act-and-the-moral-duty-owed-to-sexual-assault-victims/

4.2 c Explore feasibility of expanding access to CATCH to include victims of sexual harassment and enable Service members to self-service access to CATCH.

4.2 d Create survivor-led peer support programs that allow for in-person, virtual, and telephone interaction.

4.2 e Amplify victims' rights and services in the post-trial period.

4.3 Center the survivor to facilitate healing and restoration.

4.3 a Implement the "No Wrong Door" approach to sexual harassment, sexual assault, and domestic abuse across the Services and NGB.

4.3 b Institute a "Commander's Package" prepared by the SAPR VA with recommendations for victim care and support.

4.3 c Allow survivors flexibility to take non-chargeable time off for seeking services or time for recovery from sexual assault.

4.3 d Increase victim agency and control of the response process by maximizing adherence to survivor preference on reporting status and centering survivor preferences in expedited transfers.

4.3 e Study the methods our allies have used to make amends to survivors, including restorative engagement to acknowledge harm and potential victim compensation.

4.4 Re-Envision training and research to improve victim care and support.

4.4 a Establish a Defense Sexual Assault and Sexual Harassment Training Center of Excellence that administers a core curriculum of trauma and response trainings for all SARCs, SAPR VAs, chaplains, and other response personnel.

4.4 b Develop training to enhance the capacity of SARCs and SAPR VAs to provide culturally competent care to Service members who are racial or ethnic minorities, LGBTQ+, religious minorities, and men who experience sexual assault.

4.4 c Revise and update training modules on appropriate response to sexual assault and sexual harassment in professional military education for officers and noncommissioned officers (NCO).

4.4 d Use an action research model to identify root problems, test interventions, and create best practices and increase the administration of user satisfaction surveys to obtain continuous feedback from survivors.

Methodology

The IRC conducted a thorough review of key reports,[8] research, and survey data to determine the current state of victim care and support for Service members who have experienced sexual assault and sexual harassment. To complement these findings, they examined sexual assault and sexual harassment response policies,[9] practices, and procedures at DoD, Military Departments/Services, NGB, Department of Veterans Affairs (VA), as well as those of civilian service providers. This initial environmental scan provided context that allowed the experts to identify initial best and promising practices as well as note gaps and inconsistencies in victim care and response across the force.

Representatives from each of the Services and NGB provided the IRC's Victim Care and Support experts with invaluable information on how sexual assault and sexual harassment response procedures are implemented at the installation level. Through weekly working group meetings and requests for information, the IRC gathered detailed information from SAPR personnel on barriers to optimal victim care and support. The IRC also held discussions with the Defense Health Agency, TRICARE representatives,[10] the Army SHARP Academy, chaplains, and researchers from the VA. Additionally, the Commission's victim care and support team engaged in numerous one-on-one conversations with senior leaders and DoD policy components, Special Victims' Counsel (SVC)/Victims' Legal Counsel (VLC), forensic nurses, and other military and VA healthcare providers.

Finally, these recommendations were informed by site visits to installations, which enabled the Victim Care and Support Team to speak directly with survivors, hold discussion groups with junior enlisted personnel and non-commissioned officers (NCOs), and speak with SHARP, SAPR, and Family Advocacy Program (FAP) staff. In meeting with survivors during these visits, the IRC facilitated structured interviews through one-on-one meetings. Speaking directly with survivors provided the IRC with critical insights on the victim experience, including both strong examples of advocacy that went well, and inconsistencies or systemic problems that disrupted their healing and recovery.

---

[8] Such reports included: The Fort Hood Independent Review Committee. (2020, November 6). Report of the Fort Hood Independent Review Committee. https://www.army.mil/e2/downloads/rv7/forthoodreview/2020-12-03_FHIRC_report_redacted.pdf; DoD. (2019, April 30). Sexual Assault Accountability and Investigation Task Force. https://media.defense.gov/2019/May/02/2002127159/-1/-1/1/SAAITF_REPORT.PDF; Breslin, R., Davis, E., Hylton, K., Hill, A., Klauberg, W., Petusky, M., Klahr, A. (2019). *2018 Workplace and Gender Relations Survey of Active Duty Members: Overview Report*. Report (No. 2019-027). Alexandria, VA: Office of People Analytics, 50. https://apps.dtic.mil/sti/citations/AD1072334; Namrow, N., De Silva, S., Severance, L., Klahr, A., & Davis, L. (2018). 2016-2017 Military Investigation and Justice Experience Survey. Alexandria, VA: Office of People Analytics. https://www.sapr.mil/public/docs/reports/FY17_Annual/Annex_3_2016-2017_Military_Investigation_and_Justice_Survey.pdf

[9] The IRC also examined the policy response to intimate partner sexual violence (sexual abuse), addressed by FAP under DoD Instruction (DoDI) 6400.06.

[10] TRICARE is the health care program for uniformed service members, retirees, and their families around the world. See: https://www.tricare.mil/About

Ultimately, these conversations led the IRC to better understand what recommendations would make a difference in expanding their options for support and increasing their sense of agency in the process of seeking help.

Recommendation 4.1: Optimize the Victim Care and Support Workforce

SARCs and SAPR VAs are the heartbeat of the military's victim care and support response. SARCs serve as the single point of contact for coordinating the appropriate response and care for adult sexual assault victims at an installation or within a geographic area. SAPR VAs report to the SARC and provide adult survivors with nonclinical crisis intervention, referrals, and ongoing nonclinical support.[11] Both work closely with military healthcare providers, civilian community service providers, and other relevant personnel and organizations to ensure victims' needs are met. However, the structure of the SARC/SAPR VA workforce as it stands today is not working. This recommendation outlines the reasons why and offers proposals to optimize the workforce by centering the needs of survivors and creating personnel efficiencies.

- 4.1 a: Move SARCs and SAPR VAs from the command reporting structure;
- 4.1 b: Explore the co-location of SAPR and SHARP with other special victim services, such as FAP, to improve coordination, collaboration, and consistency in victim support;
- 4.1 c: Eliminate collateral duty for SARCs and SAPR VAs with exceptions for ships, submarines, as well as small or isolated installations that do not warrant full-time staff; and
- 4.1 d: Train more Independent Duty Corpsmen (IDCs) to be Sexual Assault Medical Forensic Examiners (SAMFEs) so patient care and evidence collection can be provided in deployed or isolated environments.

Recommendation 4.1 a: Move SARCs and SAPR VAs from the Command Reporting Structure

The IRC recommends that SARCs and SAPR VAs be removed from the command reporting structure to provide them with the independence they need to effectively advocate for sexual assault victims.

Rationale for Change: To Eliminate Bias, Protect Victim Privacy, and Empower SARCs and Victim Advocates

In the IRC's meetings with survivors, SAPR/SHARP personnel, enlisted Service members, and DoD policy representatives, the importance of this concept was repeatedly raised. This recommendation mirrors a similar one from the Fort Hood Independent Review Committee.[12]

---

[11] GAO. (2021). *Sexual Assault in the Military: Continued Congressional Oversight and Additional DOD Focus on Prevention Could Aid DOD's Efforts, Testimony Before the Subcommittee on Personnel, Committee on Armed Services, U.S. Senate.* GAO-21-463T, 7.

[12] The Fort Hood Independent Review Committee. (2020, November 6). Report of the Fort Hood Independent Review Committee. https://www.army.mil/e2/downloads/rv7/forthoodreview/2020-12-03_FHIRC_report_redacted.pdf

There are three main reasons to move SARCs and SAPR VAs from the command reporting structure:

- To eliminate perceived commander bias and influence on decisions related to the survivor's needs;
- To further protect the privacy and confidentiality of the victim; and,
- To empower SARCs and SAPR VAs to do what is in the best interest of victims without concern for how their performance ratings may be affected.

> "To ensure objectivity and fairness, the SHARP Program should operate independent from local commanders or their legal advisors."
>
> -Fort Hood Independent Review Committee

A relationship based on trust and mutual respect between local commanders and SARCs and SAPR VAs is vital for these responders to be able to effectively advocate on the survivor's behalf.[13] This cannot be overstated. When SARCs and SAPR VAs are placed in the command structure, it can result in commanders dismissing, denying, or ignoring their recommendations for survivors in the aftermath of an assault. The IRC spoke with multiple victim advocates who had experienced this firsthand.

SARCs and SAPR VAs need direct, unimpeded access to command, which is only possible when these professionals are seen as important, strategic advisors to the unit, and bringing a special expertise. Some SARCs and SAPR VAs have good relationships with their commanders and are able to work closely with them to ensure that a survivor's needs are met. This should always be the goal. There are too many instances, however, in which commanders do not understand, appreciate, or value the SARC or SAPR VA roles. This creates barriers to ensuring that victims get the help they need and does not allow the SARC or SAPR VA the access and trust from command they need to perform their job well.

Currently, SARCs and SAPR VAs are assigned to units at the brigade level (or equivalent) and report within the command structure. The purpose of this is to give Service members the option of reporting a sexual assault to the SARC or SAPR VA in their unit; someone they are familiar with and see on a regular basis. Victims may, of course, always have the option of reporting to their command if they so choose. However, some survivors are not comfortable reporting to any of these individuals. Survivors the IRC interviewed, cited numerous reasons for this, including:

- A lack of trust due to the relationship between the commander and the person who assaulted them (when the offender is in the same unit);
- Due to the relationship between the SARC or SAPR VA and the commander; or
- Because of the relationship between the SARC or SAPR VA and the person who assaulted them.

---

[13] Peebles, H., Wynn, R., Hill, A., Barry, A., Davis, E., & Klahr, A. (2019). *QuickCompass Survey of Sexual Assault Responders: Overview Report*. Report No. 2019-019. Alexandria, VA: Office of People Analytics, vi.

They perceived that their confidentiality could be compromised or that they would not be treated fairly. Privacy and confidentiality are sacred —and fundamental—to sexual assault survivors. If the confidentiality of a Restricted Report is breached, it can result in retaliation by the survivor's peers in the unit. One survivor said it this way, "[When they find out you reported a sexual assault], they put you on an island and treat you like a leper." Retaliation as a result of reporting sexual assault is real: In 2018, roughly two-thirds (64 percent) of active duty women who experienced and reported sexual assault perceived experiencing a behavior in line with retaliation—of whom nearly a quarter (21 percent) also met DoD's follow-up legal criteria for retaliation.[14]

Another important reason for removing SARCs and SAPR VAs from the command structure is so they can freely advocate for victims without fear of retaliation from their commander. The IRC heard from multiple victim advocates who spoke candidly about the retaliation they experienced from command because of their strong advocacy for their clients, or for simply adhering to SAPR/SHARP program policy. For example, one retired SARC recounted the mistreatment she endured by the commander's staff after she tried to set up a meeting with the new commander to brief him on the SAPR program, per DoD policy. The commander's staff did not consider SAPR to be important enough for this one-on-one briefing and would not allow the meeting to be scheduled. After she was finally able to brief the commander, the commander's staff retaliated by threatening to move her, withholding important information, and generally creating a toxic environment. Numerous SARCs and SAPR VAs who spoke with the IRC disclosed various levels of mistreatment and retaliation from leadership, including being ostracized, bullied, alienated, and even fired. SARCs and SAPR VAs must be able to communicate with commanders without fear of retribution.

Recommendation 4.1 b: Eliminate Collateral Duty for SARCs and SAPR VAs with Exceptions for Ships, Submarines, as Well as Small or Isolated Installations that Do Not Warrant Full-time Staff

The IRC recommends that the Services implement full-time SARC and SAPR VA positions that require specific experience and skills and include a deep understanding of trauma and how it affects victims.

Rationale for Change: Victim Advocacy is Not a Part-time, Developmental Assignment

Collateral duty in the military has long been used as a way of ensuring that certain job functions can continue even when resources are lacking. It also provides Service members with the opportunity to broaden their knowledge and skills beyond their military occupational specialty, which can contribute to a Service member's promotion potential. Personnel can be assigned to collateral duty in areas that

[14] Breslin, R., Davis, E., Hylton, K., Hill, A., Klauberg, W., Petusky, M., Klahr, A. (2019). *Workplace and Gender Relations Survey of Active Duty Members: Overview Report*. Report No. 2019-027. Alexandria, VA: Office of People Analytics, 38. https://apps.dtic.mil/sti/citations/AD1072334

are completely unrelated to their current assignment or technical expertise. For example, across the Services, collateral duty[15] sexual assault response personnel come from a range of military occupational specialties, such as aircraft maintenance or logistics. The expectation is that these Service members will spend the majority of their time in their primary job, and tack on additional hours to help staff their unit's SAPR or SHARP program. This approach is fundamentally incompatible with the tenets of victim advocacy, which is not appropriate for developmental assignments. Victim advocacy is not a "skill-building" type of job—it is an established field of expertise that requires specialized skills, knowledge, and competencies, because working with survivors can be a matter of life or death. Persons without the proper training, experience, and dedicated time should not be assigned as SARCs or SAPR VAs.

"I regularly run into commanders only wanting to assign their most dispensable leaders to SARC/ [SAPR] VA positions. And that has ended disastrously for us in some cases."

—Former SARC, as told to the IRC in an interview

In the civilian world, full-time victim advocates are specially trained professionals whose expertise is focused on the provision of support services, assistance, and counseling for victims of interpersonal violence, such as sexual assault or domestic violence.[16] Their services begin the moment a victim seeks help until the victim determines the services are no longer needed. Victim advocates who specialize in working with victims of sexual assault receive intensive training on the provision of trauma-informed care[17] and on the neurobiology of trauma.[18] Although DoD policy requires training for Service members assigned collateral duties as a SARC or victim advocate, the training provided is no substitute for direct experience working with survivors—nor can individuals without prior background in the field of victim support develop the requisite knowledge through a 40-hour course.[19,20]

---

[15] Headquarters Marine Corps. (n.d.). Human Resources and Organizational Management. https://www.hqmc.marines.mil/hrom/New-Employees/Welcome-Aboard/How-Onboarding-Works/Phase-4-Your-First-90-Days/Training-and-Workforce-Development/

[16] National Organization for Victim Assistance. (2021). *Who We Are*. https://www.trynova.org/who-we-are/mission-and-reach/

[17] Trauma-informed care shifts the focus from "What's wrong with you?" to "What happened to you?" A trauma-informed approach to care acknowledges that health care organizations and care teams need to have a complete picture of a patient's life situation—past and present—in order to provide effective health care services with a healing orientation. Source: SAMHSA. (n.d.). SAMHSA's Concept of Trauma and Guidance for a Trauma-Informed Approach. https://ncsacw.samhsa.gov/userfiles/files/SAMHSA_Trauma.pdf

[18] The neurobiology of trauma essentially refers to the effects of trauma on the brain. When someone experiences a traumatic event or experiences extreme fear, brain chemistry is altered, and the brain begins to function differently as a protective mechanism. Source: Campbell, R. (2012, December 12). The Neurobiology of Sexual Assault: Implications for Law Enforcement, Prosecution, and Victim Advocacy. *National Institute of Justice*. https://nij.ojp.gov/media/video/24056

[19] DoD. (2018). *DoDI 6495.02, Volume 1: Sexual Assault Prevention and Response Procedures*. https://www.esd.whs.mil/Portals/54/Documents/DD/issuances/dodi/649502_vol1.PDF?ver=v8IKfyy0wrK_EZ95gtv6Pw%3d%3d

[20] The D-SAACP was established to standardize sexual assault response to victims and professionalize victim advocacy roles of SARCs and SAPR VAs. See: https://www.sapr.mil/?q=d-saacp

Another concern with the Services' heavy reliance on collateral duty staffing for SAPR/SHARP is the desire and motivation for victim care and support providers to do the work. While many uniformed SAPR VAs and SARCs who met with the IRC demonstrated a strong commitment to perform this important role, across the Services, many of these individuals are assigned to these positions, and their dedication is not consistent Because of the difficult subject matter, along with the compassion and sensitivity it takes to perform this job well, it is not for just anyone. The person in this position must want to be there and must have the necessary skills to carry out the essential functions of the job. A person who is "voluntold" to serve as a SAPR VA or SARC can actually cause more harm to the survivor than if they had no victim advocate at all. Worse still, so long as the current staffing model allows Service members the ability to elect into this part time function, some may do so for other than honorable reasons. To illustrate, the IRC spoke with several survivors who had been sexually assaulted by their unit's SARC.

The use of collateral duty staff should never have been seen as a permanent solution. When DoD initially established the SAPR program in 2005, it did so without the allocation of new resources or staff to implement. For the purposes of initial staffing, the Services created SARC and SAPR VA positions as collateral duty and hired contractors to provided additional support.[21] In 2008, DoD determined that taking sexual assault reports was an inherently governmental function, and as a result, contractors were prohibited from carrying out SARC and SAPR VA duties. In Fiscal Year (FY) 2012 (FY12), the NDAA required one full-time SARC and SAPR VA per brigade-sized unit,[22] and allocating funding to provide staffing at this level. Because the need for SARCs and SAPR VAs is so great, however, the Services have continued to employ collateral duty SARCs and SAPR VAs across the force. The IRC strongly recommends DoD finally establish an enduring solution to ensuring adequate resources for full time, professional victim care and support personnel.

IRC meetings with SARCs, SAPR VAs, and survivors revealed nearly universal agreement and support for eliminating collateral duty for these positions, except in very specific cases. Collateral duty for SARCs and SAPR VAs is not ideal in the military environment. These jobs are vital to the safety, security, and well-being of the survivor and, in most cases, require a full-time commitment. For example, the IRC heard from survivors whose collateral duty SAPR VA was transferred midway through their case or was too busy with their full-time job to dedicate the time necessary to be effective. Some commanders did not allow proper time for the advocate to leave their full-time duties to assist the survivor. The IRC also learned that the Services have invested the time and resources into training collateral duty victim advocates who have never worked a single case. This is likely because more SAPR VAs were assigned to units across the installation than were actually needed, highlighting the importance of a manpower study for victim services personnel, and a detailed review of SAPR VA

[21] In 2008, an internal DoD task force determined that taking sexual assault reports was an inherently governmental function, and as a result, contractors were prohibited from carrying out SARC and SAPR VA duties.

[22] United States Congress. House Committee on Armed Services. (2011). *NDAA for FY12*. H.R. 1540, 112th Congress. Public Law 112-81. Washington: U.S. Government Publishing Office.

caseloads. In a review of SARC and SAPR VA collateral duty and permanent positions, the distribution of SARCs and SAPR VAs varied greatly across the services.[23]

To address the aforementioned findings and concerns, the IRC recommends that SARC and SAPR VA positions be a mix of uniform and civilian personnel, with the requirement that all SAPR VAs be civilians. These positions would require specific experience and skills and include a deep understanding of trauma and how it impacts victims. Transfers and rotation should be limited to the fullest extent possible to avoid interrupting established relationships with victims whose cases are still moving through the military justice system. The IRC also recommends that the only exception for collateral duty SARCs and SAPR VAs would be on vessels, or on small or isolated installations and similar contexts, such as the National Guard, that do not warrant full-time staff.

Implementation Considerations

In order to determine the ideal SARC/SAPR VA workforce, the IRC recommends a manpower study to examine all personnel—military, civilian, full time and collateral duty—that comprise the response to sexual assault in each Service. The DoD Sexual Assault Prevention and Response Office (SAPRO) has plans to conduct such a study and has completed the initial environmental scan. The IRC supports the continuation of this effort and recommends that the manpower study be a comprehensive assessment of:

- The number of sexual assault cases handled annually by each collateral duty SAPR VA across the Services and the approximate time they spent working a case from start to finish;
- The current caseloads of full-time SARCs and SAPR VAs;
- The overlap or duplication of the duties assigned to SVCs, Victim-Witness Liaisons, SARCs, and SAPR VAs, including a look at the continued relevance24 of the role of the Victim-Witness Liaison[25, 26] for sexual assault cases; and
- The optimal number of IDCs necessary to provide sexual assault medical forensic examinations on ships, submarines and other isolated areas (see Recommendation 4.1 d).

Desk Audit to Complement Manpower Study

As part of the manpower study, the IRC recommends that a sample of SARCs, SAPR VAs, SVC/VLCs, and Victim-Witness Liaison desk audits[27] be conducted to ensure the efficient use of human resources and a clear delineation and classification of job responsibilities.[28] Simply reviewing

---

[23] IRC Victim Care and Support Working Group SMEs furnished this data for each of the Services.

[24] The IRC learned that many SARCs are also doing the SAPR VA jobs and vice versa, especially when there is a personnel shortage. In addition, SVCs/VLCs may also be picking up work of SAPR VAs, especially when the victim elects to have an SVC but declines having a SAPR VA.

[25] The creation of the SVC/VLC position subsumed many of the responsibilities previously handled by the Victim-Witness Liaison.

[26] DoD. (2007). *DoDI 1030.01: Victim and Witness Assistance.* https://www.esd.whs.mil/Portals/54/Documents/DD/issuances/dodd/103001p.pdf

[27] A desk audit is an interview with the incumbent employee to obtain information about his/her duties.

[28] Having multiple points of contact makes it difficult for survivors to manage their own care. Rather than helping, the confusion can result in inertia and hopelessness.

job descriptions is insufficient, as the key is to determine what individuals in these positions are *actually* doing, regardless of what is in their job description. Many individuals are performing response duties outside or beyond what is in their job description. For example, the IRC heard from various SVC/VLCs and SARCs who were performing victim advocacy functions because there were too few full-time SAPR VAs to support the number of victims who needed assistance.

In order to recruit and retain qualified sexual assault response personnel, the IRC also recommends reviewing the current grade (GS) structure and creating new opportunities for promotion and advancement for civilian SARCs and SAPR VAs. Further, the IRC heard from many Service members who expressed interest in the idea of a new military occupational specialty (MOS) for SARCs, which the IRC recommends exploring. This would allow recruits who possess the proper skills and experience with the opportunity to make being a SARC a military career. Because military jobs require frequent transfers and relocations, the IRC does not recommend the same for SAPR VAs. Stability and consistency are very important to survivors and full-time civilian SAPR VAs can offer that.

Recommendation 4.1 c: Explore the Co-location of SAPR and SHARP with Other Special Victim Services, such as FAP, to Improve Coordination, Collaboration, and Consistency in Victim Support

The IRC recommends that DoD consider co-locating SAPR and SHARP programs with other programs and services that comprise a team of sexual assault responders, or that may benefit from closer coordination. Co-located models to address intimate partner violence and sexual violence, such as Family Justice Centers and Multi-Agency Model Centers, have emerged as promising practices to meet the needs of survivors. A recent systematic review of the research indicated a high degree of provider and survivor satisfaction with co-located models.[29]

Simply put, a state of the art "one stop shop" would give victims centralized access to a SARC or SAPR VA; a special victim counsel; a special victim criminal investigator; a special victim prosecutor; and the ability to connect with a FAP victim advocate for survivors who may have experienced sexual assault from a spouse or partner. This concept complements the recommendation from the IRC's Accountability Line of Effort (Recommendation 1.4) for the professionalization of military justice practitioners, in that an Assistant Special Victim Prosecutor would be an essential member of the co-located services team. Co-locating these services would increase collaboration and cooperation among these offices and make it easier for victims to get the help they need. In addition, sharing of resources and manpower would create personnel efficiencies. Case management reviews of Unrestricted Reports would be more easily coordinated and updates on cases could be more frequent.

[29] Rizo, C. F., Van Deinse, T., Durant, S., et al. (2021). Systematic review of research on co-location models for serving intimate partner and sexual violence survivors. *Journal of Family Violence*. https://doi.org/10.1007/s10896-021-00257-6

Co-Locate FAP with SAPR/SHARP Programs

In the military, domestic abuse/intimate partner violence and sexual assault are handled separately, even though they share similar attributes and may often serve some of the same individuals. FAP is DoD's program for addressing domestic abuse, child abuse and neglect, and problematic sexual behavior in children and youth.[30] FAP handles reports of domestic violence and child abuse and provides a range of clinical and non-clinical services, as well as victim advocacy.

Domestic abuse and sexual assault are not mutually exclusive forms of interpersonal violence—in fact, they often overlap. Roughly 32 percent of active duty women and 30 percent of wives of active duty men have experienced domestic violence in the form of sexual violence, physical violence, or stalking by a spouse or intimate partner at some point in their lifetimes.[31]

Since FAP handles these cases rather than the Services' SAPR and SHARP programs, it becomes increasingly important for these offices to work in close coordination to share information, confer on cases, make referrals, and facilitate "warm hand-offs." On some installations the FAP and SAPR/SHARP programs are already co-located, which allows for this coordination to take place more seamlessly. However, when these programs exist in disparate places, particularly if the offices are not within walking distance, communication may be hindered and a mentality of "out of sight, out of mind" may ensue. Co-location can facilitate consistency in the overall philosophy of healing for all victims of crime, better enabling FAP and SAPR response personnel to share resources and critical training information and reducing the need for victims to go to more than one place to seek the services they need. Ideally, this co-location should be in a facility that also provides other services or support that are not seen as stigmatizing to access, to further reduce barriers related to help-seeking.

> "Everyone wants to talk about reporting options, but we are trying to help people who have been traumatized. In my opinion, there is far too much focus on reporting options than on how we can help victims."
>
> –SAPR VA, as told to the IRC in a listening session

The IRC observed that the FAP and SHARP/SAPR programs seem to take different approaches to working with the individuals who come to them for help. FAP programs emphasize a comprehensive approach to victim care and wrap-

---

[30] DoD. (2019). *DoDI 6400.01: FAP.* https://www.esd.whs.mil/Portals/54/Documents/DD/issuances/dodi/640001p.pdf?ver=2019-05-01-081705-580

[31] Black, M., & Merrick, M. (2013). *Prevalence of Intimate Partner Violence, Sexual Violence, and Stalking among Active Duty Women and Wives of Active Duty Men—Comparisons with Women in the U.S. General Population, 2010.* Centers for Disease Control and Prevention, National Center for Injury Prevention and Control, 1. https://www.sapr.mil/public/docs/research/2010_National_Intimate_Partner_and_Sexual_Violence_Survey-Technical_Report.pdf

around services for victims of domestic violence, or other forms of family violence. SHARP/SAPR programs seem to be more geared toward process, like making quick decisions about restricted and unrestricted reports and expedited transfers. The current distinct approach is unfortunate, since there are many overlapping needs between domestic violence and sexual assault victims (e.g., safety planning, support and referral for accessing behavioral health, liaising with civilian providers, and being connected with an SVC/VLC).[32] The IRC observed other important differences between FAP and SHARP/SAPR: most FAP staff are civilians and there are no collateral duty FAP advocates. In discussions with SARCs and SAPR VAs, the IRC learned that trainings may place a greater emphasis on reporting options than on survivor well-being. As one SARC noted, "I have started to avoid the word "report" when referring to options when I brief [survivors]. We did a survey and found that people are more likely to connect that word to a legal or investigative action not a support action."

Co-locating FAP and SAPR services may help to address the differing approaches between the two programs and enable a more holistic response to sexual assault that emphasizes care and support as much as it does reporting options. Cross-training between FAP and SAPR personnel will support the "No Wrong Door" philosophy[33] to help ensure that survivors get the assistance they need no matter where they ask for help (see also Recommendation 4.3 a, Implement the No Wrong Door Approach).

Implementation Considerations: Co-locating Programs Can Relieve the Burden on Survivors and Increase Collaboration Across the Response Workforce

The IRC acknowledges the complexity of each Service branch's sexual assault response and does not want to presume that such a reorganization of services and functions is simple and "one size fits all." Military environments vary tremendously depending on geographic location, deployment status, Service, and other factors. As most victim service providers know, when it comes to the care and support of sexual assault victims, flexibility is key. Rather than prescribe the structure of such a program, the IRC instead offers the following guiding principles to undergird its development:

- Co-locate multi-disciplinary sexual assault services and responders where practicable to relieve the burden on survivors and put their needs front and center;
- Ensure that sexual assault services and personnel remain easily accessible to Service members and that lack of transportation[34] is never a barrier to getting help;
- Ensure coordination and collaboration among the key SAPR/SHARP personnel responsible for victim advocacy, investigation, prosecution, and SVC/VLC;

---

32 For example, a military spouse who is sexually abused by their partner may prefer to meet with a SAPR VA, rather than going to the installation FAP. While neither SAPR nor FAP personnel turn away anyone seeking services, regardless of eligibility, there is no policy requirement for victims who fall outside their scope of duty to receive the full range of services.

33 This is a person-centered approach to improving access to services and programs. At its most basic level, it refers to a system where a person who is seeking services from an organization will never encounter a "wrong door" to getting the care and support that they need. This concept will be expanded on in a subsequent recommendation in this report.

34 For instance, if a Service member's unit resides a considerable distance from a co-located service center, transportation should be made available.

- Ensure that the physical location of the SAPR/SHARP services is also home to other services (e.g., financial services, or Morale, Welfare, and Recreation programs) so as to avoid being labeled the "sexual assault building;"
- Prioritize the safety, privacy, and confidentiality of each survivor;
- Ensure that deployed, small, and isolated environments that do not have the infrastructure for co-locating services are properly staffed to respond effectively to reports of sexual assault;
- Create a mutually beneficial environment that fosters trust, respect, and reliability between the SAPR personnel and the command staff;
- Ensure that the roles and responsibilities of each SAPR/SHARP professional are clearly delineated and understood by all; and
- Create a reporting structure that reinforces accountability within the installation SAPR Program, but also between the installation SAPR/SHARP Program and DoD.

The emphasis should be on creating an environment that places the interests of the survivor first, while facilitating seamless systems coordination.

Existing Models for Co-Location

There are existing programs in place that may offer models to consider replicating. For example, the Navy's Fleet and Family Support Center was first introduced in 1979 in response to a task force that was formed to explore how to better meet the needs of the Navy family.[35] The result was a centralized location where families could get access to services for case work follow-up, financial counseling, child welfare liaison, relocation information, special assistance, and family enrichment. In another example, the SHARP Resource Center (SRC) at Joint Base Lewis-Mc Chord (JBLM) implemented a co-located services concept in 2013, based on the idea that co-locating services would eliminate the burden on survivors to travel to multiple buildings to get the care they need, and would thus facilitate a more efficient and victim-centered delivery of comprehensive, sensitive, and coordinated services.[36] The memorandum of understanding (MOU) that established the SRC stated as its mission "…to provide a sensitive and competent multi-disciplinary response to incidents of sexual assault, to help restore well-being to the victim, and bring responsible persons to justice." In 2014, the Army began a 12-site pilot program to further expand the model started at JBLM.[37] The IRC recommends that this pilot be revisited for relevant lessons learned.

The IRC believes that co-locating services and programs that serve survivors of sexual assault and related forms of interpersonal violence offers a tested model for easing the burden on survivors of sexual assault. Additionally, it would offer numerous system efficiencies and benefits for the military, if undertaken with proper thought, planning, and most of all, resources. The IRC recommends that this be piloted on select installations across each Service using an action research model (see

---

[35] Navy MWR. (2019). *The Fleet and Family Support Center: 40 Years of Meeting Your Needs…At Home and At Sea*, 5. https://www.navymwr.org/modules/media/?do=download&id=2c03dc9a-e2fd-4c7e-b3ae-410485883194

[36] Vergun, D. (2013). *New center provides comprehensive care to assault victims*. Army.mil. https://www.army.mil/article/112161/new_center_provides_comprehensive_care_to_assault_victims

[37] White, W. (2015, April 15). *Resource center synchronizes SHARP efforts*. Army.mil. https://www.army.mil/article/146500/resource_center_synchronizes_sharp_efforts

Recommendation 4.4: Re-Envision Training and Research to Improve Victim Care and Support). This would address root problems, determine the approach that works best, and evaluate the impact of co-located services on improving service delivery for survivors and increasing coordination and collaboration among the sexual assault professionals. In the evaluation, attention should also be given to the experiences victims have with seeking services away from their unit, engaging transportation, and going to a multi-service center.

Recommendation 4.1 d: Train More Independent Duty Corpsmen to be Sexual Assault Medical Forensic Examiners So Patient Care and Evidence Collection Can Be Provided in Deployed or Isolated Environments

The IRC recommends that when a sexual assault occurs on a vessel or isolated installation and immediate transport of the patient to a hospital for a full medical-forensic exam[38] is not possible or could be substantially delayed, the Navy ensure that there is a trained SAMFE in the unit to conduct the exam. The IRC recommends that all Independent Duty Corpsmen (IDCs)[39] be trained as Sexual Assault Medical Forensic Examiners (SAMFEs) so they can provide medical care and collect evidence in instances where there is no licensed provider on board, and it will take more than a few hours to transport the patient to a hospital. IDCs are specialized Naval hospital corpsmen who serve on land or sea or at isolated duty stations.

Rationale for Change: Training IDCs as SAMFEs Increases Options for Victims on Vessels or in Isolated Environments

In the acute aftermath of a sexual assault, it is critical that victims receive an immediate response to their request for assistance. They may need this assistance for many reasons: they may not be safe, may be physically injured, and/or are experiencing trauma. A delay in the response can result in a loss of evidence and further trauma for the victim. When a Service member is sexually assaulted on a ship at sea, protocol dictates that the victim be airlifted as soon as possible to the nearest port, ship, or hospital with access to trained and certified SAMFEs. There are vast options in the military for moving the victim very quickly, but sometimes the victim may have to wait 24-48 hours for the transfer to occur. Some large vessels have fully staffed health units with a dedicated SAMFE on board, but this is not always the case, particularly for smaller vessels, or at isolated installations, where a full team may not be required. The lack of capacity to provide victims with immediate medical forensic health care may not only have deleterious health consequences, but can also result in the loss, damage, or

---

38 Also referred to as a SAFE/SANE exam.

39 IDCs are highly trained and serve side-by-side with doctors, nurses, and other medical personnel. These sailors serve on land or at sea alongside Navy and Marine Corps warfighters, and at isolated duty stations where no medical officer is assigned. Source: Lyman, M. (2015, January 7). *Independent Duty Corpsman – A Specialized Lifesaver.* Navy Medicine Live. https://navymedicine.navylive.dodlive.mil/archives/10864

dilution of critical evidence. It is therefore imperative to have the option of providing medical forensic health care right away. According to the National Protocol for Sexual Assault Medical Forensic Exams, "Making decisions about whether to collect evidence and what to collect on a case-by-case basis is guided by knowledge that outside time limits for obtaining evidence vary due to factors such as the location of the evidence or type of sample collected."[40]

Implementation Considerations

IDCs are highly trained specialists who serve side-by-side with doctors, nurses, and other medical personnel. IDCs have been cleared to become SAMFEs and are eligible to enroll in the SAMFE certification program at the Military's San Antonio Training Center.[41] In fact, IDCs used to serve in the SAMFE role prior to the change in the NDAA in 2014.[42] When at sea or in other instances when the patient absolutely cannot be transferred, this training will allow them to perform this vitally important service. If the IDC requires additional technical assistance while performing the exam, they may be able to access remote support through the Defense Health Agency (DHA) ADVISOR program, where an on-call SAMFE expert can help guide the IDC and reassure the patient in real time.[43,44] IDCs should be required to take the same annual refresher courses that other medical providers take to ensure they maintain their level of competence to conduct the exams.

Because of the need to ensure the chain of custody[45] is protected, any environment where these examinations could potentially take place must have a secure, locked area to hold the evidence until it can be safely transferred to law enforcement or a storage facility, depending on the status of the

---

[40] U.S. Department of Justice, Office on Violence Against Women. (2013). *National Protocol for Sexual Assault Medical Forensic Examinations: Adults and Adolescents, Second Edition.* https://www.ojp.gov/pdffiles1/ovw/241903.pdf

[41] The Medical Education and Training Tri-Service Campus is located on Fort Sam Houston, Texas in the City of San Antonio. With 48 medical programs, and 16,500 graduates a year, it is a state-of-the-art DoD healthcare education campus that trains enlisted medical personnel. Source: Medical Education and Training Campus. (2021). https://www.metc.mil/

[42] DoD. (2014). *NDAA for FY14.* H.R. 3304 Summary of Military Justice and SAPR Provisions. https://www.hqmc.marines.mil/Portals/135/Docs/JAM/Encl%201%20-%20FY14%20NDAA%20Summary%20-%20MilJus%20and%20SAPR.pdf

[43] The only program of its type across DoD, ADVISOR provides global on-demand access to a full spectrum of medical tele-consultation services for emergent and urgent care. ADVISOR also delivers those services 24/7/365 in austere environments that have limited to no local specialty support.
Field medical personnel anywhere in the world can call one phone number and get immediate live help in 13 different medical specialties, from emergency care and critical care, to infectious diseases and toxicology. Source: Kile, M. (2021, May 27). *ADVISOR brings support to medical personnel in austere environments.* Health.mil. https://health.mil/News/Articles/2021/05/27/ADVISOR-brings-support-to-medical-personal-in-austere-environments?type=Policies

[44] The IRC learned through discussions with DHA personnel that a specific segment of ADVISOR will be dedicated to providing remote assistance for performing sexual assault forensic medical exams. This program is anticipated to launch in the coming months.

[45] The collection of samples for the sexual assault kits often establishes the first link in the chain of custody. The health care professional who has collected the samples should record an inventory of each item as part of the medical-forensic documentation. Documentation in the medical-forensic record is critical not only for victim care in the aftermath of sexual assault but also in the investigation of the crime and processing of any evidence collected during the exam. Source: U.S. Department of Justice. *National Best Practices for Sexual Assault Kits: A Multidisciplinary Approach.* U.S. Department of Justice, Office of Justice Programs, National Institute of Justice. https://cdn.ymaws.com/www.safeta.org/resource/resmgr/essential_reading/National_Best_Practices_for_.pdf

victim's report. There must also be an adequate supply of forensic evidence kits on board. Strict standard operating procedures for performing SAMFEs on ships would need to be developed to reduce the potential for rendering medical forensic evidence inadmissible.

To ensure there are enough IDCs to perform these exams, the Navy will likely need to increase this workforce, as well as enable adequate opportunities for ensuring this expanded workforce is properly trained. The IRC recommends that the Office of the Secretary of Defense work with the Department of the Navy in determining how best to include IDCs in the manpower study for victim response personnel (see Recommendation 4.1 b: Eliminate Collateral Duty for SARCs and SAPR VAs with Exceptions for Ships, Submarines, as Well as Small or Isolated Installations that Do Not Warrant Full-time Staff).

Recommendation 4.2: Expand Victim Service Options to Meet the Needs of All Survivors of Sexual Assault and Harassment in the Military

- 4.2 a: Increase access to and visibility of civilian community-based care;
- 4.2 b: Authorize Service members to access the full spectrum of Veterans Affairs (VA) services for conditions related to military sexual assault and harassment confidentially and without a referral;
- 4.2 c: Explore feasibility of expanding access to CATCH to include victims of sexual harassment and enabling Service members to self-service access to CATCH;
- 4.2 d: Create survivor-led peer support programs that allow for in-person, virtual, and telephone interaction; and,
- 4.2 e: Amplify victims' rights and services in the post-trial period.

Recommendation 4.2 a: Increase Access to and Visibility of Civilian, Community-based Care for Sexual Assault Survivors

The IRC recommends DoD and the Services pursue several strategies to meaningfully expand access to and awareness of sexual assault services provided by civilian programs. Providing information about these options supports victim choice and increases the likelihood that victims will receive some kind of care. Across the Services, stigma related to seeking sexual assault services can create an added barrier for Service members to get the help they need or to disclose their assault to anyone. Rape crisis centers offer free, confidential and in many places, virtual access to victim advocacy, safety planning, and other services. Promoting these services maximizes opportunities for Service members to seek the support they need for safety and healing.

Rationale for Change: Stronger Collaborations with Civilian Services Improves Access to Care

When a Service member is sexually assaulted, deciding where and who to turn to for help can be a hard decision. The IRC heard repeatedly from survivors who described being shunned, ostracized, or retaliated against after they reported their assault and sought services on their installation. Even Restricted Reports were not kept private—somehow the word got out and it traveled fast. It is important to note that these survivors disclosed retaliation from their peers or individuals outside their units, and not from SAPR/SHARP personnel. Still, seeking services within the installation gates introduces the potential for loss of privacy, making access to civilian services a critical option. Many survivors wanted access to services but did not seek them out for fear that others might discover what happened to them.

This fear is very real. In several of the IRC's discussions with junior enlisted Service members, individuals described watching as their friends or members of their unit were retaliated against, "coincidentally" passed over for promotions, or were forced to miss an advance training course after reporting they had been the victim of sexual assault. In 2018, the Department estimated that 38 percent of active duty women who reported a sexual assault perceived behaviors consistent with professional reprisal, including 15 percent who experienced behaviors that met legal criteria[46] for an experience of professional reprisal.[47]

For these reasons, survivors need options outside of the military community where they can obtain support, services, and, perhaps most of all—privacy they may be unable to preserve through SAPR/SHARP services. In the civilian context, confidentiality is a core principle of providing victims with services.[48] Civilian victim advocates are exempt from mandatory reporting requirements,[49] and cannot share information about a survivor's case or particular circumstances without their expressed consent. Although the military's Restricted Reporting option enables victims to access services without requiring their command or law enforcement to be notified, there is not a comparable assurance that report will be kept private.[50]

Optimizing survivor agency and choice is a central tenet of victim advocacy. Providing victims with a sense of control over what happens next in their pursuit of wellness and safety—after they have endured the ultimate violation of autonomy in experiencing sexual assault—is paramount. DoD and the Services have a profound obligation to provide the best quality of care for victims *through* the

---

[46] As outlined in the Uniform Code of Justice, 10 U.S.C. § 892.

[47] The rate of professional reprisal is a summary measure reflecting whether respondents experienced unfavorable actions taken by leadership (or an individual with the authority to affect a personnel decision) as a result of reporting sexual assault (not based on conduct or performance) and met the criteria for elements of proof for an investigation to occur. Source: Breslin, R., Davis, E., Hylton, K., Hill, A., Klauberg, W., Petusky, M., & Klahr, A. (2019). *2018 Workplace and Gender Relations Survey of Active Duty Members: Overview Report.* Report No. 2019-027. Alexandria, VA: Office of People Analytics. https://apps.dtic.mil/sti/citations/AD1072334

[48] Field, J., Goelman, D., Hart, B., Lee, R., Murphy, S., Tolhurst, K. & Valente, R. (2007). *Confidentiality: An Advocate's Guide.* Battered Women's Justice Project.
https://www.bwjp.org/assets/documents/pdfs/confidentiality_an_advocates_guide.pdf

[49] Except in certain situations, such as when there is risk to a child.

[50] Battered Women's Justice Project. (2021). *Military and Veteran-Related FAQs.* https://www.bwjp.org/our-work/projects/military-and-veterans-advocacy-program/military-and-veteran-faq.html

military, but that obligation also extends to ensuring meaningful, unencumbered access to support *outside* of the military.

At the same time, civilian victim service providers in proximity to military installations must also possess at least a basic awareness of the dynamics of military sexual assault, as well as knowledge of survivors' reporting options and limitations. The military community and each Service have distinct cultures, as well as operating procedures and programs, that civilian victim advocates must grasp in order to effectively support and care for Service members.

Implementation Considerations

Expand and Renew Partnerships between DoD SAPRO and the Department of Justice

Several years ago, the Department of Justice (DOJ) Office for Victims of Crime (OVC) and DoD SAPRO teamed up to create a training program entitled "Strengthening Military-Civilian Community Partnerships to Respond to Sexual Assault."[51] This program, funded through the Victims of Crime Act (VOCA) funds and offered through OVC's Training and Technical Assistance Center, trains local community victim advocates on building effective partnerships with local military installations to enhance and extend the system of support for sexual assault victims in the military. Advocates are trained on military systems, protocols, and culture to improve service provision to sexual assault victims in the military and to develop relationships with their military counterparts. With the knowledge gained through this training process and their own expertise in sexual assault, local community victim advocates are able to serve as knowledgeable resources to military installations.[52]

The IRC recommends expanding this OVC – DoD SAPRO training partnership so more civilian community services and military installations can benefit from this important cross-training opportunity. Right now, between four to six trainings are held each year.[53] DoD SAPRO and the DOJ signed a five-year MOU in 2017 to formalize and sustain the program. The IRC recommends strengthening the MOU and expanding the program when it comes up for renewal in 2022 with additional funding to accommodate an expansion.

Complementing this partnership, the DOJ Office on Violence Against Women (OVW) has a training and technical assistance grant program[54] to build the capacity for civilian domestic and sexual violence

---

[51] Department of Justice Office for Victims of Crime. *Advanced Military Sexual Assault Advocate Training.* https://www.ovcttac.gov/ovcttac_assets/EBlast/SAPRO_Web.HTML

[52] Office for Victims of Crime: Training and Technical Assistance Center. (2019). *Strengthening Military-Civilian Community Partnerships to Respond to Sexual Assault.* https://www.ovcttac.gov/ovcttac_assets/eblast/MilCiv_Eblast_013119.html

[53] Source: IRC Listening Session with U.S. Department of Justice Office for Victims of Crime and Office on Violence Against Women.

[54] U.S. Department of Justice, Office on Violence Against Women. (2019). *Office on Violence Against Women Fiscal Year 2019 Training and Technical Assistance Initiative Solicitation*, 8. https://www.justice.gov/ovw/page/file/1135681/download

programs to better serve military-connected victims.[55] This program enhances civilian advocates' knowledge of the military justice system, and delivers trainings for legal assistance providers and law enforcement to better serve military survivors. The IRC recommends this program be augmented in order to more effectively promote military-civilian coordinated community responses. DoD and DOJ should consider pursuing an interagency agreement or other mechanism to expand the reach of this program.[56]

Strengthen MOUs between Civilian and Military Sexual Assault Programs

DoD policy[57] requires commanders to identify and maintain a liaison with civilian sexual assault resources, and strongly encourages the use of MOUs or Memoranda of Agreement (MOA) to establish cooperation for reporting of sexual assault information, consultation on jurisdiction for prosecution, and for medical and counseling care that can be covered by military health care benefits. While collaboration with local community crisis counseling centers is also noted as one of the purpose areas of MOUs or MOAs, these seem to be less common.[58] Whether by MOU or by practice, DoD and the Services should encourage relationships with civilian providers and communicate the availability of services.

Service members' awareness of available civilian services could be improved. Some survivors told the IRC they sought services outside of the military, while others, when asked, indicated they were not aware of resources in the civilian community, and/or were unfamiliar with their local rape crisis center. Strengthening the relationships between civilian and military victim services providers will not only empower survivors with multiple options for care, but also enable the sharing of information and best practices across programs.

Recommendation 4.2 b: Authorize Service Members to Access the Full Spectrum of VA Services for Conditions Related to Military Sexual Assault and Harassment Confidentially and Without a Referral

The IRC recommends that DoD authorize all active duty Service members to confidentially access the full spectrum of Veterans Affairs (VA) services for sexual assault, without a referral.

[55] This program covers both active duty military, military dependents, and veterans.

[56] This program is funded by DOJ at $625,000 over a 36-month period.

[57] DoD. (2018). *DoDI 6495.02, Volume 1: Sexual Assault Prevention and Response Procedures.* https://www.esd.whs.mil/Portals/54/Documents/DD/issuances/dodi/649502_vol1.PDF?ver=v8IKfyy0wrK_EZ95gtv6Pw%3d%3d

[58] The IRC sought information from the Services, as well as through the state sexual assault coalitions, to informally inquire about the status or existence of formal or informal partnerships between installation SAPR/SHARP providers and civilian programs. While some communities had meaningful partnerships, they were not across the board.

Rationale for Change: Victims Should Have Full Access to All Services Available to Them

During interviews, multiple survivors noted barriers to accessing behavioral health care, including but not limited to: difficulty getting time off work; stigma about attending mental health appointments on base in uniform; fear about career repercussions; lack of knowledge about available resources; feeling overwhelmed by the process of having to seek appropriate care; and challenges in maintaining continuity of care during transitions (Permanent Changes of Station and/or Expiration of Time in Service).[59]

The IRC met with multiple survivors who expressed that they had struggled with suicidal ideation,[60] and some who received no mental health care until eventually going to the emergency room for attempting suicide. By opening up multiple avenues by which they are able to access confidential care and support, Service members will be better able to survive, thrive, and ultimately engage with DoD providers, SAPR personnel, and their chain of command. Suffering in silence and isolation adds weight to the heavy burden survivors are already carrying.

Federal law authorizes VA, in consultation with DoD, to provide Service members (including Active Duty, National Guard, and Reserve Component members) with care for physical and mental health conditions related to sexual assault and/or sexual harassment experienced during their military service without a referral from DoD.[61] The current implementation of this discretionary authority offers this access without a referral at VA Vet Centers only. As such, Service members can currently receive military sexual trauma (MST)[62]-related individual and group counseling, marital and family counseling, referral for benefits assistance, liaison with community agencies, and substance use information and referral from 300 VA Vet Centers without a referral. However, Service members are not currently able to receive medical or mental health services at the approximately 171 VA Medical Centers or 1,112 outpatient clinics nationwide without a referral.[63]

---

[59] The *2018 Health Related Behaviors Survey* found that while a higher percent of Service members is engaged in mental health care than in the general population, 6.8 percent of respondents reported unmet need for mental health treatment. Concerns about adverse professional consequences related to seeking care were commonly cited reasons for not seeking mental health care. Source: Meadows, S. O., Engel, C. C., Collins, R. L., Beckman, R. L., Breslau, J., Bloom, E. L., Dunbar, M. S., Gilbert, M., Grant, D., Hawes-Dawson, J., et al. (2021). *2018 Health Related Behaviors Survey.* Santa Monica, CA: RAND Corporation. https://www.rand.org/pubs/research_briefs/RB10116z4.html

[60] These anecdotal reports align with the literature indicating that rates of suicidality are higher in the military than in the general population (See: Ibid) and that military sexual trauma is associated with an increased risk of suicide (See: Kimerling, R., Makin-Byrd, K., Louzon, S., Ignacio, R.V., & McCarthy, J. F. (2015). Military sexual trauma and suicide mortality. *American Journal of Preventive Medicine*, *50*(6), 684–691.

[61] Counseling and treatment for sexual trauma. (1998). 38 U.S.C. § 1720D. https://www.law.cornell.edu/uscode/text/38/1720D

[62] Military Sexual Trauma (MST) is an umbrella term that encompasses both sexual assault and harassment, as defined in 38 U.S.C. § 1720D. https://www.law.cornell.edu/uscode/text/38/1720D

[63] Veterans Health Administration. (2021). *About VHA*. https://www.va.gov/health/aboutvha.asp

Expanding Service members' access to the full range of VA's MST-related services would have significant benefit for survivors. Compared to other providers, VA provides higher quality care, including mental health care,[64] on many measures,[65] and VA providers are more likely to have military cultural competence and training in evidence-based therapies for post-traumatic stress disorder and other conditions that are highly prevalent among sexual assault survivors.[66]

Increased access to VA care could also offer Service members enhanced opportunities to receive needed care virtually, which can help address some of the barriers to seeking care described above. Once the COVID-19 pandemic made in-person appointments riskier for both patients and providers, VA swiftly pivoted, resulting in a dramatic increase in virtual appointments. For example, in December 2020 alone, VHA conducted over one million virtual one-on-one appointments[67] and over 100,000 VA Video Connect group appointments.[68] To support those without adequate access, VA also launched a Digital Divide Consult[69] that can help patients access technology and/or internet connection support necessary to participate in connected care. Additionally, VA has agreements with several Internet service providers to zero-rate data expended while using the VA Video Connect telemedicine application, which further reduces potential burdens, particularly on low-income and rural patients seeking to access VA care virtually.

The IRC notes that VA-DoD Joint Executive Committee Fiscal Year 2020 Annual Report identified several barriers to implementing this discretionary authority at VA medical facilities, key among which were VA and DoD's positions on the confidentiality of care provided.[70] The IRC believes that confidentiality is required in order to offer victim-centered, trauma-informed care, and that as such, ensuring confidentiality should be a primary consideration in implementation.

---

[64] Watkins, K.E., Smith, B., Akincigil, A., Sorbero, M.E., Paddock, S., Woodroffe, A., Huang, C., Crystal, S.I., & Pincus, H.A. (2016). *The Quality of Medication Treatment for Mental Disorders in the Department of Veterans Affairs and in Private-Sector Plans.* Psychiatric Services, *67*(4). https://pubmed.ncbi.nlm.nih.gov/26567931/

[65] O'Hanlon, C., Huang, C., Sloss, E., Anhang Price, R., Hussey, P., Farmer, C., & Gidengil, C. (2017). *Comparing VA and non-VA quality of care: a systematic review.* Journal of General Internal Medicine, *32*(1): 105–121. https://doi.org/10.1007/s11606-016-3775-2

[66] Tanielian, T., Farris, C., Batka, C., Farmer, C. M., Robinson, E., Engel, C. C., Robbins, M. W., & Jaycox, L. H. (2014). *Ready to Serve: Community-Based Provider Capacity to Deliver Culturally Competent, Quality Mental Health Care to Veterans and Their Families.* Santa Monica, CA: RAND Corporation. https://www.rand.org/pubs/research_reports/RR806.html

[67] In contrast, according to an email from a Health Affairs representative, the Military Health Service provided only 367 psychotherapy appointments by telehealth in 2020.

[68] U.S. Department of Veterans Affairs. (2021, May 10). *Veterans Health Administration (VHA) Coronavirus Disease 2019 (COVID-19) Response Report - Annex A*, 105-108. https://www.va.gov/health/docs/VHA-COVID-19-Response-2021.pdf

[69] U.S. Department of Veterans Affairs. (2021). *Connecting Veterans to Telehealth Care.* https://connectedcare.va.gov/sites/default/files/telehealth-digital-divide-fact-sheet.pdf

[70] Department of Veterans Affairs and Department of Defense Joint Executive Committee Fiscal Year 2020 Annual Report: Military Sexual Trauma: Transition of Health Care and Assistance with Disability Claims.

In keeping with the goal of reestablishing individual agency in the aftermath of a traumatic event that strips survivors of choice, every effort must be made to center the victim. Key principles of this are increasing choice and control, both of which would be facilitated by allowing survivors to access VA services without a referral, confidentially.[71] The IRC also recommends that DoD authorize all Service member survivors to confidentially access the full spectrum of VA's MST-related services without a referral. Care should be provided confidentially to the fullest extent possible, including pursuing IT solutions in the joint VA-DoD electronic health record that can maximize confidentiality. Accountability mechanisms related to preserving patient privacy should be maximized and enforced.

The IRC acknowledges that provision of confidential care could pose risks to DoD, as conditions or treatment (e.g., prescription medications) that could degrade mission performance or deployment readiness of Service members would be unknown to DoD medical providers or command. However, this risk can be mitigated by ensuring Service members are aware of their responsibility to proactively communicate about these potential concerns with their SARC, SAPR VA, commander, or military health care provider as necessary when determinations about fitness for duty or deployability must be made. This is not to say that Service members should be required to notify anyone in DoD about *all* VA care they are receiving; only to note their responsibility to engage providers, commanders, or SAPR professionals in those specific circumstances. To preserve confidentiality and to remain consistent with their role as treatment provider, VA providers should not be involved in fitness for duty recommendations.

It is also important that VA's ability to serve those who have experienced both sexual harassment and sexual assault in the military[72] is made clear to the full range of SHARP, SAPR, and MEO personnel, as well as being reflected in online, training, and outreach materials.

Implementation Considerations

In order to facilitate access to VA disability compensation benefits for conditions related to sexual trauma after Service members transition out of the military, the victim care and support line of effort also recommends that DoD grant a small number of specially trained and vetted Veteran Benefits Administration (VBA) personnel access to the case-level/tabular data in the Defense Sexual Assault Information Database (DSAID). Survivors would be relieved of the burden of having to track down a copy of their report and transmit it to VBA, and VBA personnel would be able to confirm that the Service member did file a Restricted or Unrestricted Report. This could allow raters to establish the event happened during military Service and proceed to ordering a medical exam, increasing the likelihood of enhanced continuity of care and benefits.[73] Of note, data privacy and protection

---

[71] Exceptions should allow for the VA to notify DoD medical personnel when Service members exhibit signs of risk to themselves or others.

[72] The VA uses the term "military sexual trauma," which encompasses both sexual assault and sexual harassment experienced during military service. See: https://www.mentalhealth.va.gov/mentalhealth/msthome/index.asp

[73] A description of the process of applying for disability compensation for conditions related to MST is available at U.S. Department of Veterans Affairs. (2020, August). Disability Compensation for Conditions Related to Military Sexual Trauma (MST). https://www.benefits.va.gov/BENEFITS/factsheets/serviceconnected/MST.pdf

measures should be identified and included in the implementation plan to ensure maximum confidentiality and control for victims.

Recommendation 4.2 c: Explore Feasibility of Expanding Access to CATCH to include Victims of Sexual Harassment and Enabling Service Members to Self-Service Access to CATCH

DoD's Catch a Serial Offender (CATCH) Program[74] enables Service member and adult dependent victims of sexual assault who file a Restricted Report to anonymously disclose information about their offenders and discover whether the suspect may have also assaulted another person. This information may help inform their decision about whether to convert their report to Unrestricted.

In order to enhance the utility of the CATCH Program, the IRC recommends DoD examine options for expanding access in three crucial ways: first, by allowing survivors to create their own accounts; second, by expanding access to include those who have experienced sexual harassment; and third, by allowing users to extract this contemporaneous self-report of their experience to support VA disability compensation claims should they later develop Service-connected physical or mental health conditions related to the harassment or assault.

Rationale for Change: the CATCH Program Should Not Be Limited to Sexual Assault and Should be Easier to Access

It is well-established that only a minority of survivors file any sort of report,[75] for a variety of reasons (not least among them well-founded concerns about confidentiality and retaliation).[76] Limiting access to those who do file a formal Restricted Report accordingly significantly restricts the pool of survivors who are able to determine whether they were assaulted by a serial offender.

In addition, a substantial percentage of those who are sexually assaulted in the military were previously sexually harassed, often by the same individual–and yet the number of formal reports of sexual harassment is abysmally low.[77] Expanding access to survivors of sexual harassment, therefore, may

[74] DoD SAPRO. (2020). *Catch a Serial Offender (CATCH) Program*. https://www.sapr.mil/catch

[75] In 2018, roughly 30 percent of active duty women and 17 percent of active duty men who experienced a sexual assault subsequently made an official DoD report. Source: Breslin, R., Davis, E., Hylton, K., Hill, A., Klauberg, W., Petusky, M., & Klahr, A. (2019). *2018 Workplace and Gender Relations Survey of Active Duty Members: Overview Report*. Report No. 2019-027. Alexandria, VA: Office of People. https://apps.dtic.mil/sti/citations/AD1072334

[76] Reasons for not reporting sexual assault are collected in a biennial DoD survey. In 2018, 53 percent of Service members cited not wanting people to know about the incident as a reason for not reporting, and roughly one-fifth (21 percent) of women who experienced and reported sexual assault experienced a behavior in line with retaliation. Source: Id, 35-36 and viii.

[77] DoD women (47 percent) were significantly more likely than men (32 percent) to report their sexual harassment violation. Most commonly, Service members who experienced sexual harassment made an informal report (40 percent for women and 41 percent for men); however, women were more likely than men to indicate they filed a formal complaint (25 percent and 15 percent, respectively), whereas men were more likely than women to file an anonymous complaint (14 percent for men and 8 percent for women). Source: Breslin, R., Davis, E., Hylton, K., Hill, A., Klauberg, W., Petusky, M., & Klahr, A. (2019). *2018 Workplace and Gender Relations Survey of Active Duty Members: Overview Report*. Report No. 2019-027. Alexandria, VA: Office of People, 48. https://apps.dtic.mil/sti/citations/AD1072334

not only be able to identify (and increase the likelihood of victims reporting) those who are committing serial sexual harassment but also serve as a warning system of those who may be at risk of escalating their behavior up the spectrum of harm.

Implementation Considerations

The Victim Care and Support experts understand that this expansion would likely require technological, policy, and/or workforce changes to successfully implement. Because the IRC recognizes that it did not have the time available to conduct the necessary legal analysis into primary and secondary issues, it recommends a feasibility and implementation study subject to the guiding principles outlined here on how to overcome such barriers.

DoD should reexamine the university-based model that served as a prototype for the CATCH Program, which is self-service, meaning that victims have the ability to input and upload offender information into the CATCH database.[78] To ensure only military personnel and adult military dependent victims are able to enter information, registration should require verification with a .mil email address.[79]

To maximize the effectiveness of efforts to identify serial offenders, the IRC recommends any sexual misconduct on the spectrum from sexual harassment to sexual assault by the same individual be considered a "match" for notification purposes, thereby allowing survivors the agency to determine whether to convert their Restricted Report. Additionally, special victim military criminal investigators could analyze suspect information for matches and work with the Special Victim Prosecutor to develop an investigative plan to gather evidence for an arrest and prosecution. Specially trained CATCH Program representatives (one SARC per Service) should still contact individuals who input information to discuss the match and explain next steps. CATCH representatives would be able to take these reports and/or conduct a warm handoff to a SARC, SAPR VA, or EO representative as appropriate to ensure survivors not already receiving services are able to receive them.

Finally, the IRC heard directly from survivors applying for disability compensation who expressed frustration about the challenges in providing documentation of their sexual assault or sexual harassment to VA. Whether survivors ever choose to file an Unrestricted Report, they should be able to access a copy of their CATCH entry to support future disability compensation claims, should they

---

[78] Callisto. (2021). *For Survivors*. https://www.mycallisto.org/survivors

[79] DoD may also consider allowing a personal email address to be entered as well to facilitate access to their own record if needed and/or allow appropriate personnel to contact them should a potential match be identified post-transition.

later want to apply for VA benefits for conditions related to their traumatic experience and need supporting evidence.[80, 81]

Recommendation 4.2 d: Create Survivor-led Peer Support Programs that Allow for In-person, Virtual, and Telephone Interaction

The IRC recommends that DoD's Psychological Health Center of Excellence[82] (PHCoE) pilot models for peer support networks to connect sexual assault and harassment survivors at the installation level across the country, outside of the continental U.S., and on sea vessels. The purpose of these peer support programs would be to provide confidential space to survivors (whether in-person, virtually, or by phone) to connect with each other and bond over their shared experiences. The IRC envisions that this program would also offer military members who have experienced sexual assault and/or harassment the opportunity to train for and lead peer support programs under the direction of a behavioral health provider. This could be offered as an alternative collateral duty option for survivors who want to get involved in assisting their fellow Service members who have also experienced sexual assault or harassment.

Rationale for Change: Too Many Survivors Feel Isolated and Alone After Sexual Assault

Many of those who experience sexual assault and harassment in the military suffer profound isolation and loneliness in the days and months after their assault. Fear of ostracism, not being believed, and being labeled "weak" keep victims and survivors from telling others what happened to them. Victims who make a Restricted Report may be afraid to tell anyone for fear it could come to the attention of a mandatory reporter and turn Unrestricted. The IRC heard from survivors who felt so alone and hopeless after a sexual assault that they contemplated or attempted suicide. When asked what would have helped them during that challenging time, the response was often that they wished there had been someone they could talk to who could relate to their experience and offer support.

Peer support programs offer a solution that can be implemented as part of a larger victim support effort. The concept of peer support is based on the belief that people who have faced, endured, and overcome adversity can offer useful support, encouragement, hope, and mentorship to others facing similar situations.[83] An analysis of existing research on peer-led group-based interventions for sexual

---

[80] The IRC notes that the list of "markers" that VA considers acceptable for disability compensation claims for conditions secondary to MST is fairly extensive, suggesting the addition of CATCH entries may be feasible.

[81] U.S. Department of Veterans Affairs: Veterans Benefits Administration. (2020). *Disability Compensation for Conditions Related to Military Sexual Trauma (MST).* https://www.benefits.va.gov/BENEFITS/factsheets/serviceconnected/MST.pdf

[82] Psychological Health Center of Excellence. (2021). https://www.pdhealth.mil/

[83] Davidson, L., Chinman, M., Sells, D., & Rowe, M. (2006). *Peer support among adults with serious mental illness: a report from the field.* Schizophrenia Bulletin, *32*(3): 443-450. https://doi.org/10.1093/schbul/sbj043

assault victims revealed that they have a positive impact on participants' psychological, physical, and interpersonal well-being.[84]

There are numerous models of peer support, but the defining characteristic is that they are run by and for the people they serve. They are not professionally led, though they may have professional involvement in some capacity. Programs may offer self-help, mutual support, support groups, and mentoring.[85] The military offers peer support through Military OneSource,[86] but is not able to offer this program to survivors of sexual assault because the service providers running the programs are mandatory reporters and unable to maintain a Restricted Report. The DoD Safe Helpline offers a Safe HelpRoom,[87] a secure, anonymous moderated community forum where survivors of sexual assault can support each other in a safe, online environment through group chats. Due to inconsistent use, the Safe HelpRoom's 24-hour capacity plans to be discontinued.[88] There is also a "local" Safe HelpRoom, which empowers local SARCs and SAPR VAs to operate their own online, moderated sessions. Though these options for peer support may meet the needs of survivors who are comfortable communicating through a chat function, having a service that provides in-person, virtual, or telephonic options to connect with peers in their area would give survivors more choices, especially in the case of mentoring or one-on-one peer support.

Implementation Considerations

The IRC's victim care and support line of effort recommends that special attention be paid to developing peer support options for Service members who are LGBTQ+, from communities of color, men, religious minorities, and others who have difficulty finding individuals who can relate and understand their unique experiences. The importance of those connections is exemplified by feedback from participants in the VA-developed program, the Women Veterans Network (WoVeN)—a model DoD might explore in the development of pilots. WoVeN operates primarily through Boston University School of Medicine and was created to help female veterans connect with each other to provide support in their shared struggles and experiences with MST. Former Service members describe WoVen this way:

---

[84] Konya, J., Perôt, C., Pitt, K., Johnson, E., Gregory, A., Brown, E., Feder, G., & Campbell, J. (2020). *Peer-led groups for survivors of sexual abuse and assault: a systematic review.* Journal of Mental Health. https://www.tandfonline.com/doi/full/10.1080/09638237.2020.1770206

[85] Joyful Heart Foundation. (2007). *Peer support guidebook: tools for creating and maintaining safe and successful peer-led groups for adults with histories of sexual abuse.* https://www.joyfulheartfoundation.org/sites/default/files/Basic-Programs-EngagingMen-1in6-peer-support-guidebook.pdf

[86] Military OneSource. (2020). *Military OneSource Peer-to-Peer Support: Talk to Someone Who Gets It.* https://www.militaryonesource.mil/confidential-help/specialty-consultations/peer-to-peer/military-onesource-peer-to-peer-support-talk-to-someone-who-gets-it/

[87] DoD Safe Helpline. (2021). *Safe HelpRoom.* https://www.safehelpline.org/safe-helproom

[88] The IRC learned this through discussion with DoD SAPRO.

- "I learned about WoVeN from one of my friends … an Army Veteran who was searching for women veteran activities and found the website. I thought 'Here's that connection I've been missing, here's that sisterhood I can get back.' WoVeN is something especially for 'us.'"

Since its inception in 2017, WoVen has hosted nearly 3,000 women in its network.[89]

Recommendation 4.2 e: Amplify Victims' Rights and Services in the Post-Trial Period

The IRC recommends that education and training on post-conviction support for victims of sexual assault be widely offered and incorporated into a DoD core curriculum for SAPR and SHARP professionals (See: Recommendation 4.4: Re-Envision Training and Research to Improve Victim Care and Support), so that all victims, no matter where they are in the military justice process, are aware of their post-conviction rights. The DoD should explore the creation of an automated system to notify victims and SAPR/SHARP personnel about critical dates and offender movement.

Rationale for Change: Victims' Needs and Rights Do Not End at Conviction or Acquittal

In both the civilian and military justice systems, there is the public perception that victim involvement in a case ends after the trial or plea. This could not be further from the truth. In fact, there are several points in the post-conviction process when victims need support and guidance on how to exercise their post-conviction rights.

The post-conviction period is often referred to as "post-trial" in the military and covers the time from conviction (by plea or following a trial) until the offender has finished taking any legal actions that could impact their conviction, sentence, or criminal record. The military has one form[90] that a victim must complete about their notification preferences in the post-conviction period. They sign this form once the trial proceedings have concluded after a plea or conviction. There is also a brochure that must be provided to victims at this time that contains information about obtaining a record of the trial, tracking the confinement location of the offender, the convening authority action, appellate review, clemency and parole considerations and notification rights. According to DoD Directive (DD) form 2703,[91] "Victims also have the right to be notified in writing of the following changes in the prisoner's status: transfer to another facility, parole, escape, release from confinement, or death while in confinement. If the prisoner is released on temporary home leave (e.g., to visit a dying parent), the confinement facility will make every effort to notify the victim in advance."

---

[89] WoVeN. (2021). Women Veterans Network. https://www.wovenwomenvets.org/

[90] DoD. (2013). *DD Form 2704*. https://www.esd.whs.mil/Portals/54/Documents/DD/forms/dd/dd2704.pdf

[91] DoD. (2016). *DD Form 2703*. https://www.esd.whs.mil/Portals/54/Documents/DD/forms/dd/dd2703.pdf

Victim notification and input is extremely important during the post-conviction period. Arguably, how a victim is notified is as important as the notification itself. Best practices for victim notification are described by the DOJ National Institute of Justice (NIJ)[92]:

- "Victim notification should be undertaken with care and sensitivity, using a victim-centered and trauma-informed approach. Utilizing victim advocacy services is beneficial. Depending on how much time has passed since the assault, a victim may be in a very different stage of life and may not have disclosed past events to the people currently in her/his life. Notifications may trigger painful and emotional memories or be an unwelcome intrusion, especially in cases where the assault took place many years ago, there has been no communication between the victim and law enforcement and the notification is unexpected, or when notification may compromise the victim's privacy."

Implementation Considerations

Although there is policy on informing victims of their post-conviction rights, the IRC observed that there is little attention given to training SVCs/VLCs and SAPR VAs on post-conviction support for victims. The IRC recommends that a training module on post-conviction rights and support for victims be developed and incorporated into the core SAPR/SHARP training curriculum described in Recommendation 4.4. In addition, there is no automated system to notify victims of upcoming hearings or prisoner movement, nor are there systems to alert SVC/VLCs and SAPR VAs about critical dates that are approaching.[93] The Services should explore the feasibility and cost to implement an automated notification system, which could help to alleviate the frustration among survivors, their advocates and counsel who are "left in the dark" when it comes to the timing of these important, sensitive events.

Recommendation 4.3: Center the Survivor to Facilitate Healing and Restoration

- 4.3 a: Implement the "No Wrong Door" approach to sexual harassment, sexual assault, and domestic abuse across the Services and NGB;
- 4.3 b: Institute a "Commander's Package" prepared by the SAPR VA with recommendations for victim care and support;
- 4.3 c: Allow survivors flexibility to take non-chargeable time off for seeking services or time for recovery from sexual assault;
- 4.3 d: Increase victim agency and control of the response process by maximizing adherence to survivor preference on reporting status and centering survivor preferences in expedited transfers; and,

---

[92] U.S. Department of Justice. *National Best Practices for Sexual Assault Kits: A Multidisciplinary Approach.* U.S. Department of Justice, Office of Justice Programs, National Institute of Justice. https://cdn.ymaws.com/www.safeta.org/resource/resmgr/essential_reading/National_Best_Practices_for_.pdf

[93] This information was provided to the IRC in an individual interview with the SVC.

- 4.3 e: Study the methods our allies have used to make amends to survivors, including restorative engagement to acknowledge harm and potential victim compensation.

Recommendation 4.3 a: Implement the No Wrong Door Approach to Sexual Harassment, Sexual Assault, and Domestic Abuse Across the Services

The IRC recommends that DoD codify the "No Wrong Door" (NWD) approach into the Victim and Witness Assistance DoDI 1030.2[94] and DoDI 6495.02,[95] and ensure the Services apply it to every point in which a survivor of sexual assault may seek assistance. The NWD approach[96] is a person-centered approach to improving access to services and programs. At its most basic level, NWD refers to a system where a person who is seeking services from an organization will never encounter a "wrong door" to getting the care and support that they need. Even if they reach the wrong department, whoever receives that contact is trained to ensure that the person receives a "warm handoff" to the appropriate place.

> "When someone isn't able to use a SARC that's in the building next door because of where and how that SARC is funded, that's an issue."
>
> –SARC, as told to the IRC in an interview

Rationale for Change: Victims Should Never Be Turned Away When Seeking Help

A "warm handoff" refers to the transfer of care between two members of a team, where the handoff occurs in front of the "client," demonstrating the established relationship between the two team members. NWD is used most often in the medical and social services, where there are many moving parts and where finding the right programs and services can be confusing and frustrating. It is used to enhance accountability, build trust, strengthen the continuity of care, and increase client satisfaction.

NWD has been incorporated in many SHARP, SAPR, and FAP offices across the Services, but not in an official and consistent way. The warm handoff becomes especially important when victims are unsure of exactly what happened to them and do not know where to turn for help. It is critical that they not be turned away or expected to know where to go for help. Being met with a "We can't help you here" or "That doesn't fall under this office; here's a phone

---

[94] DoD. (2020, September 2). DoDI 1030.02: Victim and Witness Assistance. https://www.esd.whs.mil/Portals/54/Documents/DD/issuances/dodi/103002p.pdf

[95] DoD. (2018). DoDI 6495.02, Volume 1: Sexual Assault Prevention and Response Procedures. https://www.esd.whs.mil/Portals/54/Documents/DD/issuances/dodi/649502_vol1.PDF?ver=v8lKfyy0wrK_EZ95gtv6Pw%3d%3d

[96] Office of Crime Victims Advocacy. (2012, March). *Victims of Crime: Indicators of Success.* https://ovc.ojp.gov/sites/g/files/xyckuh226/files/pubs/InnovativePractices/Practices_Indicators%20of%20success-508.pdf

number for you to call" all but ensures that the survivor will go no further and stop seeking help altogether.

Implementation Considerations

In addition to codifying the NWD approach into DoD policy,[97] the IRC recommends the Services apply this principle of victim care and support to every point in which a survivor of sexual assault may seek assistance, including:

- On joint bases where there may be confusion about which SAPR support services a military member can use or if the survivor decides to report their assault to a different branch of the military[98];
- In situations when a survivor of sexual assault reports an assault to FAP and vice versa;
- When an assault occurs on a particular installation and the survivor is expedited to a different installation;
- When a sexual assault survivor presents at an emergency room hospital run by a Service other than theirs; and,
- When a survivor of sexual harassment goes to the SAPR office instead of the Equal Employment Opportunity office.

The key is to ensure that if a survivor has mustered up the courage and strength to come forward, whoever is on the receiving end will personally ensure that the survivor is connected to the people and services most appropriate. A survivor should never hear the words, "I can't help you."

Finally, the IRC emphasizes the importance of NWD to victims of domestic violence-related sexual assault. Current FAP and SAPR policies[99] draw a line of demarcation between delivery of services for sexual assault depending on the relationship between the victim and the perpetrator. FAP maintains responsibility for handling sexual assault cases that occur within the context of a marriage, between persons currently or formerly cohabitated, and for persons who have a child together. SAPR/SHARP, by contrast, maintains responsibility for adult, non-partner sexual assault cases.

---

[97] DoD. (2020, September 2). *DoDI 1030.02: Victim and Witness Assistance.* https://www.esd.whs.mil/Portals/54/Documents/DD/issuances/dodi/103002p.pdf

[98] For example, one SARC from a joint base told the IRC during a listening session: "I have learned the hard way that not everybody gets the same access. For example, one Air Force member had to use an Air Force SVC rather than our Navy VLC — she had to make an appointment over a week away, then never received a call and had to remind the SVC to call her back. Our VLC had availability the very next day and easily could have answered her questions if there were more consistency between services."

[99] DoD. (2018). *DoDI 6495.02, Volume 1: Sexual Assault Prevention and Response Procedures.* https://www.esd.whs.mil/Portals/54/Documents/DD/issuances/dodi/649502_vol1.PDF?ver=v8IKfyy0wrK_EZ95gtv6Pw%3d%3d, 3.

Unfortunately, this distinction can restrict choices for survivors of domestic abuse-related sexual assault and has also resulted in a concerning policy gap in eligibility for victim services of any kind for dating partners or other intimate partners who fall outside the DoD definition for intimate partner.

- To remedy this, as well as reinforce the concept of No Wrong Door, **the IRC strongly recommends the reissuance of DoDI 6400.06**, "Domestic Abuse Involving DoD Military and Certain Affiliated Personnel," which expands the DoD definition for "intimate partner" to include dating partners in eligibility for FAP services, and contains several measures to improve coordination between FAP and SAPR/SHARP to maximize victims' options in seeking support for intimate partner-related sexual assault.[100]

Recommendation 4.3 b: Institute a "Commander's Package" from the SAPR VA with Recommendations for Victim Care and Support

In the case of an Unrestricted Report, the IRC recommends that a special package be prepared within 24 hours by the SAPR VA (through the SARC) for the commander that contains recommendations for the sexual assault survivor's immediate and ongoing care.

Rationale for Change: Victims Need Support and Validation in the Aftermath of Sexual Assault

The purpose behind this recommendation is to convey critical information and obtain buy-in up front from the commander for any of the needs the survivor may have. It relieves the burden on the survivor from having to bring these needs to command, and it provides command with thoughtful recommendations to consider based on best practices for crime victims. This concept is not unlike a doctor producing a "medical profile"[101] for a commander after a Service member has suffered an injury and cannot participate in routine activities for a selected amount of time.

Implementation Considerations

The "Commander's Package" should contain:

- A list of the points of contact assigned to the survivor (SVC, SARC, SAPR VA);
- Upcoming appointments with SARCs, SAPR VAs, SVCs; and,
- Any special needs the survivor may have.

It should also contain recommendations for the commander's review and approval on topics including, but not limited to:

- Non-chargeable time off (described in 4.3 c);
- Counseling;
- Changing accommodations;

---

[100] DoD. (2007). *DoDI 6400.06: Domestic Abuse Involving DoD Military and Certain Affiliated Personnel.* https://www.esd.whs.mil/Portals/54/Documents/DD/issuances/dodi/640006p.pdf

[101] DoD. (2020, September 4). *DoDI 6120.03, Volume 2. Medical Standards for Military Service: Retention.* https://www.esd.whs.mil/Portals/54/Documents/DD/issuances/dodi/613003v2p.pdf?ver=2020-09-04-120013-383

- Safety/security enhancements for their living quarters; and,
- Expedited transfer of victim or alleged offender.

If the commander disagrees with any of the recommendations from the SAPR VA, they must prepare a written justification for why they are not approving the recommendations included in the Commander's Package. The next level of leadership must review the justification to determine if it has merit. If the determination is made that the commander's denial of any of the recommendations is justified, command must communicate why the decision was made to the survivor in the presence of their SARC, SAPR VA, or SVC, whoever they prefer to have with them. The survivor can decide not to have this meeting in person; the choice is theirs. Its purpose is to establish accountability in the event the commander does not accept the recommendations from the SAPR VA.

Recommendation 4.3 c: Allow Survivors Flexibility to Take Non-chargeable Time Off for Seeking Services or Time for Recovery from Sexual Assault

The IRC recommends the Services institute policies to enable commanders to grant survivors of sexual assault non-chargeable time off to enable them time to attend medical appointments, meet with their SAPR VA, or rest and recover from the acute impacts of trauma.

Rationale for Change: Recovery from Trauma is Not a Linear Process and Impacts Everyone Differently

Not having appropriate time for processing, healing, and recovery came up repeatedly in our interviews with survivors. Their experiences are reinforced by DoD data:

- Fewer than half of DoD active duty women indicated that their leadership made them feel supported to a large extent after they reported their experience of sexual assault (38 percent) or provided them flexibility to attend an appointment related to their sexual assault (48 percent) to a large extent.
- Just 41 percent of DoD women indicated that their leadership expressed concern for their well-being to a large extent.[102]

One survivor told the IRC that her commander required her to go back to work after being up for 24 hours due to emergency care she required after her sexual assault. She stated, "It doesn't get better right away; you need to be gentle with survivors of sexual assault." Another described wishing she had a break upon returning from deployment to Iraq, where she was sexually assaulted. Another survivor, whose case resulted in a not guilty verdict, told the IRC how difficult it was for her to go right back to work the next day—that she wished she had had a few days to fully process the result of the trial and prepare herself mentally for her return to the unit. Another survivor told the IRC that she was rushed by her command to decide whether she wanted to request an expedited transfer, or

[102] Breslin, R., Davis, E., Hylton, K., Hill, A., Klauberg, W., Petusky, M., Klahr, A. (2019). 2018 Workplace and Gender Relations Survey of Active Duty Members: Overview Report. Report (No. 2019-027). Alexandria, VA: Office of People Analytics. Retrieved from: https://apps.dtic.mil/sti/citations/AD1072334, 37

she would lose her opportunity to do so. This survivor stated that she would have preferred more time to think about whether the expedited transfer was right for her and whether it would have ramifications for her career growth and mobility. Being rushed into decision-making or into going back to work after sexual assault can be daunting for the survivor and can cause severe anxiety and angst. The need for this time can occur at any point following a sexual assault, and for each survivor, it may be different.

Implementation Considerations

Allowing flexibility for a survivor to take non-chargeable time off at the time of their choosing is in keeping with the victim-centered approach to working with victims of crime. The non-chargeable time off would be short-term (e.g., ranging from one hour, up to three days). Longer durations of absence would require a recommendation from a physician or psychologist, much like the current "convalescent leave" policy that is in place.[103] The purpose for including this as a recommendation is to reinforce to commanders that allowing survivors to take this time is crucial for establishing a path to healing and to building resilience.

> Less than half of Service women victims felt their leadership allowed them time to attend appointments related to their sexual assault.
>
> –2018 DoD Workplace & Gender Relations Survey

The request for non-chargeable time off would be part of the Commander's Package (See: Recommendation 4.3 b: Institute a "Commander's Package" from the SAPR VA with Recommendations for Victim Care and) from the SAPR VA. The IRC is aware that it is already within a commander's discretion to allow for this time. However, it appears that many commanders will not grant the time off unless they know exactly where the Service member is going and how they will use the time. Service members refer to this as "toxic accountability." The result is that many survivors feel unsupported by their command to be able to pursue the necessary time and space to access care and recover. This recommendation seeks to restore support from command and enable survivors time to heal.

Recommendation 4.3 d: Increase Victim Agency and Control of the Response Process by Maximizing Adherence to Survivor Preference on Reporting Status and Centering Survivor Preferences in Expedited Transfers

Interviews with survivors revealed that many felt they lacked control over the response process after reporting a sexual assault. This included those who inadvertently told someone who they were unaware was a mandatory reporter and those whose Restricted Report became Unrestricted against

---

[103] DoD. (2009, June 16; *rev.* 2021, January 15). *DoDI 1327.06: Leave and Liberty Policy and Procedures*, 18. https://www.esd.whs.mil/Portals/54/Documents/DD/issuances/dodi/132706p.pdf?ver=5f-RKMr_XQ3tXqk5w3TVcg%3D%3D

their wishes. For many, this loss of agency was a traumatizing continuation of the stripping away of bodily autonomy that occurred during the assault itself.

Rationale for Change: Victim Choice is Essential for Healing and Recovery

Accordingly, the IRC recommends several steps to restore agency and control to victims' reporting preferences.

1. To help maximize the chances that survivor's initial wishes are considered, **DoD should reexamine who is included in the list of mandatory reporters and enhance training and education on this topic**. Even among NCOs, there was confusion about whether they are considered mandatory reporters for those who are subordinate to them in rank but not their direct subordinates, as well as for their peers. Given that Military OneSource is presented as a source of confidential nonmedical counseling, it is also unclear whether they should be listed as having a mandatory reporting requirement under SAPR.[104]

2. **DoD should strengthen efforts to keep a report Restricted if that is the survivor's desire**. While it may be in the best interests of the Department and Services to increase the number of Unrestricted Reports in order to hold perpetrators accountable, it is imperative to maximize survivor agency in this decision. They may need time to develop a deeper understanding of their options, activate their support network, and initiate behavioral health before being in a position to make a truly informed decision. Both officers and NCOs should be cautioned against pressuring individuals to disclose why they may not want to be around another Service member or exhibit behavior changes in their presence, which may lead to survivors feeling forced to share details that inadvertently lead to a report being Unrestricted. In addition, once a survivor has selected the Restricted Reporting option, every effort should be made to maintain that option, regardless of third-party actions.

3. Both survivors and SAPR personnel shared a number of frustrations related to the expedited transfer process; accordingly, the IRC **recommends revising the expedited transfer procedures in DoDI 6495.02 Volume 1 to affirm the centrality of victim preferences.**[105] For example, many SAPR professionals noted that commanding officers often assume the victim will want a transfer, rather than asking the victim for their desired outcome. While many victims would prefer a transfer, others would prefer to stay where they have an established support network. In addition, while DoD policy affirms that commanders can transfer the alleged offender for the purpose of maintaining good order and discipline, the IRC heard that this option was

[104] DoD. (2018). *DoDI 6495.02, Volume 1: Sexual Assault Prevention and Response Procedures.* https://www.esd.whs.mil/Portals/54/Documents/DD/issuances/dodi/649502_vol1.PDF?ver=v8lKfyy0wrK_EZ95gtv6Pw%3d%3d, 109

[105] Id, 51-56.

comparatively less utilized in most Services, compared to moving victims.[106] Additional clarity should be provided about how and when commanders should consider this option, with renewed emphasis on the preference to center survivor preferences.

Implementation Considerations

Strengthen Efforts to Maintain a Restricted Report

The Defense Advisory Committee on Investigations, Prosecution, and Defense of Sexual Assault in the Armed Forces (DAC-IPAD) determined in its 2018 Annual Report[107] that in certain circumstances,[108] the victim should have the ability to limit further reporting or investigation; in effect, Restricting what was an Unrestricted Report. In its 2019 Annual Report,[109] the DAC-IPAD recommended (recommendation 14) that the Secretary of Defense establish a working group to assess this issue. In 2019, the DoD Sexual Assault Accountability and Investigation Task Force made a recommendation similar to the DAC-IPAD's 2018 determination.[110] The IRC believes that such a policy is important, and that after this new policy is published and implemented, the Department should evaluate its effectiveness, and amend the policy as may be necessary to make this an important tool for victims.

Improve the Expedited Transfer Process

When survivors who have filed Unrestricted Reports do want an expedited transfer, they should be made aware (by SAPR professionals, in revamped training materials and online) that under the DoDI, they are to submit the request to their commanding officers. One survivor reported that their SARC did not submit the expedited transfer request in a timely manner, and another shared that their unit executive officer was unwilling to put the request forward for various reasons. In both cases, once the commanding officer learned of the request, it was handled expeditiously, affirming the importance of ensuring survivors know they can submit the request to the official responsible for granting or denying the request on a specified timeline themselves. The IRC also learned that the DoD does not currently track data on how long it takes for an expedited transfer to occur. It is imperative that DoD

---

106 The IRC was encouraged to learn from the Navy that this option was beginning to be used more frequently in at least one fleet.

107 Defense Advisory Committee on Investigation, Prosecution, and Defense of Sexual Assault in the Armed Forces. (2018). *Annual Report*. https://dacipad.whs.mil/images/Public/08-Reports/DACIPAD_Report_02_Final_20180330_Web_Amended.pdf

108 For example, third-party reporting of a sexual assault, or disclosure of a sexual assault by a victim while seeking assistance from a member of the chain of command without realizing that doing so made the disclosure an Unrestricted Report.

109 Defense Advisory Committee on Investigation, Prosecution, and Defense of Sexual Assault in the Armed Forces. (2019). *Annual Report*. https://dacipad.whs.mil/images/Public/08-Reports/DACIPAD_Report_03_Final_20190326_Web.pdf

110 The report of the Task Force, including that recommendation, was approved by the Secretary of Defense on May 1, 2019. Meanwhile, in section 540K of the NDAA for FY20, Congress directed a report on this issue. That report was issued on June 23, 2020, indicating that a policy similar to that recommended by the Task Force and the DAC-IPAD was under development.

begin tracking this information so there is an official record of how long it takes for these expedited transfers to be completed and this information can be monitored and studied.[111]

Additional information should also be provided about other options available to move those who report being sexually assaulted, such as the fast safety move and humanitarian grounds, both in an appendix to the DoDI and in training for commanders.[112] These options could also be made as part of the Commander's Package, described in Recommendation Recommendation 4.3 b: Institute a "Commander's Package" from the SAPR VA with Recommendations for Victim Care and , in the event an expedited transfer is not the best option for the survivor.

Finally, DoD policy[113] should provide additional clarity on what constitutes a credible report. This is currently defined as "either a written or verbal report made in support of an Expedited Transfer that is determined to have credible information," though how that determination should be made is not explained. Credible information is further defined as "Information that, considering the source and nature of the information and the totality of the circumstances, is sufficiently believable to presume that the fact or facts in question are true."[114] This definition leaves open the possibility that victims who have a history of behavioral problems or collateral offenses such as underage drinking—the very individuals who may be at greatest risk for being preyed upon by serial predators—will not be considered adequately credible or believable when seeking an expedited transfer, potentially deepening their trauma and harming their chances of recovery.

Recommendation 4.3 e: Study the Methods Our Allies Have Used to Make Amends to Survivors, Including Restorative Engagement to Acknowledge Harm and Potential Victim Compensation

The IRC recommends that the DAC-IPAD study methods for restorative engagement[115] with survivors. These strategies can help survivors heal from the trauma of sexual assault and the institutional betrayal they may have experienced when their cases were poorly handed.

---

[111] DoD should utilize DSAID to track the date the survivor requested an expedited transfer through command, the date on which the command decided to approve or deny the request, and the date any such transfer occurred.

[112] Id, 51-52.

[113] DoD. (2013, March 28, *rev.* 2021, April 9). *DoDI 6495.021, Volume 1. Sexual Assault Prevention and Response: Program Procedures*. https://www.esd.whs.mil/Portals/54/Documents/DD/issuances/dodi/649502_vol1.PDF

[114] Id, 106.

[115] Government of Canada. (2021, April 1). *Restorative Engagement*. https://www.canada.ca/en/department-national-defence/services/benefits-military/health-support/sexual-misconduct-response/restorative-engagement.html; Government of Canada (2021, April 1). *Key Information on Restorative Engagement*. https://www.canada.ca/en/department-national-defence/services/benefits-military/health-support/sexual-misconduct-response/restorative-engagement/key-info.html

Rationale for Change: Acknowledging Victim Harm Can Be Life-Altering in the Healing Journey

The credibility of the U.S. military as a force that promotes the meaningful participation of women in defense and security is undermined so long as it allows a culture of mistreatment, degradation, and sexual harm in its ranks.

The U.S. Five Eyes Partners[116] have found ways to acknowledge the harm that survivors of sexual assault have endured during Service, including financial redress. DoD should seek to learn from the Canadian Armed Forces and the Australian Defense Force,[117] both of whom are using restorative engagement to provide survivors with an opportunity to be heard by a senior officer and share their experience through a facilitated, trauma-informed dialogue.

The purpose of restorative engagement is to create a safe space to allow survivors' lived experiences of sexual misconduct to be heard, responded to, and acknowledged by DoD and leaders from their branch of Service; contribute to culture change within the military workplace by increasing awareness and understanding of the experiences of survivors and the context within which harm has occurred; and begin the process of restoring the relationship between survivors and the U.S. military.[118] Restorative engagement can promote greater institutional accountability by facilitating a concrete process by which DoD and the Services could recognize the betrayal felt by some of its own.

Implementation Considerations

In both the Canadian and Australian models, restorative engagement also includes some form of financial compensation to acknowledge economic losses incurred by survivors as a result of the harm they experienced. While the IRC recognizes the distinct legal context[119] of these models, it is relevant to note that in the U.S., Service members are not covered by the protections of Title VII of the Civil Rights Act of 1964,[120] which means they cannot take legal action to stop harassment or get restitution for harassment from their employer. Additionally, they are also barred from suing the military or the

---

[116] Five Eyes is a strategic military and intelligence partnership between Australia, Canada, New Zealand, the United Kingdom, and the U.S.

[117] Australia Commonwealth Ombudsman. (n.d.). *Reporting abuse in Defence*. https://www.ombudsman.gov.au/How-we-can-help/australian-defence-force/reporting-abuse-in-defence

[118] Government of Canada. (2021, April 1). *Restorative Engagement*. https://www.canada.ca/en/department-national-defence/services/benefits-military/health-support/sexual-misconduct-response/restorative-engagement.html; Government of Canada. (2021, April 1). *Key Information on Restorative Engagement*. https://www.canada.ca/en/department-national-defence/services/benefits-military/health-support/sexual-misconduct-response/restorative-engagement/key-info.html

[119] The Restorative Engagement program is part of the Canadian Armed Forces (CAF)-Department of National Defence (DND) Sexual Misconduct Class Action Settlement (the Settlement). Restorative Engagement provides class members the opportunity to share their experience of sexual misconduct in the military workplace with a Senior Defence Representative from the DND/CAF or Staff of the Non-Public Funds.

[120] Civil Rights Act of 1964, Public Law 88–352; 78 Stat. 241. (1964). https://www.govinfo.gov/content/pkg/STATUTE-78/pdf/STATUTE-78-Pg241.pdf#page=1

U.S. Government under the Federal Tort Claims Act (FTCA) based on what is known as the *Feres* Doctrine.[121] This bar has prohibited such claims since 1950, despite repeated attempts to have the U.S. Supreme Court reconsider.[122] Further, while the VA provides compensation and health care to those diagnosed with specific medical conditions resulting from a military sexual assault, a compensation fund that addresses and acknowledges challenges aside from health and behavioral outcomes, such as loss of pay and pension benefits, does not exist. The DAC-IPAD should evaluate the steps our allies have taken to compensate survivors and their potential applicability to the U.S. context.

Recommendation 4.4: Re-Envision Training and Research to Improve Victim Care and Support

- 4.4 a: Establish a Defense Sexual Assault and Sexual Harassment Training Center of Excellence that administers a core curriculum of trauma and response trainings for all SARCs, SAPR VAs, chaplains, and other response personnel;
- 4.4 b: Develop training to enhance the capacity of SARCs and SAPR VAs to provide culturally competent care to Service members who are racial or ethnic minorities, LGBTQ+, religious minorities, and men who experience sexual assault;
- 4.4 c: Revise and update training modules on appropriate response to sexual assault and sexual harassment in professional military education for officers and NCOs; and,
- 4.4 d: Use an action research model to identify root problems, test interventions, and create best practices and increase the administration of user satisfaction surveys to obtain continuous feedback from survivors.

Recommendation 4.4 a: Establish a Defense Sexual Assault and Sexual Harassment Training Center of Excellence

Using the SHARP Academy as a model, the IRC recommends the development of a core curriculum through a Defense Sexual Assault and Sexual Harassment Center of Excellence. This core curriculum would be required for all persons in the military to complete before taking on a role where they will be working directly with sexual assault victims (e.g., SARC, SAPR VAs, chaplains).

---

[121] *Feres v. United States*, 340 U.S. 135 (1950) wherein the United States Supreme Court held that the Government is not liable "under the FTCA for injuries to servicemen where the injuries arise out of or are in the course of activity incident to service."

[122] Doe v. United States, 539 U.S. (2021) (cert. denied); wherein a U.S. Military Academy cadet sued the Government over a sexual assault endured while she was a student. The case asked the court to consider whether (1) *Feres v. United States*, which held that the Federal Tort Claims Act broadly precludes claims for injuries "incident to service," was wrongly decided and should be overruled; and (2) whether, alternatively, *Feres* should be limited so as not to bar tort claims brought by Service members injured by violations of military regulations, during recreational activities, or while attending a service academy.

> "If we are going to take this role seriously, we need to upgrade how we treat training and education."
>
> – SARC, as told to the IRC in a listening session

Rationale for Change: Core Training for all Response Personnel Creates Consistency in the Provision of Care Across the Services

In the many conversations the IRC held with individuals involved in the response to sexual assault and harassment, we learned that continuous, high quality training for SARCs and SAPR VAs was difficult to come by and was frequently described as "outdated," "inadequate," and even "out of compliance." Some individuals who are particularly passionate go out of their way to seek outside civilian resources for training. Many SARCs and SAPR VAs indicated that they had formed connections with civilian community advocacy groups in order to expand their knowledge base and skills and sought mentors within these organizations.

Training is not consistent across the Services and only the Army has a dedicated "SHARP Academy,"[123] a centralized training facility in Leavenworth, Kansas, where SHARP personnel go to receive their training. The SHARP Academy offers a variety of courses and curricula geared toward different audiences, such as program managers, SARCs, SAPR VAs, and SHARP Instructors.[124] They partner with the National Organization for Victim Assistance on their curricula development and credentialing requirement courses. Feedback from SARCs and SAPR VAs who attended the SHARP Academy were highly complementary of their experience there.[125]

> "I sought out volunteer work at a civilian agency so I could be a better military advocate."
>
> – SAPR VA, as told to the IRC in a listening session

SAPR personnel at one location noted that once training had been made virtual due to the pandemic, attendance had increased significantly, but that online options were being eliminated. Ensuring the availability of virtual platforms for training should be prioritized long-term due to the convenience of this modality.

In addition, the victim care and support line of effort recommends DoD conduct a thorough assessment of the extent and effectiveness of the training that chaplains

---

123 U.S. Army Combined Arms Center. (n.d.). *SHARP Academy*. https://usacac.army.mil/schools-and-centers/sharp-academy

124 SHARP instructors must participate in a five-week follow-on course to SARC/VA Career Course and serve as instructors for the SHARP Foundation course for units. SHARP instructors also assist the commands with executing their SHARP annual unit refresher training and present SHARP senior leader briefs (SLB) as required/needed. Source: U.S. Army Combined Arms Center. (n.d.). *Course Descriptions*. https://usacac.army.mil/schools-and-centers/sharp-academy/crsdescription

125 One SARC told the IRC, "By creating the consistency, we also expand our ability to have a broader base of colleagues to support us and a diverse pool of knowledge to pull from. I think standardizing is only part of it, the other part is exploring ways to allow the SARCs and [SAPR] VAs across Services to work together to leverage diversity and creativity of all SARCs."

receive on appropriate response to sexual assault and harassment. Some survivors reported that the confidential support they received from caring chaplains was invaluable, and the Chaplains Religious Enrichment Development Operation, a retreat program for sexual assault survivors in Norfolk, received high praise from SAPR professionals. However, this positive experience was not universal: others reported poor and even harmful interactions with chaplains. Chaplains themselves reported differing amounts of training related to sexual assault response. Given that on deployments and ships, chaplains are at times the only source of confidential support available, it is imperative they receive a more comprehensive, thorough, and consistent training; whether they adhere to core principles taught therein should also be assessed.

Implementation Considerations

A DoD Center of Excellence would not keep the Services from offering their own custom training to complement or build onto the core curriculum. However, having a common curriculum across the Services, administered by DoD SAPRO, will improve the consistency, professionalism, and quality of the responses across the board. A standardized curriculum would also strengthen the ability to realize the "no wrong door" philosophy by ensuring that all persons serving in victim care and support roles have a baseline set of knowledge, skills, and abilities in working with survivors. The IRC notes that DoD SAPRO is currently exploring a similar concept for a common curriculum and encourages the development of a cross-Service training center to administer it.

Recommendation 4.4 b: Develop Training to Build the Capacity of SARCs and SAPR VAs to Provide Culturally Competent Care to Service Members from Communities of Color, LGBTQ+ Service Members, Religious Minorities, and Men

As part of the core curriculum for response personnel, the IRC recommends including specialized training modules that build capacity of SARCs and victim advocates to provide culturally competent care and support to Service member survivors who are persons of color, LGBTQ+ Service members, religious minorities, and men.[126]

Rationale for Change: The Military Must Ensure Compassionate, Competent Care for the Diverse Needs of Survivors

The IRC met with survivors whose experiences with sexual assault and sexual harassment were impossible to divorce from their race or ethnicity. Another survivor described to the IRC how difficult it was, as a man, to report the sexual assault and ask for help, because he feared stigma from peers, who would scrutinize his sexuality.

---

[126] Culturally competent and specific services provide culturally relevant and linguistically specific services and resources to communities, especially racial and ethnic minority groups. 34 U.S.C. § 12291(a)(6) and (7).

Victims of sexual harassment and sexual assault can experience these harms differently, in connection with their gender, sexual orientation or gender identity, race, ethnicity, or other characteristics of who they are. For example, new data from RAND shows that just 12 percent of Service members identify as "other than heterosexual," but account for 43 percent of sexual assaults in the military.[127] Approximately one in three Black Service members report experiencing past-year racial/ethnic harassment.[128]

Further, while women are disproportionately the victims of sexual assault, many men Service members are also victims, and their unique experiences are not always understood or addressed. In addition, bias and lack of cultural competence on the part of victim service providers can create barriers to seeking and receiving appropriate mental health care.[129]

The IRC heard an example of this bias from several SARCs and SAPR VAs, who shared that some trainings they had attended largely excluded content on LGBTQ+ survivors. Some instructors avoid using the term "LGBTQ" or deliberately skipped LGBTQ+ training sections altogether to avoid discussing content with which they seemed uncomfortable.[130] These accounts indicate a lack of awareness and understanding about the importance of enhancing access to services and resources for all victims, including those who face barriers to using traditional services and may be reluctant to report their assaults or receive care.

Implementation Considerations

The IRC strongly recommends the development of culturally competent strategies and training modules to ensure that SARCs, SAPR VAs, chaplains, and other military response personnel provide victim-centered services that address the needs of survivors from marginalized or underserved populations.

In 2016, the Department released the DoD Plan to Prevent and Respond to Sexual Assault of Military Men to "guide [the] development of research-informed, gender-specific techniques to increase Service member understanding of how sexual assault affects men; ensure DoD response services meet the

---

127 Morral, A.R. & Schell, T.L. (2021). *Sexual Assault of Sexual Minorities in the U.S. Military.* Santa Monica, CA: RAND Corporation. https://www.rand.org/pubs/research_reports/RRA1390-1.html

128 Daniel, S., Claros, A.Y., Namrow, N., Siebel, M., Campbell, A., McGrath, D., & Klahr, A. (2019). *2017 Workplace and Equal Opportunity Survey of Active Duty Members: Executive Report.* Report No. 2018-023. Alexandria, VA: Office of People Analytics. https://taskandpurpose.com/app/uploads/2021/01/27/2017-Workplace-and-Equal-Opportunity-Survey-Report.pdf

129 National Alliance on Mental Illness. (2021). *Black/African American.* https://www.nami.org/Your-Journey/Identity-and-Cultural-Dimensions/Black-African-American

130 IRC Listening Session with SARCs and SAPR VAs.

needs of Service men; and encourage Service men's engagement with the response system."[131] The IRC recommends using this guide to inform the development of specialized modules on male victims.

In addition, the DoD recently released a new Victim Advocacy Training Guide that includes culturally competent elements to address the intersectionality of survivors' identities and experiences, and efforts are underway to include non-clinical encounter skills for response personnel as well. The IRC supports these efforts and recommends the Department enhance them by establishing formal relationships with community-based programs that provide culturally specific services. Additionally, the Department should utilize the federally funded organizations who specialize in providing culturally specific Training and Technical Assistance (TTA) to sexual and domestic violence providers. For example, the DoD should partner with the Department of Justice's OVW[132] and OVC,[133] as they fund a variety of TTA providers across the nation who assist with curriculum development and skill-building that is geared towards specific, underserved populations.

Recommendation 4.4 c: Revise and Update Training Modules on Appropriate Response to Sexual Assault and Sexual Harassment in Professional Military Education (PME) for Officers and NCOs

PME related to sexual assault and sexual harassment response must be updated and modernized with certain core modules standardized across the Services. In particular, it is imperative that all leaders (both officers and enlisted) be trained on the neurobiology of trauma.[134]

Rationale for Change: Commanders Will Never Understand Sexual Assault if They Don't Understand the Science of Trauma

Those who lack understanding of common physiological responses to traumatic experiences often judge victims' reactions in a more negative light and can worsen the recovery trajectory by questioning how survivors behaved in the midst of an assault and thus enhancing self-blame.

Training and education about how to adequately support survivors of sexual harassment and assault across the board should be enhanced to align with the other recommendations in this report: for example, to ensure commanders better understand the importance of centering victim choice and agency throughout the response process. The vast majority of uniformed personnel who spoke to the

---

[131] DoD SAPRO. (2016). *Fact Sheet: DoD Plan to Prevent and Respond to Sexual Assault of Military Men.* https://sapr.mil/sites/default/files/Fact_Sheet_DoD_Plan_to_Prevent_and_Respond_to_Sexual_Assault_of_Military_Men.pdf

[132] The DOJ Office on Violence against Women (OVW) administers the Culturally Specific Services Program (CSSP).

[133] The DOJ Office for Victims of Crime (OVC) funds the National Center for Culturally Responsive Victim Services. This Center facilitates the delivery of national-scale, high quality training and technical assistance to increase access to victim services and victim compensation for victims of crime in areas that have been historically underserved, marginalized, and adversely affected by inequality, including communities of color. https://ovc.ojp.gov/funding/opportunities/o-ovc-2021-32002

[134] Campbell, R. (2012, December 12). The Neurobiology of Sexual Assault: Implications for Law Enforcement, Prosecution, and Victim Advocacy. National Institute of Justice. https://nij.ojp.gov/media/video/24056

IRC affirmed the crucial role commanders play in setting the tone of how others in the unit will respond when an allegation of sexual harassment or assault is made.

Survivors and roundtable discussions with junior enlisted personnel and NCOs widely confirmed that those Service members who report a sexual assault are treated differently (ostracized by peers and/or leaders, particularly if the accused is well-liked, or being treated as "fragile"). Additionally, all training should be culturally competent and address the increased risk for experiencing assault and harassment among LGBTQ+ survivors. Another extraordinarily widespread experience shared with the IRC by survivors, junior enlisted personnel, NCOs and officers, is the extent of gossip and its detrimental impact on both survivors and accused. While it may be impossible to eradicate gossip, training should emphasize the importance of maximizing privacy and the role of leaders in attempting to suppress—rather than actively participate in—spreading private information or rumors

During roundtable discussions, NCOs across the services also noted that much of the training they received was focused on the same universal SAPR training, such as understanding the differences between Restricted and Unrestricted Reports. Many disclosed that they were unclear whether they were mandatory reporters for those subordinate to them in rank but who did not report directly to them or for their own peers, leading to uncertainty about who they could turn to if they were assaulted, or whether they could provide emotional support to another without being obligated to report that a friend was assaulted.

Implementation Considerations

During some of the roundtables held with individuals at the E-5 to E-6 level, NCOs began informally advising one another on what types of response would have been most appropriate when someone approached them in the aftermath of an experience of harassment or assault. Accordingly, more thorough modules related to sexual harassment and sexual assault response should be incorporated into lower levels of NCO Professional Development, and SAPR personnel should set aside time to engage with junior NCOs in small groups at the unit level to practice response scenarios.

Finally, the victim care and support line of effort recommends that as new training is developed, assessment of its effectiveness be built in from the beginning.

Recommendation 4.4 d: Use an Action Research Model to Identify Root Problems, Test Interventions, and Create Best Practices, with Input from Survivors

There must be careful, ongoing monitoring of program outcomes to ensure interventions are delivering the anticipated results. Direct feedback from survivors should also be routinely and methodically gathered to improve services.

Rationale for Change: Stronger Program Evaluations and Feedback Mechanisms Will Lead to Improved Services for Survivors

DoD has invested millions of dollars in conducting surveys, gathering data, and funding studies to better inform its understanding of sexual harassment and assault in its ranks. From prevalence studies to climate surveys, to large-scale military workplace studies, there are a plethora of data and information that underscore the pervasive nature of sexual harassment and sexual assault in the Services. However, there is little research evidence on victim care and support interventions that are being implemented at the installation level. There are numerous programs and approaches that the military has undertaken to improve the response and the care that victims receive after sexual assault.

For example, the DoD Safe Helpline, embedded behavioral health specialists, collateral duty SARCs and SAPR VAs, and SVC/VLC, to name just a few.[135] The military collects quantitative data and anecdotal information on these programs, but there are no scientific evaluations to show whether they are truly working to improve the response to sexual assault. In other words, what is the impact of these interventions? Are they the right interventions and are they being administered in the right dosages? Research is necessary to know what works. It is not enough to implement practices that have been labeled as "best" or "promising"—an evaluation component should be built into the implementation whenever a new intervention is undertaken.

Action Research Collaborative

As a way of building an evidence base for its efforts to address sexual assault and sexual harassment, the IRC recommends that DoD form a collaborative action research partnership with the DOJ to conduct an independent series of action research projects. Action research requires a very specific methodology that engages researchers and practitioners working together to tackle the issue at hand and create positive change. According to the DOJ NIJ, action research uses this collaborative approach to:

- Understand circumstances in their local context;
- Plan a response;
- Implement the response; and
- Modify the response based on the results of the evaluation.[136]

There are distinct benefits to using an action research model:

- Increased understanding of the target problem through data collection and analysis;
- Improved problem-solving strategies that focus on identified problem elements;

---

[135] DoD SAPRO. (2020). *FY21-FY25 Research Agenda.* https://www.sapr.mil/sites/default/files/public/docs/research/FY21-25_DoD_SAPR_Research_Agenda_FINAL.pdf

[136] U.S. Department of Justice. (2016). *Forming an Action Research Team to Address Sexual Assault Cases.* National Institute of Justice. https://www.ojp.gov/pdffiles1/nij/249232.pdf

- Pooled agency resources that conserve costs and expand the range of practitioner capabilities and expertise;
- Program refinement and system improvement; and,
- More knowledgeable evaluation of interventions."[137]

Using an action research model to identify problems and create solutions could enable the military to gain deep insight into how a policy or program is truly working at the installation level, leaving room for improvement and enhancement to the program along the way. It is recommended that DoD SAPRO take the lead in working with the NIJ to undertake an action research approach to assess the root problems of sexual harassment and sexual assault in the military as a way of generating new and innovative ideas for creating the change necessary to meaningfully shift the culture.

User Satisfaction and Survivor Feedback: Another Evaluation Tool

The IRC engaged in numerous briefings, meetings, and one-on-one phone calls with DoD behavioral healthcare leaders regarding the mental healthcare provided to survivors of sexual assault. The passion and commitment to this work is evident. These professionals provided specific information regarding the implementation of improvements and pilot programs to increase the ease with which survivors access mental healthcare services. However, one area these healthcare professionals noted as lacking involved information about survivors' satisfaction with behavioral health services. This type of feedback could contribute to ensuring that what patients deem important is centered in the behavioral health services they receive.

Gathering survivor feedback through user satisfaction ratings is critical for giving behavioral health providers the opportunity to learn to what degree they are meeting the expectations of their patients and where there are gaps or shortfalls. It is essential that behavioral health providers seek the views of their patients to set and sustain appropriate standards of care and take action when those standards are not met. Patient satisfaction is a key indicator of the quality of the care they are receiving and also helps to determine how satisfied a patient is with the treatment received. These results, especially when patients are given the option of giving open-ended comments, can provide valuable insights to inform the approach of the health care team.

Military Treatment Facilities (MTFs) currently use a single patient satisfaction survey (the Joint Outpatient Experience Survey, or JOES) to measure overall satisfaction with their visit that is not specific to care for survivors of sexual assault.[138]

---

[137] Mock, L. F. (2010). Action Research for Crime Control and Prevention. In Klofas, J., Hipple, N.K., & McGarrell, E. (eds.). *New Criminal Justice: American Communities and the Changing World of Crime Control*, 97. https://www.ojp.gov/ncjrs/virtual-library/abstracts/action-research-crime-control-and-prevention-new-criminal-justice

[138] JOES is sent to a sample of patients seen in direct care at MTFs, daily. The Survey asks questions about access, provider communication, satisfaction with care, satisfaction with the facility, etc. Source: Email correspondence with Defense Health Agency personnel (2021, June 14).

Implementation Considerations

Action Research Collaborative

Through an interagency agreement, DoD funding could be transferred to NIJ to develop, in conjunction with DoD SAPRO, an evaluation plan that will identify and prioritize the programs to be studied along with a timeline for their execution and the delivery of the results. As part of the collaborative effort, DOJ would assist DoD in developing evaluation plans for the programs and interventions recommended by the IRC to ensure that moving forward there will be a method in place for determining their effectiveness from the start. Resources for dedicated staff at both Departments should be allocated to ensure that the partnership is properly staffed and sustainable over the life of the collaborative.

Obtaining Survivor Feedback

The IRC recommends that custom user satisfaction ratings be developed and administered for behavioral health programs that are providing care to sexual assault patients to routinely gather information that can help to improve their services. Surveys can be administered on a continuous basis by text, an app, or by email and should be able to be completed anonymously. It is also recommended that the DoD's Defense Health Agency's PHCoE take the lead both on developing the surveys as well as working with the various MTFs to implement their use. Developing custom user satisfaction ratings for current programs such as inTransition,[139] intensive out-patient treatment, and the embedded behavioral health providers that deliver services within the military units is a recommended first step upon which to build.

Conclusion

It is quite simple, actually. Fundamentally, and at the very minimum, survivors need information, they need to be heard and they need services. These are their rights. For so many survivors of sexual assault in the military, these rights have been overlooked, rejected, and dismissed. Their stories of being violently assaulted were heart-wrenching to hear and learning about how they were treated afterwards by their peers and leaders will forever haunt the members of this IRC.

Victim care and support across the Services needs serious repair and attention. The IRC identified many issues that led to this conclusion: the inconsistency in the quality and professionalism of the care that survivors receive; the fear of retaliation and ostracism as a result of reporting an assault and survivors' lack of trust in command to protect and defend them; barriers that keep victims from seeking or accessing appropriate and timely assistance; ignorance on the part of leadership and peers about the impact of trauma from sexual assault; outdated and/or inconsistent training for service providers; and a lack of evidence from research and evaluation about what works.

---

139 inTransition is a free, voluntary, and confidential program by the Defense Health Agency that provides care continuity support by assisting Service members/veterans in transitioning their mental healthcare. Source: Psychological Health Center of Excellence. (2021). inTransition: About us. https://www.pdhealth.mil/resources/intransition

Survivors told the IRC they want easy access to medical and behavioral health services, frequent updates on the status of their case, check-ins on their safety and security, and assurance that their rights are being upheld. They want respect and they want to be believed. Most of all, they want to feel safe.

It is the hope of the Victim Care and Support experts that these recommendations will be taken seriously, accepted, and implemented to the greatest extent possible. The survivors that met with the IRC had dreamed their entire lives of serving their country through military Service. Remarkably, even after being assaulted, most wanted to stay in the military and continue what they had started. This resilience and commitment speaks volumes about the honor and pride that comes with being a military Service member. It is imperative that the military's leadership acknowledge this and begin immediately to do what is necessary to protect and defend its own.

Appendix F: Areas for Further Study

The Independent Review Commission (IRC) on Sexual Assault in the Military attempted to address as many issues as possible under its Charter; however, given the limitations of a 90-day timeframe, not all concerns raised by stakeholders could be fully addressed. Below are several areas that have been identified for further study.

Military Service Academies

This report would not be complete without mention of the Military Service Academies. While the most recent data show an overall decrease in sexual assaults in the Service Academies for the academic program year 2019-2020,[1,2] the IRC regrets that its time constraints did not allow for a separate and in-depth focus on these schools; however, the IRC did keep the Academies in mind while framing its recommendations. Because the cadets and midshipmen are on active duty and subject to the Uniform Code of Military Justice (UCMJ), they will benefit from the changes to the Code recommended in this report. Implementation of the IRC's recommendations should include an analysis of their unique requirements.

Long-term Behavioral Health and Victim Care

In the civilian population, stigma is a significant barrier to seeking behavioral health services. It is even more so in the military community, where military culture sets the expectation that Service members should be able to handle problems on their own.[3] A 2014 RAND study on improving the Department of Defense (DoD) approach to stigma reduction concluded that there is still much unknown about the influence that stigma has on help-seeking behavior.[4] However, many survivors who spoke with or wrote to the IRC cited this as the reason they never reported their sexual assault. Some commanders reinforced this message by telling survivors of sexual assault to "get over it," or "keep your head up." One survivor recalled her commander telling her that "her personal issues don't matter." Survivors also reported hesitating to seek behavioral health services because of the perceived risk of losing medical or disability benefits or being declared "unfit for duty." When the stigma of behavioral health impedes a survivor's ability to get care, their mental health may worsen to the point where it negatively impacts their careers, relationships, and their physical health, not to mention military readiness. While the IRC was unable to devote significant effort on this issue, it is hoped that

---

[1] DoD. (2021, February). *Annual Report on Sexual Harassment and Violence at the Military Service Academies: Academic Program Year 2019-2020*, 5.

[2] It is difficult to know if these statistics demonstrate true decline, since the Coronavirus pandemic affected normal operations at the Military Service Academies. Classes were suspended in March 2020 and activities were canceled.

[3] Kaplan, D. (2019). *Reducing Military Mental Health Stigma to Improve Treatment Engagement: Guidance for Clinicians*. Psychological Health Center of Excellence, Department of Defense. https://www.pdhealth.mil/news/blog/reducing-military-mental-health-stigma-improve-treatment-engagement-guidance-clinicians

[4] Acosta, J. et al. (2014). *Mental Health Stigma in the Military*. RAND Corporation, 2014. http://www.eachmindmatters.org/wp-content/uploads/2015/02/RAND_RR426.pdf

DoD will continue to study the influence that stigma has on survivors' use of behavioral health services.

Administrative Separation Boards, Grade Determination Boards, and Boards of Inquiry

The IRC heard from many survivors (and several commanders) about their frustrations with the Service's various administrative boards within the sexual assault paradigm when an offender is not criminally prosecuted, but instead receives nonjudicial punishment or a letter of reprimand—neither of which trigger a punitive discharge—and then goes to an administrative board for processing. Typically, the offender will either be processed for involuntary separation or face a board of inquiry (for officers) or grade determination board (a board convened to determine the highest rank/grade a Service member served satisfactorily in). Though these boards vary in function, their objectives may have lasting impacts on the respondent and victims of sexual assault. For the respondent, the stakes are high. At risk is a Service member's career, reputation, pay and future benefits.[5] These administrative boards are comprised of Service members hand-selected by command[6] and with no legal training. Because there was no data for the IRC to examine, the anecdotal concerns we heard from military sexual assault survivors resounded with unanimity: these Boards are not impartial and more often than not, decide to retain Service members with substantiated incidents of sexual harassment or assault. For survivors and the American public, these retention decisions are an anathema to the Service's core values. Because the IRC is acutely aware of due process rights of respondents, yet heard the real frustrations of sexual assault victims, an extensive review of the Service's Administrative and allied Boards should be conducted by the Defense Advisory Committee on Investigations, Prosecution, and Defense of Sexual Assault in the Armed Forces (DAC-IPAD) to determine if systemic issues of equity and accountability exist.

Victim Collateral Misconduct

Victims of sexual assault may have engaged in misconduct leading up to, or associated with, the sexual assault incident. Examples of minor misconduct include, but are not limited to, underage drinking, extramarital sex (infidelity),[7] fraternization, and patronizing an off-limits establishment or location. The thorny issue of whether, and how, to dispose of such misconduct rests with the victim's commander—which can create a chilling effect on victims' decisions to come forward and report their assault, or simply seek services.

---

5 See, for example, DAC-IPAD testimony of LTC (Ret.) Joseph Morse on October 4, 2018 who testified, "If I had remained in the Army, been promoted, and retired as a colonel, my retirement pay would have approximately doubled over the remainder of my lifetime."

6 The commander who selects the board members is typically at higher level than the commander who issued the nonjudicial punishment or reprimand, which may result in a process that is frustrating for both victim and the commander who issued disciplinary action for the substantiated allegation.

7 UCMJ, Article 134.

DoD is in the process of issuing a "Safe-to-Report" policy as directed by section 539A of the National Defense Authorization Act for Fiscal Year 2021 regarding collateral misconduct of victims of sexual assault and may include an outright prohibition on punishing victims who engage in minor collateral misconduct. In the meantime, the Services have regulations governing victim collateral misconduct. The regulations range from having commanders "consider" deferring discipline until all investigation are complete[8] to "encouraging" commanders to defer discipline until final disposition of the sexual assault case[9] to "balancing objectives of holding members accountable for their own misconduct with the intent to avoid unnecessary trauma to sexual assault victims and the goal of encouraging sexual assault reporting."[10]

In 2019, pursuant to congressionally-required data collection, the Services provided their first sets of data over a two-year period detailing the number of instances in which a covered individual was suspected of misconduct, the number of instances in which adverse action was taken against the covered individual, and the percentage of investigations of sexual offenses that involved an accusation or adverse action against a covered individual.[11] The data[12] provided demonstrates the urgency for implementation of the "Safe-to-Report" policy:

- In 91.6 percent of cases where a victim engaged in collateral misconduct in the Marine Corps, the command took adverse action;
- The Air Force doled out punishment to victims in 34.6 percent of cases; and
- The Navy issued punishments in 42.3 percent of cases.

Beyond this initial set of data, little—if anything—is known as to how commanders are making adverse action determinations. The next report is due to Congress on September 20, 2021. If the new DoD policy includes a prohibition on imposing adverse action for a victim's minor collateral misconduct, the IRC believes that the Department should consider examining and assessing whether retroactive expungement of such records for victims who did not receive the protections afforded by the new policy would best attain justice. Applications for expungement, reviews of cases, and determinations could be made by the Military Department Boards for the Correction of Military/Naval Records. Additionally, the IRC is concerned that having commanders make decisions regarding minor misconduct may not effectively serve victims. Conversely, the Department should consider what role—if any—the proposed Special Victim Prosecutor (see Recommendation 1.1) would have in determining collateral misconduct.

---

[8] Army Regulation 600-20, Chapter 7-11(n)(4).

[9] SECNAVINST 1752.4C, Enclosure 7, Collateral Misconduct in Sexual Assault Cases.

[10] AFI90-6001, 6.4 Victim Collateral Misconduct.

[11] The term 'covered individual' means an individual who is identified in the case files of a military criminal investigative organization as a victim of a sexual offense that occurred while that individual was serving on active duty as a member of the Armed Forces.

[12] 2019 Report on Allegations of Collateral Misconduct Against Individuals Identified as the Victim of Sexual Assault in the Case Files of a Military Criminal Investigative Organization.

Guard and Reserve

The IRC notes that recent independent investigations of sexual harassment and sexual assault in the Guard and Reserve have surfaced troubling findings.[13] These components face special jurisdictional challenges by their very nature that simply do not resonate with the Active Duty component. The IRC recognizes the unique nature of authority over the National Guard and applauds the efforts of the National Guard Bureau (NGB) to have the states adopt a model state code of military justice that is patterned after the UCMJ. The IRC recommends that the NGB modify its model state code of military justice to include any changes made by Congress to the UCMJ as a result of IRC recommendations, and encourage the states to adopt the modified model state code. In the alternative, DAC-IPAD should conduct an in-depth study into military justice for non-military specific crimes in the 21st Century as it pertains to the Guard and Reserve. This study should consider the utility of standing courts[14] and non-military specific offenses like sexual assault in today's military. The study should include comparative analyses of systems in other countries,[15] and whether those models might be helpful to solve the complex issues involving the Guard and Reserve within the sexual assault paradigm.

The IRC notes that NGB leadership is highly motivated to take on sexual assault prevention and response and helped educate the IRC on the specific issues facing the Guard and Reserve components. DoD and Congress should support the Guard's efforts to find solutions to the complex state and federal jurisdictional questions surrounding sexual harassment and assault of Guard members.

Civilian Workforce

While the IRC focused its efforts on military personnel, it is well established that there remain significant challenges in how the Department manages civilian employee sexual assault and sexual harassment. Most recently, the GAO report, "Sexual Harassment and Assault: Guidance Needed to Ensure Consistent Tracking, Response, and Training for DoD Civilians," identified gaps related to visibility of incidents, tracking of data, uniformity of response resources, and the quality of training content.[16] For example, DoD data does not include comprehensive statistics on sexual assault involving all DoD civilian employees except when a Service member is the suspect. Further, while DoD civilian employees outside of the continental U.S. are afforded the option to file an Unrestricted Report, this is not a requirement, so all incidents are not captured. Without guidance that addresses

[13] See, e.g., Myers, M. (2020, August 24). *Mishandling of misconduct reports, retaliation a pattern across the National Guard.* Military Times. https://www.militarytimes.com/news/your-military/2020/08/24/mishandling-of-misconduct-reports-retaliation-a-pattern-across-the-national-guard/

[14] The IRC is aware of the United States Supreme Court decision, *Ex parte* Milligan, 71 U.S. (4 Wall.) 2 (1866).

[15] "Over the years, the French Military Justice System has progressively led to a system in which military justice is combined with that of ordinary justice. During times of peace, the jurisdiction of all military courts is abolished. During times of war, military courts have primary jurisdiction to deal with offences." Source: France: Military Justice System, by Edith Palmer, The Law Library of Congress, Global Legal Research Center, July 2013.

[16] GAO. (2021). *Sexual Harassment and Assault: Guidance Needed to Ensure Consistent Tracking, Response, and Training for DoD Civilians.* https://www.gao.gov/assets/gao-21-113.pdf

these areas, DoD will not definitively know the true extent of sexual assault among the DoD civilian workforce.[17]

The Department employs nearly 900,000 DoD civilians across the globe–"more civilians by far than any other government organization [and] more civilian employees than at least four states have residents."[18] Considering many civilians are working in blended environments with Service members, this issue warrants serious attention., It is imperative the federal civilian workforce at DoD is supported by a mature workplace violence program with appropriate oversight to prevent, respond to, and comprehensively track data involving workplace-related sexual harassment incidents and sexual assault crimes. To this end, the IRC recommends a continued focus on, and even higher prioritization of, implementing the recent GAO recommendations in the shortest timeframe feasible. This will complement the implementation of the IRC recommendations and allow DoD components the advantage of aligning program updates that serve all DoD personnel.

---

[17] Ibid.

[18] Davidson, J. (2021). *Most reports by civilians of sexual assault go unrecorded in Defense Department database*. The Washington Post. https://www.washingtonpost.com/politics/defense-civilians-sexual-assault/2021/02/19/306c0150-729e-11eb-a4eb-44012a612cf9_story.html

Appendix G: IRC Founding Documents

February 26, 2021 Secretary of Defense Memorandum

SECRETARY OF DEFENSE
1000 DEFENSE PENTAGON
WASHINGTON, DC 20301-1000

FEB 2 6 2021

MEMORANDUM FOR SENIOR PENTAGON LEADERSHIP
COMMANDERS OF THE COMBATANT COMMANDS
DEFENSE AGENCY AND DOD FIELD ACTIVITY DIRECTORS

SUBJECT: Immediate Actions to Counter Sexual Assault and Harassment and the Establishment of a 90-Day Independent Review Commission on Sexual Assault in the Military

Sexual assault and harassment remain persistent and corrosive problems across the Total Force. I have reviewed the responses to my initial tasking on January 23, 2021. The submissions reflect some action in this space but the effort is far short of what is required to make lasting change. I expect every member of our Total Force to be part of the solution and leaders — both civilian and military — across the Department to take direct accountability to drive meaningful change. To make real progress, we must consider outside views and ideas, to the extent practicable, and be transparent about where we have fallen short.

To carry out President Biden's direction, I am ordering several immediate actions and the establishment of a *90-Day Independent Review Commission on Sexual Assault in the Military (IRC)* to address sexual assault and harassment in the military.

IMMEDIATE ACTIONS

- **Assess Compliance with Sexual Assault and Harassment Policies and Integrated Violence Prevention Efforts:** I direct the Secretaries of the Military Departments to ensure compliance with all existing policies on sexual assault and harassment, and accelerate violence prevention activities. Using guidance and tools provided by the Under Secretary of Defense for Personnel and Readiness (USD(P&R)), the Secretaries of the Military Departments will assess compliance with current policies, including the newest integrated violence prevention policy (DoD Instruction 6400.09, "DoD Policy on Integrated Primary Prevention of Self-Directed Harm and Prohibited Abuse or Harm"), and alignment — *at the ground level* — with prevention best practices as outlined in the Prevention Plan of Action. Within 120 days, the Secretaries of the Military Departments will submit reports to me on compliance and provide plans to address any deficiencies identified.

- **Conduct Evaluations at High Risk Installations:** A *High Risk Installation Evaluation Report* and its findings will be submitted to me through USD(P&R), as soon as feasible. In addition, quarterly reports will be submitted to me on the new Command Climate survey data, on those installations and units that are of greatest concern, as well as those that are showing promise. The USD(P&R) will issue a plan of action and milestones to meet these requirements by March 15, 2021.

- **Establish a Violence Prevention Workforce:** To build and prepare a DoD-wide violence prevention community of practice, the Secretaries of the Military Departments will identify and resource personnel whose duties are dedicated to the prevention of interpersonal violence and self-harm. Using the template provided by the USD(P&R), the Military Departments will submit to me a report by October 1, 2021, describing the constellation and distribution of their prevention workforce, planned resourcing and sustainment, and required staffing changes at all levels. In addition, the Military Departments will ensure that at least half of their identified violence prevention workforce receives initial training by December 31, 2021, and that the entire workforce is trained by June 30, 2022.

90-Day Independent Review Commission on Sexual Assault in the Military (IRC)

The IRC, which is anticipated to be led by Lynn Rosenthal, will conduct an independent, impartial assessment of the Department's efforts. The Deputy Secretary of Defense will chair the Commission's Executive Support Committee. The Executive Support Committee will ensure the Independent Review Commission has all necessary support and resources. Members of the Executive Support Committee will include the Undersecretary of Defense for Personnel and Readiness and other senior Service and OSD leadership as necessary.

Within 7 days, the Deputy Secretary of Defense, supported by the USD(P&R), will provide a charter for my signature that formalizes the role of the IRC and the membership of the Executive Support Committee. The IRC shall ensure the Department receives vital input from key stakeholders, both inside and outside of the Department, in order to appropriately inform its assessment.

The IRC will pursue three Lines of Effort (LOEs), with accompanying Working Groups that receive information from internal and external stakeholders, including military survivors of sexual trauma, prevention and response practitioners, and outside experts. To further ensure independent views inform the Commission, each Working Group will be led by a subject matter expert with experience and expertise to guide and lead the group with impartiality. Additional membership will include representatives from the Office of the USD(P&R), Military Departments, National Guard Bureau, Joint Staff, and related Department components. Working Groups will review previous DoD and outside efforts (e.g., studies, assessments, reports), including recommendations from members of Congress. The LOEs for the IRC will be:

- **Line of Effort 1: Accountability.** The IRC, via the LOE 1 Working Group, will examine the role of the military justice system, as codified in the Uniform Code of Military Justice (UCMJ) in addressing the prevalence of sexual assault and harassment, in building trust and encouraging survivors to report, and its efficacy in bringing alleged perpetrators to justice. It will also assess feasibility, opportunities, and risks from changes to the commander's role in prosecution. ***No later than 60 days from initial meeting, the IRC will provide a report that includes actionable recommendations to ensure the UCMJ - and associated processes, roles and responsibilities - align with our goals to prevent sexual assault and harassment and promote appropriate accountability, fairness to all individuals involved, and good***

order and discipline.

- **Line of Effort 2: Prevention.** The IRC, via the LOE 2 Working Group, will conduct a comprehensive assessment of ongoing prevention efforts to determine where gaps may exist and where additional resources may be needed. ***Within 90 days from initial meeting, the IRC will provide recommendations to mitigate any gaps found in our prevention efforts and ensure the Military Departments, Services, and National Guard Bureau account for their implementation of policies and programs designed to prevent sexual assault and associated risk factors.*** The recommendations provided should achieve an enduring, Department-wide prevention infrastructure in which leaders are equipped with the data, people, resources, policy, and tools that the Military Departments and Services need to stop sexual assault and other readiness-detracting behaviors before they occur.

- **Line of Effort 3: Climate and Culture.** The IRC, via the LOE 3 Working Group, will review evidence-based approaches to improve climate to ensure that all Service members are able to serve with dignity and respect, and that all victims feel safe to report without fear of reprisal from leadership or peers. ***Within 60 days from initial meeting, the IRC shall provide recommendations to ensure all military members have the skills, tools, and necessary data to promote climates of dignity, respect, and inclusion.*** While I recognize the climate assessment responsibilities of command, recommendations must inform and enable all members to detect and address those behaviors that can give rise to sexual assault, such as sexual harassment, hazing, bullying, and gender discrimination.

Additional LOEs and accompanying Working Groups may be added at the discretion of the IRC Lead.

My Point of Contact for these efforts is Dr. Elizabeth Van Winkle [redacted]

Our people and our readiness are inextricably linked. Each member of the Total Force must commit themselves to support this cause. Even the best policies and programs will not be effective when members of our military do not uphold our values and expectations. We must, and will, do better.

March 23, 2021 Secretary of Defense Memorandum

DEPUTY SECRETARY OF DEFENSE
1010 DEFENSE PENTAGON
WASHINGTON, DC 20301-1010

MAR 2 3 2021

MEMORANDUM FOR SENIOR PENTAGON LEADERSHIP
COMMANDERS OF THE COMBATANT COMMANDS
DEFENSE AGENCY AND DOD FIELD ACTIVITY DIRECTORS

SUBJECT: Independent Review Commission on Sexual Assault in the Military Structure and Membership

On February 26, 2021, the Secretary of Defense announced his intent to establish a 90-day Independent Review Commission (IRC) on Sexual Assault in the military. Today, I am pleased to provide additional details on the structure of the IRC and designate the personnel that will be participating in this critical effort.

The IRC structure is tiered to ensure its independence, while also providing its experts with access to the support and resources of the Department at every stage of the process. These tiers include the following:

- Executive IRC
- IRC Advisory Support Team
- Line of Effort (LOE) Working Group Consultative Teams
- LOE Working Group Subject Matter Experts (SME) and Support Teams

The Executive IRC is led by the IRC Chair, Lynn Rosenthal, and is the deliberative body of the IRC that will ultimately provide recommendations to the Secretary of Defense and the President of the United States. The Executive IRC is composed of Highly Qualified Experts (HQE) and a Detailee that have been chosen by Ms. Rosenthal to participate in this effort. The Executive IRC will also include experts from a limited number of other Federal agencies as well as participation from the Deputy Secretary of Defense. Additional information about the HQEs and Detailee who will be a part of the Executive IRC is provided at TAB A.

The IRC Advisory Support Team is structured to ensure the IRC has the support of the highest levels of DoD leadership. Additional information on the membership of the Advisory Support Team, as well as the IRC structure and full membership, is provided at TAB B.

The Working Group Consultative Teams includes the Department leadership who oversee the offices of primary responsibility in the Office of the Secretary of Defense (OSD) for sexual assault and harassment prevention and response. These OSD Component leads are complemented by the Military Department and Service leaders who will be responsible for implementing the IRC's ultimate recommendations.

The Working Group SMEs and Support Teams include at least two personnel from each of the military Services and Joint Staff, along with OSD personnel, to support the work of the IRC on a full-time basis. These SMEs were nominated by the military Services and selected in consultation with the IRC Chair based on their expertise in preventing and responding to sexual assault and harassment in the military. This group will also include a military sexual assault survivor to provide the critical lived-experience and perspective from this community. The full list of SMEs supporting the IRC is also included at TAB B. The IRC Chair may appoint additional personnel to the IRC at her discretion.

The IRC will commit to making recommendations that will, with the support of the Department, result in meaningful and lasting progress on this persistent and corrosive problem across the military.

Attachments:
As stated

INDEPENDENT REVIEW COMMITTEE

EXECUTIVE IRC		
IRC Chair	Lynn Rosenthal	IRC Lead HQE
	Cindy Dyer	Accountability Co-Lead
	Brig Gen James Schwenk (ret)	Accountability Co-Lead
	Meghan Tokash	Accountability Co-Lead
	Dr. Debra Houry	Prevention Co-Lead
	Neil Irvin	Prevention Co-Lead
	Maj Gen James Johnson (ret)	Prevention Co-Lead
	Lt Col Bridgette Bell	Climate and Culture Co-Lead
	Kris Fuhr	Climate and Culture Co-Lead
	Dr. Kyleanne Hunter	Climate and Culture Co-Lead
	Indira Henard	Victim Care and Support Co-Lead
	Kristina "Kris" Rose	Victim Care and Support Co-Lead
	Kayla Williams	Victim Care and Support Co-Lead
OSD	Dr. Kathleen Hicks	Deputy Secretary of Defense
ADDITIONAL IRC MEMBERS		
OSD/P&R	Ms. Virginia Penrod	Acting Under Secretary, Personnel and Readiness
OSD/OGC	Ms. Beth George	Acting General Counsel
OSD	Mr. Bishop Garrison	Senior Advisor to Secretary of Defense for Human Capital
IRC ADVISORY SUPPORT TEAM		
Joint Staff	*Gen Mark Milley*	*Chairman of the Joint Chiefs of Staff*
Army	*Hon John Whitley*	*Acting Secretary of the Army*
	Gen J. McConville	*Chief of Staff of the Army*
Air Force	*Hon John Roth*	*Acting Secretary of the Air Force*
	Gen CQ Brown	*Chief of Staff of the Air Force*
Space Force	*Gen John Raymond*	*Chief of Space Operations*
Navy	*Hon Thomas Harker*	*Acting Secretary of the Navy*
	Adm. Michael Gilday	*Chief of Naval Operations*

INDEPENDENT REVIEW COMMITTEE

Marine Corps	*General David Berger*	*Commandant of the Marine Corps*
NG	*Gen D. Hokanson*	*Chief of the National Guard Bureau*
ASD(LA)	*Mr. Louis Lauter*	*Acting Assistant Secretary of Defense, Legislative Affairs*
ASD(PA)	*Mr. John Kirby*	*Assistant to the Secretary of Defense, Public Affairs*
ASD (SO/LIC)	*Mr. Christopher Maier*	*Acting Assistant Secretary, Special Operations/Low Intensity Conflict*
OSD/OFR	*Dr. Elizabeth Van Winkle*	*Executive Director, Office of Force Resiliency*
OSD/OGC	*Mr. Paul Koffsky*	*Acting Principal Deputy General Counsel*
DHRA/SAPRO	*MG Clem Coward*	*Director, Sexual Assault Prevention and Response Office*
OSD/P&R	*Ms. Beth Foster*	*Senior Advisor, USD(P&R)*

LINE OF EFFORT WORKING GROUPS

LOE 1: ACCOUNTABILITY WG		LOE 2: PREVENTION WG		LOE 3: CLIMATE AND CULTURE WG		LOE 4: VICTIM CARE AND SUPPORT WG	
LEAD	Cindy Dyer	LEAD	Dr. Debra Houry	LEAD	Lt. Col. Bridgette Bell	LEAD	Indira Henard
LEAD	Brig. Gen James Schwenk (ret)	LEAD	Neil Irvin	LEAD	Kris Fuhr	LEAD	Kris Rose
LEAD	Meghan Tokash	LEAD	Maj Gen James Johnson (ret)	LEAD	Dr. Kyleanne Hunter	LEAD (VA Rep)	Kayla Williams
WG CONSULTATIVE TEAM		**WG CONSULTATIVE TEAM**		**WG CONSULTATIVE TEAM**		**WG CONSULTATIVE TEAM**	
Dr. Nathan Galbreath, Deputy Director, SAPRO		Dr. Andra Tharp, Senior Advisor, OFR		MG Clem Coward, Director, SAPRO		Dr. Nathan Galbreath, Deputy Director, SAPRO	
Mr. Dwight Sullivan, DoD OGC Representative		Ms. Susan Sutherland, DoD OGC Representative		Ms. Maria Fried, DoD OGC Representative		Ms. Maria Fried, DoD OGC Representative	
Mr. Mark Lewis, Army M&RA		Mr. Jim Helis, Director, Army Resilience		Lt Gen Gary Brito, Army G-1		Mr. Jim Helis, Director, Army Resilience	
Ms. Catherine Kessmeier, Navy M&RA		RDML Putnam Browne, Director 21st Century Sailor Program		VADM John Nowell, Navy N-1		Ms. Melissa Cohen, DON SAPRO Director	
Mr. John Fedrigo, AF M&RA		Brig Gen Claude Tudor, Director, Air Force Resilience		Lt Gen Brian Kelly (BK), Air Force A-1		Brig Gen Claude Tudor, Director, Air Force Resilience	
COL Eric Widmar, Joint Staff Legal		Ms. Marie Balocki, Director, USMC Family Programs		LtGen David Ottignon, USMC M-1		Ms. Marie Balocki, Director, USMC Family Programs	
COL Traci Winston, NGB SAPR		RADM Matt Kleiman, NGB SAPR		Brig Gen Shawn Campbell, Space Force S-1		COL Stephanie Navas, Director, NGB SAPR	
CAPT Vasilios Tasikas, USCG Mr. Mark Jamison, Deputy, USCG		Ms. Lisa Arfaa, VCJCS Representative		MG Eric Little, NGB J1		Chief Nolita Whiten, Navy	
				Maj Gen Lenny Richoux, J-1		Ms. Kimberly Lahm, OASD(HA)	
				Joanne Bass, Chief Master Sergeant of the Air Force		Lt Col Tom Brockmann, Joint Staff Surgeon	
WG SUPPORT TEAM		**WG SUPPORT TEAM**		**WG SUPPORT TEAM**		**WG SUPPORT TEAM**	
LTC Rebecca Farrell (OTJAG)	Army SME	Dr. Eren Watkins	Army SME	Dr. Jenna Newman	Army SME	Ms. Angela Pate,	Army SME
CDR Daniel Leary, JAGC, USN	Navy SME	Dr. Monique Clinton-Sherrod	Navy SME	Dr. Monique Clinton-Sherrod	Navy SME	Tonya D. McKennie	Navy SME
Maj Ryan Lipton	USMC SME	Dr. Linda Love	USMC SME	LtCol Anne Braden	USMC SME	Maj John Lewis	USMC SME
Col Shaun Speranza	Air Force SME	Maj Leah Pound	Air Force SME	Marci Curry	Air Force SME	Maj Lauren Shure,	Air Force SME
N/A	Space Force SME	Mr. Scott Crum	Space Force SME	SMSgt Elisha Peters	Space Force SME	Paula Krause	Space Force SME
Col Traci Winston	NGB SME	Ms. Amber Spotten	NGB SME	LtCol Erik Anker	NGB SME	Ms. Amber Spotten	NGB SME
Ms T.L. Williams	Army CID SME			Dr. Yuko Whitestone	SO/LIC SME		
Elizabeth Heisey	NCIS SME						
Julie Lecea Alternates: Ashlee Wega	AFOSI SME						
Steve Torres							

WORKING GROUP SUPPORT STAFF

ADMIN/LOGISTIC SUPPORT		*REPORT WRITING/BRIEFING DEVELOPMENT*		*STRATEGIC COMMUNICATIONS*	
Schedulers/Note Takers	DHRA	**Lead Report Manager**	DHRA/SAPRO	Communications Expert	**OFR**
Moderators	DHRA	**Report Writers**	DHRA	Communications Expert	**DHRA/SAPRO**
Military Admin	Mil Services – Admin/level	**Editor/Formatter**	DHRA	Lisa Lawrence	**OSD(PA)**
Cailin Crockett *Senior Advisor to the IRC Chair*				CMSgt Jason Jenkins	**OSD(LA)**

Independent Review Commission Charter

Charter for
90 Day Independent Review Commission
on Sexual Assault in the Military

A. Official Designation: This effort shall be known as the *90 Day Independent Review Commission (IRC) on Sexual Assault in the Military.*

B. Mission: The mission of the IRC, and associated Line of Effort (LOE) Working Groups, is to report to the Secretary of Defense and the President of the United States with recommendations on how to advance efforts to counter military sexual assault and harassment in the areas of: accountability; prevention; climate and culture; and victim care and support. The IRC shall ensure the LOE Working Groups receive vital individual input from key stakeholders, both inside and outside of the Department, in order to appropriately inform recommendations. The IRC and its LOE Working Groups shall provide their objective and independent analysis and recommendations without interference or fear of reprisal or other adverse action by any person or entity external to them.

C. Scope and Focus of Activities: The IRC, and associated LOE Working Groups, will do the following:

- Evaluate military policies, programs, and processes
- Review and assess best-practices of industry, academia, and other external organizations
- Review previous DoD and external efforts (e.g., studies, assessments, reports), including prior recommendations from key stakeholders
- Generate recommended policy changes and propose actions to improve prevention and response efforts on sexual assault, harassment, and other readiness-detracting behaviors

The IRC will provide actionable recommendations on the following focus areas:

- LOE 1 - Accountability: Assess the role of the Uniform Code of Military Justice in addressing the prevalence of sexual assault and harassment, survivor likelihood of reporting, and ability to appropriately bring alleged perpetrators to justice. The review will include a prioritized assessment of the feasibility, opportunities, and risks from changes to the commander's role in military justice.

- LOE 2 – Prevention: Conduct a comprehensive assessment of ongoing prevention efforts to determine where gaps may exist and where additional resources may be needed. The recommendations provided should achieve an enduring, Department-wide prevention infrastructure in which leaders are equipped with the data, people, resources, policy, and tools that the Military Departments and Services need to stop sexual assault and other readiness-detracting behaviors before they occur.

- LOE 3 – Climate and Culture: Review implementation of existing support policies and resources; and identify and propose evidence-based approaches to improve climate and culture to ensure that all Service members feel safe, empowered to use available support services, are able to report without fear of reprisal from leadership or peers, and are able to serve with dignity and respect.

OSD001940-21/CMD002982-21

- LOE 4 – Victim Care and Support: Conduct a review of clinical and non-clinical victim services to ensure they are comprehensive, evidence-based, and available to all victims regardless of reporting status. The recommendations should include both mental and physical health care that is trauma-informed and victim-centered.

D. Deliverables: Each IRC LOE Working Group will provide periodic updates on interim findings, and a final report of recommendations, to the IRC. A final, consolidated report will be subsequently briefed to the Workforce Management Group (described in Section F below), provided to the Secretary of Defense and the President of the United States, and upon approval, publicly released. Timelines for reports and briefings are provided in Section F below.

The IRC's success will be defined by:

- Actionable improvements to policies, programs, and processes
- Recommendations to the Secretary of Defense and the President of the United States regarding policies, statutes, and resources to combat sexual assault and other readiness-detracting behaviors

E. Governance and Management: The IRC will be chaired by Ms. Lynn Rosenthal and led by a group of HQEs in order to ensure that independent, impartial experts can assess the totality of the Department's efforts. The IRC will include the full-time Highly Qualified Experts (HQE) from each LOE, an Advisory Support Team to include the Military Departments and Services, and other relevant internal stakeholders and subject matter experts. The deliberative body of the IRC, however, will be limited to the impartial HQEs along with the Deputy Secretary of Defense.

Final recommendations across all lines of efforts will be made to the Secretary of Defense and the President of the United States within 90 days of the first meeting.

The IRC's four LOE Working Groups will be led by full-time HQEs and informed by a broad range of stakeholders and subject matter experts providing individual advice and recommendations, as well as previous studies and recommendations, including recent recommendations by Members of Congress and reviews at Defense installations such as Fort Hood. As applicable, the working groups will receive individual briefings from internal and external stakeholders, including military survivors of sexual assault and harassment, prevention and response practitioners, and outside experts.

All media activities—including but not limited to off-the-record, on-the-record, taped, and/or televised interviews—will be coordinated through the Assistant to the Secretary of Defense for Public Affairs. DoD will not in any way direct or shape the views expressed by the IRC or Working Group members during such media activities.

IRC Chair Rosenthal will facilitate IRC updates for external stakeholders and media, after the updates are routed to the President and Secretary of Defense.

F. Membership and Activities: Members of the IRC and LOE Working Groups will consist of impartial HQEs as well as internal stakeholders and subject-matter-experts, who are full-time, or permanent part-time, Federal officers or employees, or active duty members of the Armed Forces.

The IRC will brief the findings and final recommendations to the forthcoming Workforce Management Group (WMG), as the internal DoD entity ultimately responsible for implementation of IRC recommendations.

H. Congressional Engagement: Upon request, the IRC may engage with Members of Congress and the Committees on Armed Services to inform them of the IRC's progress and to provide an opportunity for the IRC to receive input. The IRC may, upon request, brief the findings and final recommendations to Members of Congress and the Committees on Armed Services once the report is approved by the Secretary of Defense and the President of the United States.

I. Specific activities and timelines include:

Line of Effort 1 – Accountability Working Group. The Accountability Report recommendations will be briefed to the full IRC, to include the IRC Advisory Support Team, no later than (NLT) 21 days after the initial kick off meeting, with the final report delivered to the Secretary of Defense and the President of the United States within 45 days after initial kick off meeting.

Line of Effort 2 – Prevention Working Group. The Prevention Report recommendations will be briefed to the full IRC, to include the IRC Advisory Support Team, NLT 45 days after the initial kick off meeting with the final report delivered to the Secretary of Defense and the President of the United States within 90 days after initial kick off meeting.

Line of Effort 3 – Climate and Culture. The Climate and Culture recommendations will be briefed to the full IRC, to include the IRC Advisory Support team, NLT 30 days after the initial kick off meeting with the final report delivered to the Secretary of Defense and the President of the United States within 60 days after initial kick off meeting.

Line of Effort 4 – Victim Care and Support. The Victim Care and Support recommendations will be briefed to the full IRC, to include the IRC Advisory Support team, NLT 45 days after the initial kick off meeting with the final report delivered to the Secretary of Defense and the President of the United States within 90 days after initial kick off meeting.

J. Designated personnel from the Office of the Under Secretary of Defense for Personnel and Readiness (USD(P&R)) and the Military Departments will provide administrative and logistical support, as well as the requisite expertise, to the IRC and the four LOE working groups, including: scheduling, note taking, summary reports, interim report development, briefings, final report development, and designated subject-matter experts. USD(P&R) will coordinate the administrative and logistical support.

K. Timelines: The IRC will convene no later than 22 March. The IRC and LOE working group meetings will be scheduled until completion of the mission and as necessary. Tentative timelines are as follows:

(TEN) 22 Mar 21 IRC Meeting: Kickoff

12 April 21	*LOE 1 Accountability Report briefed to IRC and IRC Advisory Support Team*
21 April 21	*LOE 3 Climate and Culture Report briefed to IRC and IRC Advisory Support Team*
6 May 21	**LOE 1 Accountability Report Routed to Secretary of Defense and the President of the United States**
17 May 21	*LOE 2 Prevention, and LOE 4 Victim Care and Support, briefed to IRC and IRC Advisory Support Team*
21 May 21	**LOE 3 Climate and Culture Report Routed to Secretary of Defense and the President of the United States**
21 June 21	**IRC Submits Final Report and Recommendations to the President of the United States** (*includes LOE 2 Prevention and LOE 4 Victim Care and Support Reports*).

The IRC and the IRC Advisory Support team will meet approximately bi-weekly, and the LOE working groups will meet as often as required to support the full activities of the IRC. Special meetings may be called as necessary.

H. Duration: This charter is effective upon signature.

I. Termination Date: 30 June, 2021 or as determined by the SECDEF.

J. Charter Modification: The SECDEF reserves the authority to modify this charter.

L. Approval:
Date: MAR 05 2021

OSD001940-21/CMD002982-21

Independent Review Commission Staff & Members

Figure 1. IRC Chair and Senior Advisors

IRC Chair	Biography
Lynn Rosenthal	Lynn Rosenthal is the president of The Center for Family Safety and Healing, which takes an integrated team approach to breaking the cycle of family violence and child abuse. Rosenthal, a nationally known champion for the prevention of family violence, previously served at the Biden Foundation as the director, Violence Against Women Initiatives. From 2009-2015, she was the first-ever White House Advisor on Violence Against Women, coordinating efforts to address domestic and sexual violence. In this capacity, Rosenthal co-chaired the White House Task Force to Protect Students from Sexual Assault and led interagency collaboration to spark new prevention initiatives. Rosenthal also served as vice president for Strategic Partnerships at the National Domestic Violence Hotline, executive director of the National Network to End Domestic Violence and held leadership positions at state domestic violence coalitions in Florida and New Mexico.
Senior Advisors	**Biography**
Sasha Rutizer	Sasha Rutizer is a Senior Trial Attorney at the Department of Justice in the Human Rights and Special Prosecutions Section where she prosecutes sexual assault, gender based violence, human rights violations, and other crimes committed outside the United States that fall within the Military Extraterritorial Jurisdiction Act and Special Maritime and Territorial Jurisdiction. Prior to joining DOJ she was a Senior Attorney at the National District Attorneys Association within the National Center for Prosecution of Child Abuse advising and training prosecutors around the country.
Cailin Crockett	Cailin Crockett leads prevention policy for intimate partner violence and child abuse for the DoD Family Advocacy Program, serving active duty military and their partners and children, in support of mission readiness and the National Defense Strategy. In this role, she works closely with the Defense Sexual Assault Prevention and Response Office, the Defense Suicide Prevention Office, and the Office for Diversity, Equity, and Inclusion as part of the DoD Prevention Collaboration Forum, a Secretary of Defense initiative to promote primary prevention. Prior to joining DoD, she held roles at the U.S. Departments of Justice, Health and Human Services, and the White House, advising on intimate partner and sexual violence policies and programs. She is a Truman National Security Fellow, and a Bloomberg American Health Initiative Fellow.

Figure 2. IRC Line of Effort HQEs

Line of Effort	HQE	Biography
Accountability	Cindy Dyer	Cindy Dyer is a nationally recognized expert on violence against women. She recently served as vice president for human rights at Vital Voices, an international nongovernmental organization dedicated to advancing the rights of women and girls globally. Between 2007 and 2009, she served as the director of the U.S. Department of Justice Office on Violence Against Women. Dyer was nominated to this position by President George W. Bush on Aug. 2, 2007 and confirmed by the Senate on Dec. 19, 2007. Dyer is also an experienced prosecutor and recognized expert on sexual assault and domestic violence. Prior to her service at the Justice Department, Dyer was chief prosecutor of the Family Violence Division of the Dallas County District Attorney's Office. She has received numerous awards and honors for her service to victims, including Prosecutor of the Year from the Greater Dallas Crime Commission.
	James Schwenk	Retired Brig. Gen. James Schwenk was commissioned as an infantry officer in the Marine Corps in 1970. He attended law school at the Washington College of Law, American University. As a judge advocate, he served in the Office of the Secretary of Defense, the Office of the Secretary of the Navy, and Headquarters, Marine Corps; as staff judge advocate for Marine Forces Atlantic, II Marine Expeditionary Force, Marine Corps Air Bases West, and several other commands; and participated in several hundred courts-martial and administrative discharge boards. Upon retirement in 2000, Schwenk joined the Defense Department Office of General Counsel as an associate deputy general counsel, retiring after 49 years of federal service in 2014.
	Meghan Tokash	Meghan Tokash is an assistant U.S. attorney at the Department of Justice serving the Western District of New York as the supervisor of the district's Special Victim Unit. Previously, she served as an active duty judge advocate in the U.S. Army Judge Advocate General's Corps for eight years, prosecuting cases related to homicide, rape, sexual assault, domestic violence and child abuse. Tokash was selected to serve as one of 15 special victim prosecutors when she worked in the Army's first Special Victim Unit at the Fort Hood Criminal Investigation Division Office. She deployed to Iraq as the senior trial counsel for U.S. Forces Iraq, and prosecuted sexual assault cases across U.S. Army Europe and U.S. Army Central Command in courthouses from Kuwait to Afghanistan to Shaw Air Force Base, South Carolina. Tokash was an attorney advisor for the Judicial Proceedings Panel prior to her 2017 appointment by Secretary of Defense Ash Carter to serve on the Defense Advisory Committee on the Investigation, Prosecution and Defense of Sexual Assault in the Armed Forces. Tokash served as a member of the Case Review Working Group whose work culminated by issuing a comprehensive report and recommendations in October 2020 pertaining to investigative case file reviews for military adult penetrative sexual assault offense cases closed in fiscal year 2017.
Prevention	Dr. Debra Houry	Dr. Debra Houry is the director of the National Center for Injury Prevention and Control at the Centers for Disease Control and Prevention, where she leads innovative research and science-based programs to prevent injuries and violence and to reduce their consequences. Houry previously served as an associate professor and emergency physician at Emory University. She has

Line of Effort	HQE	Biography
		authored more than 90 peer-reviewed publications and book chapters on injury prevention and violence. She has received many national awards, including the first Linda Saltzman Memorial Intimate Partner Violence Researcher Award from the Institute on Violence, Abuse and Trauma, and the Academy of Women in Academic Emergency Medicine's Researcher Award. She was recently elected as a member of the National Academy of Medicine, which is considered one of the highest honors in the fields of health and medicine.
	Neil Irvin	Neil Irvin is the executive director of Men Can Stop Rape, an internationally recognized organization that mobilizes men to use their strength for creating cultures free from violence, especially men's violence against women and girls. Previously, Irvin served as the vice president of national programs for MCSR and was the architect of the Men of Strength Club, an award-winning, Centers for Disease Control and Prevention-evaluated primary prevention program for boys, paving the way for Strong Moves, the country's largest primary prevention program for boys. As executive director, he has spearheaded innovative programs and initiatives for the organization such as the Healthy Masculinity Action Project, which reached over 62 million people, and the ASK smartphone technology platform, which has served over 82 million people. Irvin has served on the Department of Justice's National Advisory Committee and the Biden Foundation's Leadership Committee, and as a member of the U.S. delegation at the United Nations 25th Commission on the Status of Women, the NBA's Domestic Violence Committee, the steering committee for It's On Us, The George Washington University's Global Women's Leadership Council, and the NoVo Foundation's Move to End Violence initiative.
	Maj. Gen. James Johnson (ret.)	Retired Air Force Maj. Gen. James Johnson presently serves as governance chairman for The Flag and General Officers' Network, a not-for-profit veterans corporation enabling admirals and general officers to network and provide public service. He is also an independent leadership consultant and a mission readiness advocate, promoting evidence-based, bipartisan public policy solutions to prepare youth for life. Between 2015 and 2018, Johnson served as the director for Air Force Sexual Assault Prevention and Response and then as director of the Integrated Resilience Office, Headquarters U.S. Air Force. The Integrated Resilience Office provides strategic solutions for optimal well-being and resilience, with special focus on the most effective primary prevention and response to interpersonal and self-directed violence.
Climate and Culture	LTC Bridgette Bell	Army LTC Bridgette Bell graduated from the U.S. Military Academy at West Point, New York, in the Class of 2004. She is a combat veteran with over 16 years of service as a leader in human resources. Her military career includes positions with the 108th Air Defense Artillery Brigade and the Special Troops Battalion of the 4th Brigade Combat Team, 1st Cavalry Division. While deployed to Mosul, Iraq, she dealt with trauma survivors firsthand as her unit's primary responder for sexual assault victims. As a company commander at Fort Myer, Virginia, she provided for the welfare and unique needs of over 240 assigned and 1,200 attached soldiers in the Military District of Washington. She attended the Naval Postgraduate School, then returned to West Point to teach engineering psychology in the Department of Behavioral Sciences and Leadership. She continued serving in higher education as the executive officer for the Army ROTC at Jackson State University. Bell's research includes a

Line of Effort	HQE	Biography
		master's thesis on the Army Suicide Prevention Program and working with the Trauma Recovery Program at the G.V. (Sonny) VA Medical Center in Jackson, Mississippi. She is a 2017 Pat Tillman Foundation Military Scholar pursuing a Ph.D. in clinical psychology from Jackson State University. She plans to specialize in trauma, grief and multicultural psychology and apply the intersection of human resources and psychology to solve complex problems.
	CPT Kris Fuhr (ret.)	Kris Fuhr is a 1985 graduate of the U.S. Military Academy at West Point, New York. As a captain in the Army, Fuhr was the first woman to command a forward-deployed, ground-based intelligence company on the inner German border. Fuhr is a senior volunteer leader for the Ranger School Support Group at Fort Benning, Georgia, providing virtual and in-person support to students and over 6,000 family members. She is also a volunteer senior mentor with the Army on issues regarding the integration of women into combat arms and the leader of a mentorship network for over 700 women who serve as infantry and armor officers and Ranger candidates.
	Dr. Kyleanne Hunter	Dr. Kyleanne Hunter is an assistant professor of military and strategic studies. She is an adjunct senior fellow at the Center for a New American Security, co-director of the Athena Leadership Project and a nonresident fellow at the Brute Krulack Center for Creativity and Innovation at Marine Corps University. Hunter is a Marine Corps combat veteran with multiple combat deployments as an AH-1W Super Cobra attack pilot. She finished her active-duty time in the Marine Corps' Legislative Liaison Office in the House of Representatives. She holds a Bachelor of Science in foreign service from Georgetown University's Walsh School of Foreign Affairs Service, and a Master of Arts and a doctorate from University of Denver's Josef Korbel School of International Studies. She was the former chair of the Employment and Integration Subcommittee for the Defense Advisory Committee on Women in the Services.
Victim Care and Support	Dr. Indira Henard	Dr. Indira Henard is the executive director of the DC Rape Crisis Center, which is the oldest rape crisis center in the country. Henard has been involved in the violence against women movement for 20 years. Henard's direct service experience in various gender-based violence programs has helped to inform her policy analysis that has led to coordinating public policy initiatives, organizing and planning space for survivor-led advocacy, and educating local and international communities around civic participation within the violence against women movement. Prior to joining the D.C. Rape Crisis Center, Henard served as a Senate aide for then-Senator Barack Obama on Capitol Hill, as well as special assistant on his presidential campaign. Henard was most recently awarded the 2020 Washingtonian of the Year Award, as well as Mayor Muriel Bowser's 2020 Washington Women of Excellence Award.
	Kristina Rose	Kristina "Kris" Rose has more than 35 years of experience working on crime victimization and criminal justice issues in government, nonprofit and corporate environments. During her 19 years at the Department of Justice, she served as the deputy director at the Office for Victims of Crime, as the acting director and deputy director for the National Institute of Justice, and as the chief of staff for the Office on Violence Against Women. In 2016, Rose was invited to work at the White House as a senior policy advisor on violence against women in the Office of the Vice President. Prior to that, as part of a DOJ leadership program,

Line of Effort	HQE	Biography
		she had the opportunity to spend nearly a year as a victim advocate in the U.S. Attorney's Office in Washington, D.C., working hands-on with victims of all violent crimes. She most recently served as the director of strategic partnerships for Healing Justice and executive director for End Violence Against Women International. She received her Bachelor of Arts in sociology from George Mason University and her Master of Science in criminal justice from Northeastern University.
	Kayla Williams	Kayla Williams is the assistant secretary, Office of Public and Intergovernmental Affairs at the Department of Veterans Affairs. Prior to that, she was a senior fellow and director of the Military, Veterans and Society Program at the Center for a New American Security, focused on issues facing veterans, military readiness and civil-military relations. Previously, Williams served as the director of the Center for Women Veterans at VA, where she was the primary advisor to the secretary on department policies, programs and legislation affecting women veterans. Williams was enlisted for five years as an Arabic linguist, serving in a military intelligence company of the 101st Airborne Division.

Figure 3. IRC Executive Officers

IRC Executive Officers
Todd Charette
Trevor Powell
Christina Trader

Made in United States
Orlando, FL
07 November 2026

90337544R10168